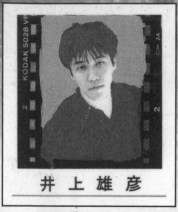

井 上 雄 彦

Takehiko Inoue

IT'S DECEMBER 1992 AS I WRITE THIS, AND THE
POPULARITY OF THE NBA IN JAPAN IS AT AN
ALL-TIME HIGH,* BUT WHAT ABOUT *JAPANESE*
BASKETBALL? CAN YOU EVEN NAME *ONE*
JAPANESE BASKETBALL PLAYER?

*WE WEAR NBA LOGOS ON OUR CLOTHES AND
WATCH NBA STARS ON OUR TVS. THE TERM
"STREET BALL" HAS EVEN MADE ITS WAY INTO
THE VERNACULAR!

Takehiko Inoue's *Slam Dunk* is one of the most
popular manga of all time, having sold over 100
million copies worldwide. He followed that series
up with two titles lauded by critics and fans
alike—*Vagabond*, a fictional account of the life
of Miyamoto Musashi, and *Real*, a manga about
wheelchair basketball.

SLAM DUNK
Vol. 11: Even a Fluke

SHONEN JUMP Manga Edition

STORY AND ART BY TAKEHIKO INOUE

English Adaptation/Kelly Sue DeConnick
Translation/Joe Yamazaki
Touch-up Art & Lettering/James Gaubatz
Cover & Graphic Design/Sean Lee
Editor/Kit Fox

VP, Production/Alvin Lu
VP, Sales & Product Marketing/Gonzalo Ferreyra
VP, Creative/Linda Espinosa
Publisher/Hyoe Narita

Printed in the U.S.A.

Published by VIZ Media, LLC
P.O. Box 77010
San Francisco, CA 94107

10 9 8 7 6 5 4 3 2 1
First printing, August 2010

www.viz.com

THE WORLD'S
MOST POPULAR MANGA
www.shonenjump.com

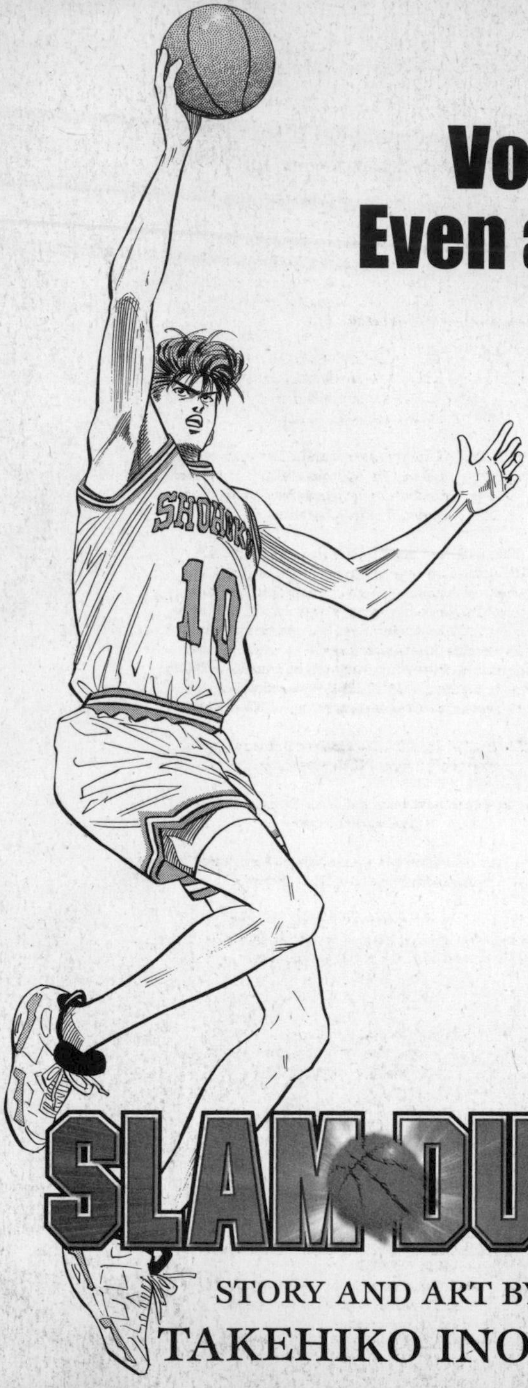

SHOHOKU
10

Vol. 11: Even a Fluke

SLAM DUNK

STORY AND ART BY

TAKEHIKO INOUE

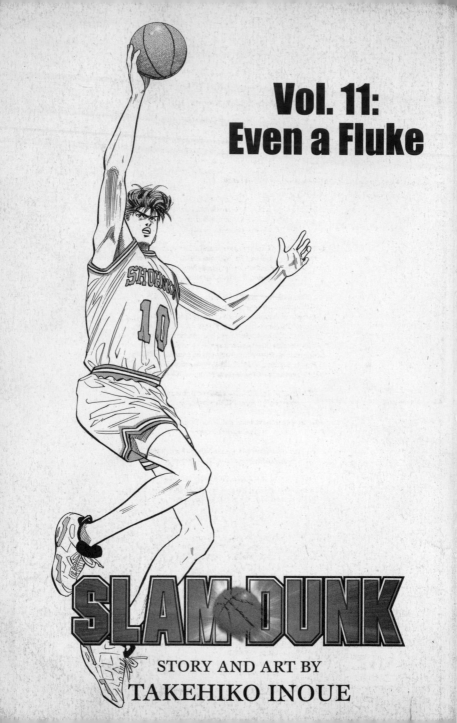

Character Introduction

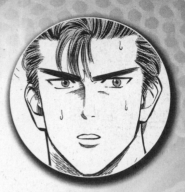

Hanamichi Sakuragi
A first-year at Shohoku High School, Sakuragi is in love with Haruko Akagi.

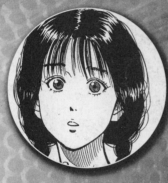

Haruko Akagi
Also a first-year at Shohoku, Takenori Akagi's little sister has a crush on Kaede Rukawa.

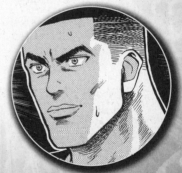

Takenori Akagi
A third-year and the basketball team's captain, Akagi has an intense passion for his sport.

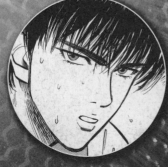

Kaede Rukawa
The object of Haruko's affection (and that of many of Shohoku's female students!), this first-year has been a star player since junior high.

Sakuragi's Friends

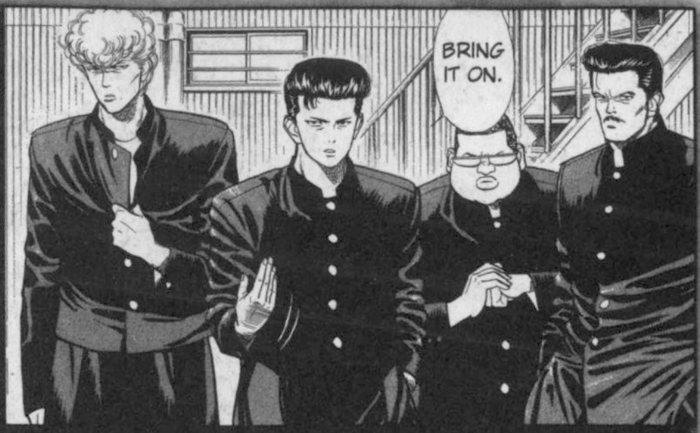
BRING IT ON.

Ohkusu Mito Takamiya Noma

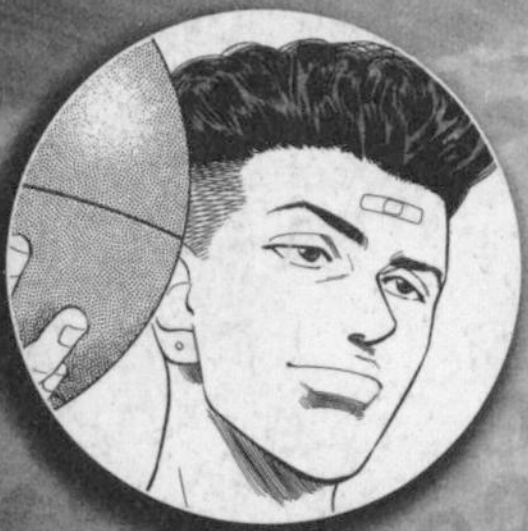

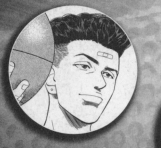

Ryota Miyagi
A problem child with a thing for Ayako.

Ayako
Basketball Team Manager

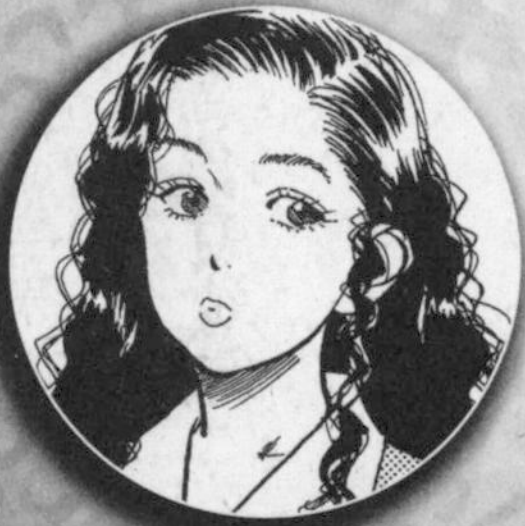

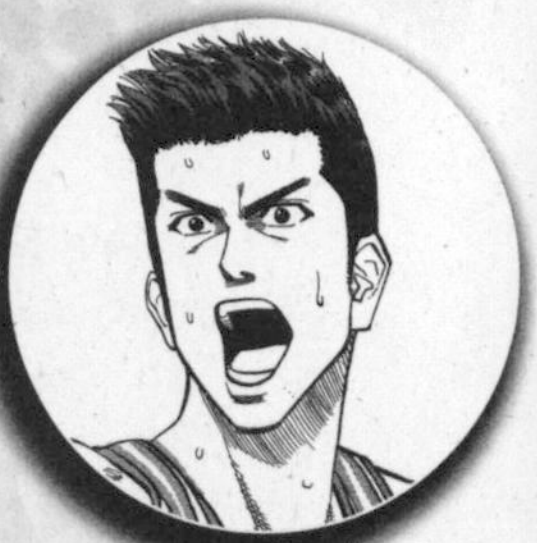

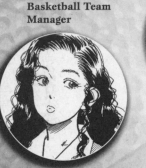

Hisashi Mitsui
An MVP during junior high.

Our Story Thus Far

Hanamichi Sakuragi is rejected by close to 50 girls during his three years in junior high. In high school, he joins the basketball team in order to get closer to his beloved Haruko, whose brother is the team captain. However, the endless fundamental drills do not suit his personality, and he and Captain Akagi frequently butt heads.

After a good showing in their first exhibition game, the team already has its sights set on Nationals when Ryota Miyagi reclaims his position as Point Guard.

Not yet over his feud with Miyagi, former b-baller Hisashi Mitsui and his gang invade the gym and try to start a brawl, but Coach Anzai gets through to Mitsui and convinces him to rejoin the team. With Mitsui and Miyagi both back on board, Shohoku advances through the prefectural tournament to play powerhouse school Shoyo. At halftime, our boys are down by nine points...

Vol. 11:
Even a Fluke

Table of Contents

#90 SHOYO AND FUJIMA

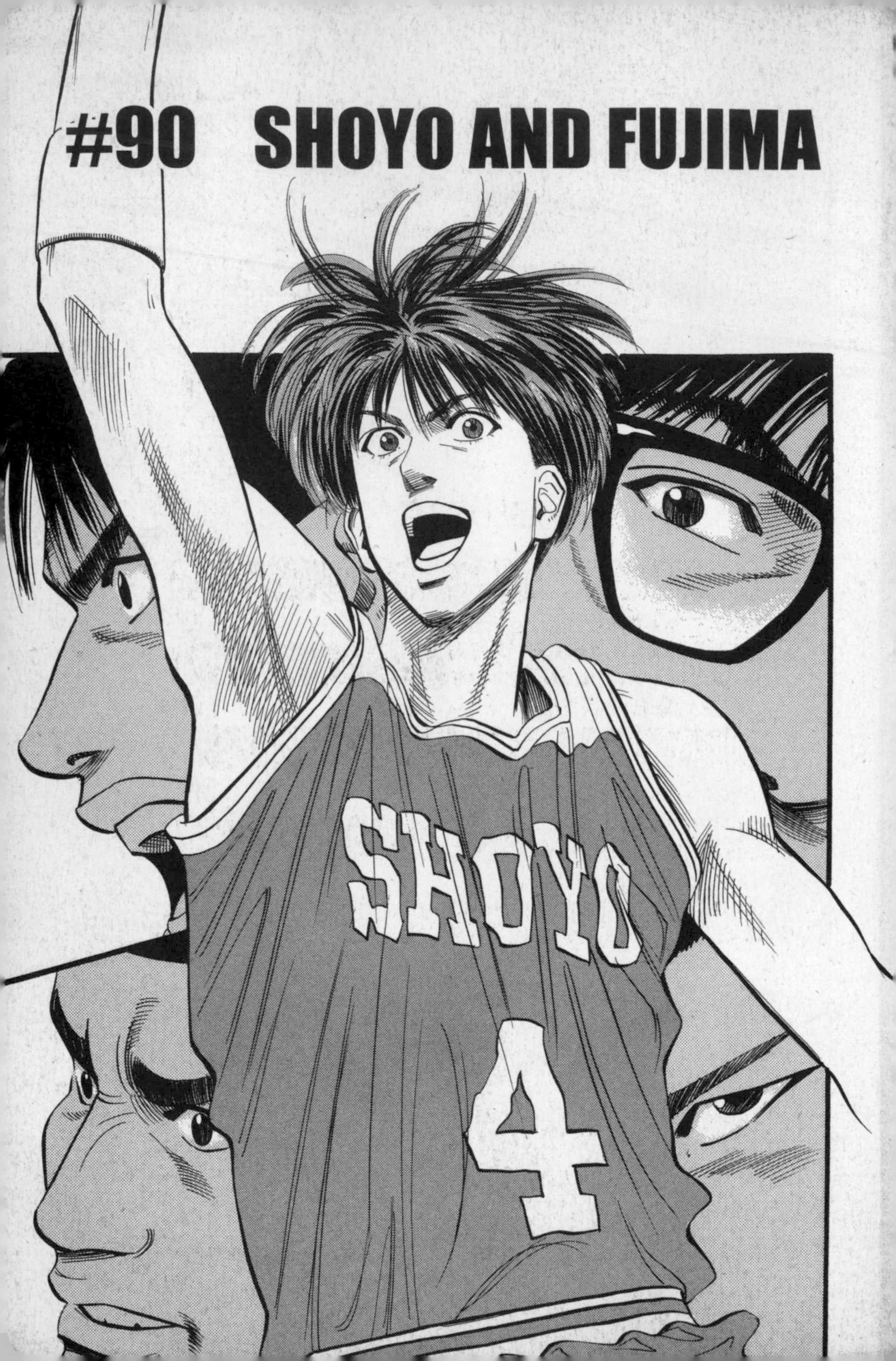
SHOYO
4

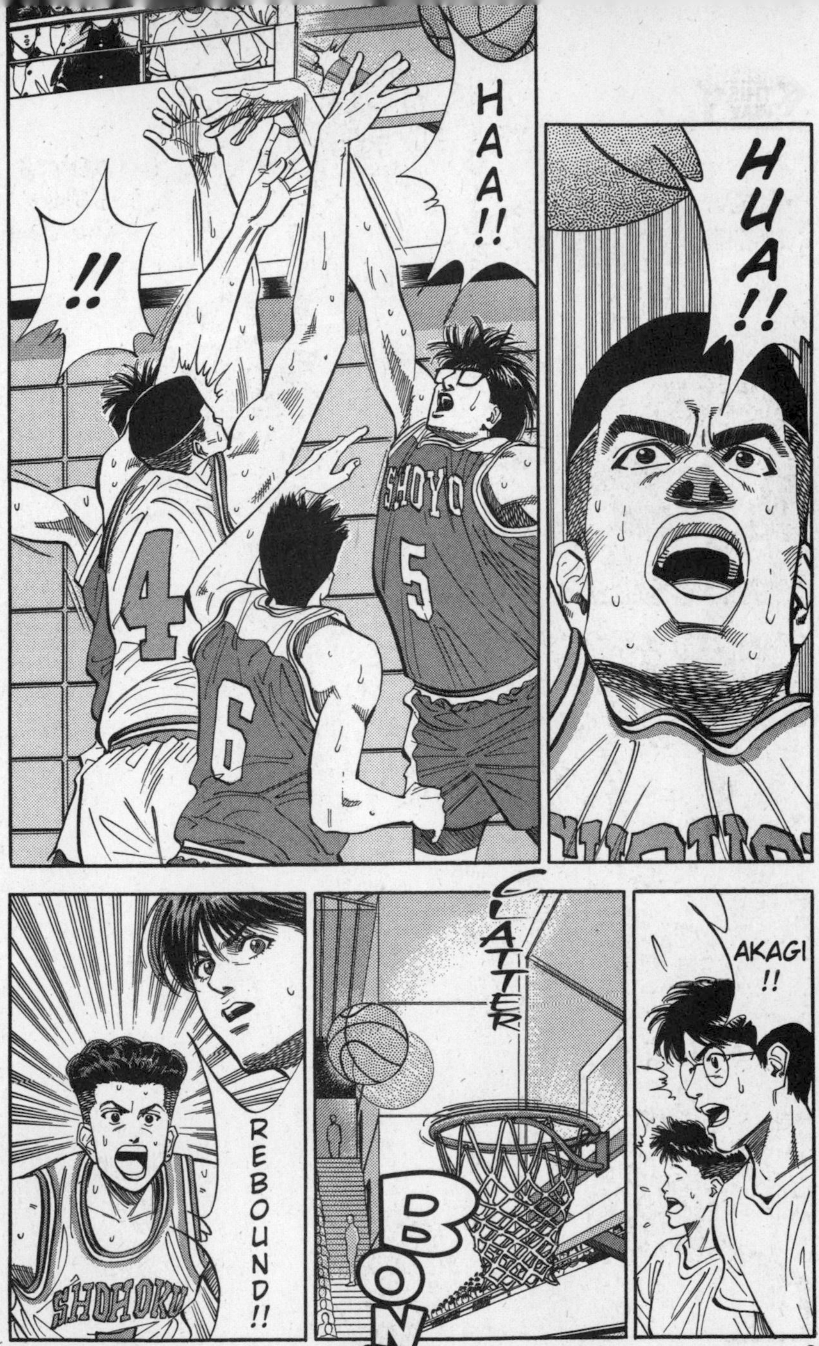
HUA!!
HAA!!
!!
AKAGI!!
CLATTER
BONK
REBOUND!!

READ THIS WAY

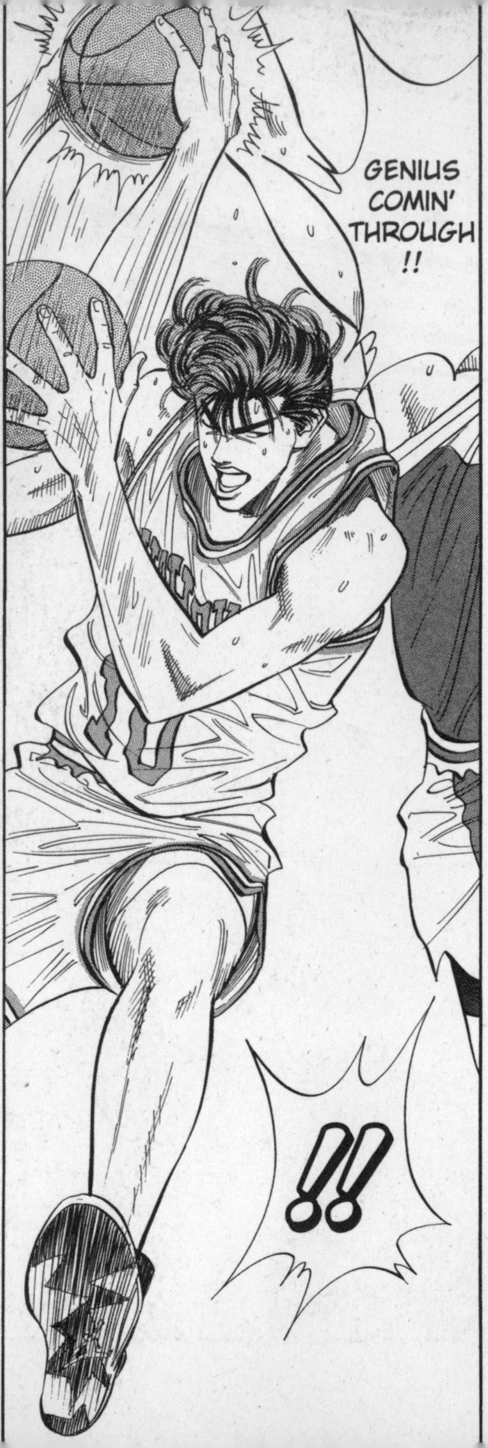
GENIUS COMIN' THROUGH!!
!!

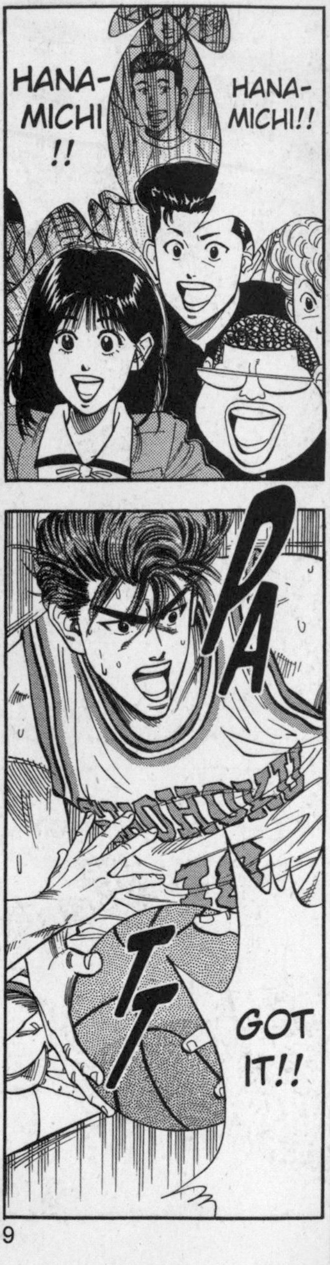
HANA-MICHI!!
HANA-MICHI!!
PA
GOT IT!!

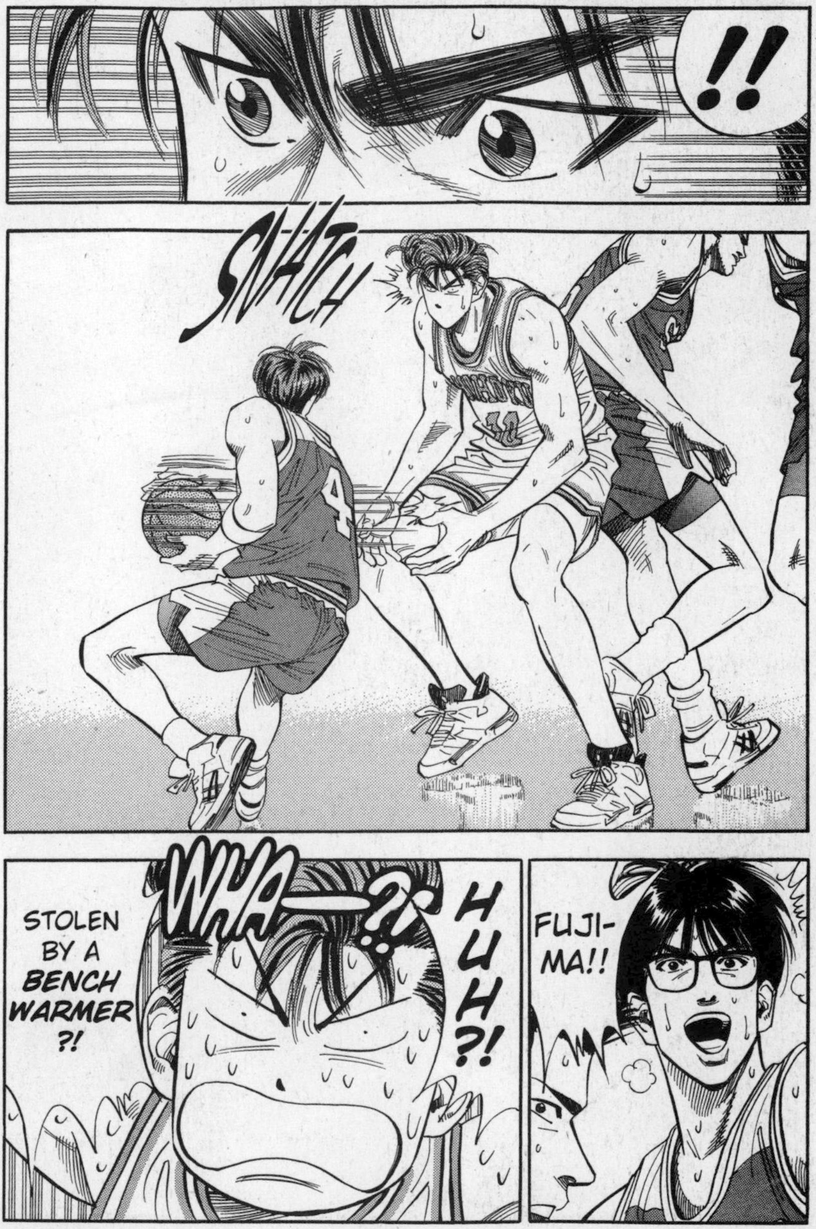
!!
SNATCH
FUJI-MA!!
HUH?!
WHA—?!
STOLEN BY A BENCH WARMER ?!

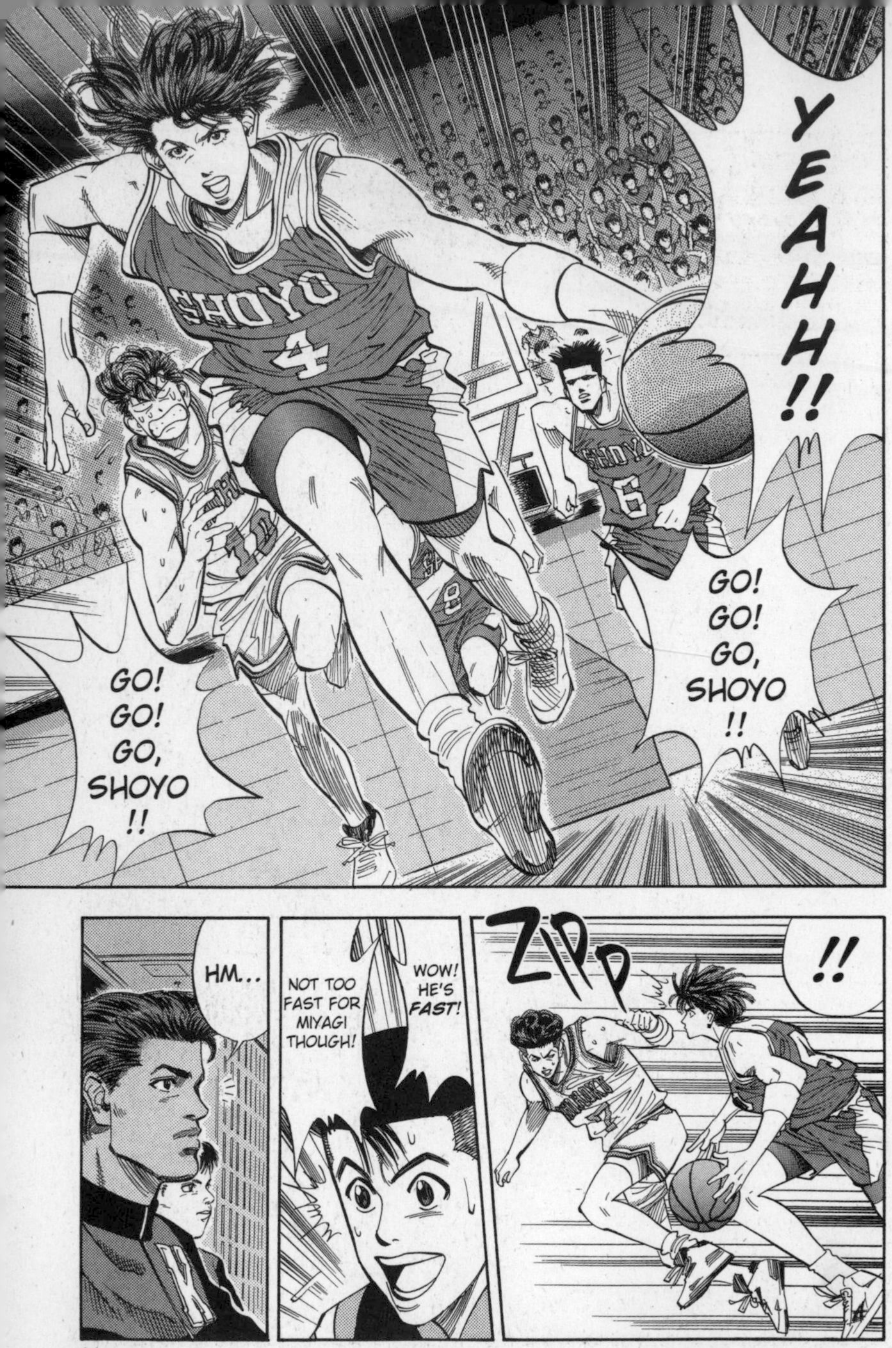
YEAHH!!
GO! GO! GO, SHOYO!!
GO! GO! GO, SHOYO!!
ZIPD
!!
WOW! HE'S FAST!
NOT TOO FAST FOR MIYAGI THOUGH!
HM...

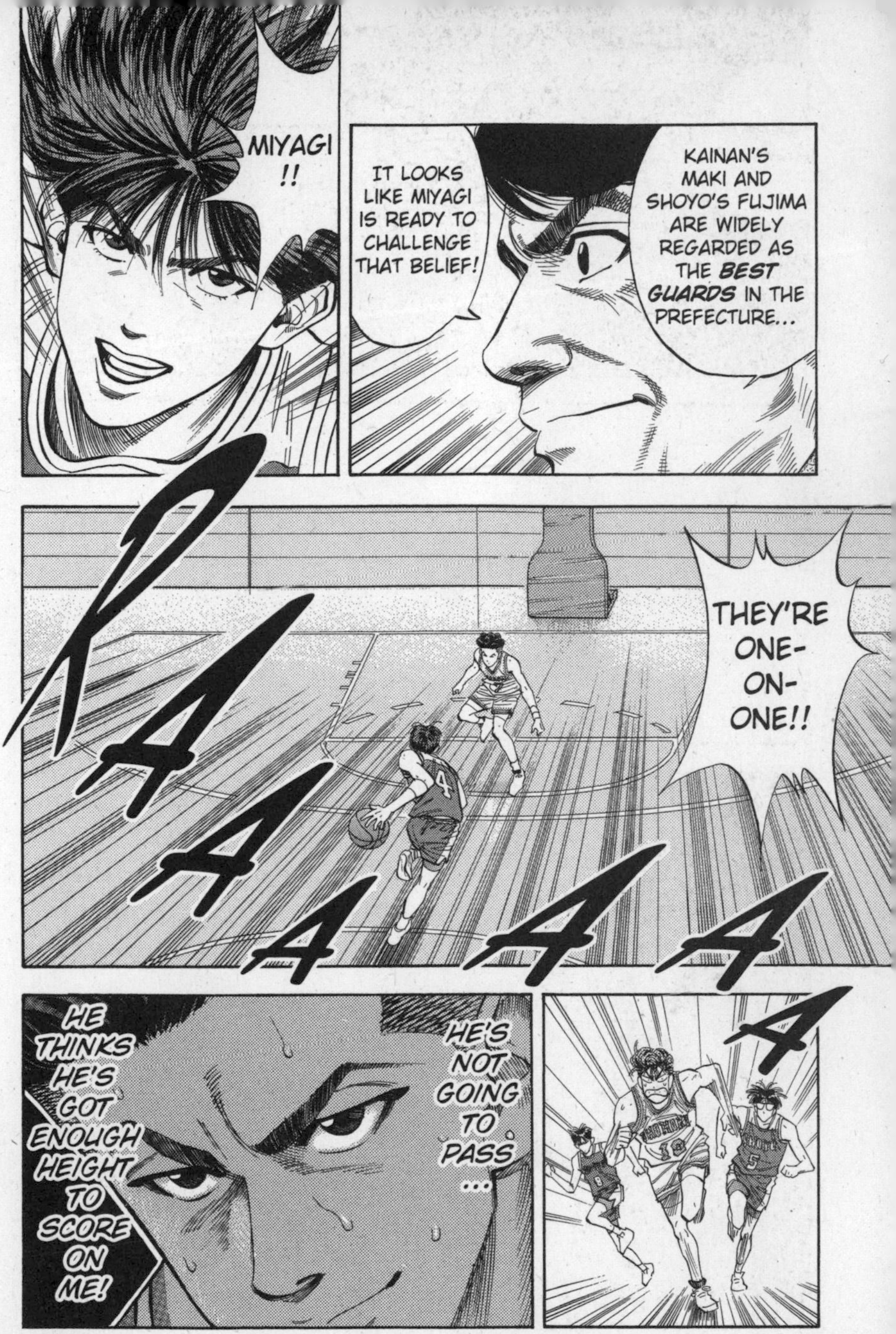
KAINAN'S MAKI AND SHOYO'S FUJIMA ARE WIDELY REGARDED AS THE **BEST GUARDS** IN THE PREFECTURE...
IT LOOKS LIKE MIYAGI IS READY TO CHALLENGE THAT BELIEF!
MIYAGI !!
THEY'RE ONE-ON-ONE!!
WAAAAAA
HE'S NOT GOING TO PASS...
HE THINKS HE'S GOT ENOUGH HEIGHT TO SCORE ON ME!

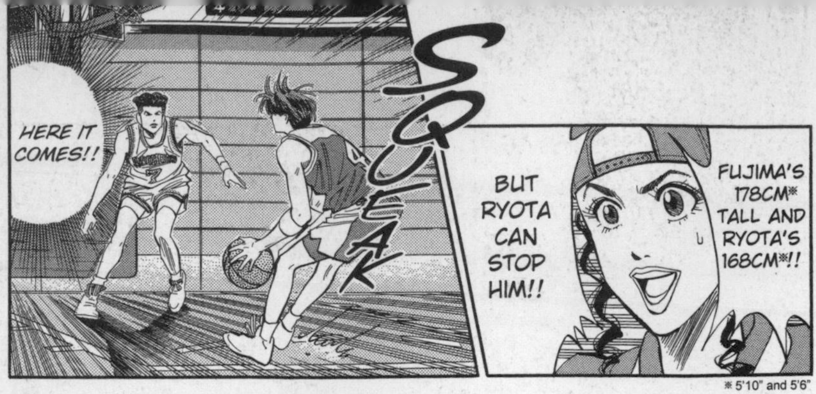
FUJIMA'S 178CM※ TALL AND RYOTA'S 168CM※!!
BUT RYOTA CAN STOP HIM!!
SQUEAK
HERE IT COMES!!

※ 5'10" and 5'6"

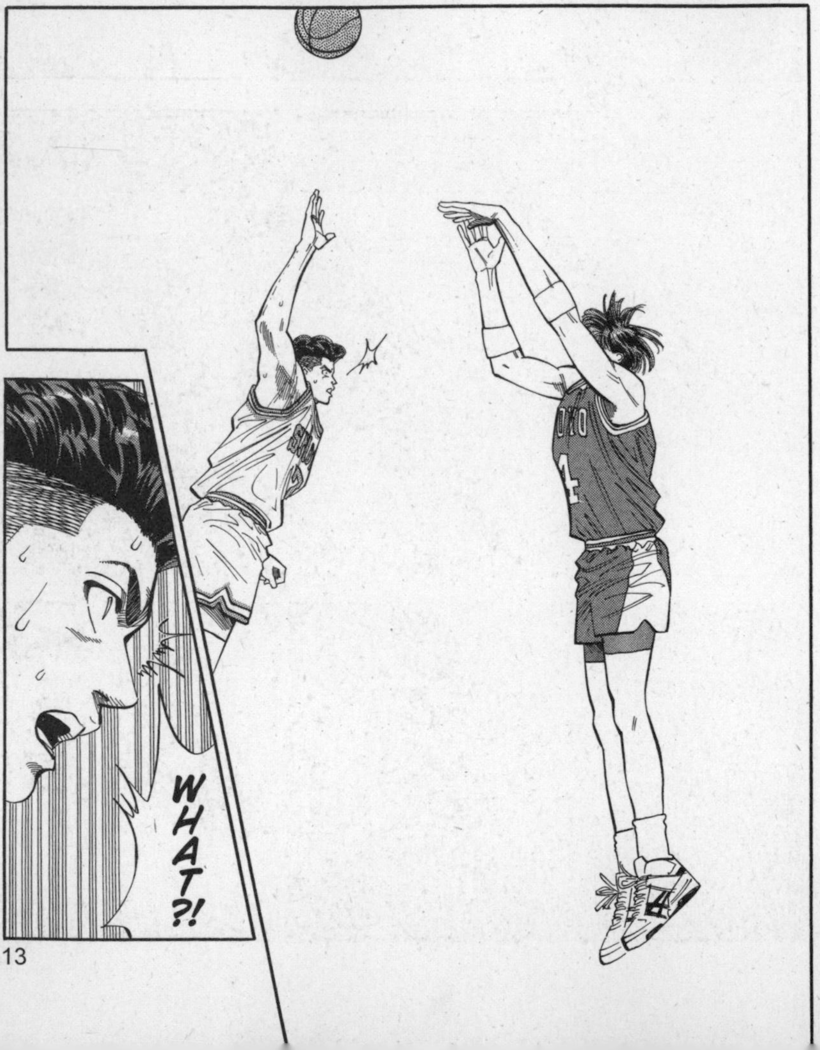
WHAT?!

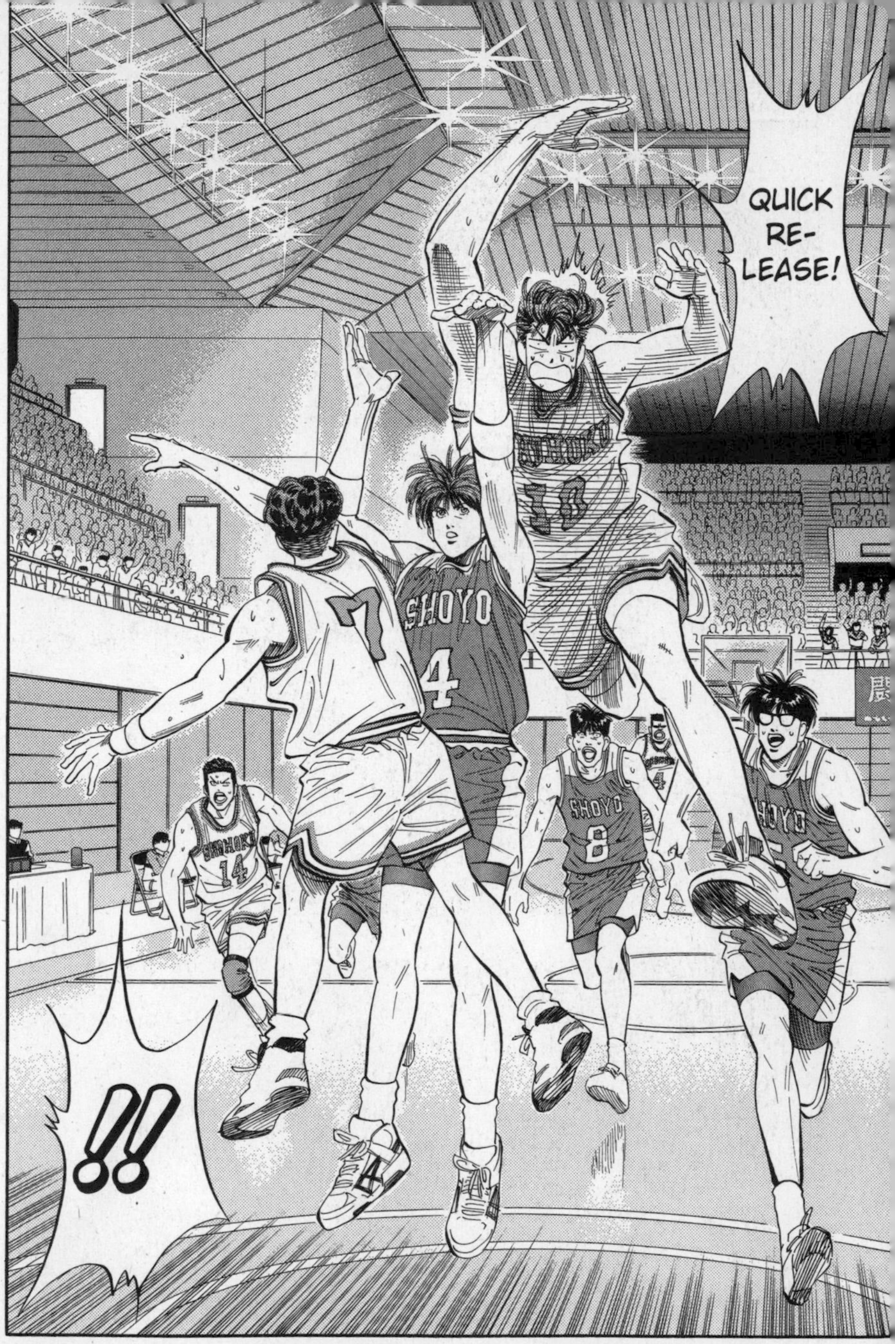
QUICK RE-LEASE!
!!

READ THIS WAY

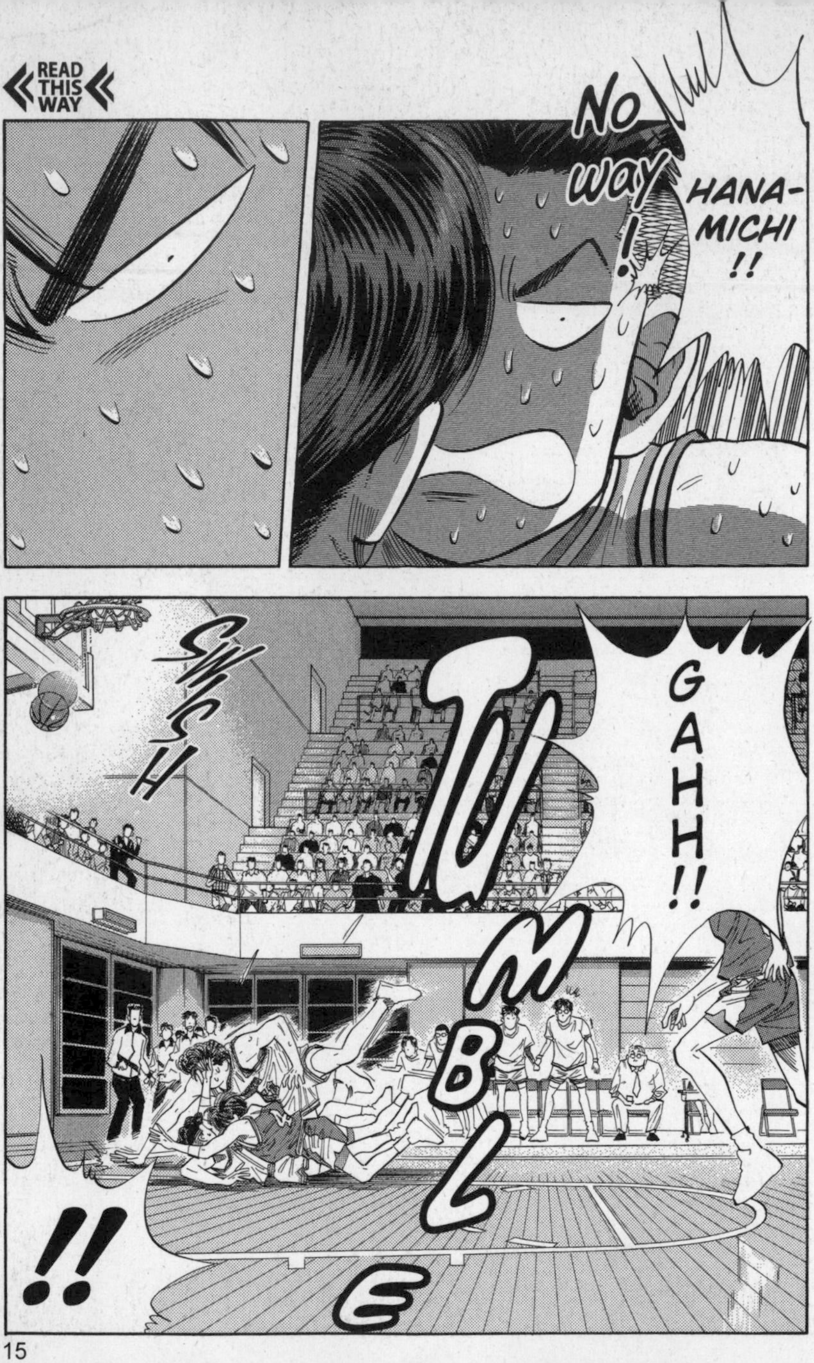

HANA-MICHI!!
No way!
GAHH!!
TUMBLE
SWISH
!!

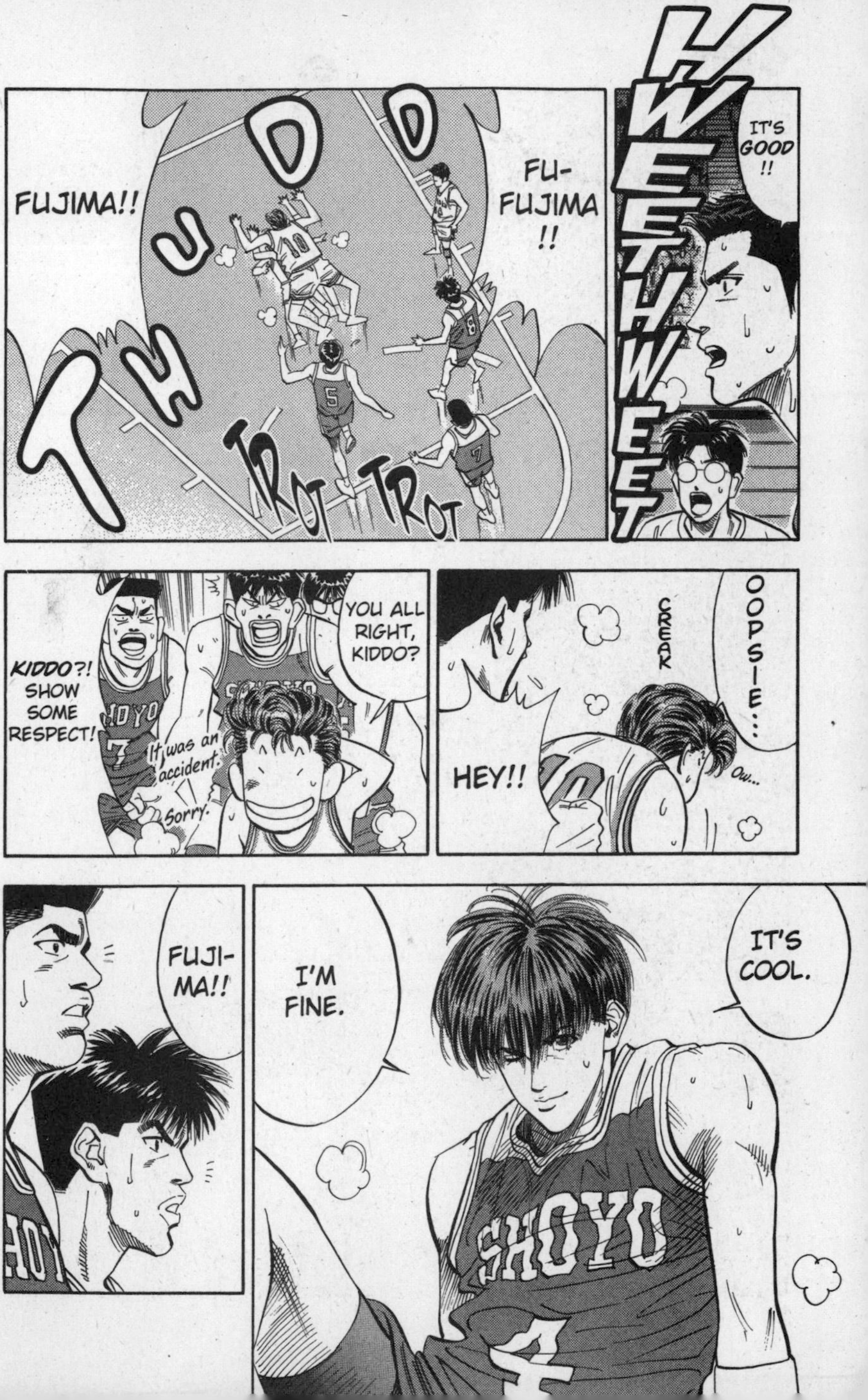
HWEETWHWEET
IT'S GOOD!!
FU-FUJIMA!!
FUJIMA!!
THUD
TROT TROT
OOPSIE...
CREAK
HEY!!
Ow...
YOU ALL RIGHT, KIDDO?
KIDDO?! SHOW SOME RESPECT!
It was an accident.
Sorry.
IT'S COOL.
I'M FINE.
FUJI-MA!!

READ THIS WAY

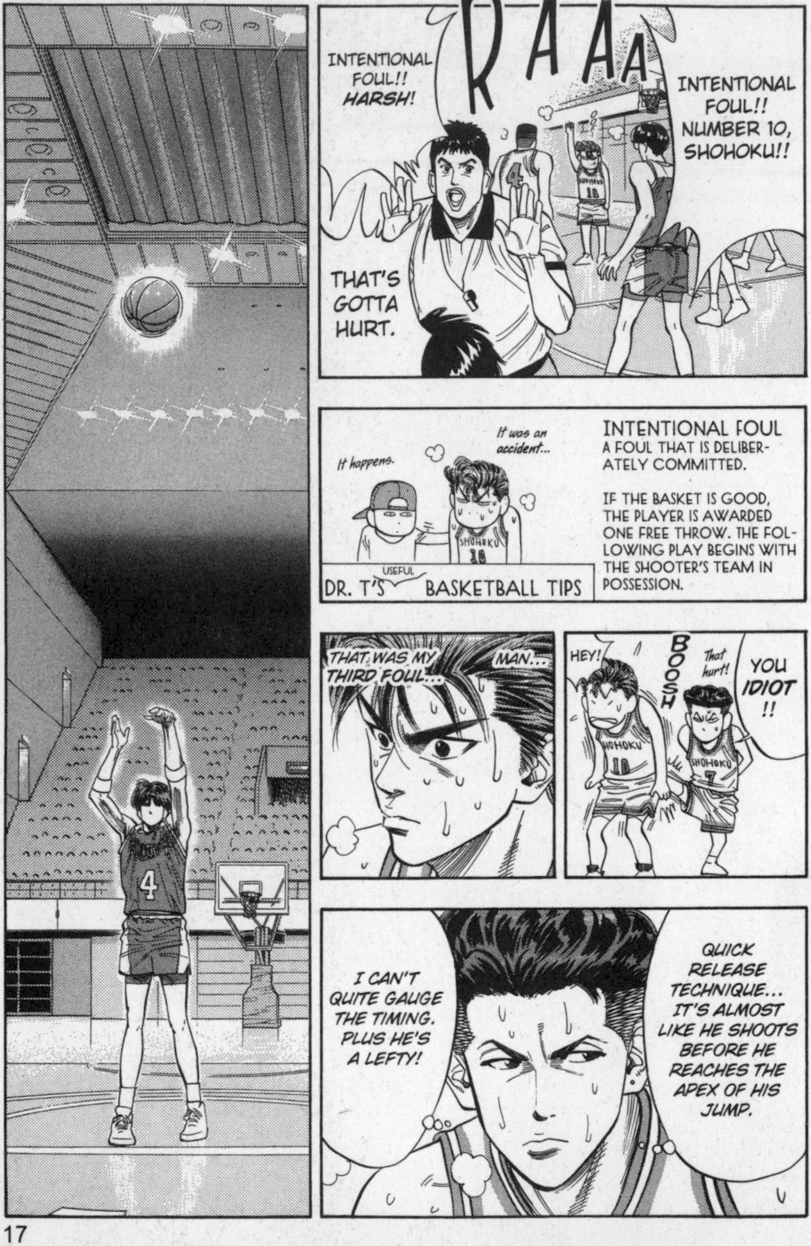

INTENTIONAL FOUL!! NUMBER 10, SHOHOKU!!
RAAA
INTENTIONAL FOUL!! *HARSH!*
THAT'S GOTTA HURT.
INTENTIONAL FOUL
A FOUL THAT IS DELIBERATELY COMMITTED.
IF THE BASKET IS GOOD, THE PLAYER IS AWARDED ONE FREE THROW. THE FOLLOWING PLAY BEGINS WITH THE SHOOTER'S TEAM IN POSSESSION.
It was an accident...
It happens.
DR. T'S USEFUL BASKETBALL TIPS
YOU *IDIOT* !!
That hurt!
BOOSH
HEY!
MAN...
THAT WAS MY THIRD FOUL...
QUICK RELEASE TECHNIQUE... IT'S ALMOST LIKE HE SHOOTS BEFORE HE REACHES THE APEX OF HIS JUMP.
I CAN'T QUITE GAUGE THE TIMING. PLUS HE'S A LEFTY!

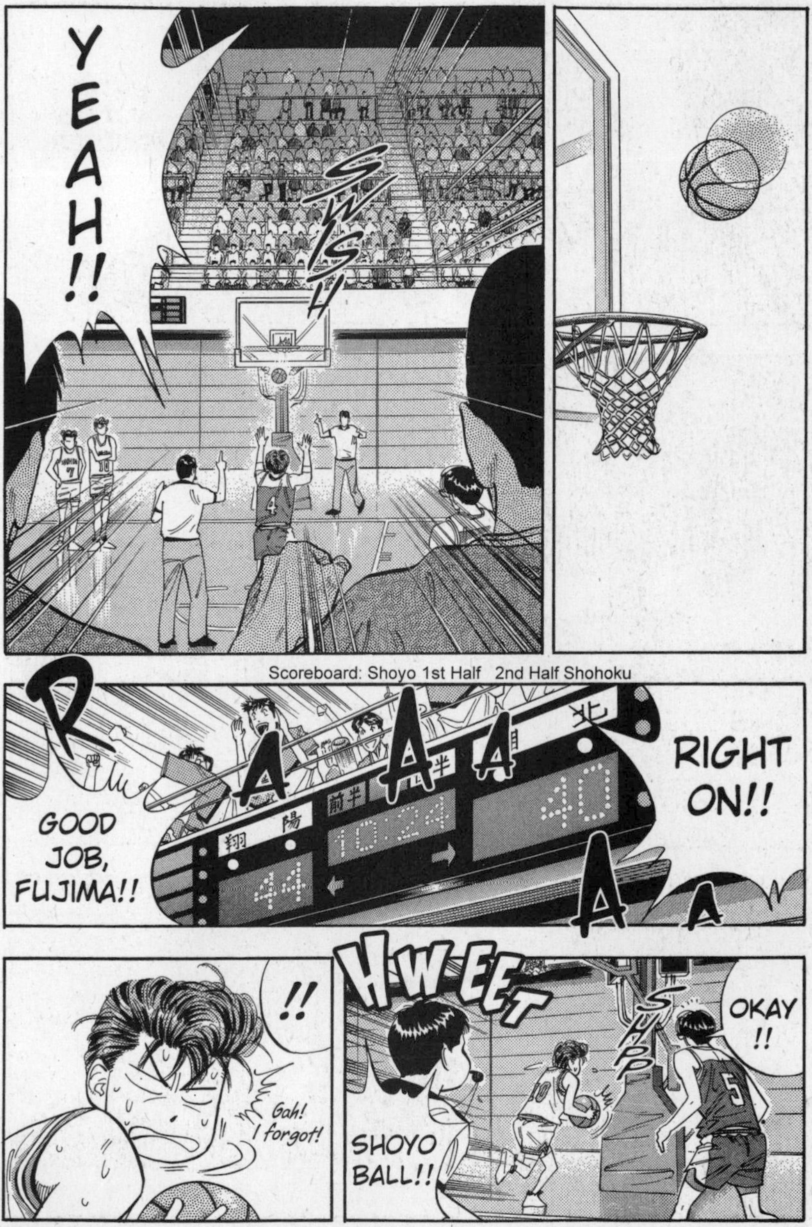
YEAH!!
SWISH
Scoreboard: Shoyo 1st Half 2nd Half Shohoku
RIGHT ON!!
RAAAAA
GOOD JOB, FUJIMA!!
HWEET
OKAY!!
SHPP
SHOYO BALL!!
!!
Gah! I forgot!

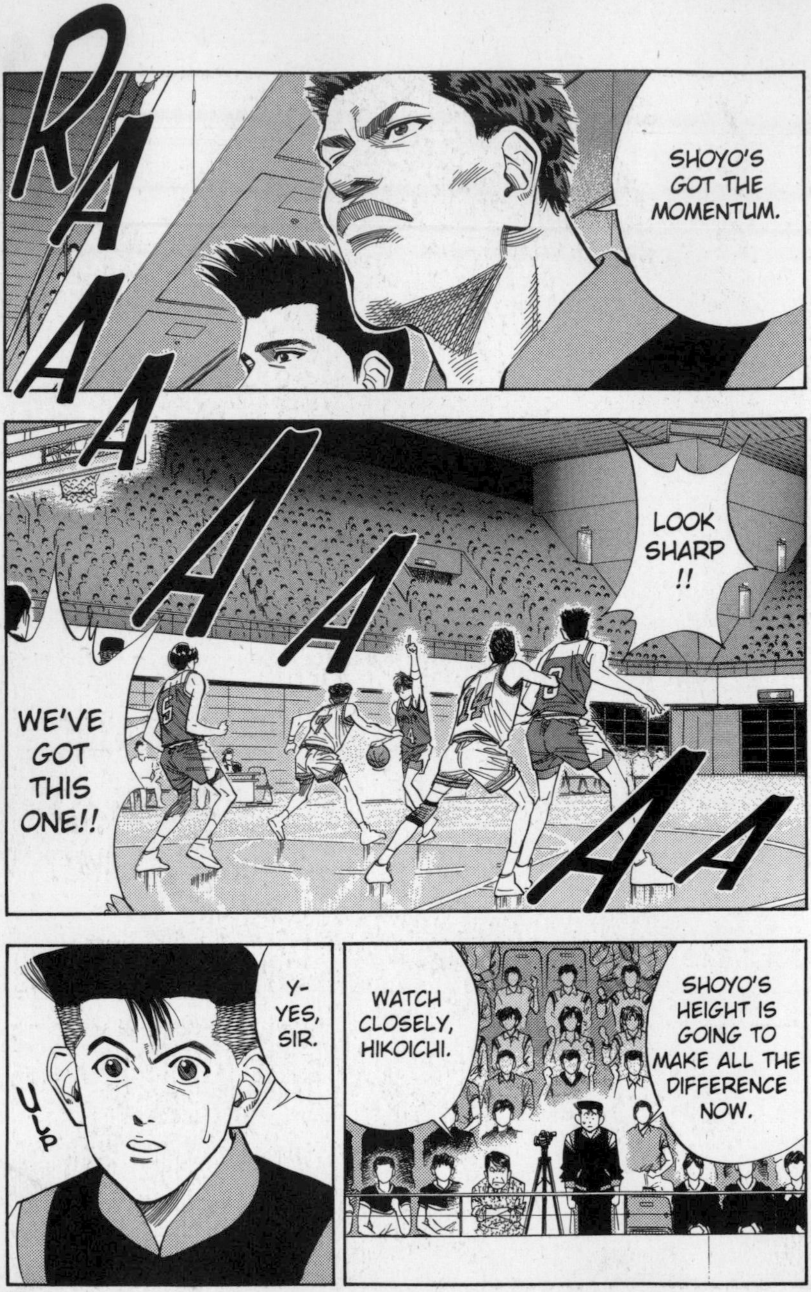
RAAAAAAAAA
SHOYO'S GOT THE MOMENTUM.
LOOK SHARP!!
WE'VE GOT THIS ONE!!
SHOYO'S HEIGHT IS GOING TO MAKE ALL THE DIFFERENCE NOW.
WATCH CLOSELY, HIKOICHI.
Y- YES, SIR.
ULP

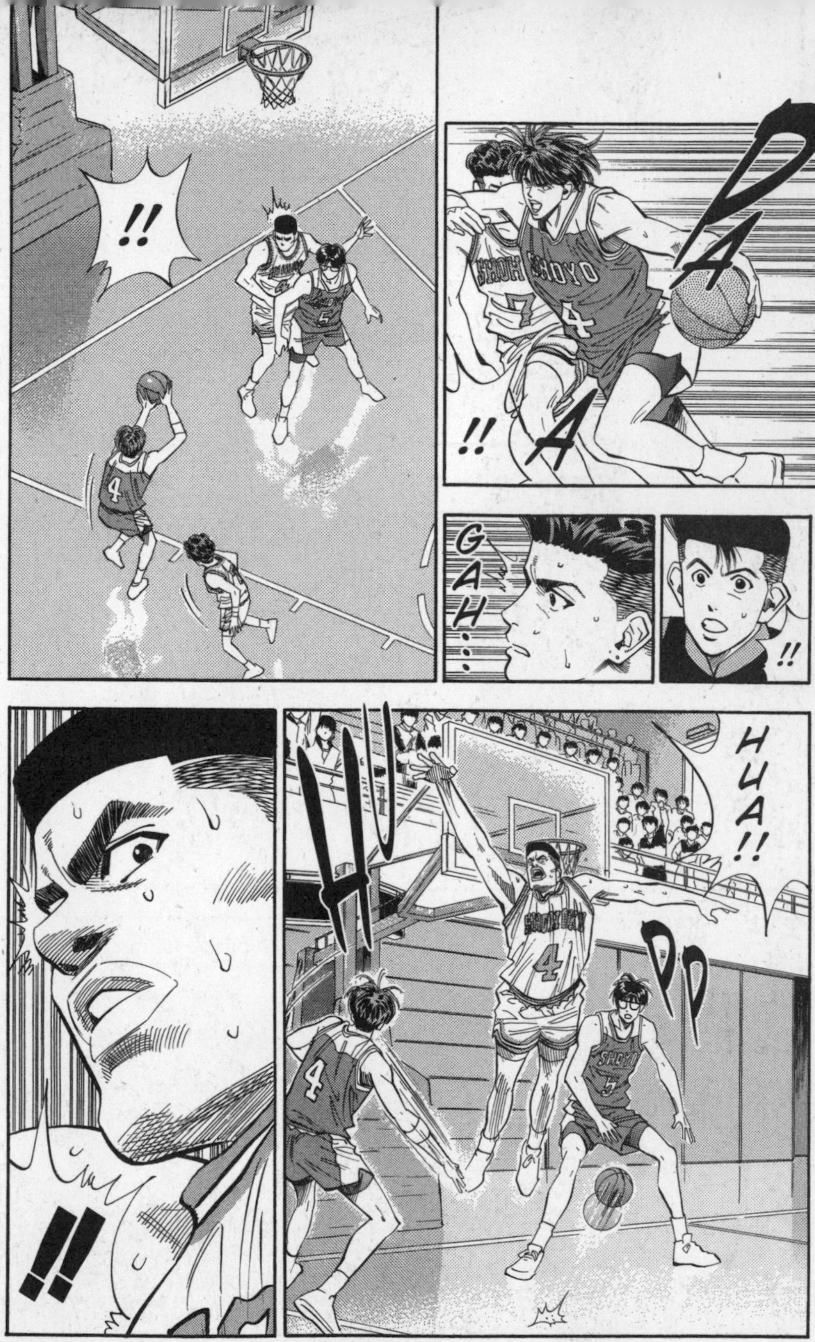
DA
A
!!
!!
GAH...
!!
HUA!!
H
DD
!!

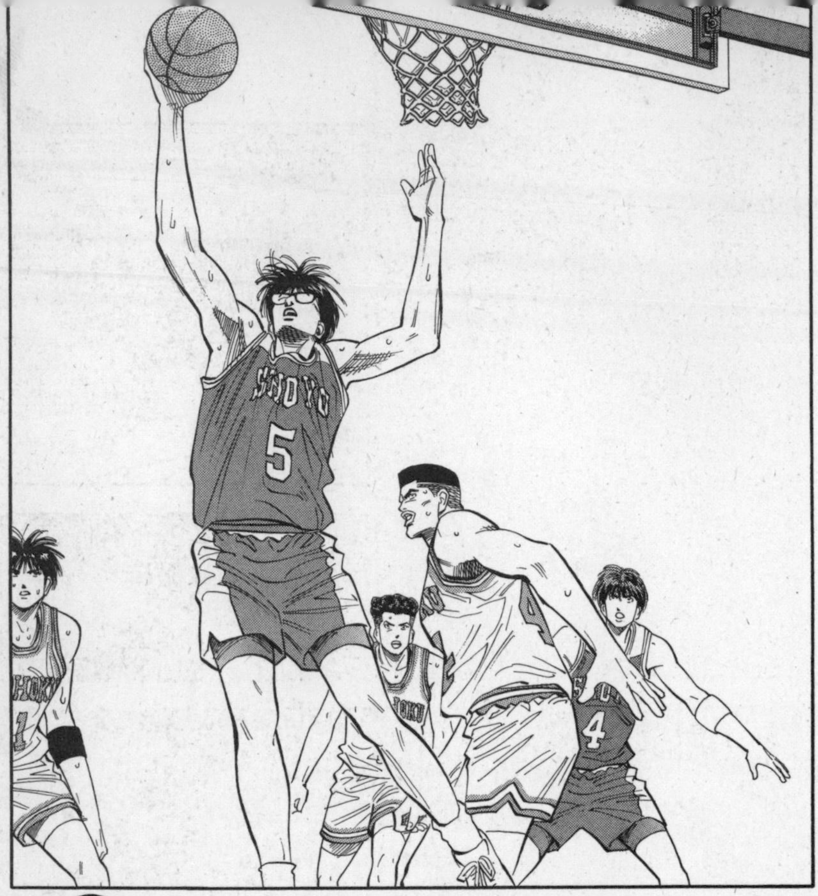

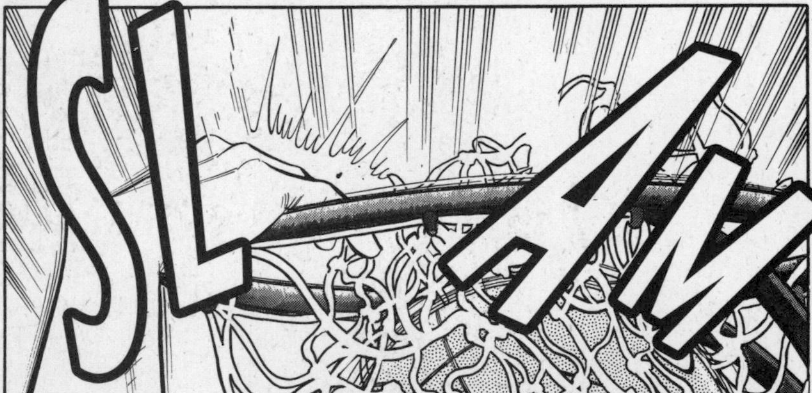
SLAM

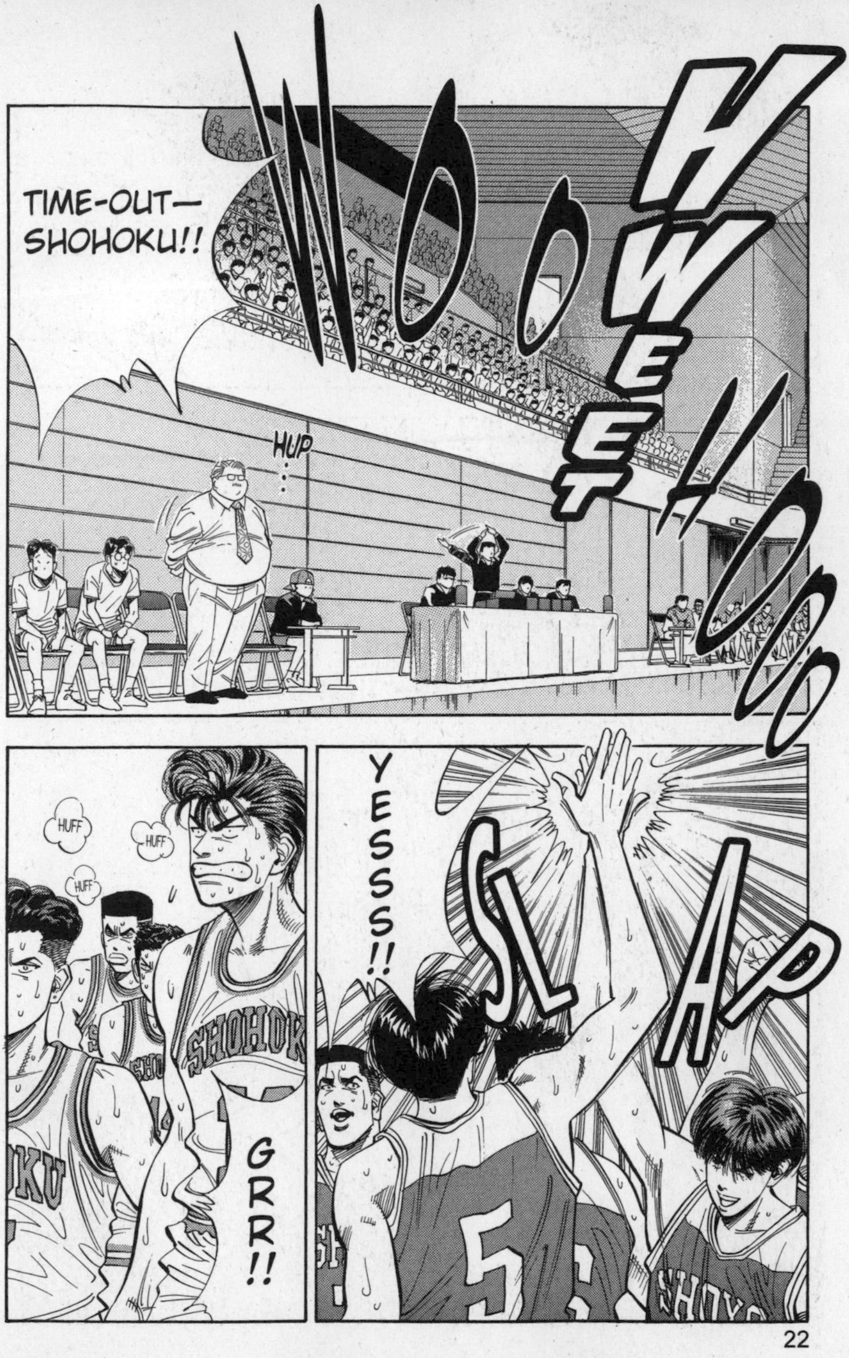
FWEET
WOOOHOOOO
TIME-OUT—SHOHOKU!!
HUP
YESSS!!
SLAP
HUFF
HUFF
HUFF
GRR!!

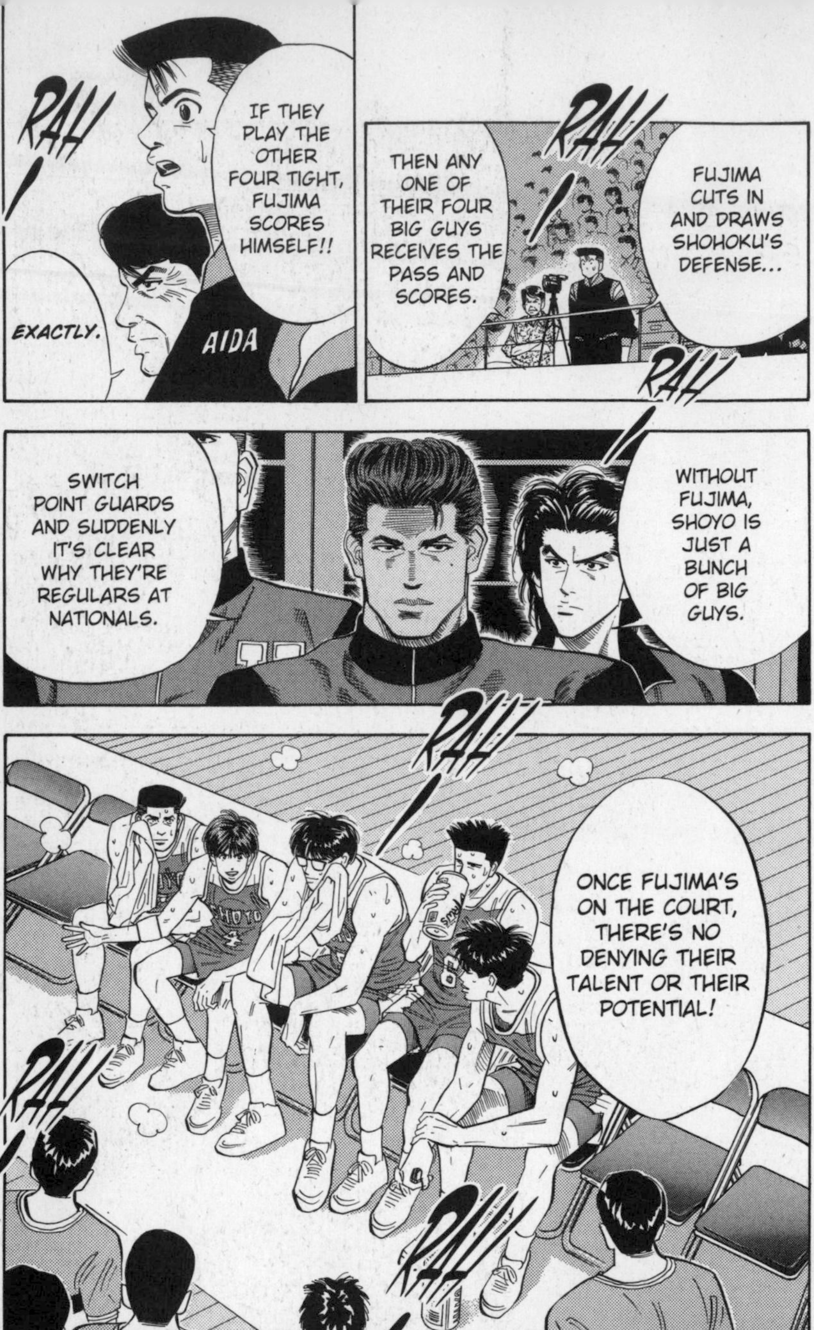
RAH!
FUJIMA CUTS IN AND DRAWS SHOHOKU'S DEFENSE...
RAH!
THEN ANY ONE OF THEIR FOUR BIG GUYS RECEIVES THE PASS AND SCORES.
IF THEY PLAY THE OTHER FOUR TIGHT, FUJIMA SCORES HIMSELF!!
RAH!
EXACTLY.
AIDA
RAH!
WITHOUT FUJIMA, SHOYO IS JUST A BUNCH OF BIG GUYS.
SWITCH POINT GUARDS AND SUDDENLY IT'S CLEAR WHY THEY'RE REGULARS AT NATIONALS.
RAH!
ONCE FUJIMA'S ON THE COURT, THERE'S NO DENYING THEIR TALENT OR THEIR POTENTIAL!
RAH!
RAH!

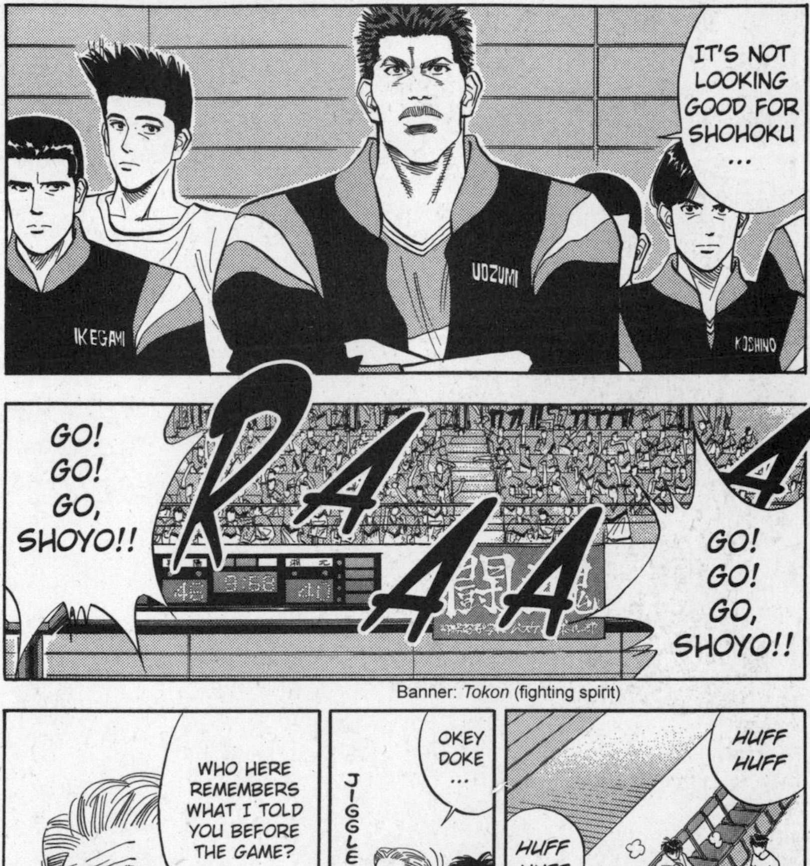
IT'S NOT LOOKING GOOD FOR SHOHOKU ...
IKEGAMI
UOZUMI
KOSHINO
GO! GO! GO, SHOYO!!
RAAAAA
GO! GO! GO, SHOYO!!

Banner: *Tokon* (fighting spirit)

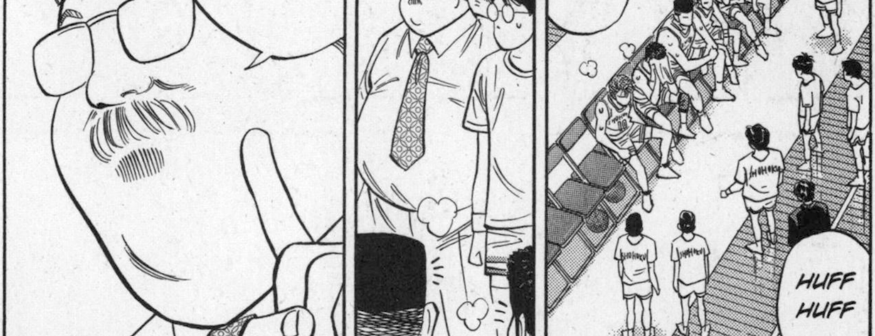
HUFF HUFF
HUFF HUFF
HUFF HUFF
OKEY DOKE ...
JIGGLE...
WHO HERE REMEMBERS WHAT I TOLD YOU BEFORE THE GAME?

READ THIS WAY

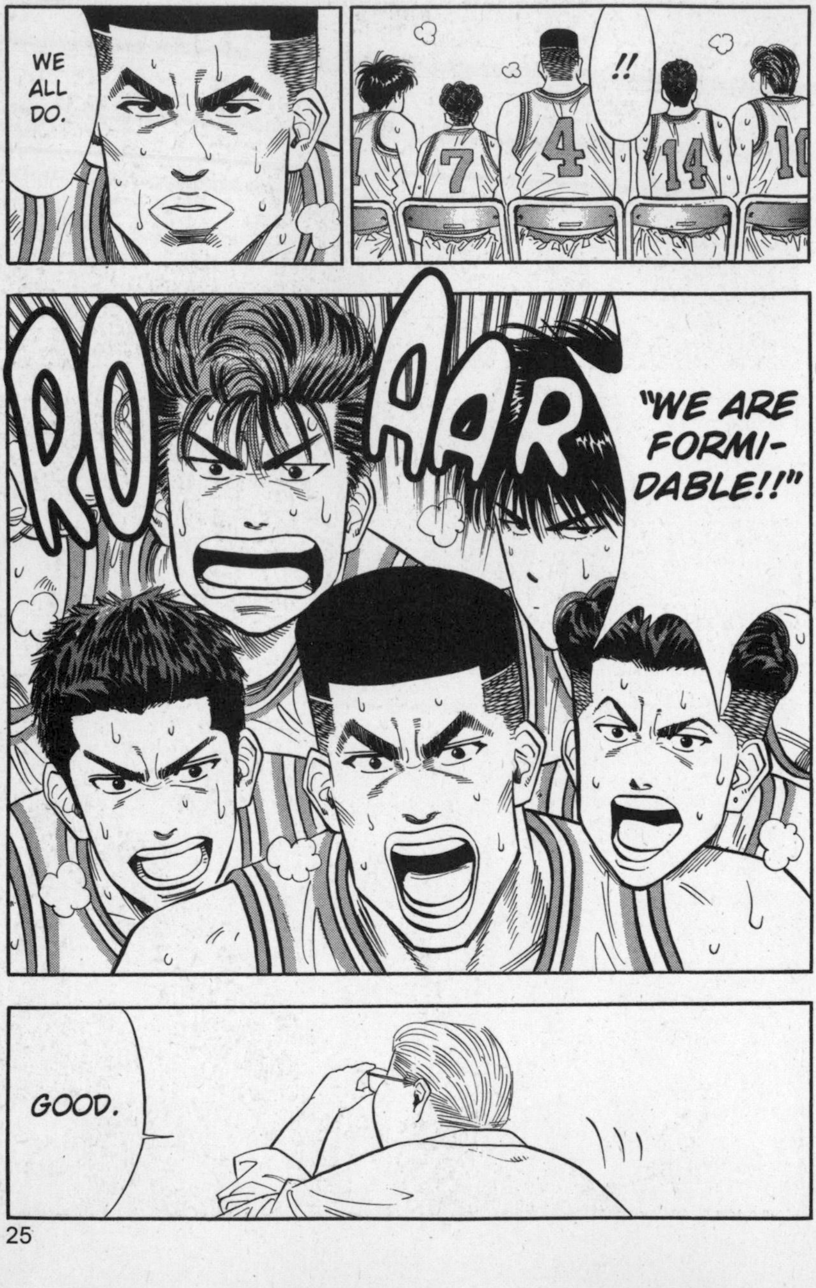
!!
WE ALL DO.
ROAAR
"WE ARE FORMIDABLE!!"
GOOD.

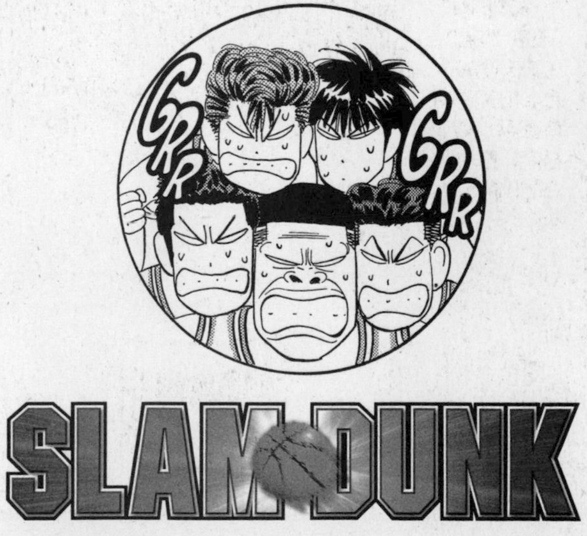
GRR
GRR

SLAM DUNK

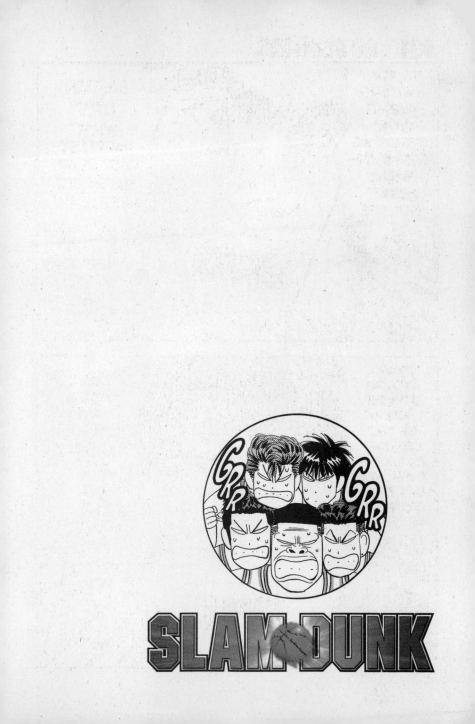

#91 60 SECONDS

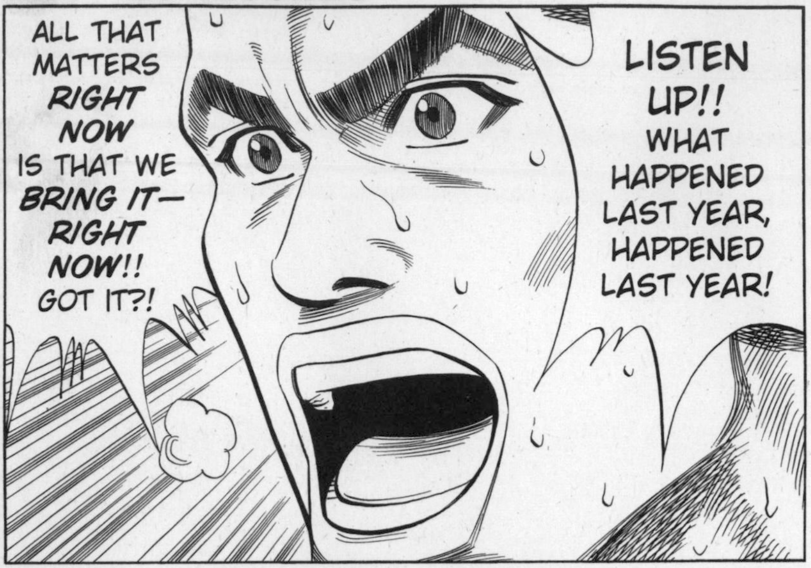
LISTEN UP!! WHAT HAPPENED LAST YEAR, HAPPENED LAST YEAR!
ALL THAT MATTERS RIGHT NOW IS THAT WE BRING IT— RIGHT NOW!! GOT IT?!

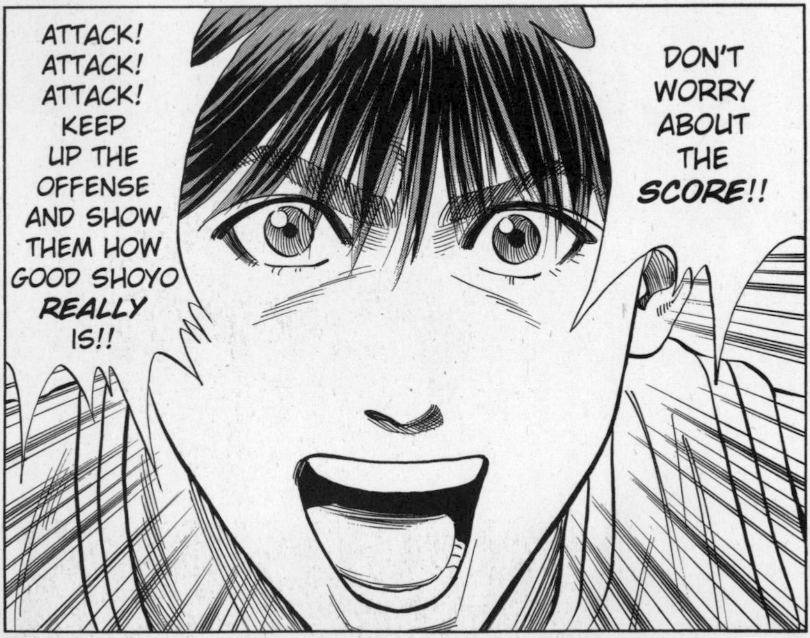
DON'T WORRY ABOUT THE SCORE!!
ATTACK! ATTACK! ATTACK! KEEP UP THE OFFENSE AND SHOW THEM HOW GOOD SHOYO REALLY IS!!

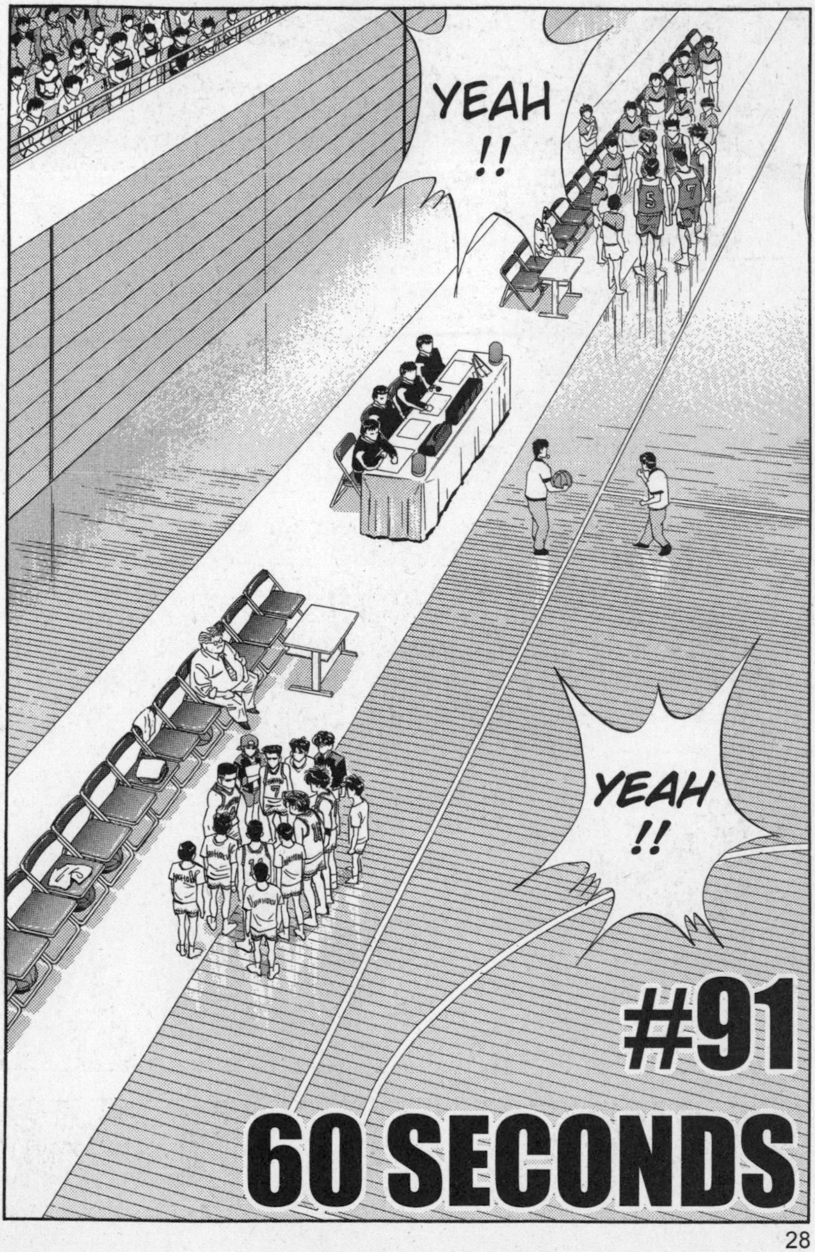
YEAH !!
YEAH !!
#91
60 SECONDS

READ THIS WAY

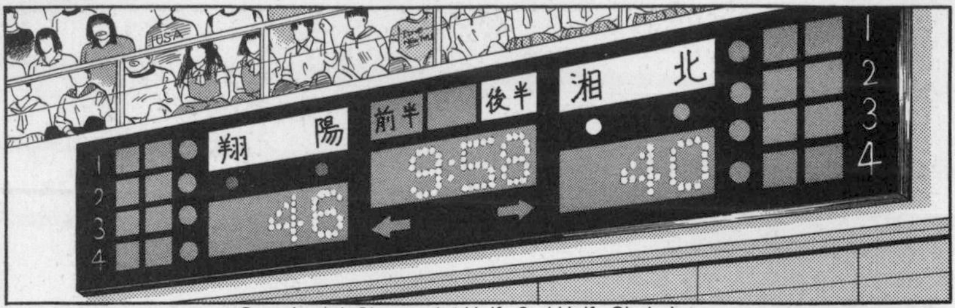
翔陽
前半
後半
湘北
9:58
46
40

Scoreboard: Shoyo 1st Half 2nd Half Shohoku

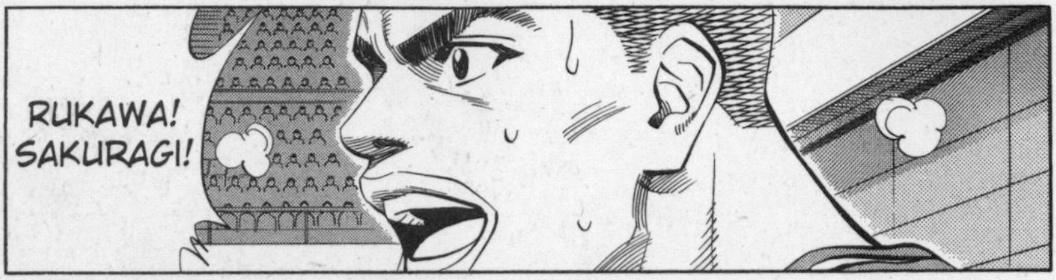
RUKAWA! SAKURAGI!

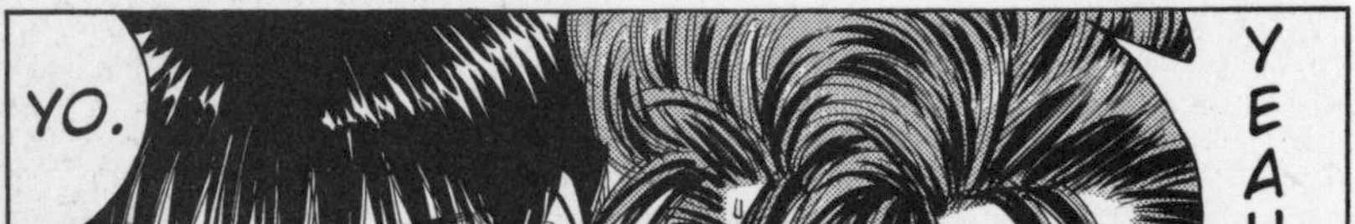
YEAH!!
YO.

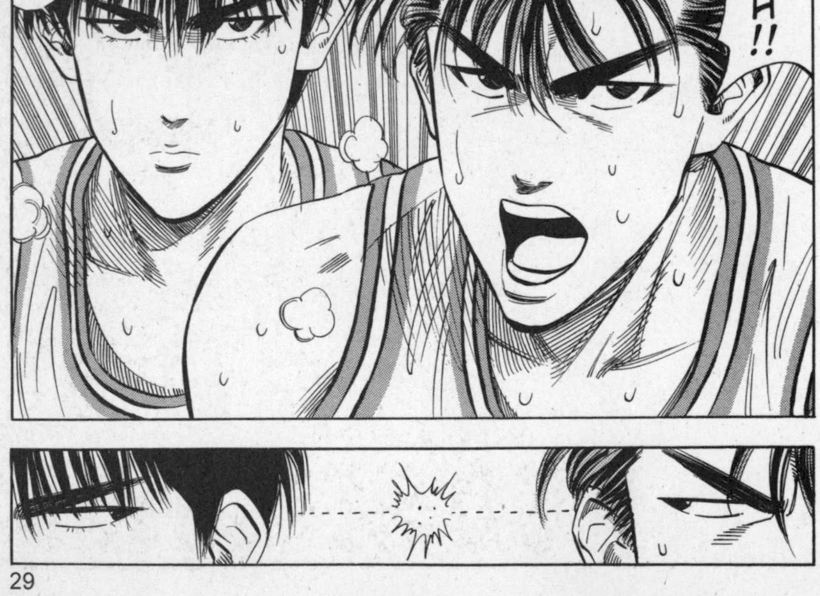

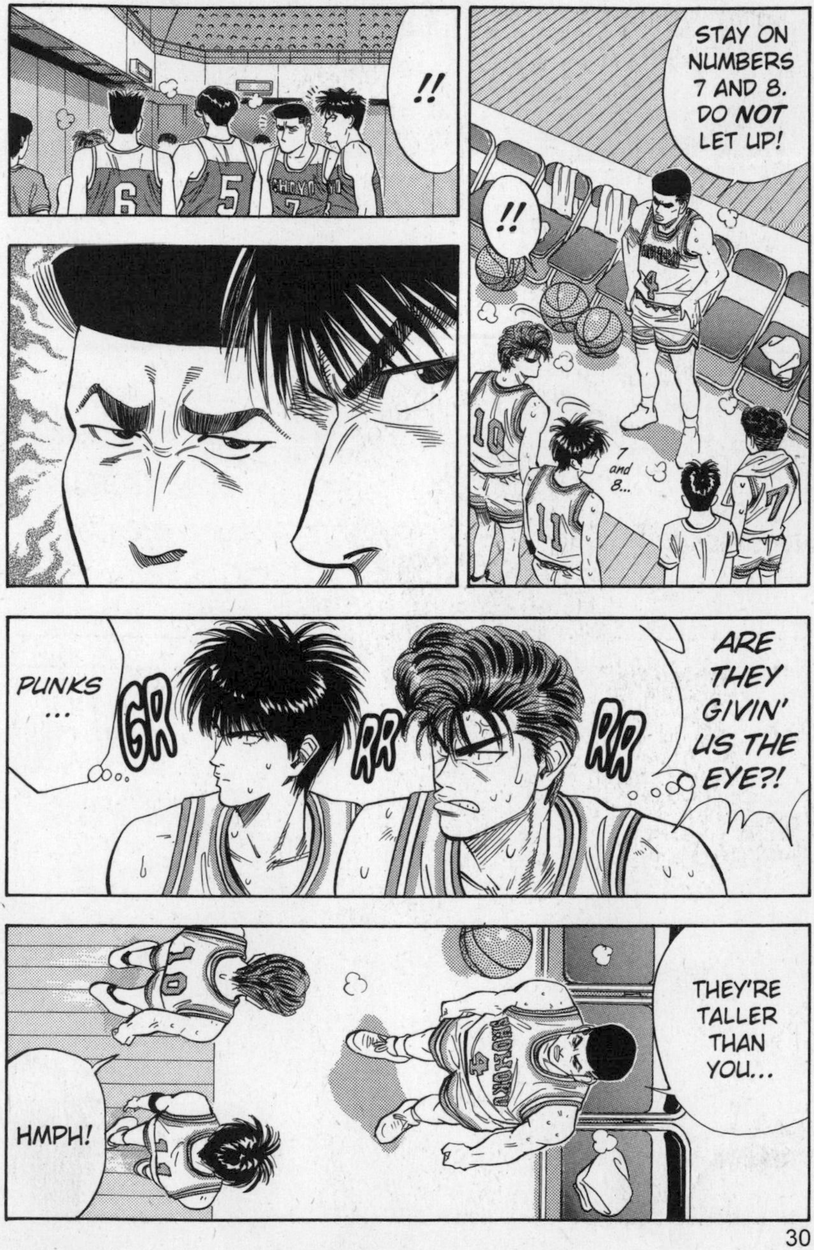
STAY ON NUMBERS 7 AND 8. DO NOT LET UP!
!!
7 and 8...
!!
ARE THEY GIVIN' US THE EYE?!
GR RR RR
PUNKS...
THEY'RE TALLER THAN YOU...
HMPH!

READ THIS WAY

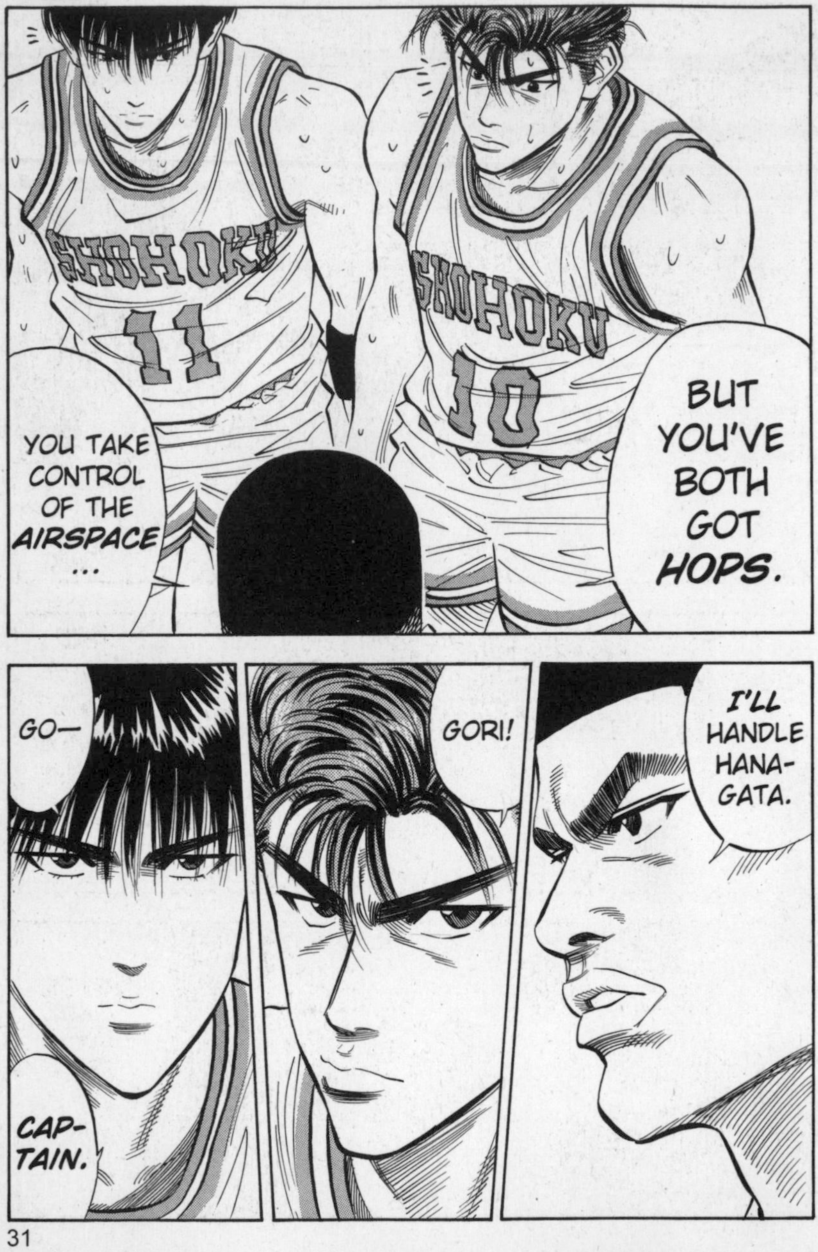
BUT YOU'VE BOTH GOT HOPS.
YOU TAKE CONTROL OF THE AIRSPACE ...
I'LL HANDLE HANA-GATA.
GORI!
GO—
CAP-TAIN.

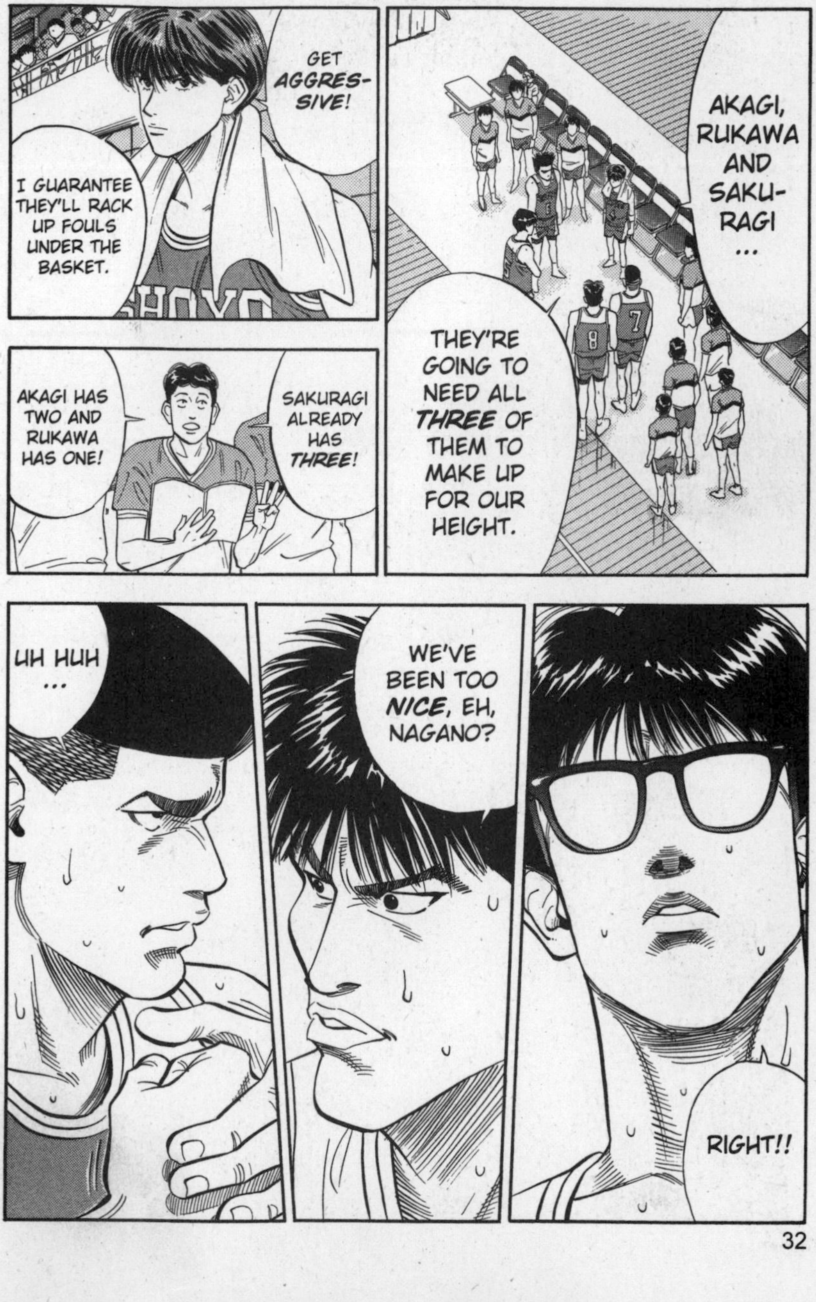
AKAGI, RUKAWA AND SAKURAGI ...
THEY'RE GOING TO NEED ALL THREE OF THEM TO MAKE UP FOR OUR HEIGHT.
GET AGGRESSIVE!
I GUARANTEE THEY'LL RACK UP FOULS UNDER THE BASKET.
SAKURAGI ALREADY HAS THREE!
AKAGI HAS TWO AND RUKAWA HAS ONE!
RIGHT!!
WE'VE BEEN TOO NICE, EH, NAGANO?
UH HUH ...

READ THIS WAY

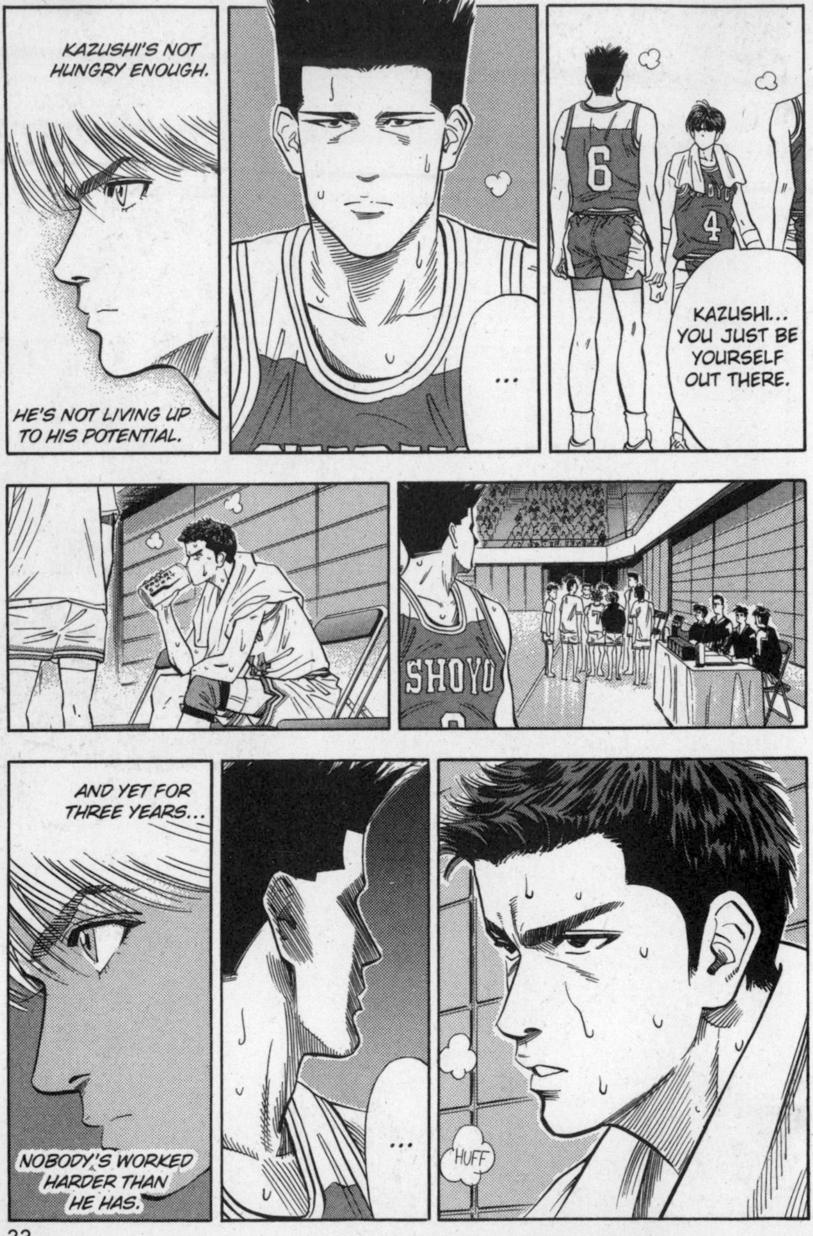
KAZUSHI... YOU JUST BE YOURSELF OUT THERE.
...
KAZUSHI'S NOT HUNGRY ENOUGH.
HE'S NOT LIVING UP TO HIS POTENTIAL.
SHOYO
HUFF
...
AND YET FOR THREE YEARS...
NOBODY'S WORKED HARDER THAN HE HAS.

FUJI-MA!
BOX-AND-ONE DEFENSE※. LET ME TAKE MITSUI.
!
YOU SURE ABOUT THAT?
MITSUI GOT MVP IN JUNIOR HIGH, YOU KNOW.

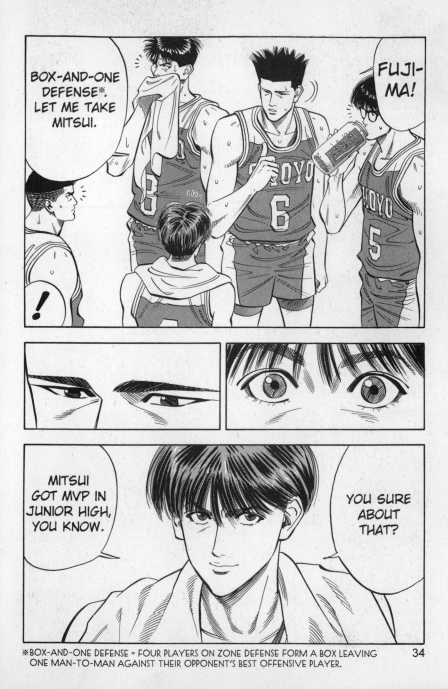

※BOX-AND-ONE DEFENSE = FOUR PLAYERS ON ZONE DEFENSE FORM A BOX LEAVING ONE MAN-TO-MAN AGAINST THEIR OPPONENT'S BEST OFFENSIVE PLAYER.

READ THIS WAY

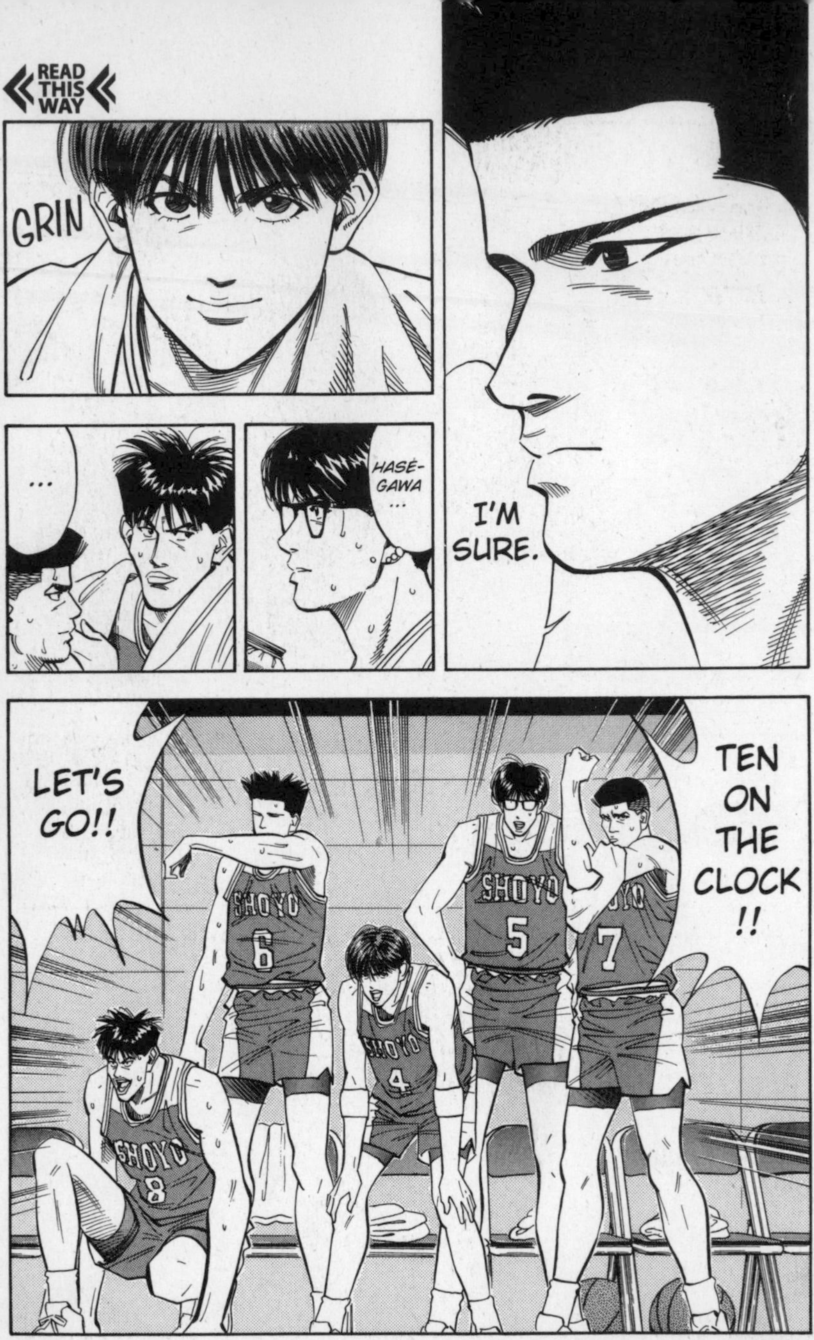
I'M SURE.
GRIN
HASE-GAWA ...
...
TEN ON THE CLOCK !!
LET'S GO!!

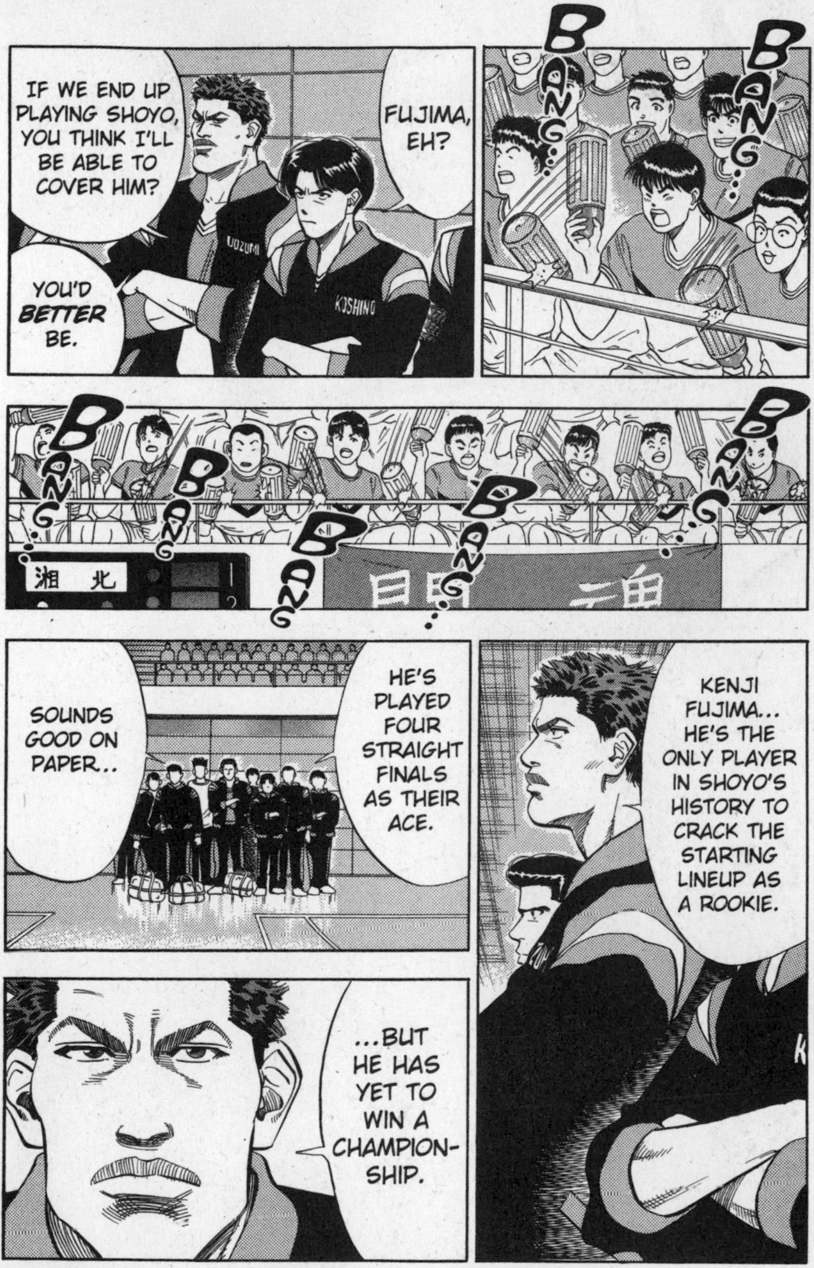
BANG...
BANG...
FUJIMA, EH?
IF WE END UP PLAYING SHOYO, YOU THINK I'LL BE ABLE TO COVER HIM?
UOZUMI
KOSHINO
YOU'D **BETTER** BE.
BANG...
BANG...
BANG...
BANG
BANG...
湘北
KENJI FUJIMA... HE'S THE ONLY PLAYER IN SHOYO'S HISTORY TO CRACK THE STARTING LINEUP AS A ROOKIE.
HE'S PLAYED FOUR STRAIGHT FINALS AS THEIR ACE.
SOUNDS GOOD ON PAPER...
...BUT HE HAS YET TO WIN A CHAMPIONSHIP.

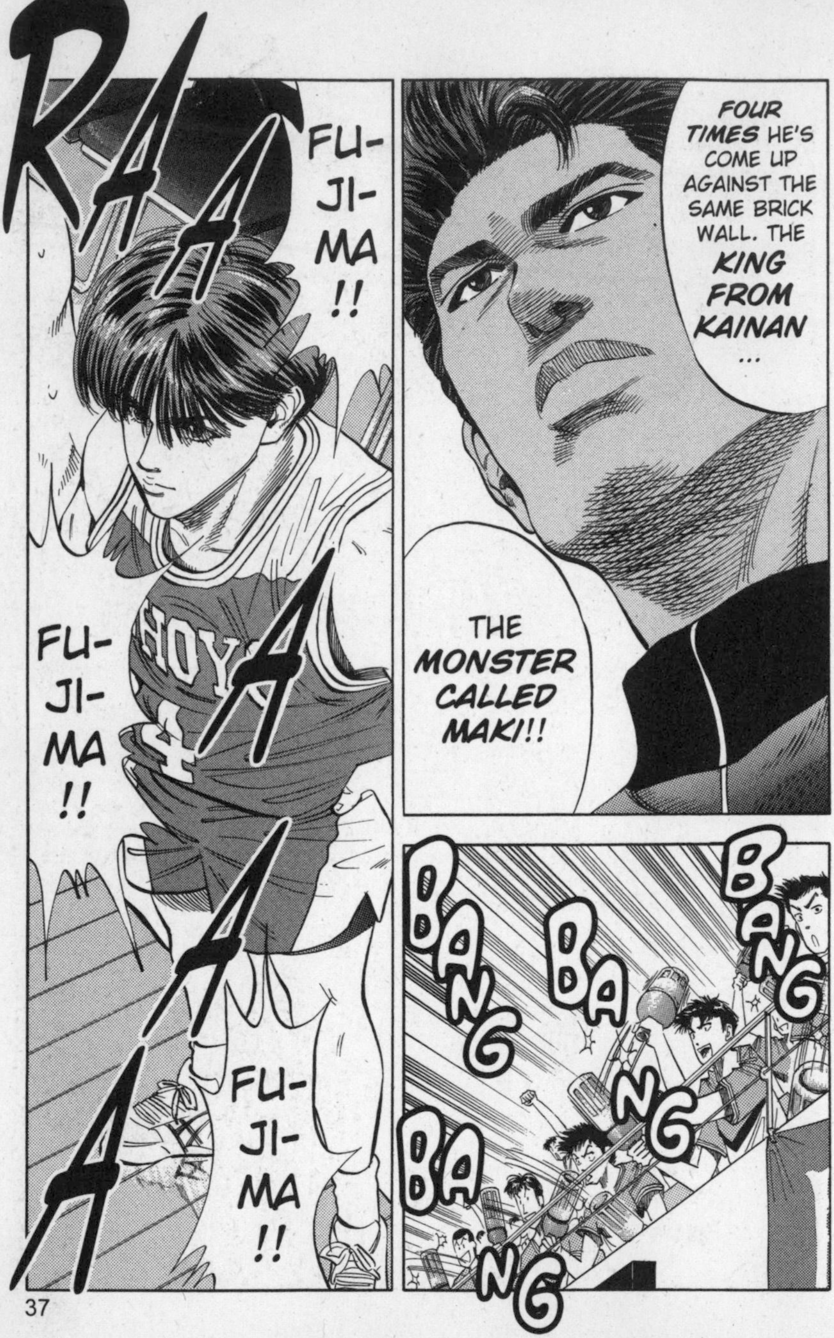

FOUR TIMES HE'S COME UP AGAINST THE SAME BRICK WALL. THE KING FROM KAINAN ...
THE MONSTER CALLED MAKI!!
BANG
BANG
BANG
BANG
BANG
RAAAAA
FU-JI-MA!!
FU-JI-MA!!
FU-JI-MA!!

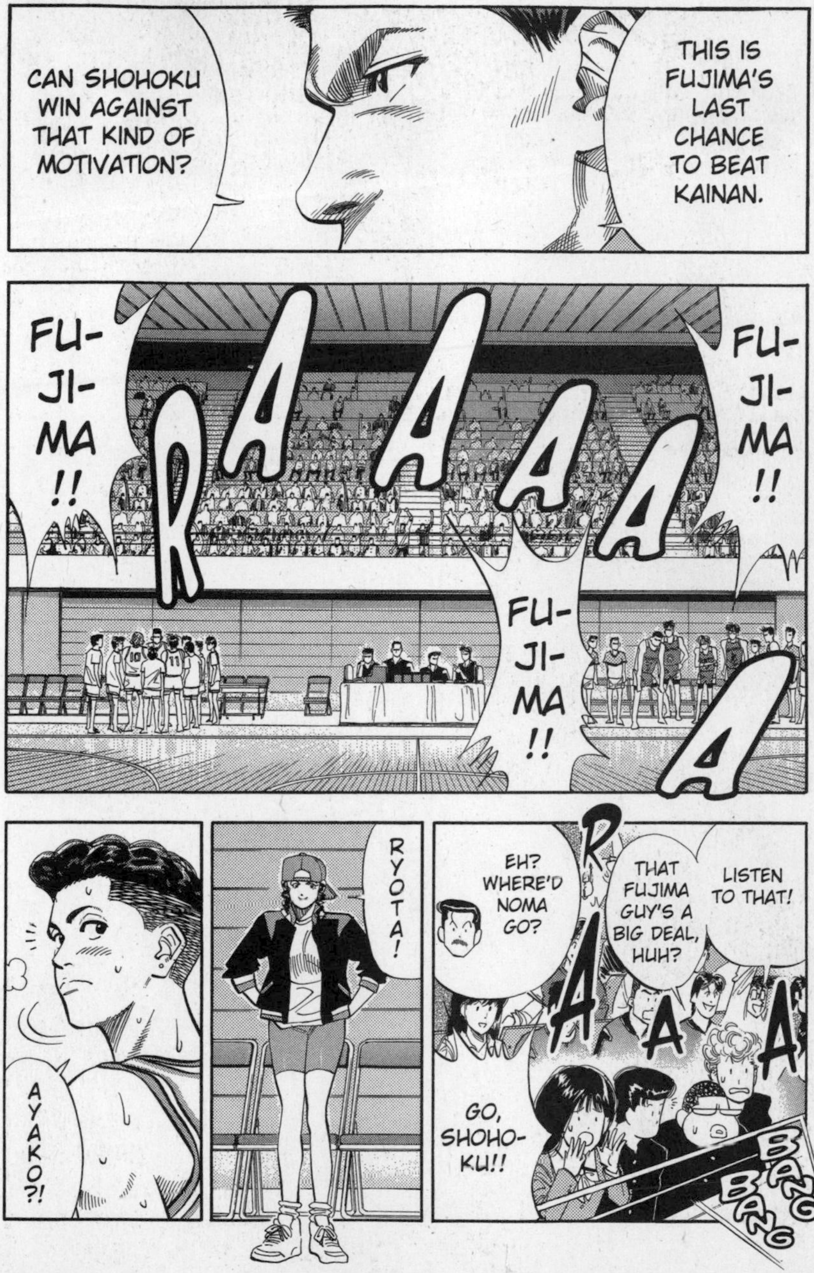
THIS IS FUJIMA'S LAST CHANCE TO BEAT KAINAN.
CAN SHOHOKU WIN AGAINST THAT KIND OF MOTIVATION?
FU-JI-MA!!
FU-JI-MA!!
FU-JI-MA!!
RAAAAAA
LISTEN TO THAT!
THAT FUJIMA GUY'S A BIG DEAL, HUH?
EH? WHERE'D NOMA GO?
RAAA
GO, SHOHOKU!!
BANG BANG
RYOTA!
AYAKO?!

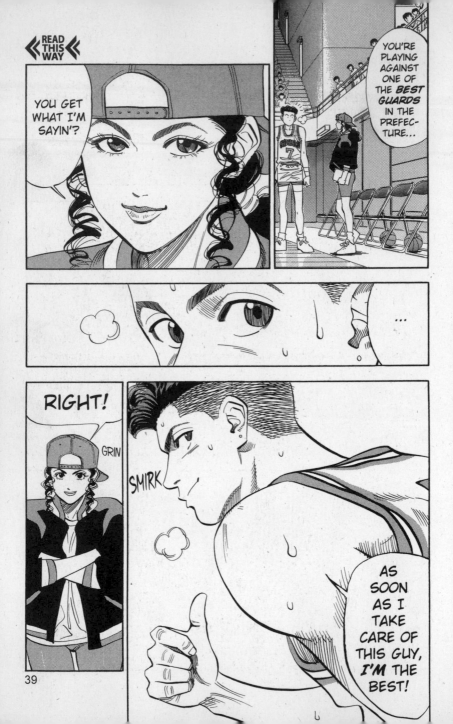

YOU'RE PLAYING AGAINST ONE OF THE **BEST GUARDS** IN THE PREFECTURE...

YOU GET WHAT I'M SAYIN'?

...

RIGHT!

GRIN

SMIRK

AS SOON AS I TAKE CARE OF THIS GUY, *I'M* THE BEST!

39

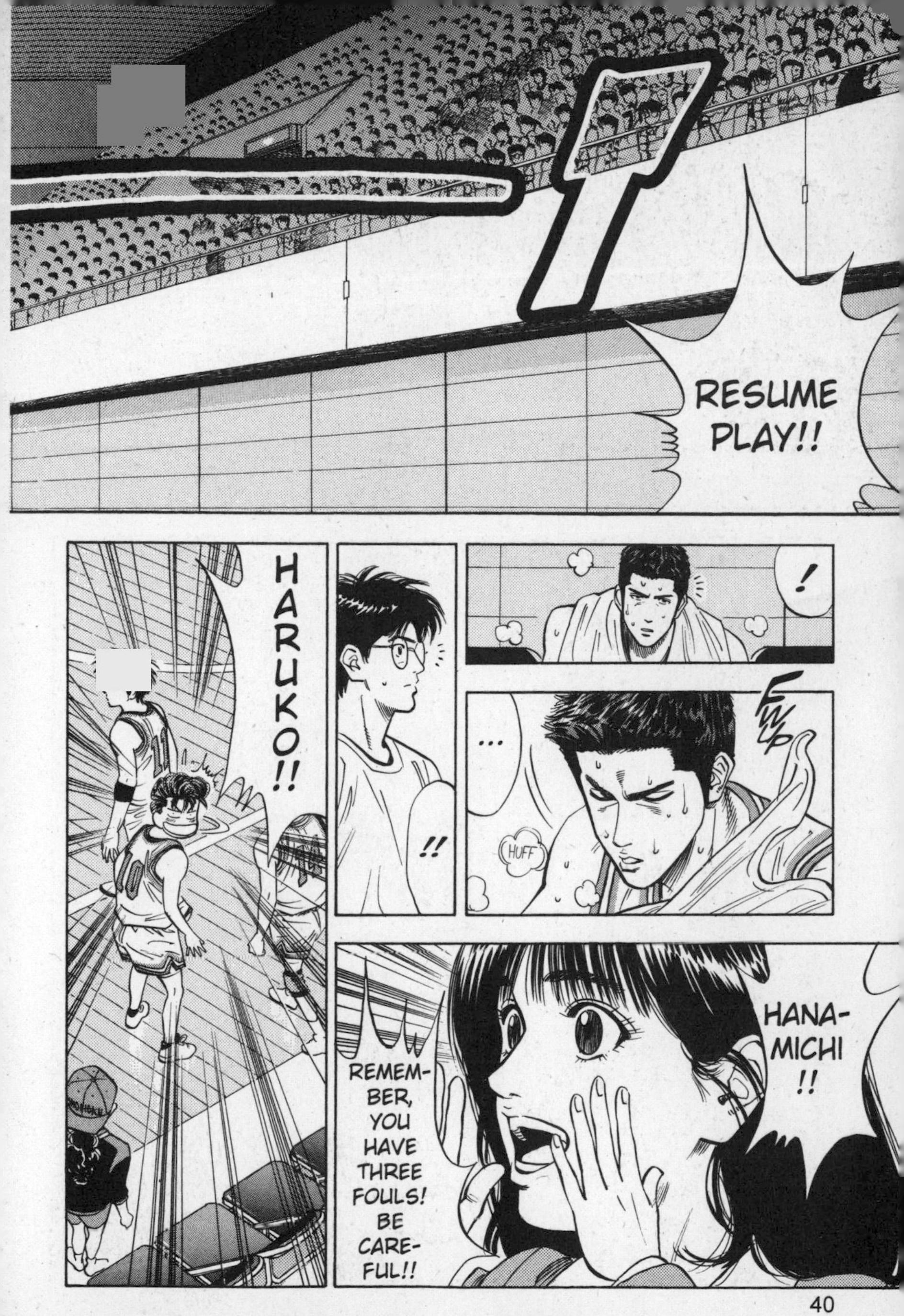
RESUME PLAY!!
!
...
FWUP
HUFF
!!
HANA-MICHI!!
REMEMBER, YOU HAVE THREE FOULS! BE CAREFUL!!
HARUKO!!

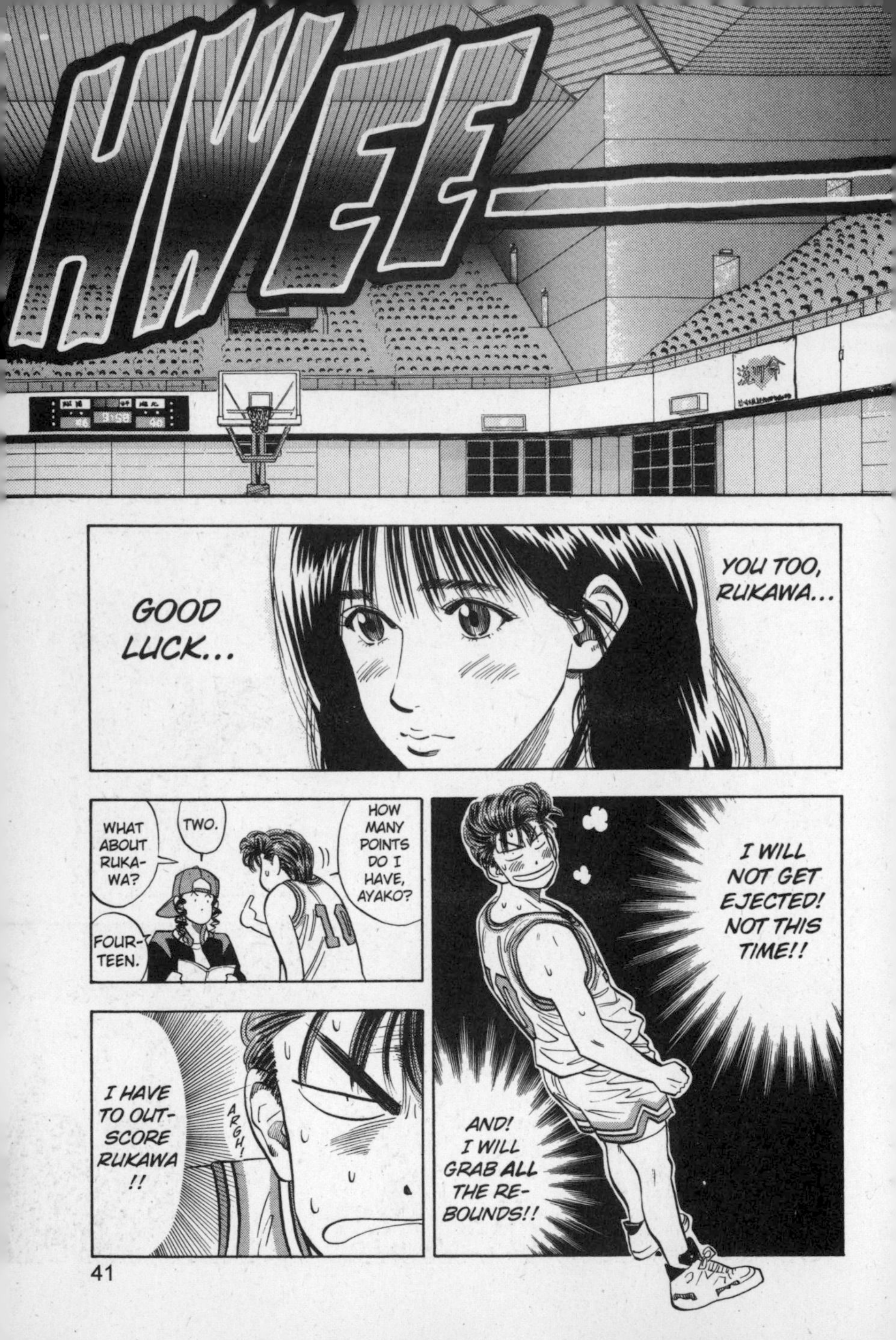
HWEE—
GOOD LUCK...
YOU TOO, RUKAWA...
I WILL NOT GET EJECTED! NOT THIS TIME!!
AND! I WILL GRAB ALL THE RE-BOUNDS!!
HOW MANY POINTS DO I HAVE, AYAKO?
TWO.
WHAT ABOUT RUKA-WA?
FOUR-TEEN.
ARGH!
I HAVE TO OUT-SCORE RUKAWA!!

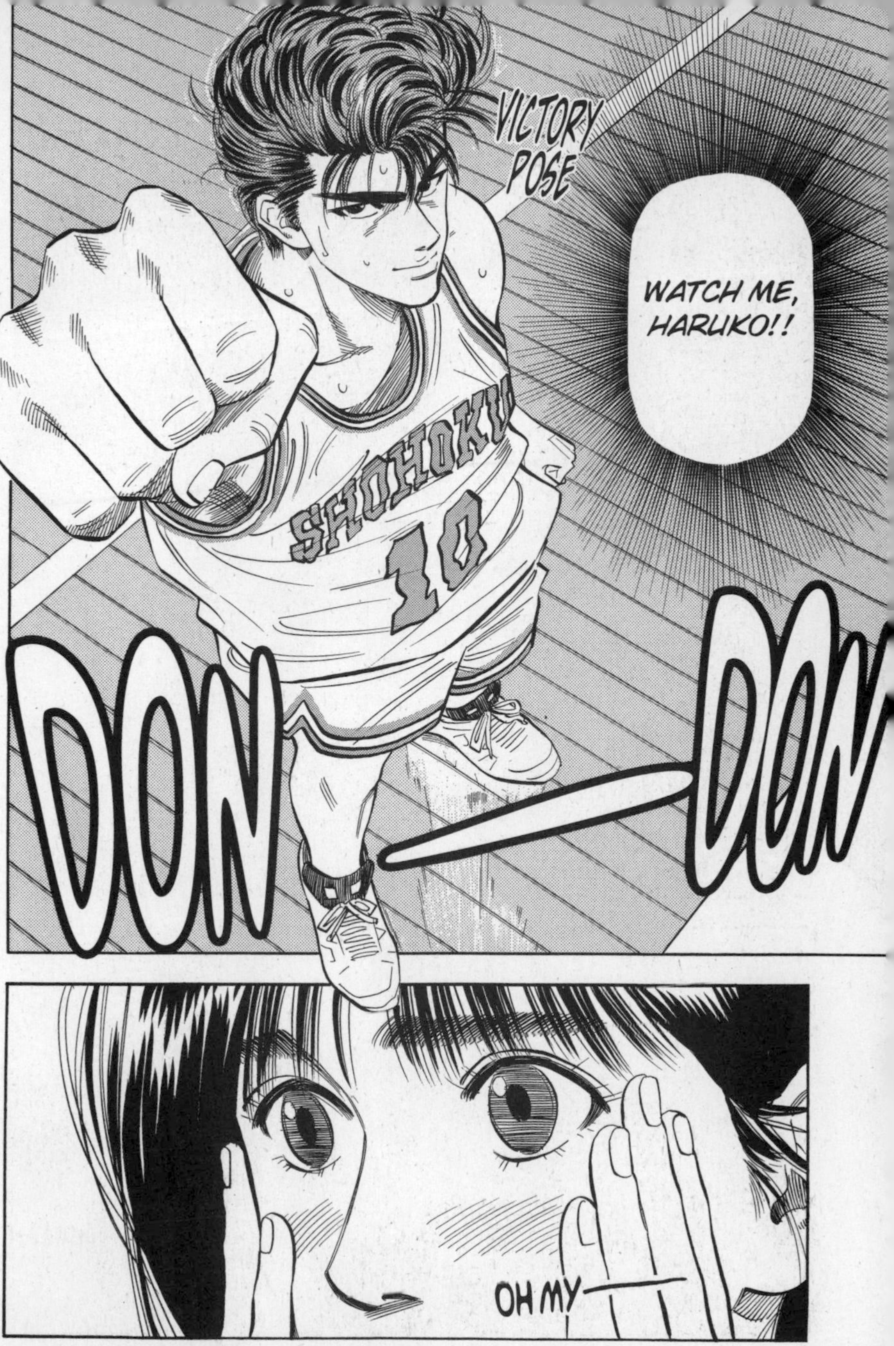
VICTORY POSE
WATCH ME, HARUKO!!
DON DON
OH MY—

READ THIS WAY

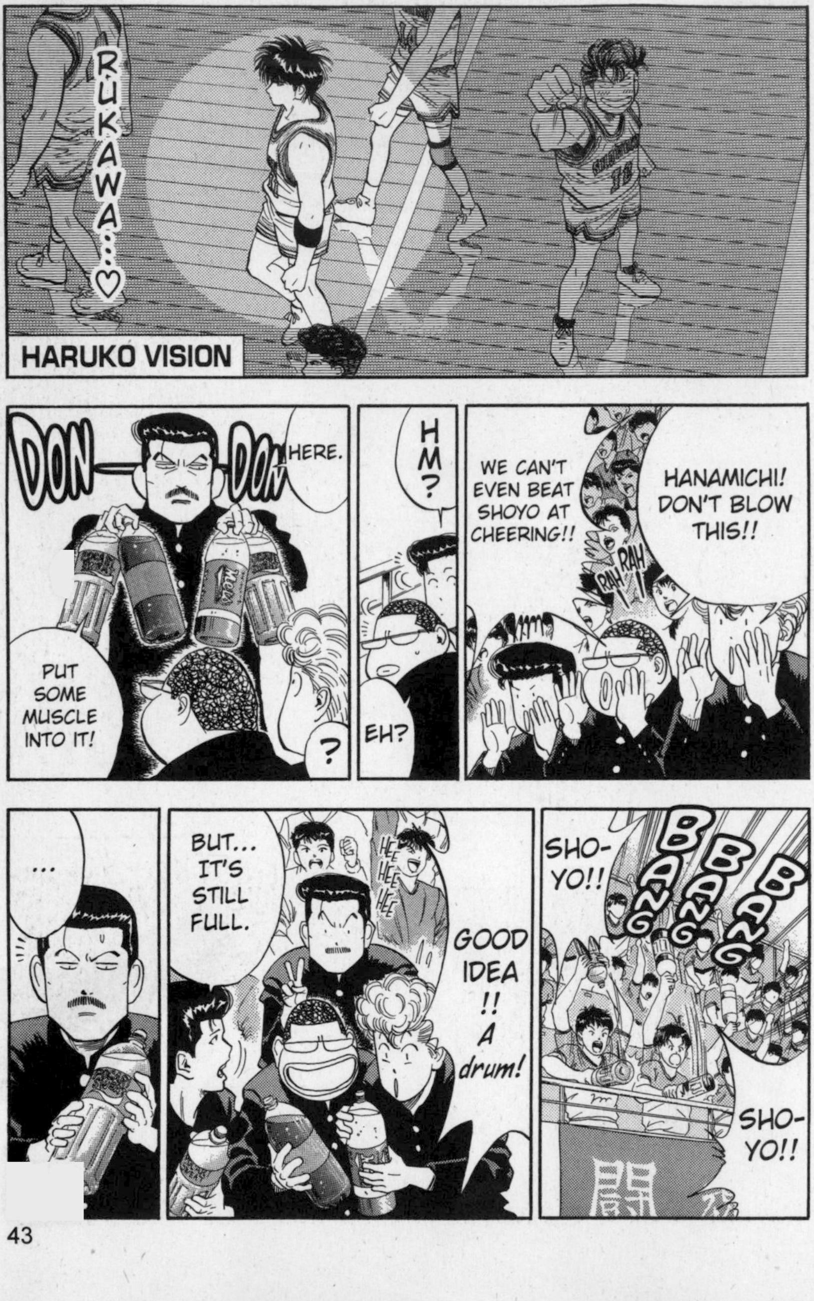
RUKAWA...♡
HARUKO VISION
HANAMICHI! DON'T BLOW THIS!!
RAH
RAH
WE CAN'T EVEN BEAT SHOYO AT CHEERING!!
HM?
EH?
HERE.
DON
DON
PUT SOME MUSCLE INTO IT!
?
BANG
BANG
BANG
SHO-YO!!
SHO-YO!!
BUT... IT'S STILL FULL.
HEE HEE HEE
GOOD IDEA!! A drum!
...

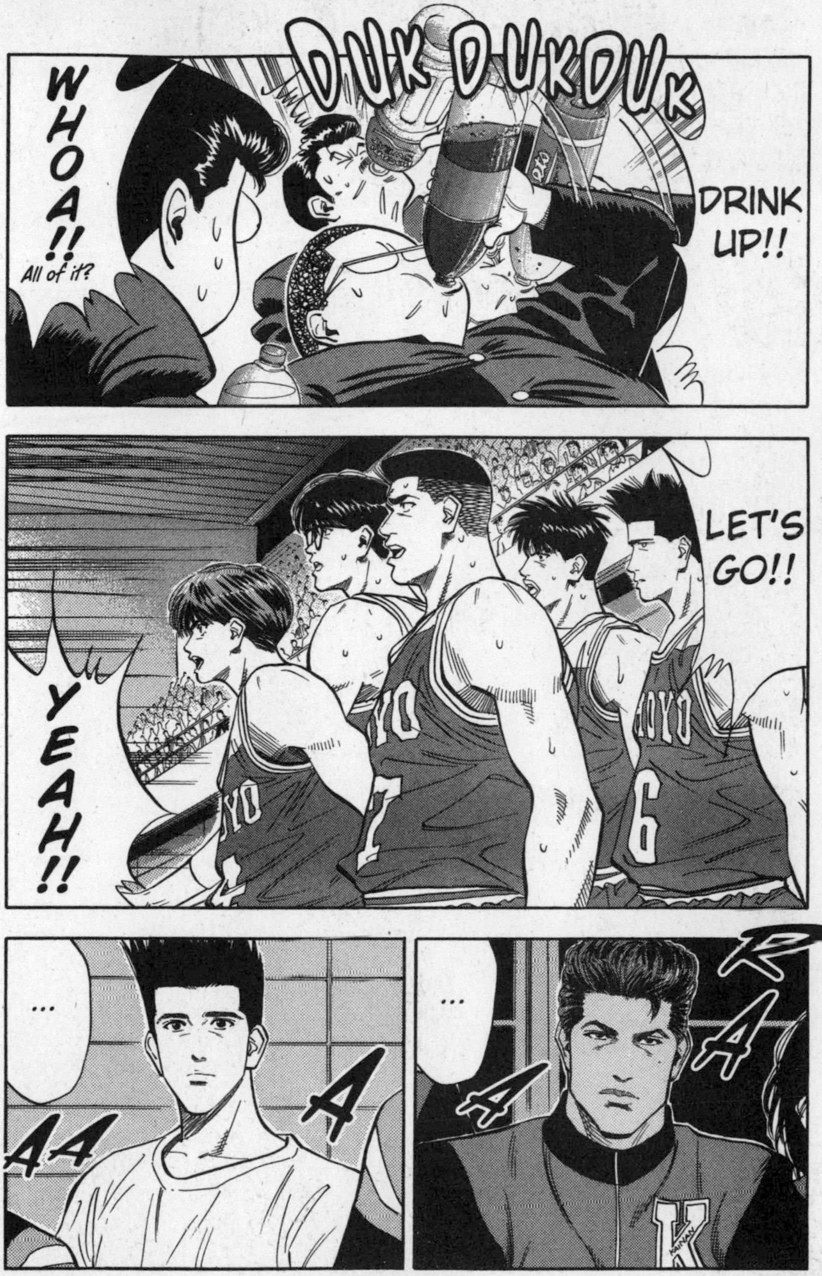
DUK DUKDUK
DRINK UP!!
WHOA!!
All of it?
LET'S GO!!
YEAH!!
...
RAAA
...
A
AA

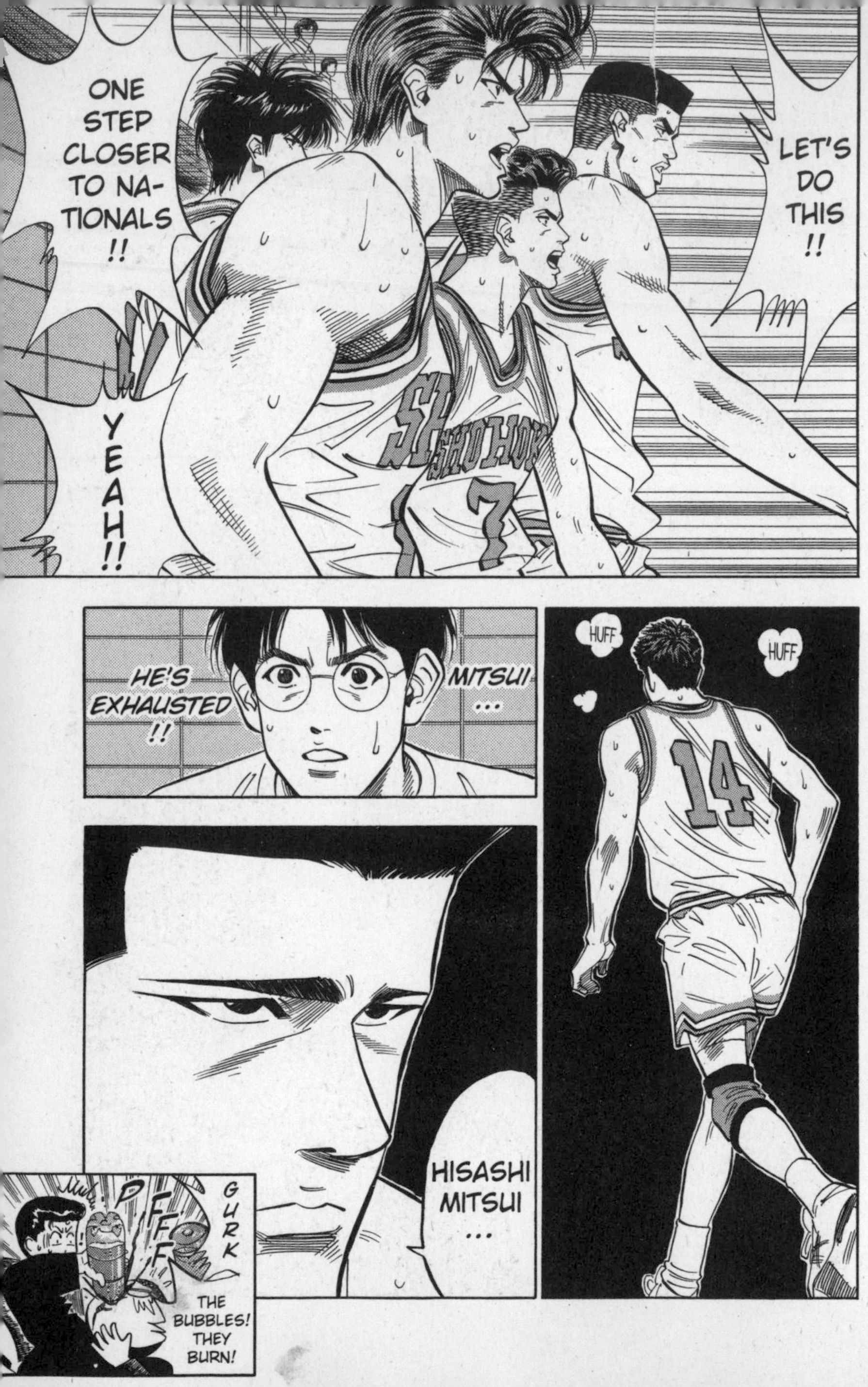
LET'S DO THIS!!
ONE STEP CLOSER TO NATIONALS!!
YEAH!!
HUFF
HUFF
MITSUI...
HE'S EXHAUSTED!!
HISASHI MITSUI...
GURK
PFFF
THE BUBBLES! THEY BURN!

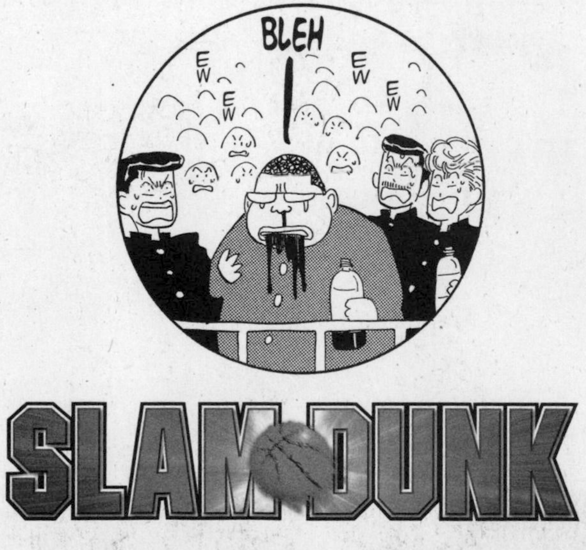
BLEH
EW
EW
EW
EW

SLAM DUNK

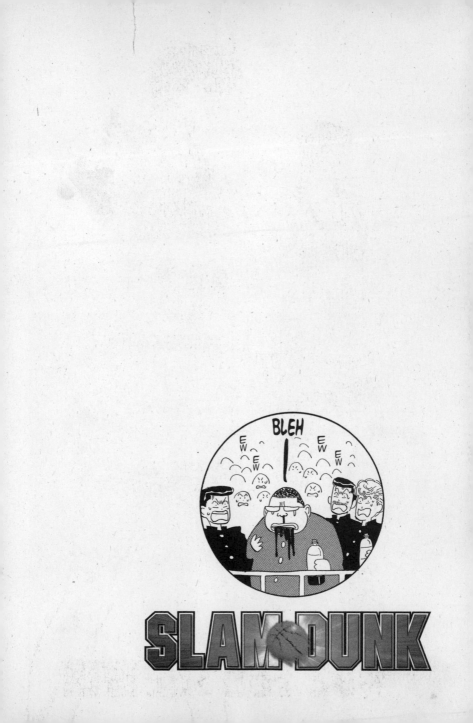

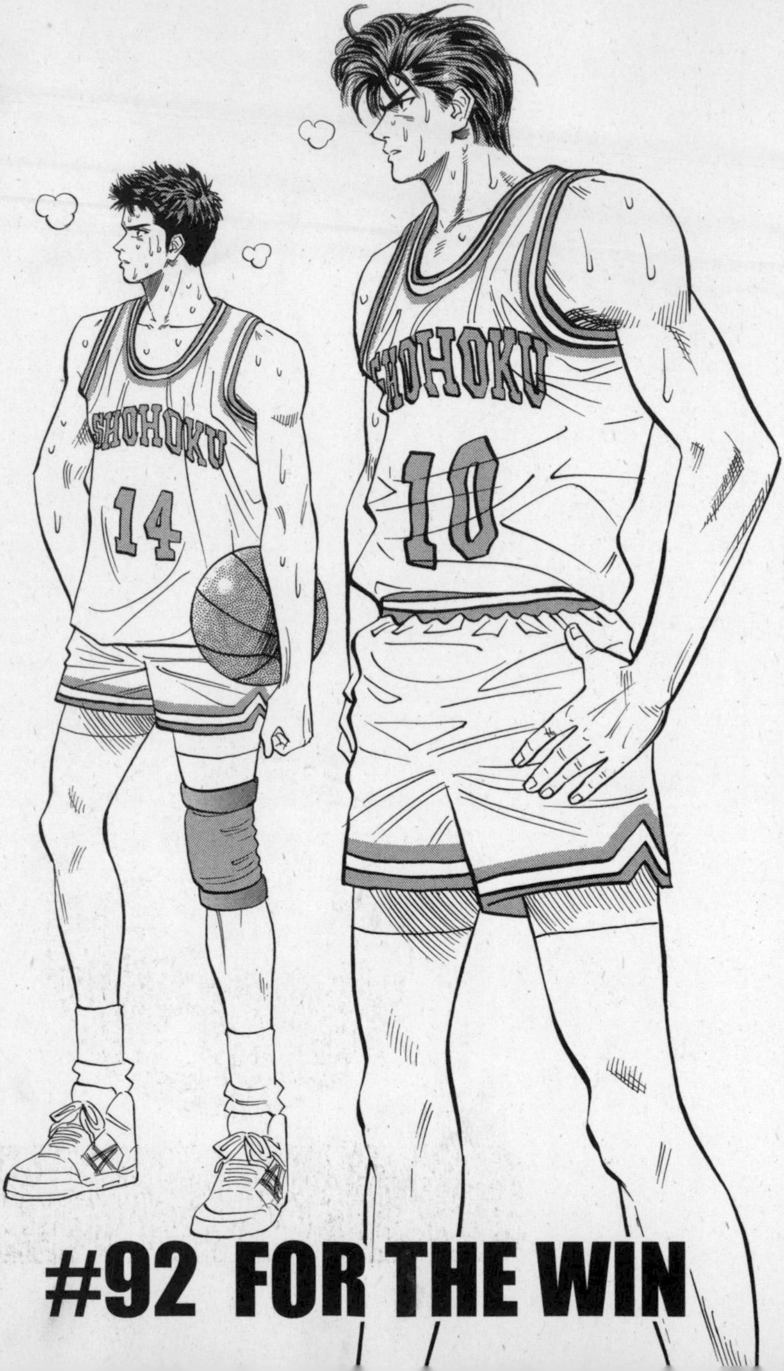
SHOHOKU
10
SHOHOKU
14

#92 FOR THE WIN

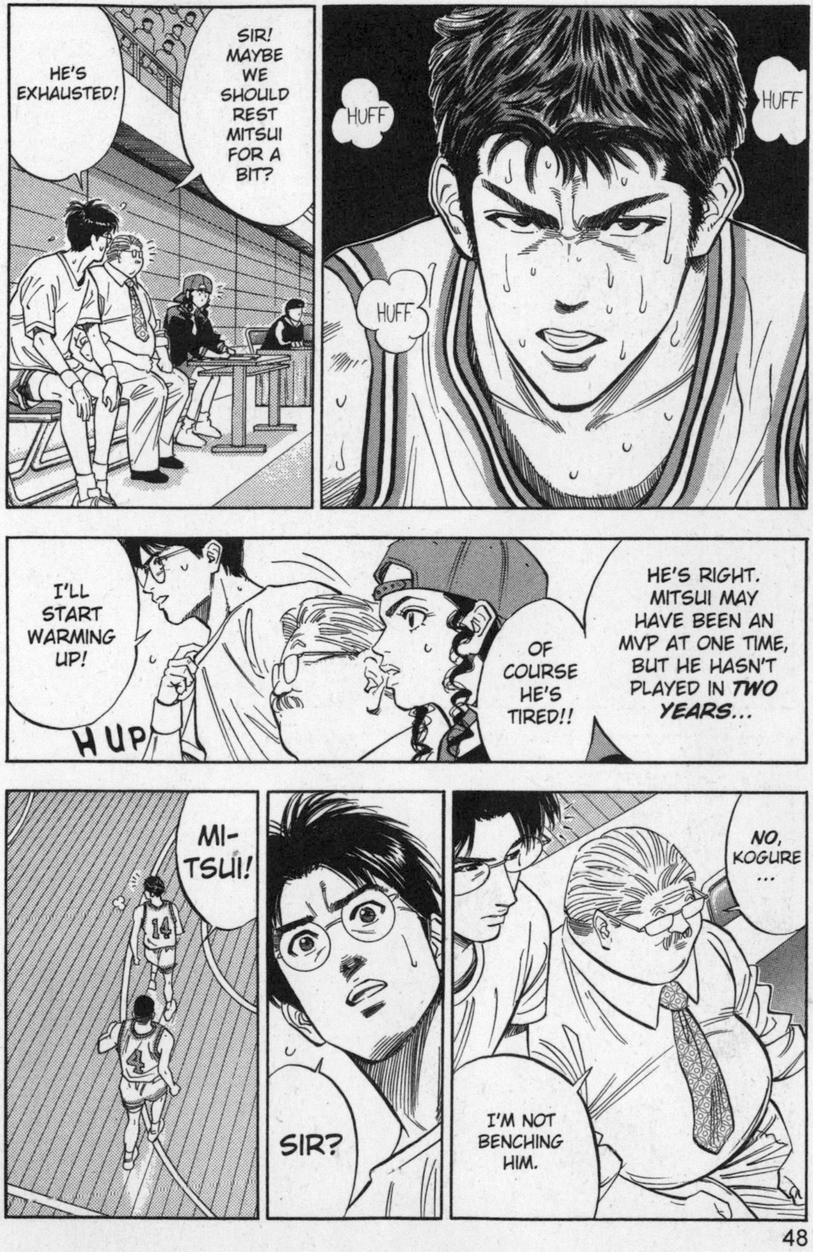
HUFF
HUFF
HUFF
SIR! MAYBE WE SHOULD REST MITSUI FOR A BIT?
HE'S EXHAUSTED!
HE'S RIGHT. MITSUI MAY HAVE BEEN AN MVP AT ONE TIME, BUT HE HASN'T PLAYED IN TWO YEARS...
OF COURSE HE'S TIRED!!
I'LL START WARMING UP!
HUP
NO, KOGURE ...
I'M NOT BENCHING HIM.
SIR?
MI-TSUI!

READ THIS WAY

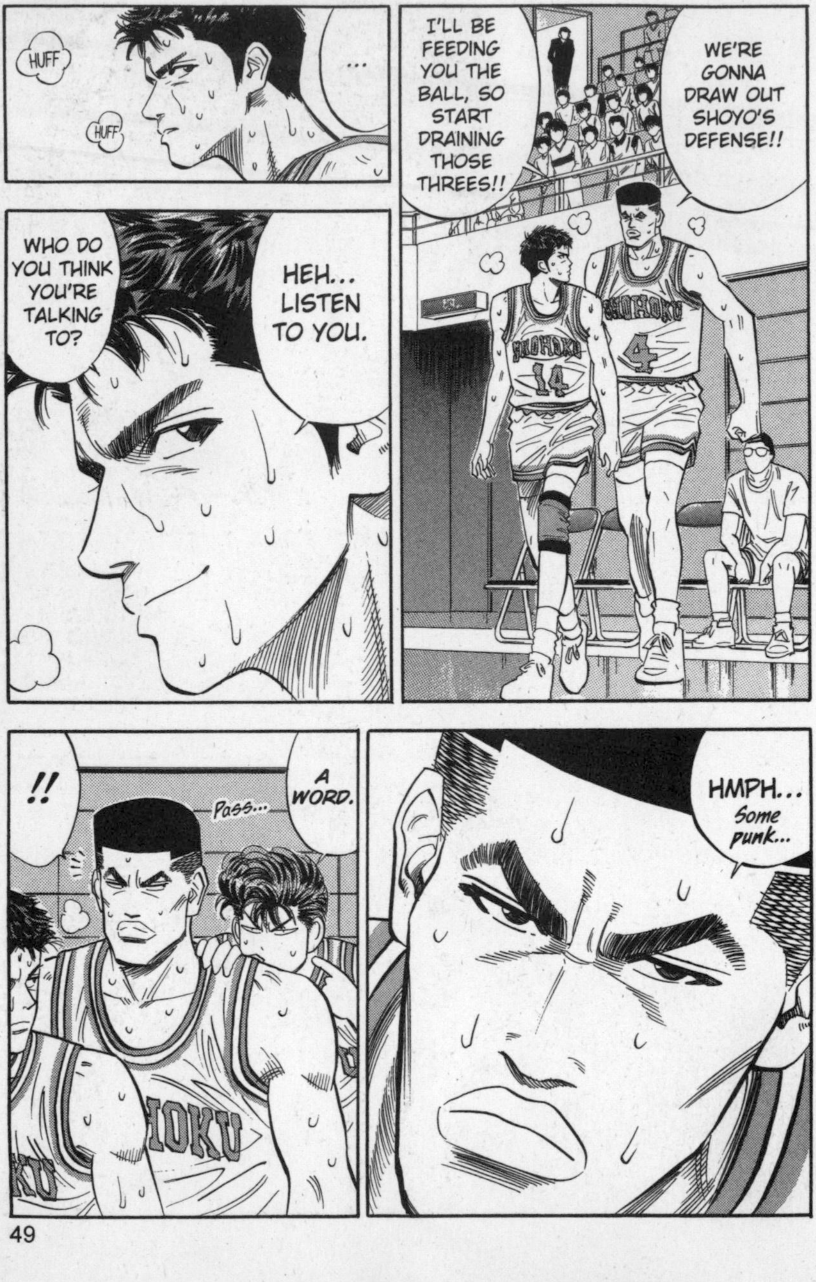

WE'RE GONNA DRAW OUT SHOYO'S DEFENSE!!
I'LL BE FEEDING YOU THE BALL, SO START DRAINING THOSE THREES!!
HUFF
HUFF
...
HEH... LISTEN TO YOU.
WHO DO YOU THINK YOU'RE TALKING TO?
HMPH... Some punk...
A WORD.
Pass...
!!

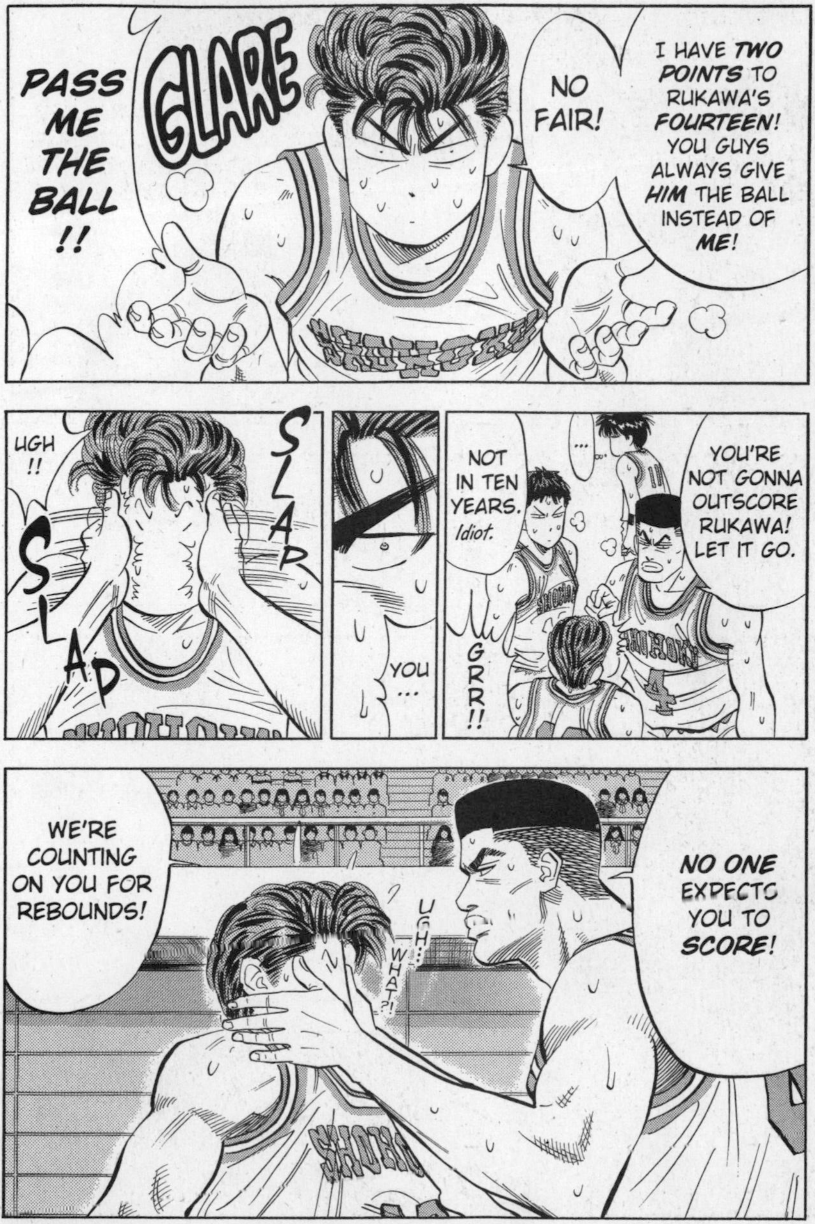
I HAVE TWO POINTS TO RUKAWA'S FOURTEEN! YOU GUYS ALWAYS GIVE HIM THE BALL INSTEAD OF ME!
NO FAIR!
GLARE
PASS ME THE BALL!!
YOU'RE NOT GONNA OUTSCORE RUKAWA! LET IT GO.
...
NOT IN TEN YEARS. Idiot.
GRR!!
SLAP
YOU...
UGH!!
SLAP
NO ONE EXPECTS YOU TO SCORE!
UGH...
WHAT?!
WE'RE COUNTING ON YOU FOR REBOUNDS!

READ THIS WAY

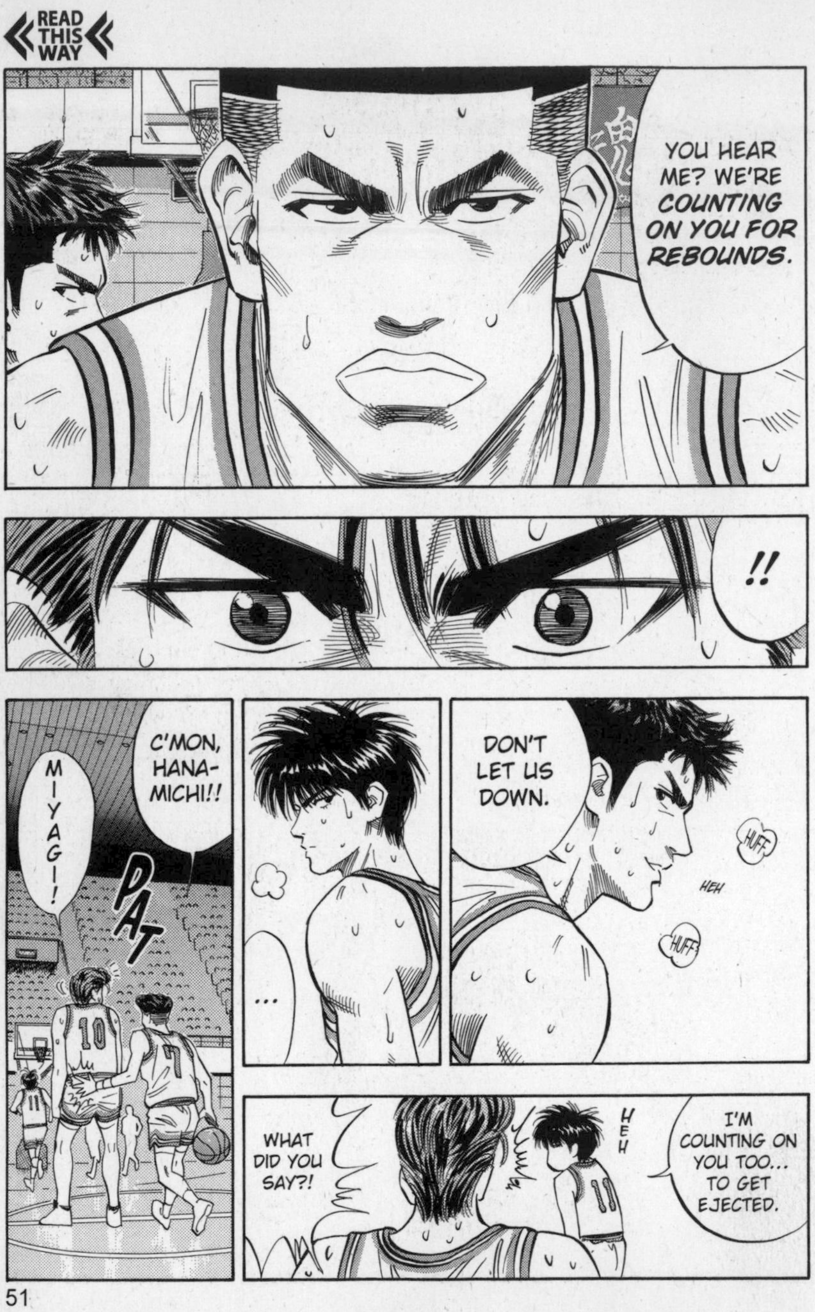

YOU HEAR ME? WE'RE COUNTING ON YOU FOR REBOUNDS.
!!
DON'T LET US DOWN.
HUFF
HEH
HUFF
...
I'M COUNTING ON YOU TOO... TO GET EJECTED.
HEH
WHAT DID YOU SAY?!
C'MON, HANA-MICHI!!
MIYAGI!
PAT

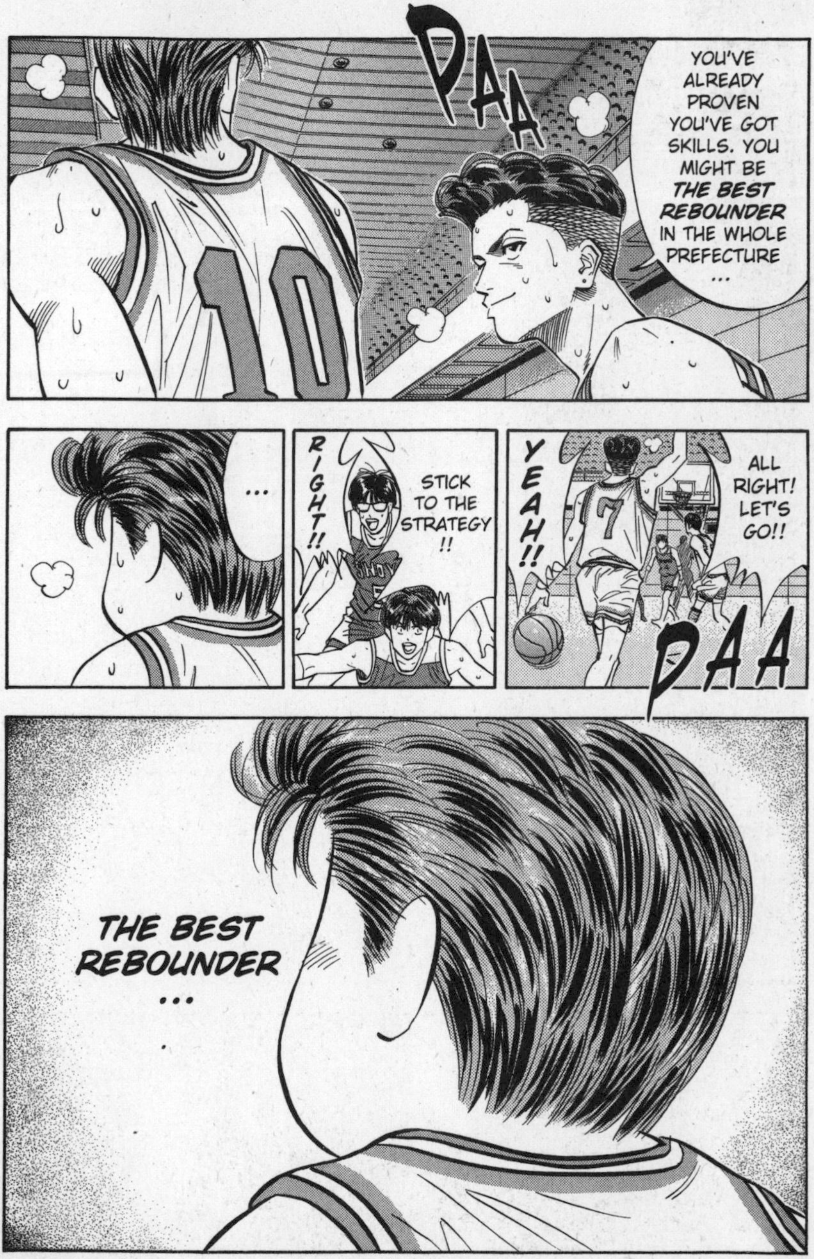
PAA
YOU'VE ALREADY PROVEN YOU'VE GOT SKILLS. YOU MIGHT BE *THE BEST REBOUNDER* IN THE WHOLE PREFECTURE ...
ALL RIGHT! LET'S GO!!
YEAH!!
DAA
STICK TO THE STRATEGY !!
RIGHT!!
...
THE BEST REBOUNDER ...

READ THIS WAY

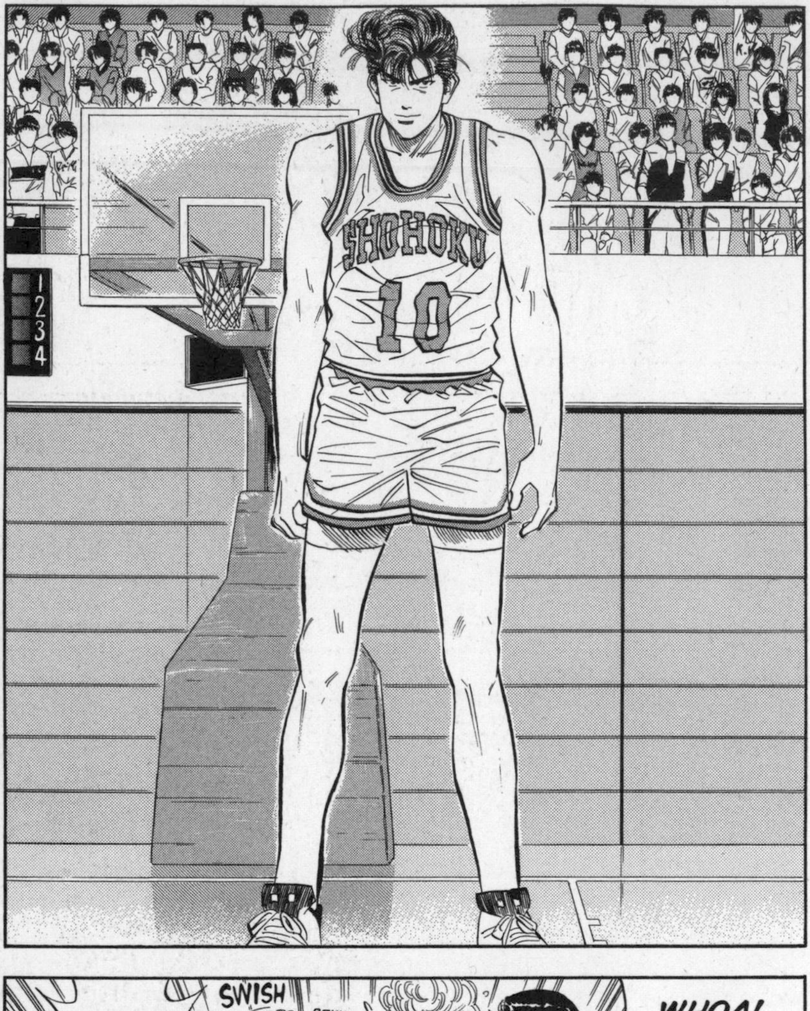
SHOHOKU
10

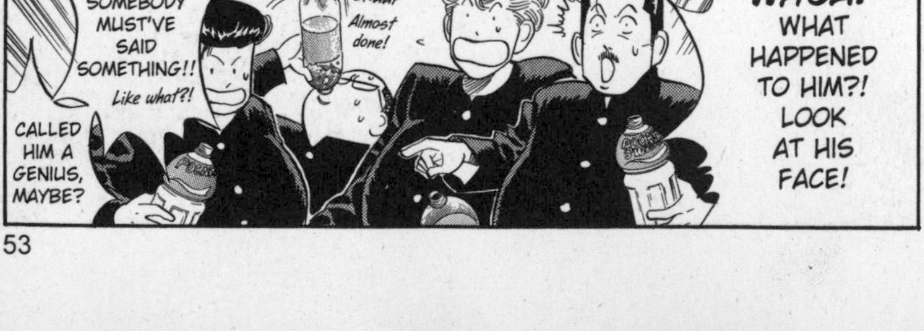
WHOA! WHAT HAPPENED TO HIM?! LOOK AT HIS FACE!
BRULP
Almost done!
SWISH
SOMEBODY MUST'VE SAID SOMETHING!!
Like what?!
CALLED HIM A GENIUS, MAYBE?

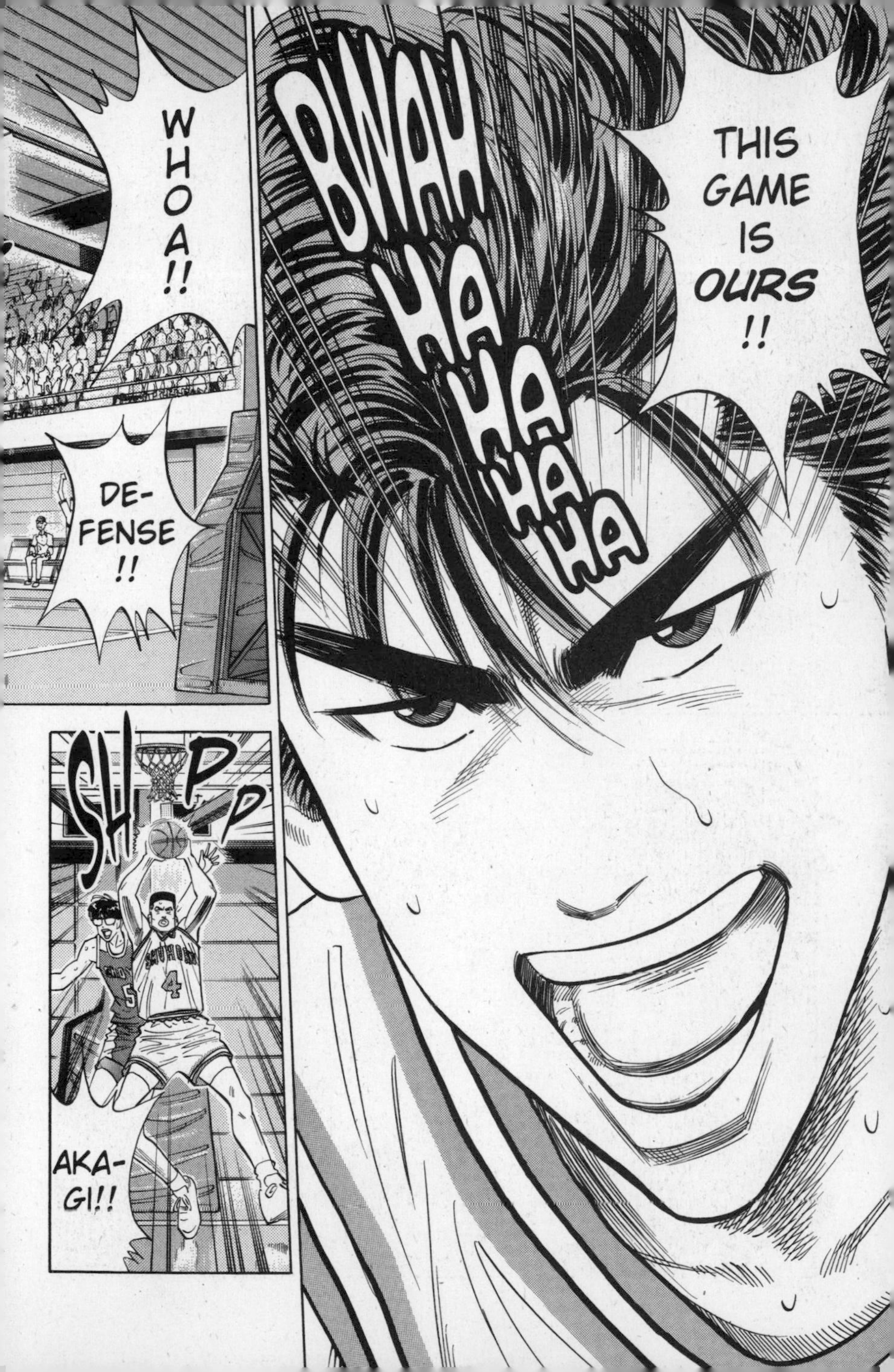
BWAH HA HA HA HA HA
THIS GAME IS OURS!!
WHOA!!
DE-FENSE!!
SHPP
AKA-GI!!

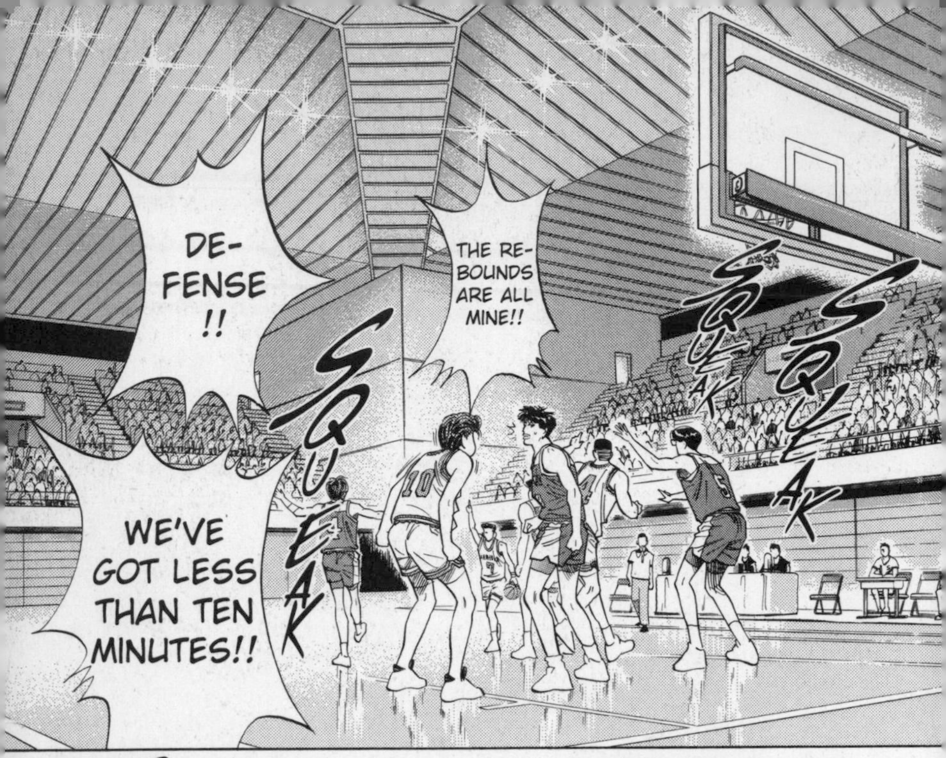

SQUEAK
SQUEAK
THE RE-
BOUNDS
ARE ALL
MINE!!
DE-
FENSE
!!
SQUEAK
WE'VE
GOT LESS
THAN TEN
MINUTES!!

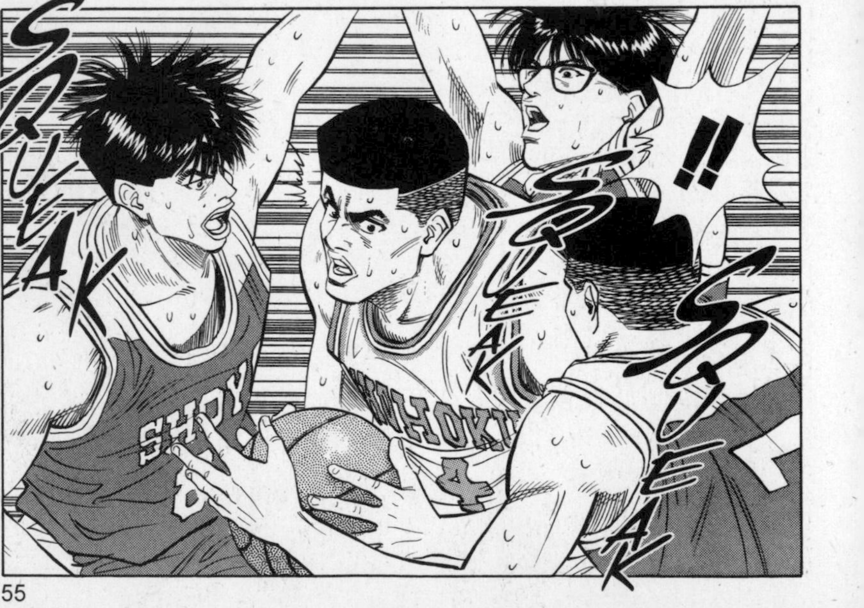

SQUEAK
!!
SQUEAK
SQUEAK

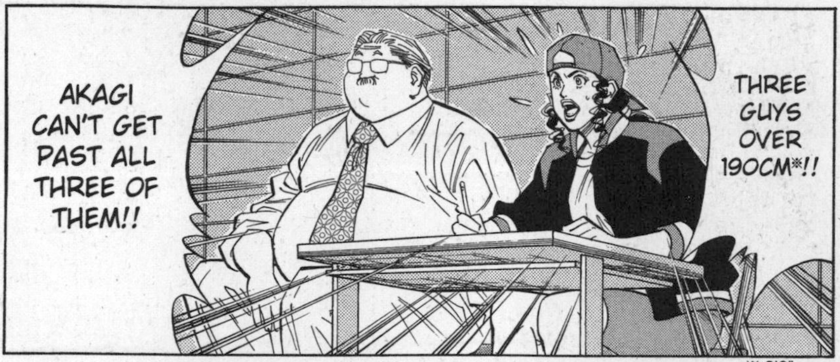
THREE GUYS OVER 190CM※!!
AKAGI CAN'T GET PAST ALL THREE OF THEM!!

※ 6'3"

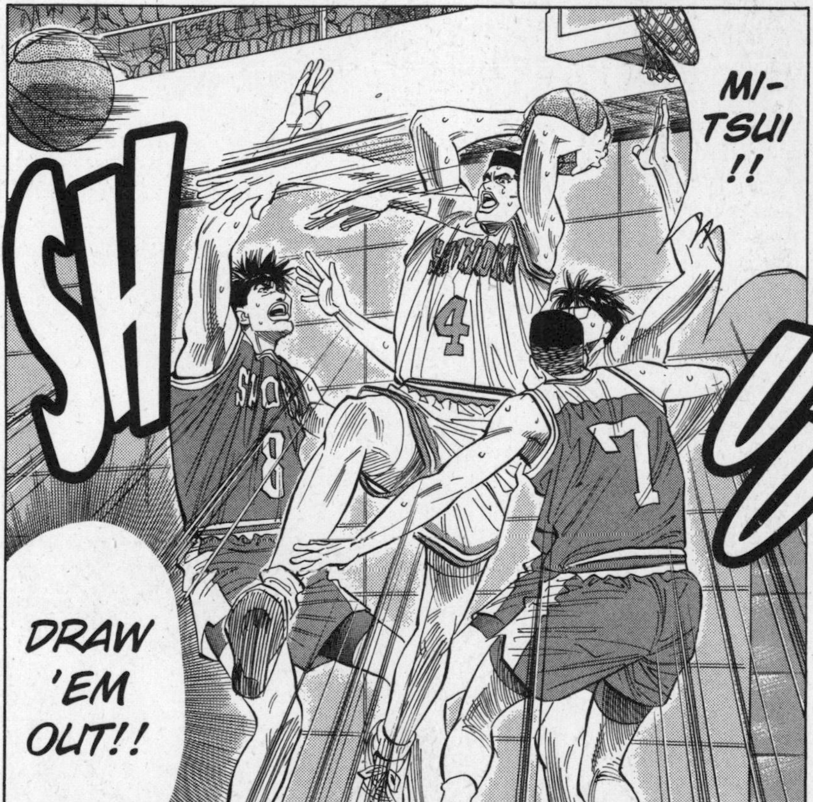
MI-TSUI!!
SHUU
DRAW 'EM OUT!!

READ THIS WAY

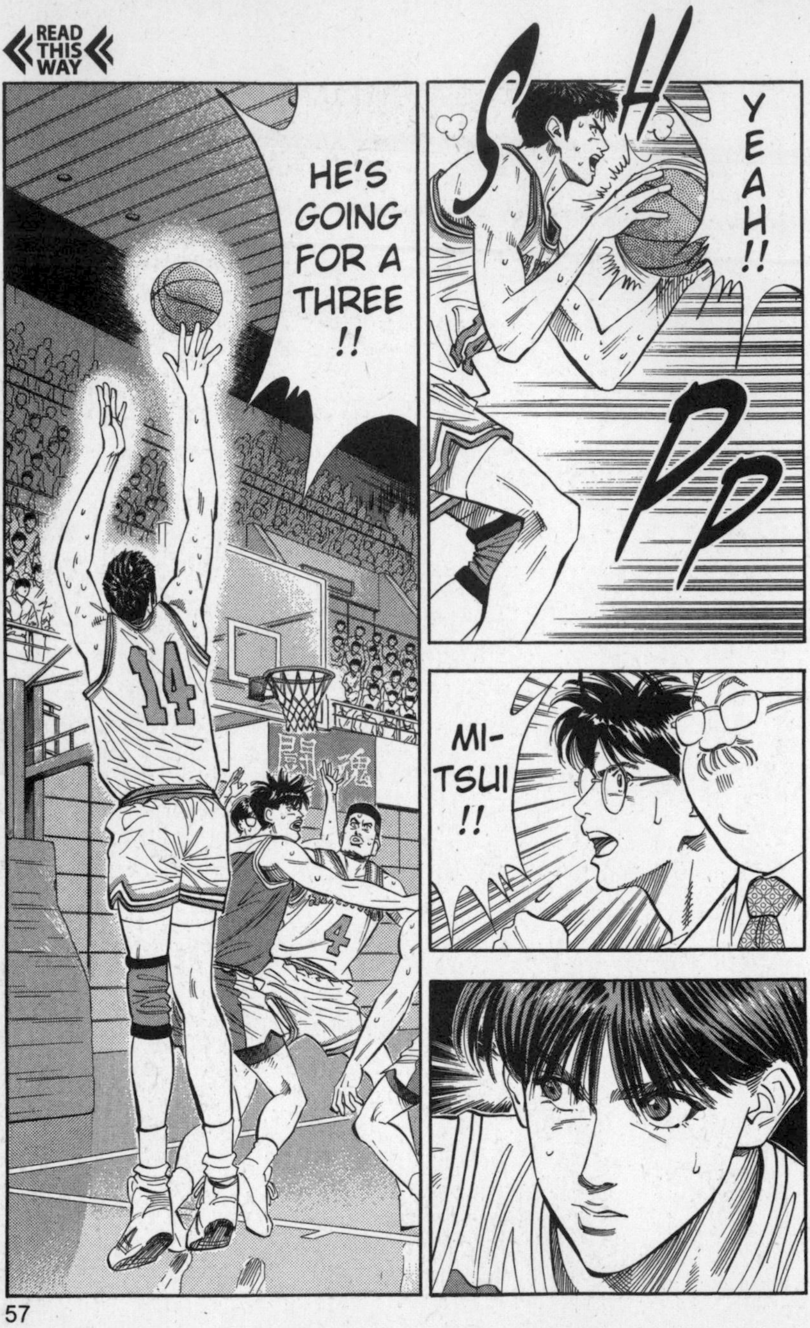
SH
YEAH!!
PP
MI-TSUI!!
HE'S GOING FOR A THREE!!

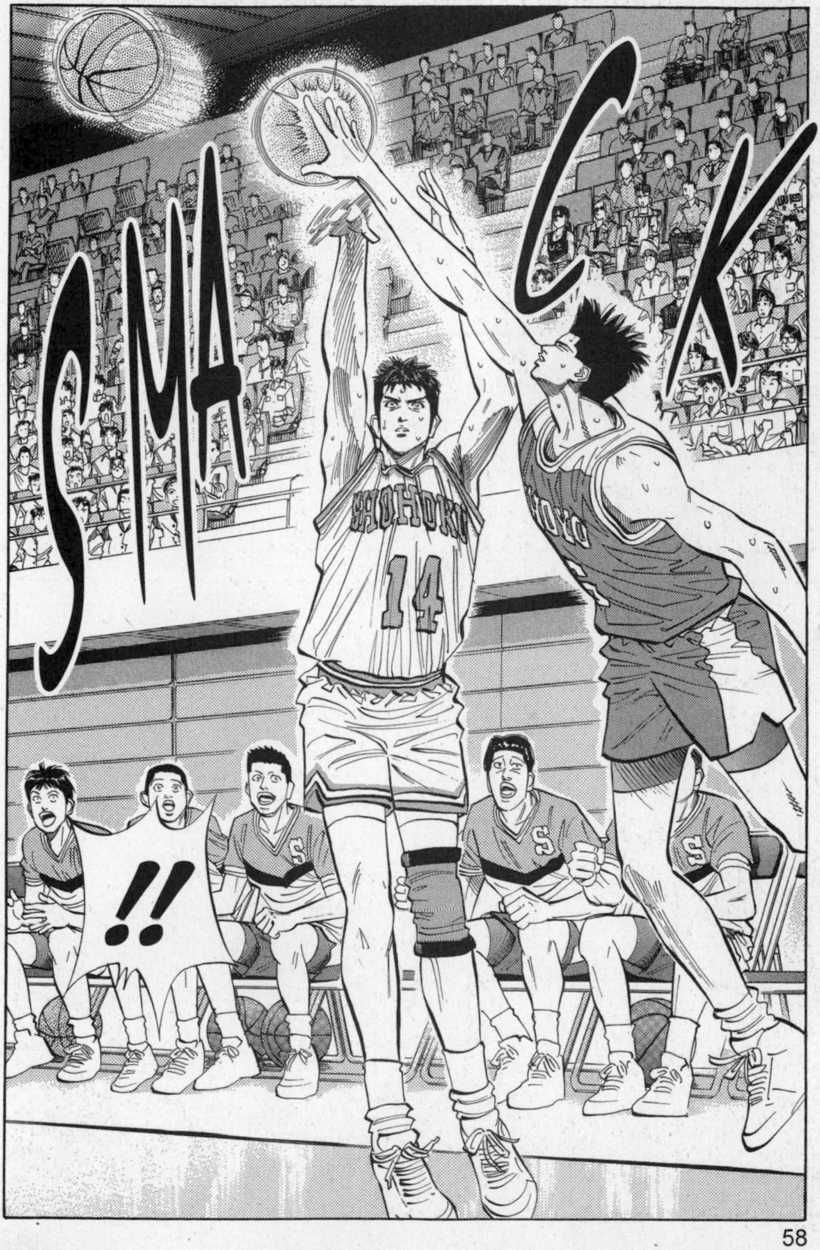
SMACK
!!

READ THIS WAY

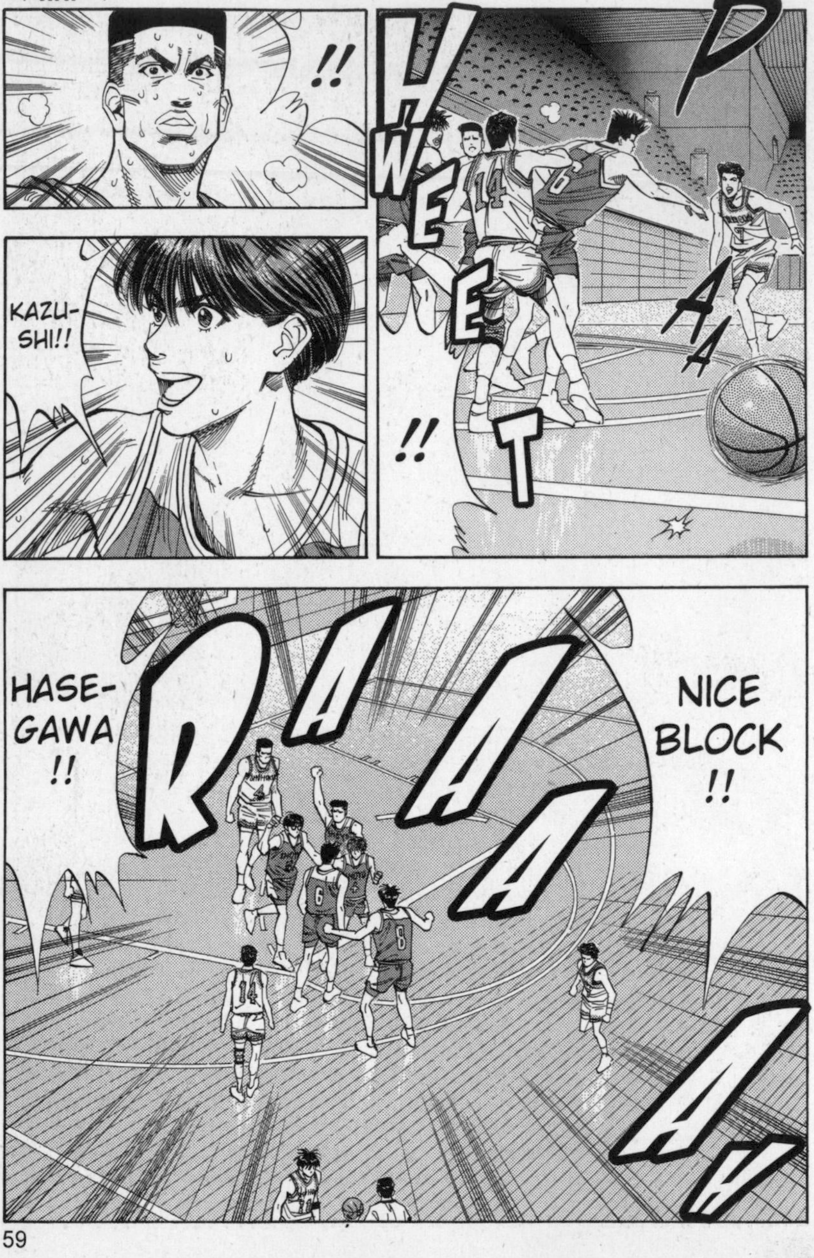

HWEET
PAAA
!!
!!
KAZU-SHI!!
NICE BLOCK!!
RAAAAAH
HASE-GAWA!!

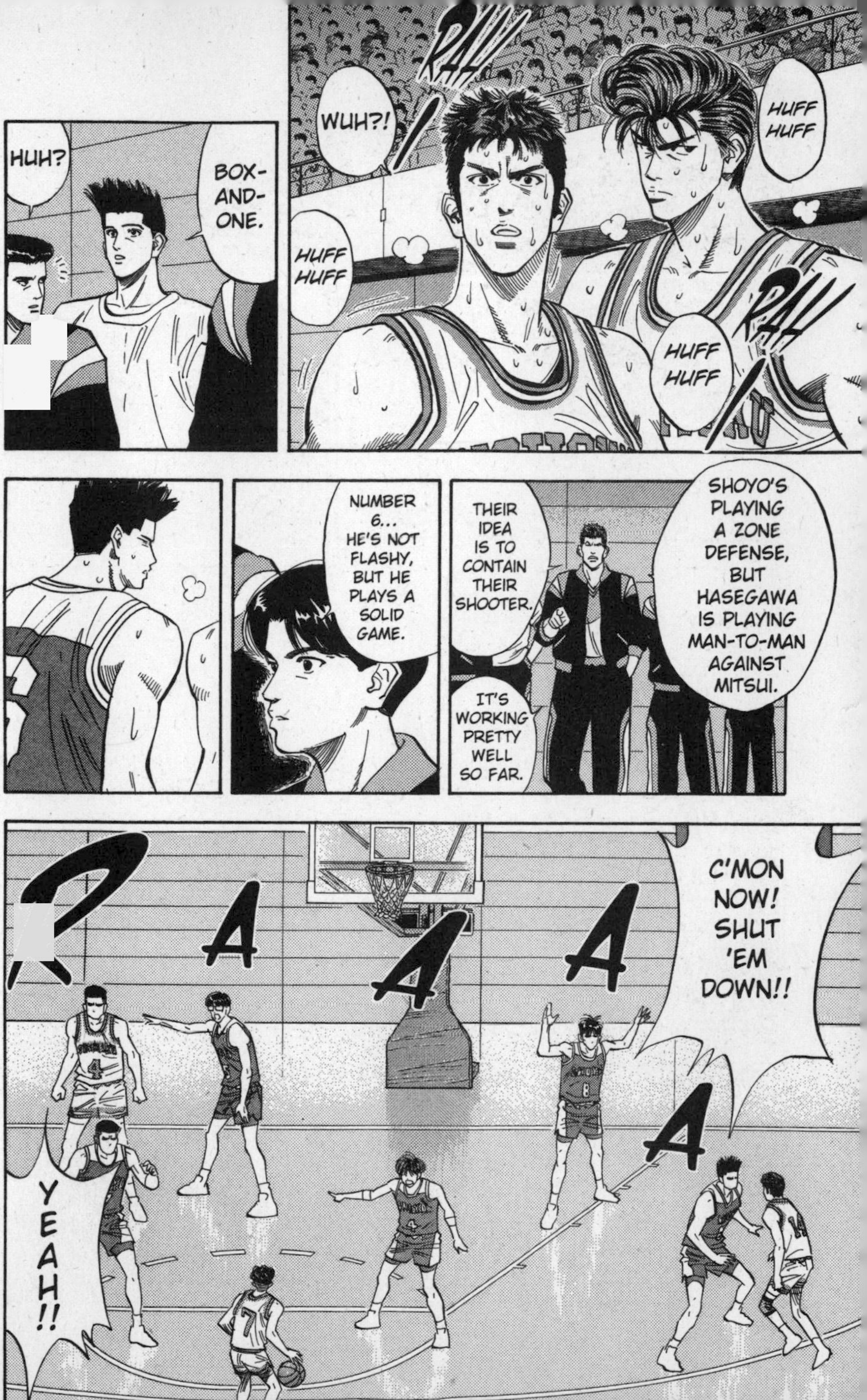
HUFF HUFF
RAH
WUH?!
RAH
HUFF HUFF
HUFF HUFF
BOX-AND-ONE.
HUH?
SHOYO'S PLAYING A ZONE DEFENSE, BUT HASEGAWA IS PLAYING MAN-TO-MAN AGAINST MITSUI.
THEIR IDEA IS TO CONTAIN THEIR SHOOTER.
IT'S WORKING PRETTY WELL SO FAR.
NUMBER 6... HE'S NOT FLASHY, BUT HE PLAYS A SOLID GAME.
C'MON NOW! SHUT 'EM DOWN!!
RAAAAA
YEAH!!

READ THIS WAY

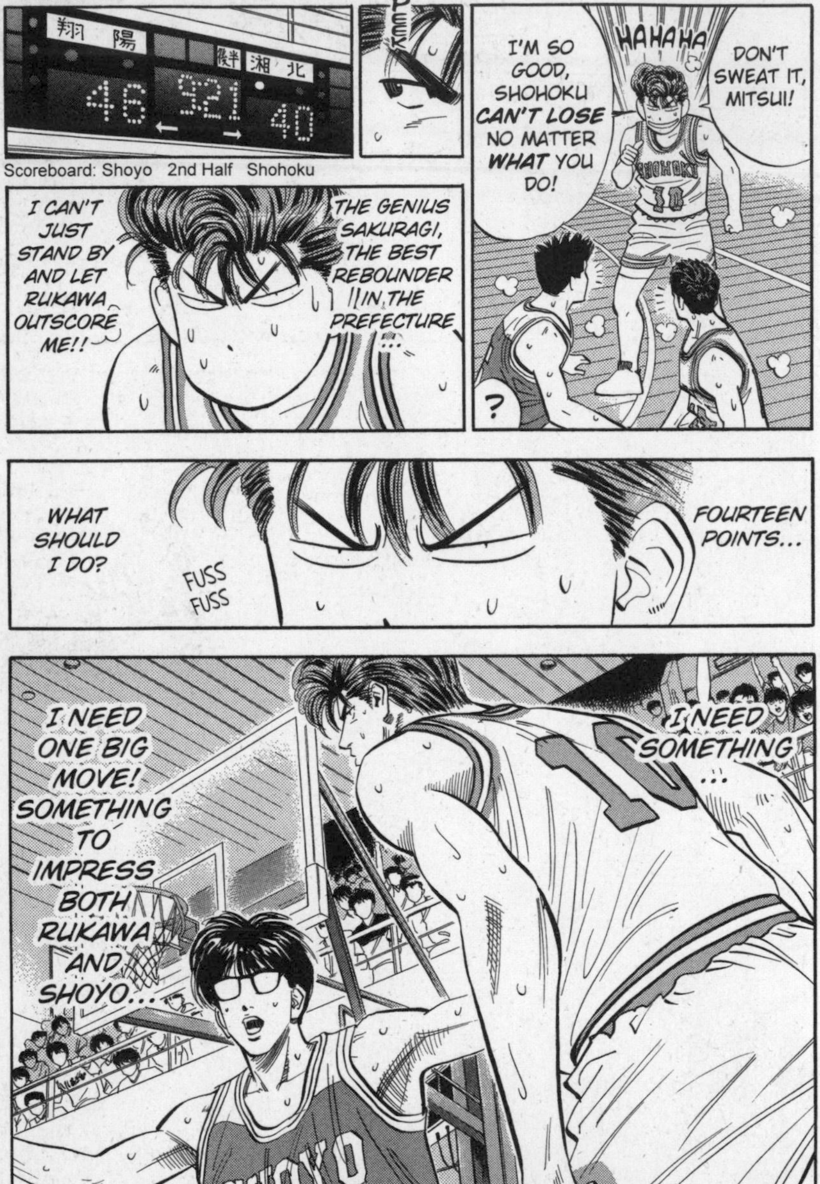
DON'T SWEAT IT, MITSUI!
HAHAHA
I'M SO GOOD, SHOHOKU CAN'T LOSE NO MATTER WHAT YOU DO!
?
PEEK
翔陽 後半 湘北
46 921 40
Scoreboard: Shoyo 2nd Half Shohoku
THE GENIUS SAKURAGI, THE BEST REBOUNDER IN THE PREFECTURE...
I CAN'T JUST STAND BY AND LET RUKAWA OUTSCORE ME!!
FOURTEEN POINTS...
FUSS FUSS
WHAT SHOULD I DO?
I NEED SOMETHING...
I NEED ONE BIG MOVE! SOMETHING TO IMPRESS BOTH RUKAWA AND SHOYO...

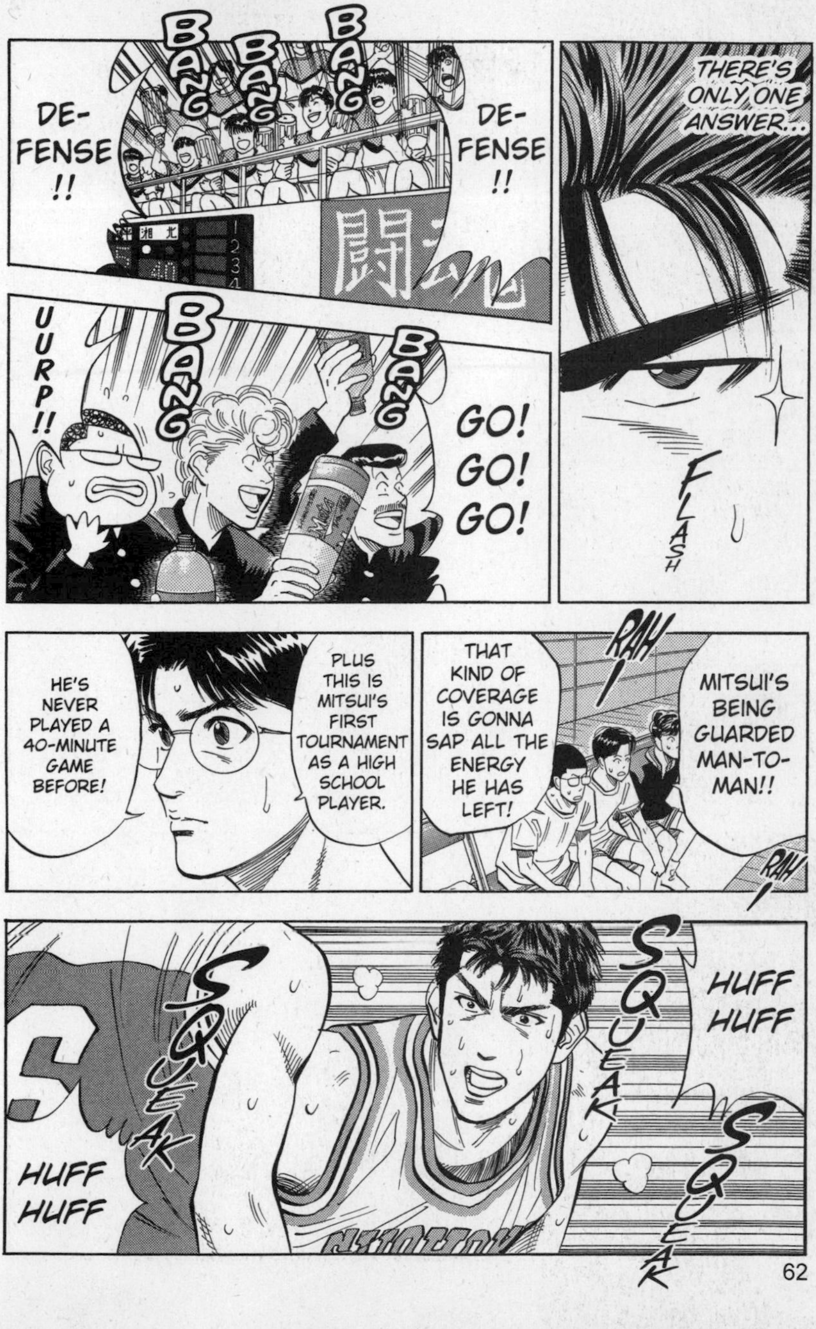

THERE'S ONLY ONE ANSWER...
FLASH
DE-FENSE!!
BANG
BANG
BANG
DE-FENSE!!
BANG
BANG
UURP!!
GO! GO! GO!
RAH
MITSUI'S BEING GUARDED MAN-TO-MAN!!
THAT KIND OF COVERAGE IS GONNA SAP ALL THE ENERGY HE HAS LEFT!
RAH
PLUS THIS IS MITSUI'S FIRST TOURNAMENT AS A HIGH SCHOOL PLAYER.
HE'S NEVER PLAYED A 40-MINUTE GAME BEFORE!
HUFF HUFF
SQUEAK
SQUEAK
SQUEAK
HUFF HUFF

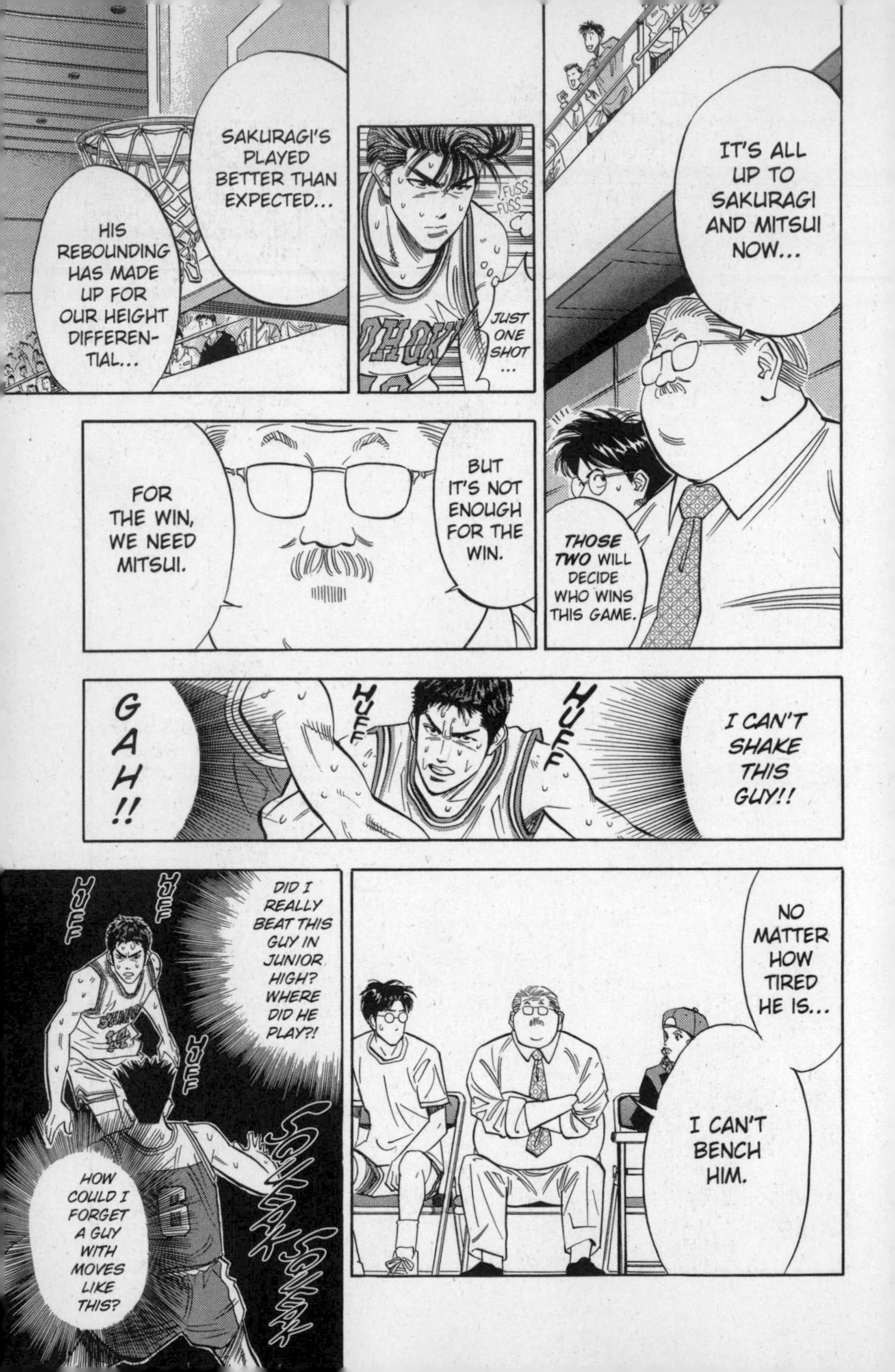
IT'S ALL UP TO SAKURAGI AND MITSUI NOW...
FUSS FUSS
JUST ONE SHOT...
SAKURAGI'S PLAYED BETTER THAN EXPECTED...
HIS REBOUNDING HAS MADE UP FOR OUR HEIGHT DIFFERENTIAL...
THOSE TWO WILL DECIDE WHO WINS THIS GAME.
BUT IT'S NOT ENOUGH FOR THE WIN.
FOR THE WIN, WE NEED MITSUI.
I CAN'T SHAKE THIS GUY!!
HUFF
HUFF
GAH!!
NO MATTER HOW TIRED HE IS...
I CAN'T BENCH HIM.
DID I REALLY BEAT THIS GUY IN JUNIOR HIGH? WHERE DID HE PLAY?!
HUFF
HUFF
HUFF
HOW COULD I FORGET A GUY WITH MOVES LIKE THIS?

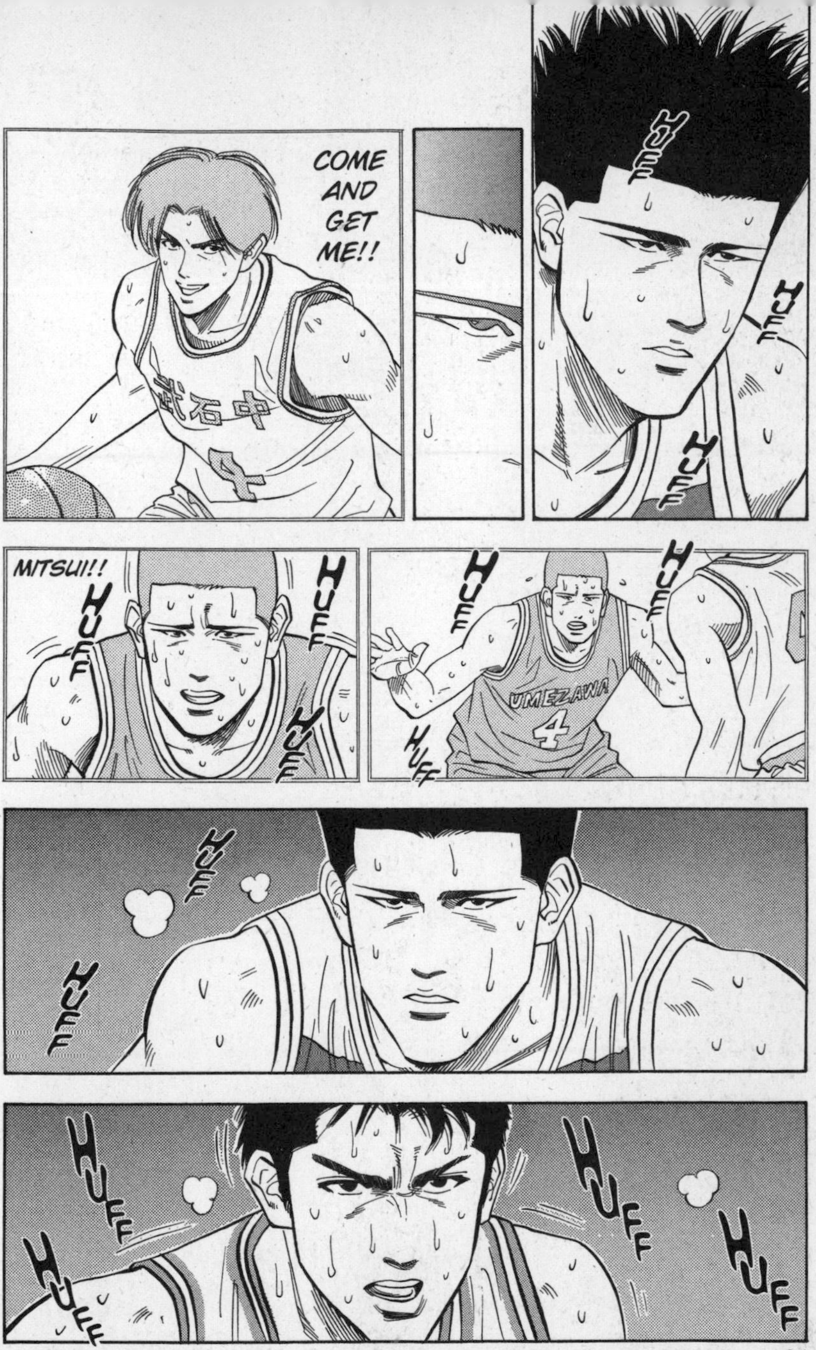
HUFF
HUFF
HUFF
COME AND GET ME!!
HUFF
HUFF
HUFF
MITSUI!!
HUFF
HUFF
HUFF
HUFF
HUFF
HUFF
HUFF
HUFF
HUFF
HUFF

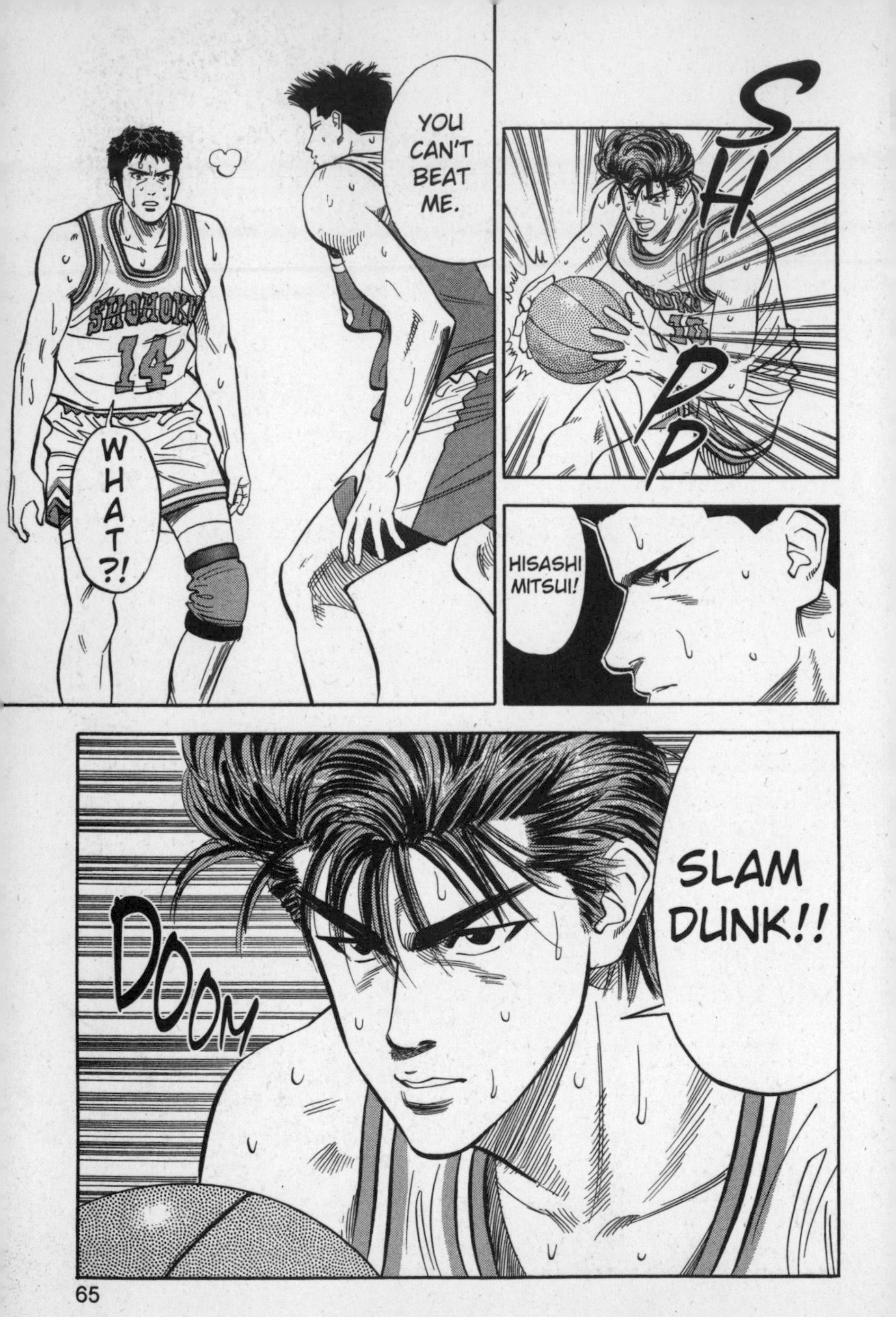
SHDP
HISASHI MITSUI!
YOU CAN'T BEAT ME.
WHAT?!
SLAM DUNK!!
DOOM

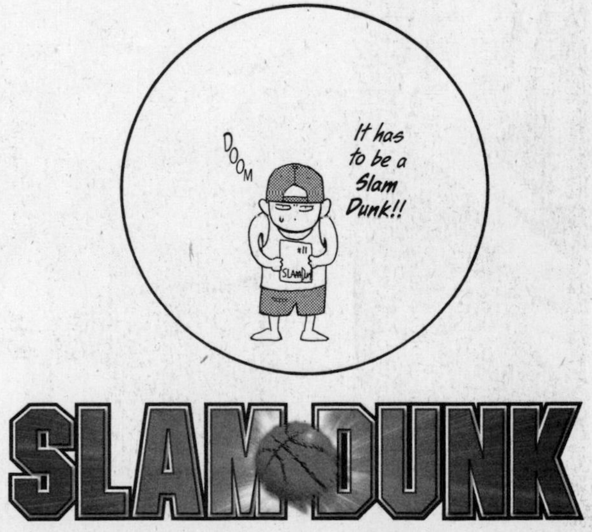
It has to be a Slam Dunk!!
DOOM

SLAM DUNK

#93 MITSUI'S LIMIT

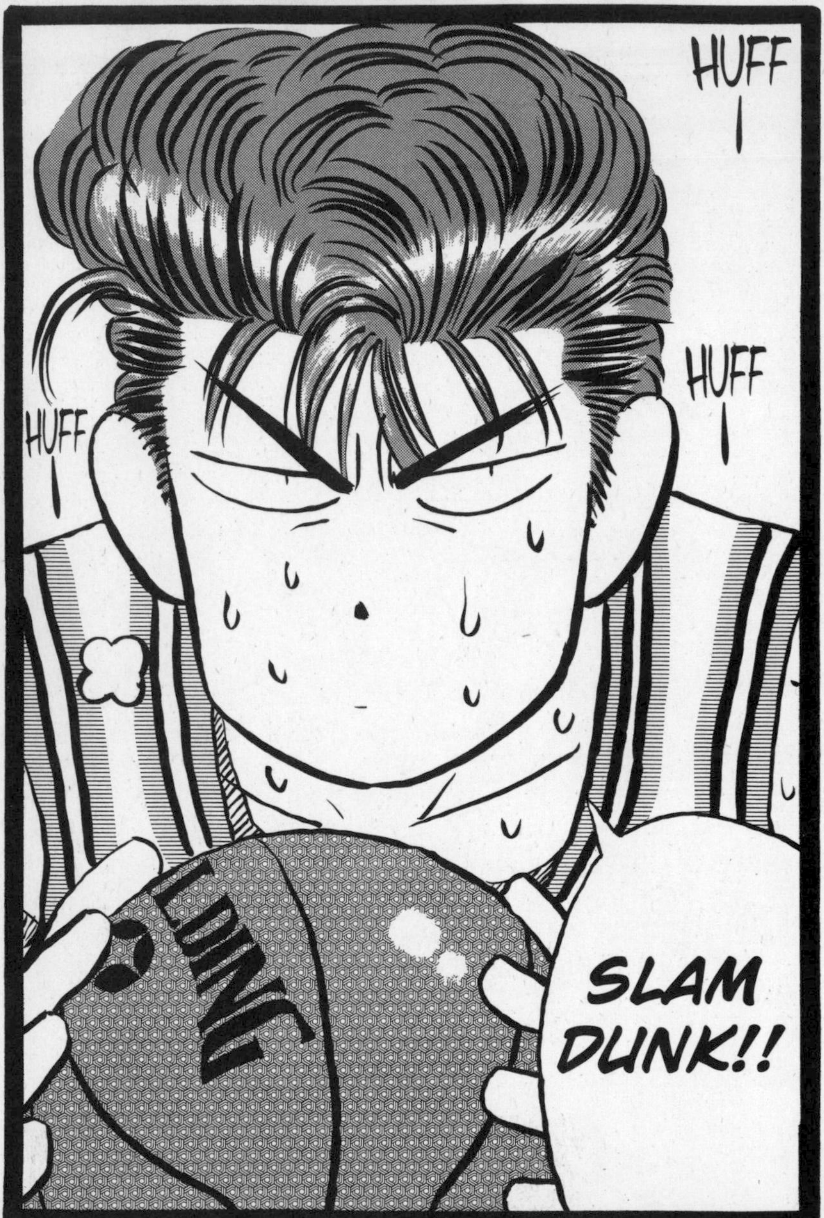
HUFF
HUFF
HUFF
SLAM DUNK!!

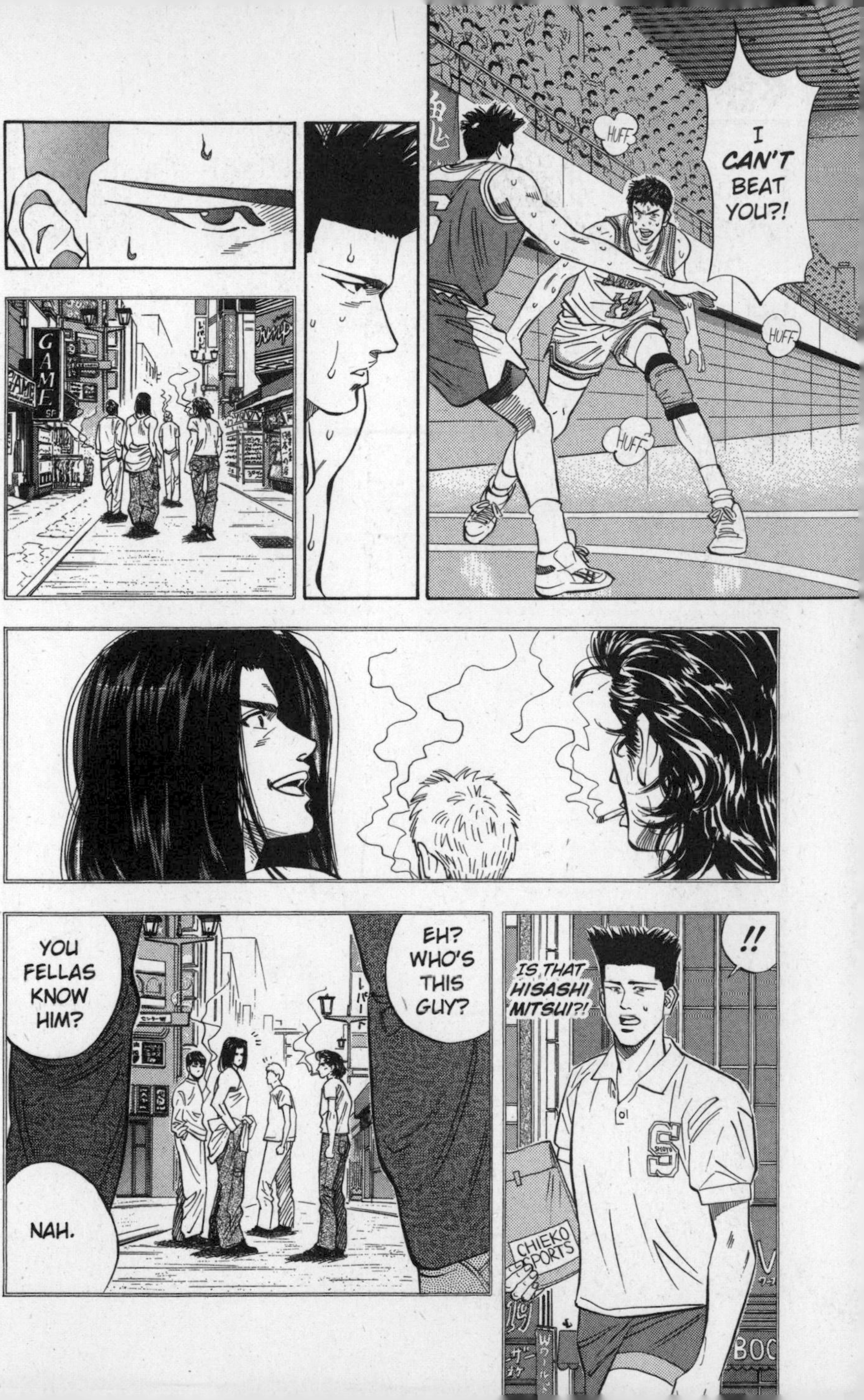
HUFF
I CAN'T BEAT YOU?!
HUFF
HUFF
GAME
!!
IS THAT HISASHI MITSUI?!
CHIEKO SPORTS
EH? WHO'S THIS GUY?
YOU FELLAS KNOW HIM?
NAH.

READ THIS WAY

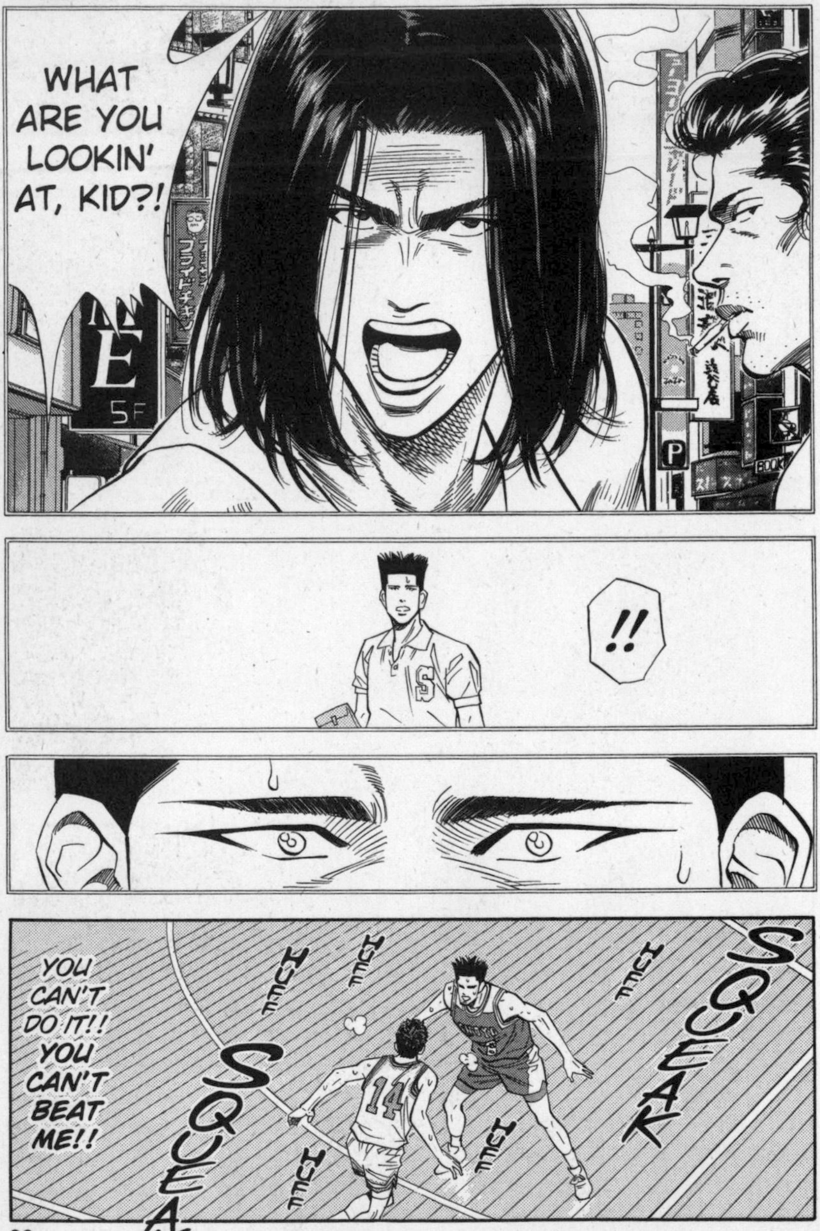
WHAT ARE YOU LOOKIN' AT, KID?!
!!
SQUEAK
TTTCH
HUFF HUFF
SQUEAK
TTTCH
HUFF
YOU CAN'T DO IT!! YOU CAN'T BEAT ME!!

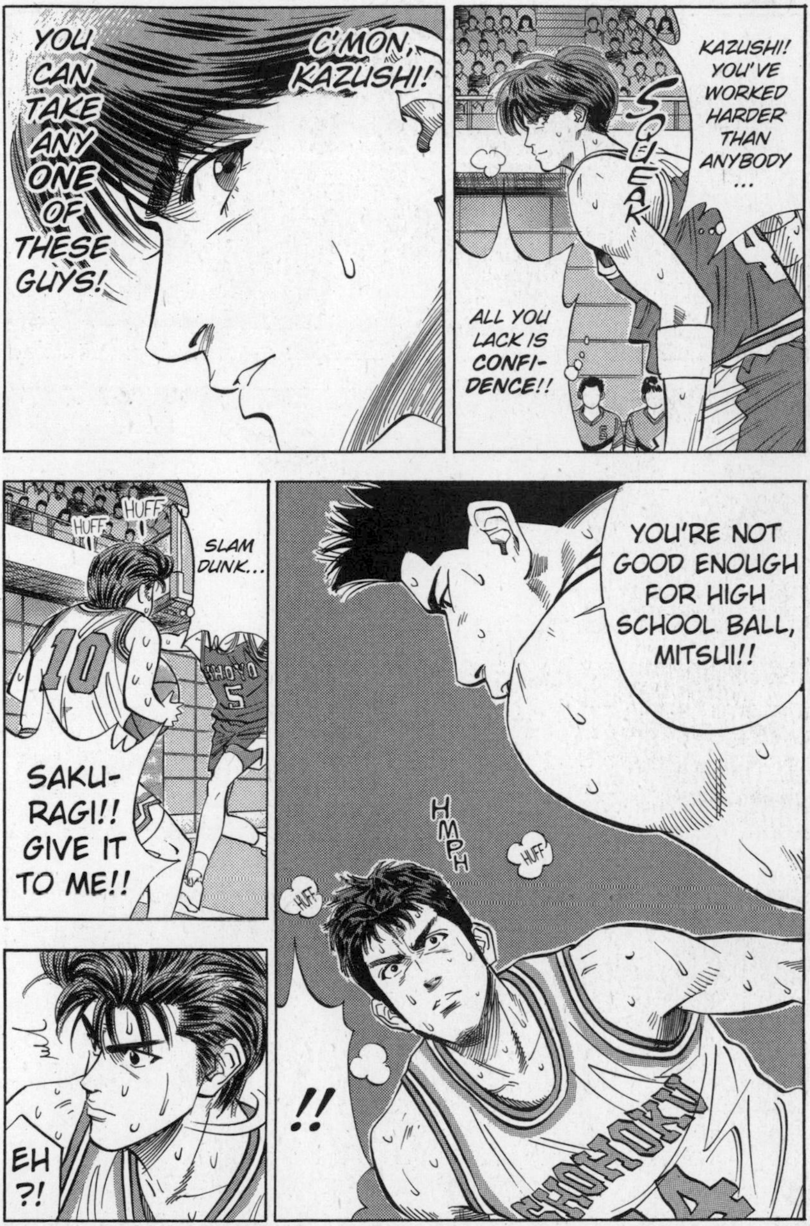
KAZUSHI! YOU'VE WORKED HARDER THAN ANYBODY...
SQUEAK
ALL YOU LACK IS CONFIDENCE!!
C'MON, KAZUSHI!
YOU CAN TAKE ANY ONE OF THESE GUYS!
YOU'RE NOT GOOD ENOUGH FOR HIGH SCHOOL BALL, MITSUI!!
HMPH
HUFF
HUFF
!!
HUFF
HUFF
SLAM DUNK...
SAKURAGI!! GIVE IT TO ME!!
EH ?!

READ THIS WAY

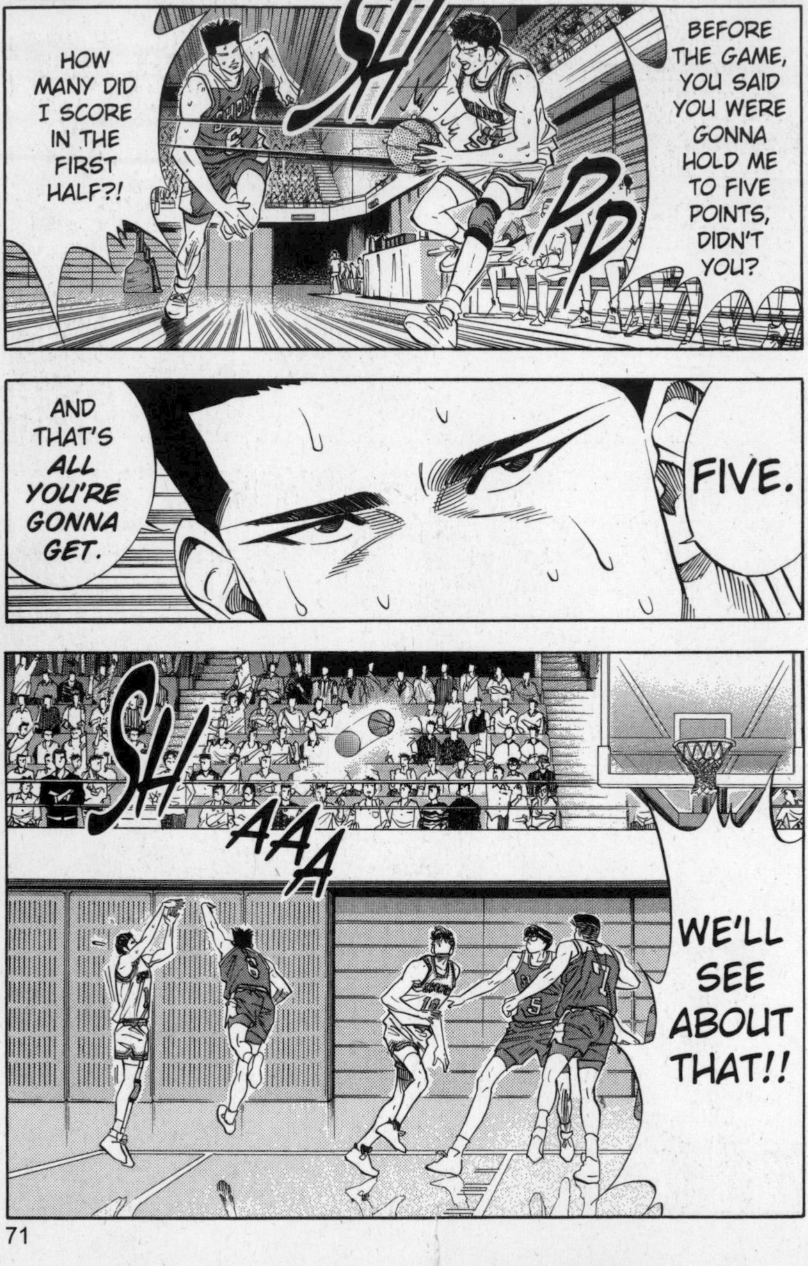
BEFORE THE GAME, YOU SAID YOU WERE GONNA HOLD ME TO FIVE POINTS, DIDN'T YOU?
SH
PP
HOW MANY DID I SCORE IN THE FIRST HALF?!
FIVE.
AND THAT'S *ALL YOU'RE GONNA GET.*
WE'LL SEE ABOUT THAT!!
SHAAA

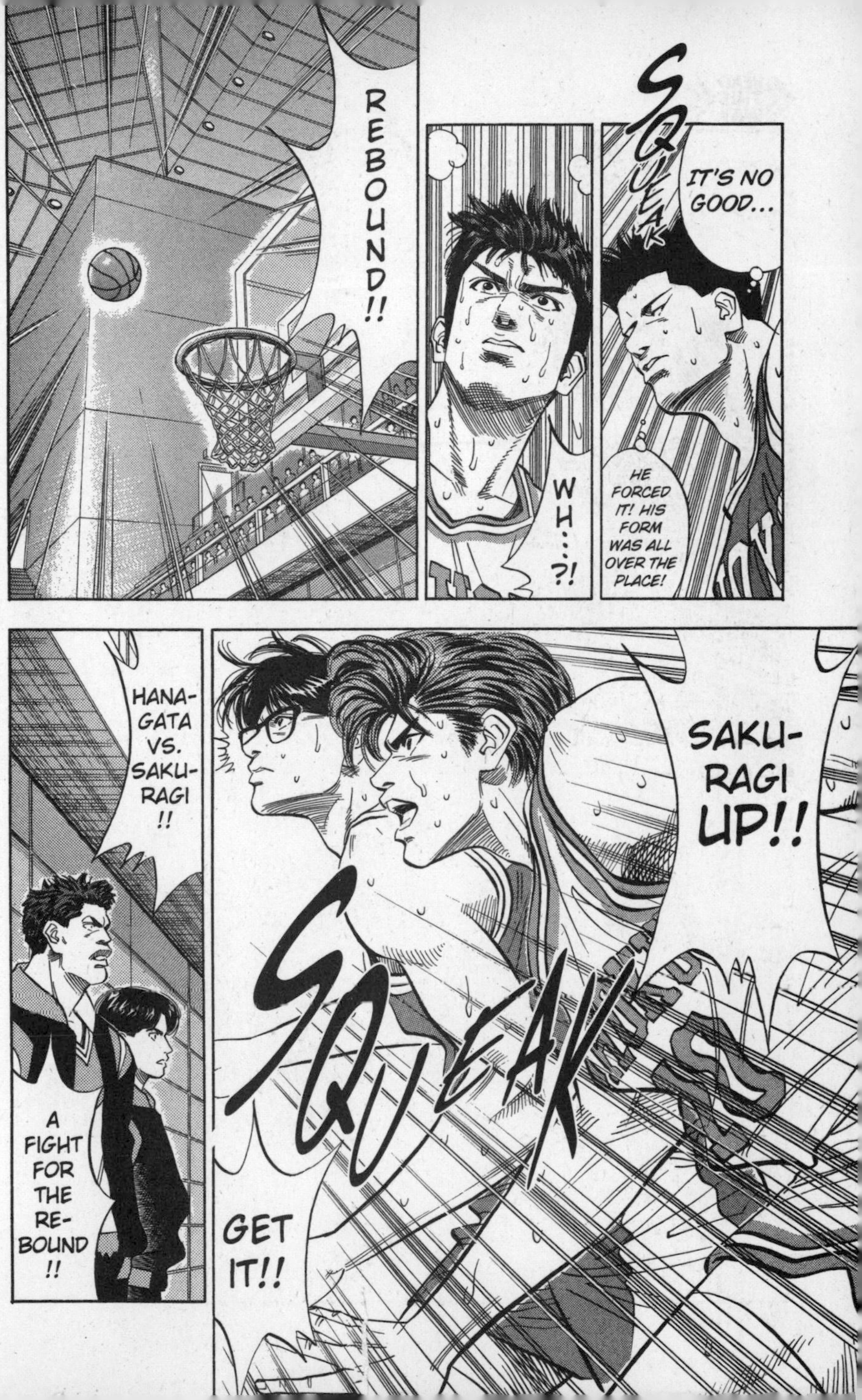
SQUEAK
IT'S NO GOOD...
HE FORCED IT! HIS FORM WAS ALL OVER THE PLACE!
WH...?!
REBOUND!!
SAKURAGI UP!!
SQUEAK
GET IT!!
HANAGATA VS. SAKURAGI!!
A FIGHT FOR THE REBOUND!!

READ THIS WAY

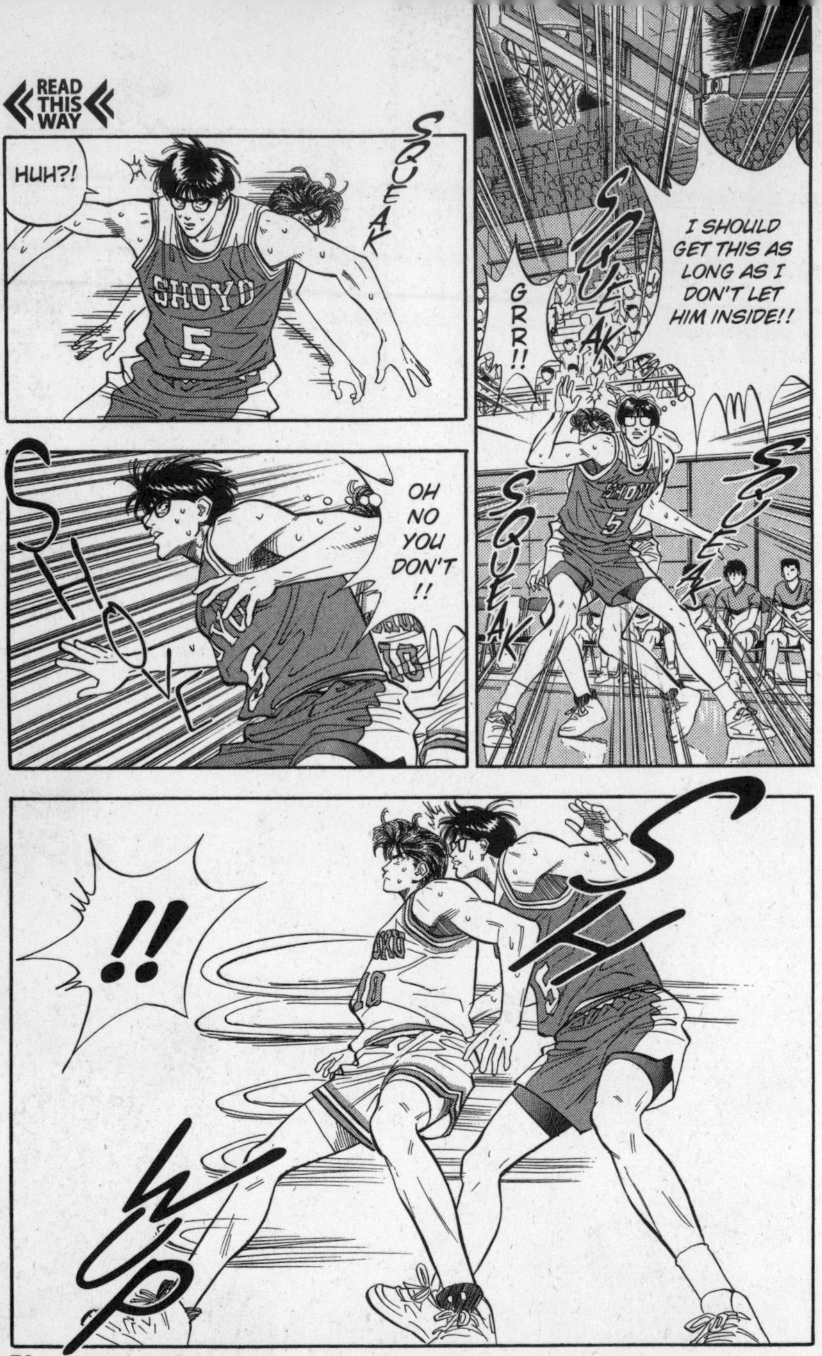

I SHOULD GET THIS AS LONG AS I DON'T LET HIM INSIDE!!
SQUEAK
GRR!!
SQUEAK
SQUEAK
SQUEAK
SQUEAK
HUH?!
OH NO YOU DON'T!!
SHOVE
SH
!!
WUP

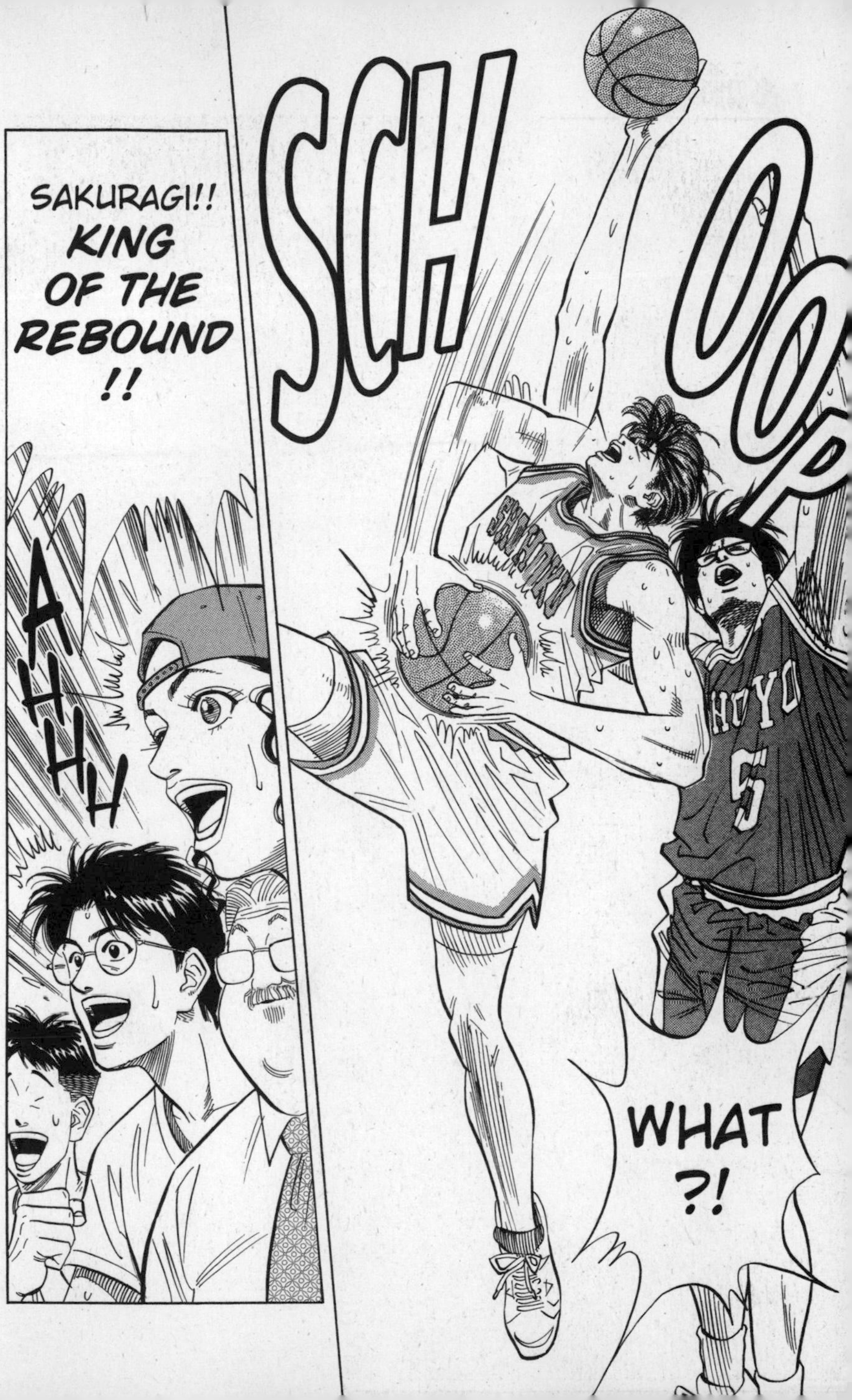
SCHOOP
WHAT ?!
SAKURAGI!! KING OF THE REBOUND !!
AHHHH

READ THIS WAY

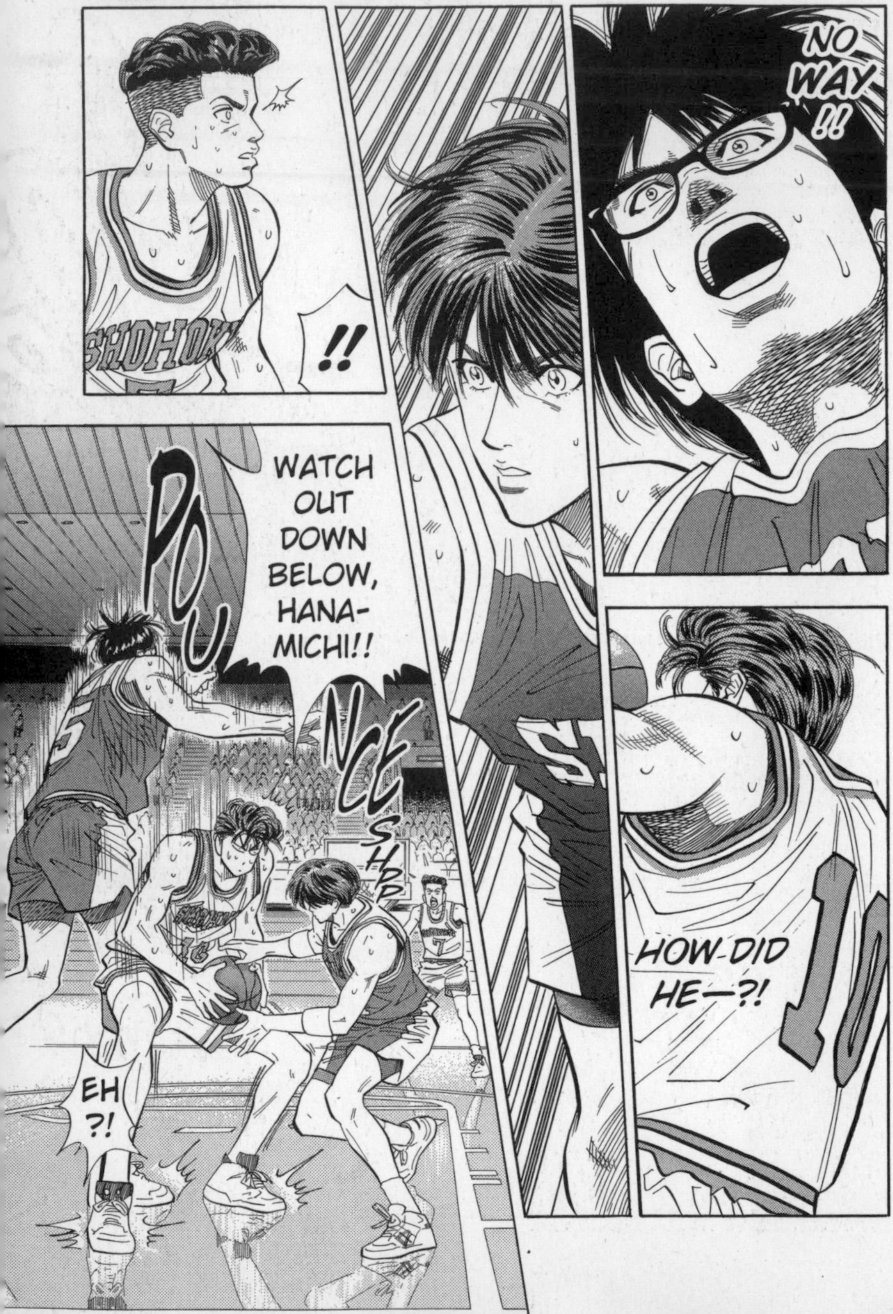
NO WAY!!
HOW DID HE—?!
!!
WATCH OUT DOWN BELOW, HANAMICHI!!
POUNCE
SHPP
EH?!

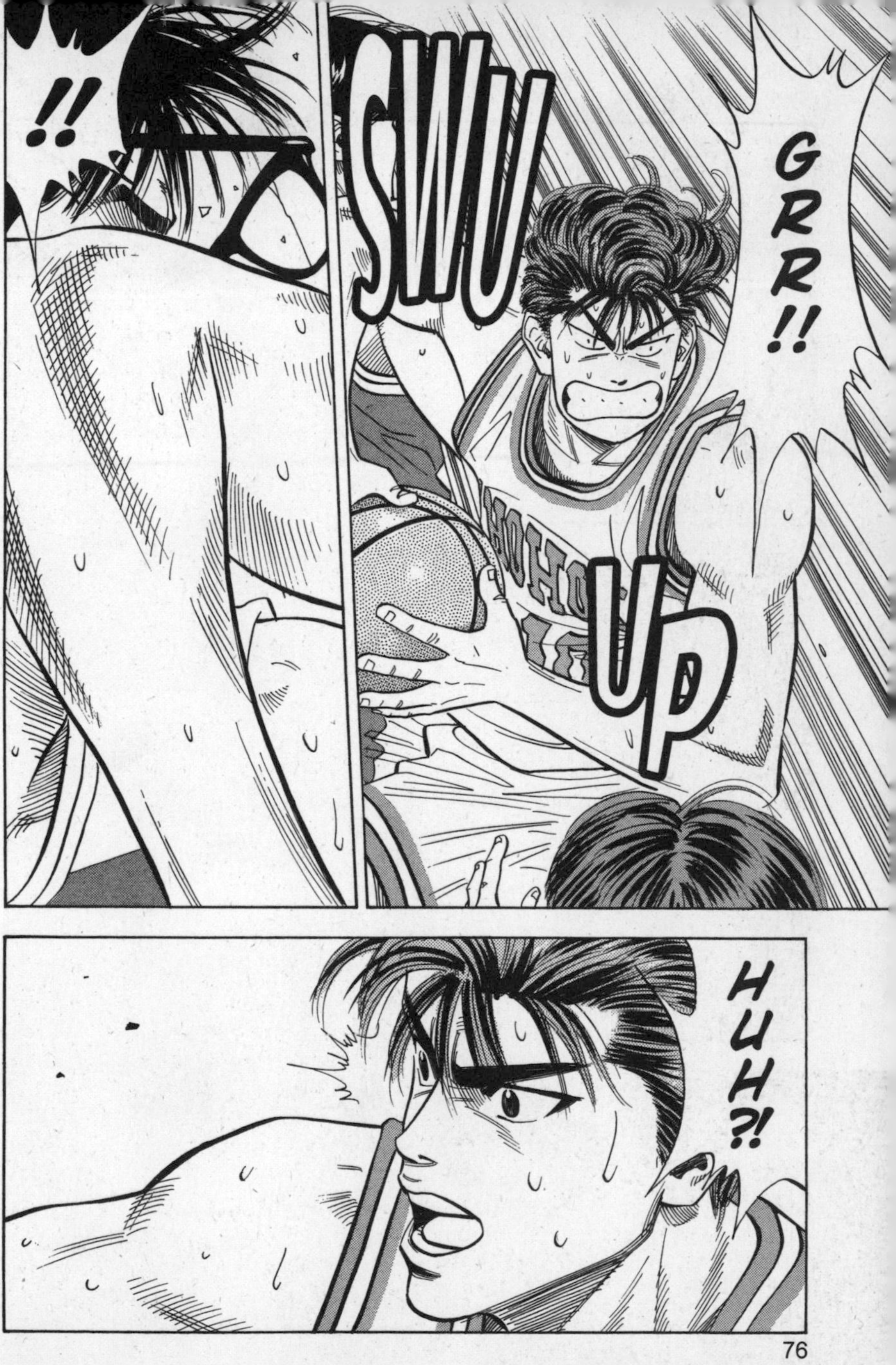
GRR!!
SWU
UP
!!
HUH?!

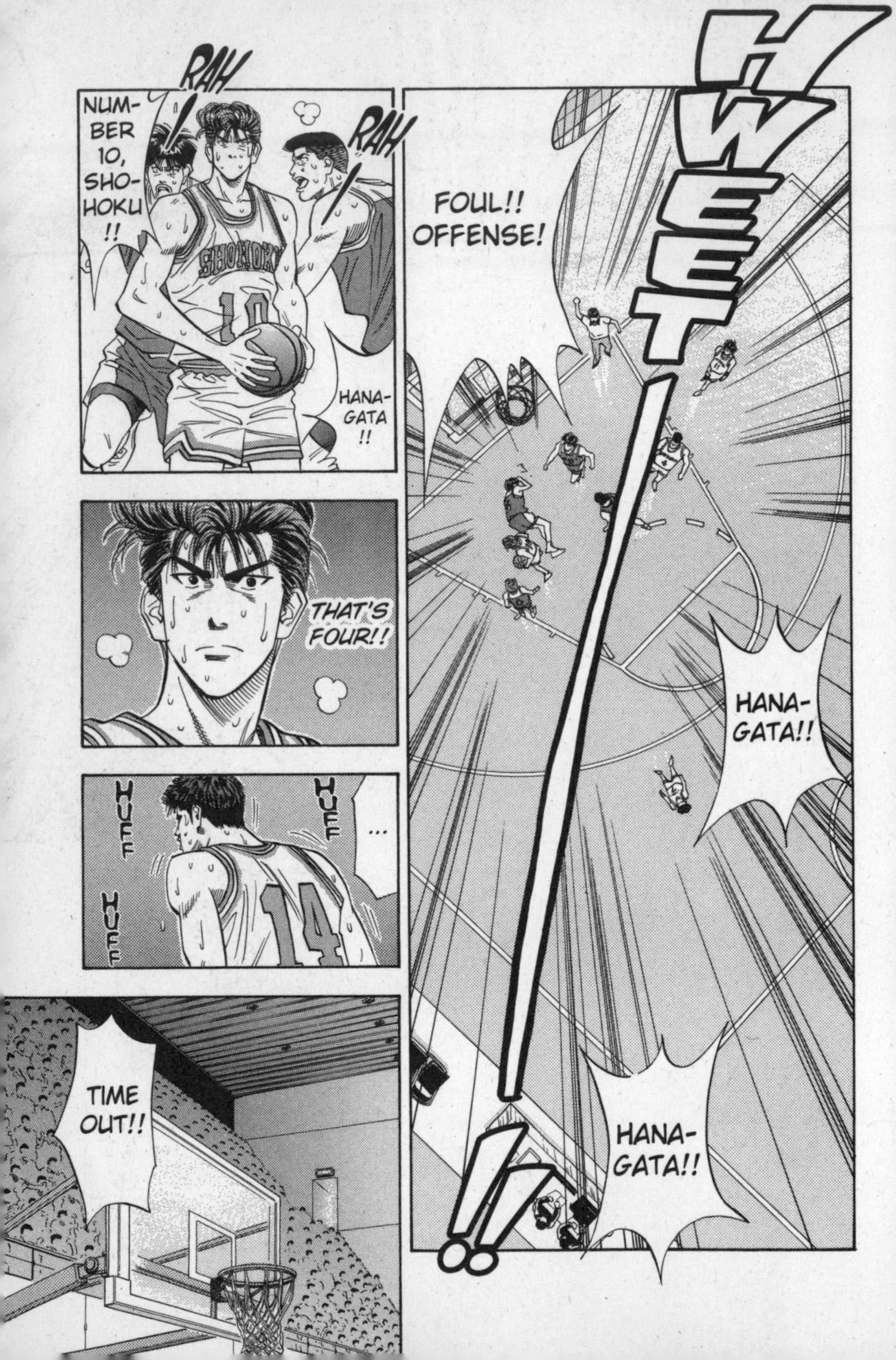
HWEET!!
FOUL!! OFFENSE!
HANA-GATA!!
HANA-GATA!!
RAH
RAH
NUM-BER 10, SHO-HOKU !!
HANA-GATA !!
THAT'S FOUR!!
HUFF
HUFF
HUFF
...
TIME OUT!!

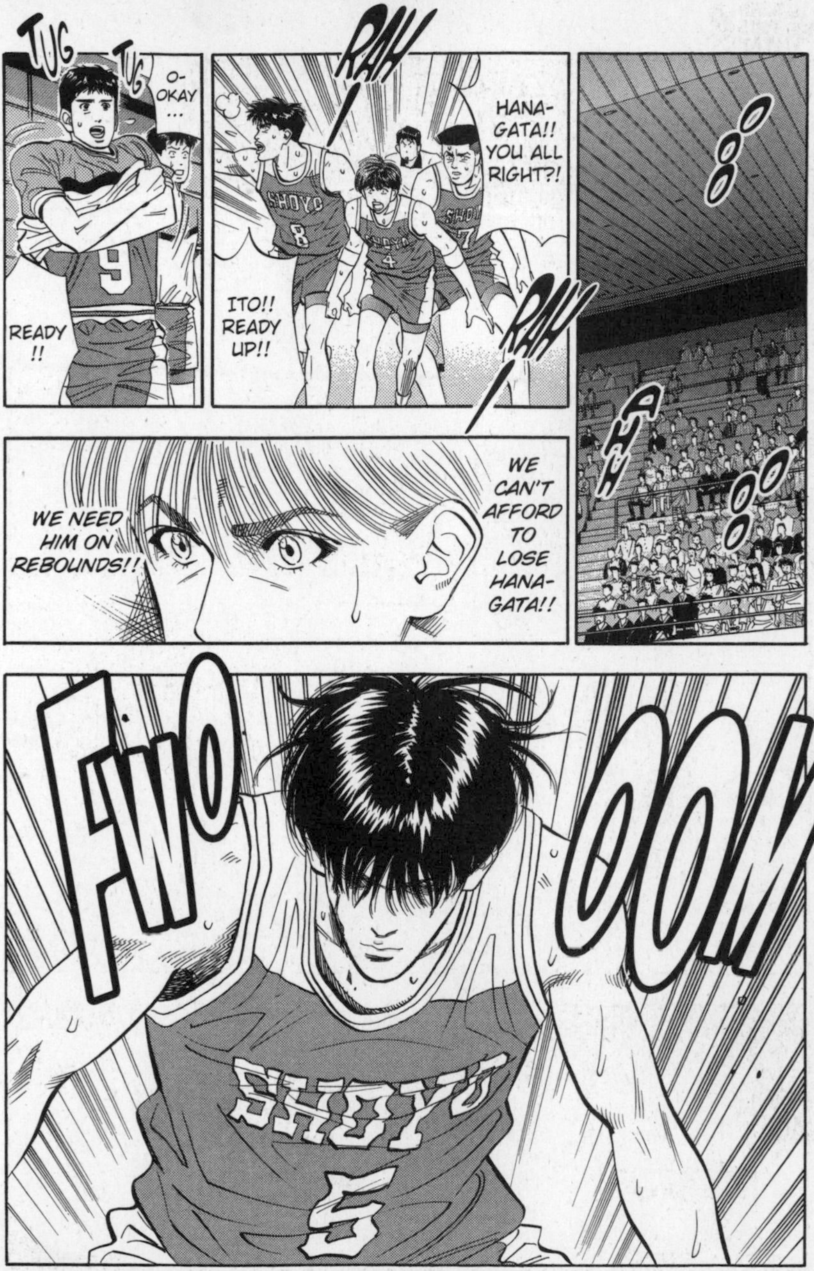
OOO
AHH
OOO
RAH!
HANA-GATA!! YOU ALL RIGHT?!
ITO!! READY UP!!
RAH!
TUG
TUG
O-OKAY ...
READY !!
WE CAN'T AFFORD TO LOSE HANA-GATA!!
WE NEED HIM ON REBOUNDS!!
FWOOOM

READ THIS WAY

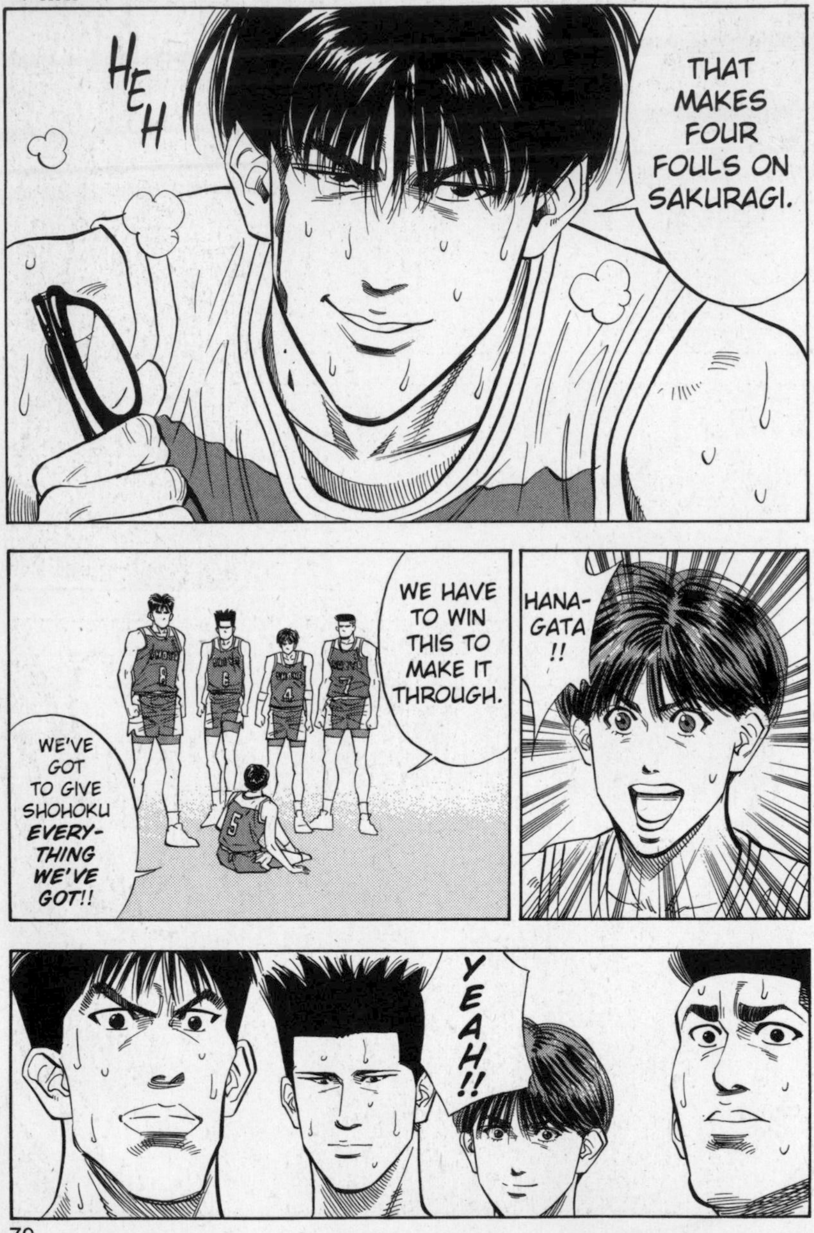

THAT MAKES FOUR FOULS ON SAKURAGI.
HEH
HANA-GATA!!
WE HAVE TO WIN THIS TO MAKE IT THROUGH.
WE'VE GOT TO GIVE SHOHOKU EVERYTHING WE'VE GOT!!
YEAH!!

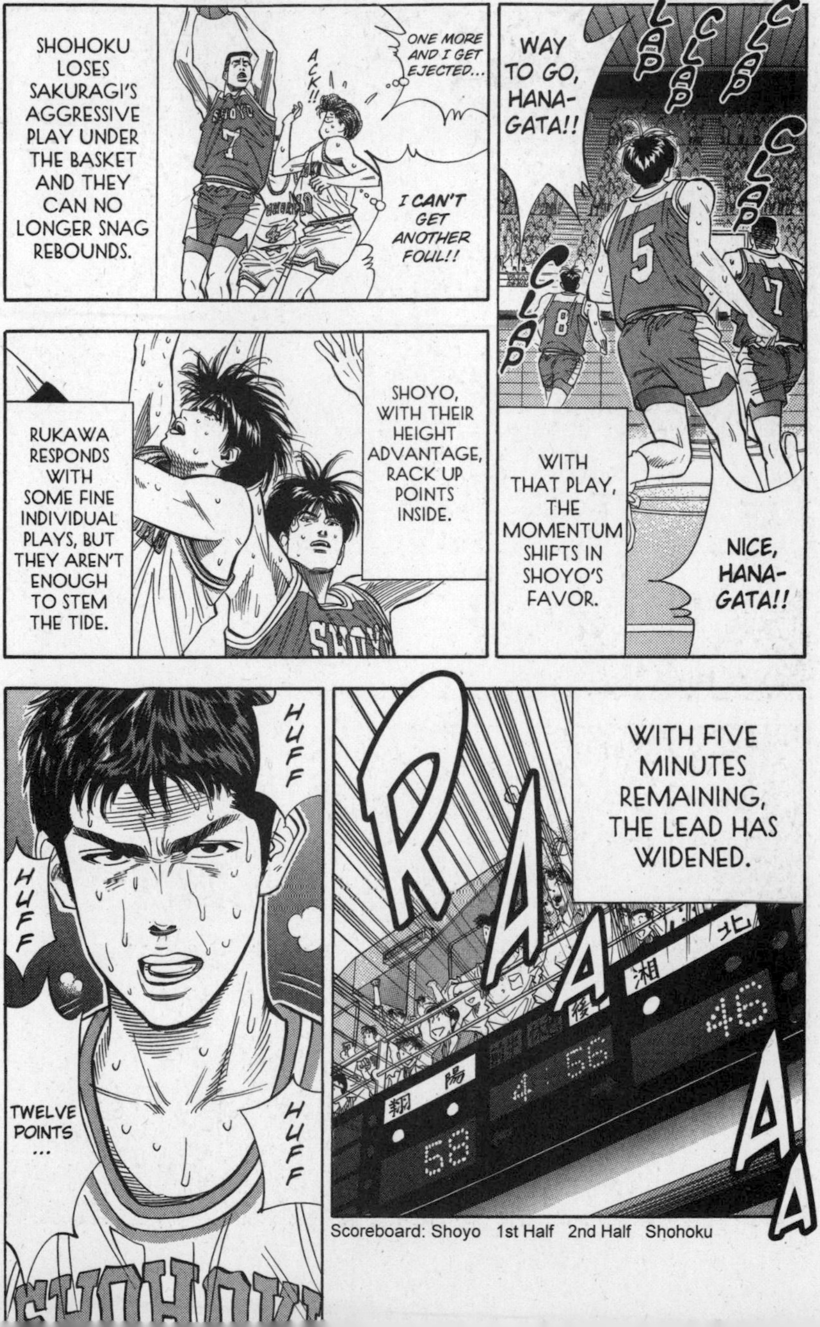
CLAP CLAP CLAP CLAP CLAP
WAY TO GO, HANAGATA!!
WITH THAT PLAY, THE MOMENTUM SHIFTS IN SHOYO'S FAVOR.
NICE, HANAGATA!!
SHOHOKU LOSES SAKURAGI'S AGGRESSIVE PLAY UNDER THE BASKET AND THEY CAN NO LONGER SNAG REBOUNDS.
ONE MORE AND I GET EJECTED...
ACK!!
I CAN'T GET ANOTHER FOUL!!
SHOYO, WITH THEIR HEIGHT ADVANTAGE, RACK UP POINTS INSIDE.
RUKAWA RESPONDS WITH SOME FINE INDIVIDUAL PLAYS, BUT THEY AREN'T ENOUGH TO STEM THE TIDE.
WITH FIVE MINUTES REMAINING, THE LEAD HAS WIDENED.
RAAAA
翔陽
58
4:56
湘北
46
HUFF HUFF
TWELVE POINTS...
HUFF HUFF
Scoreboard: Shoyo 1st Half 2nd Half Shohoku

READ THIS WAY

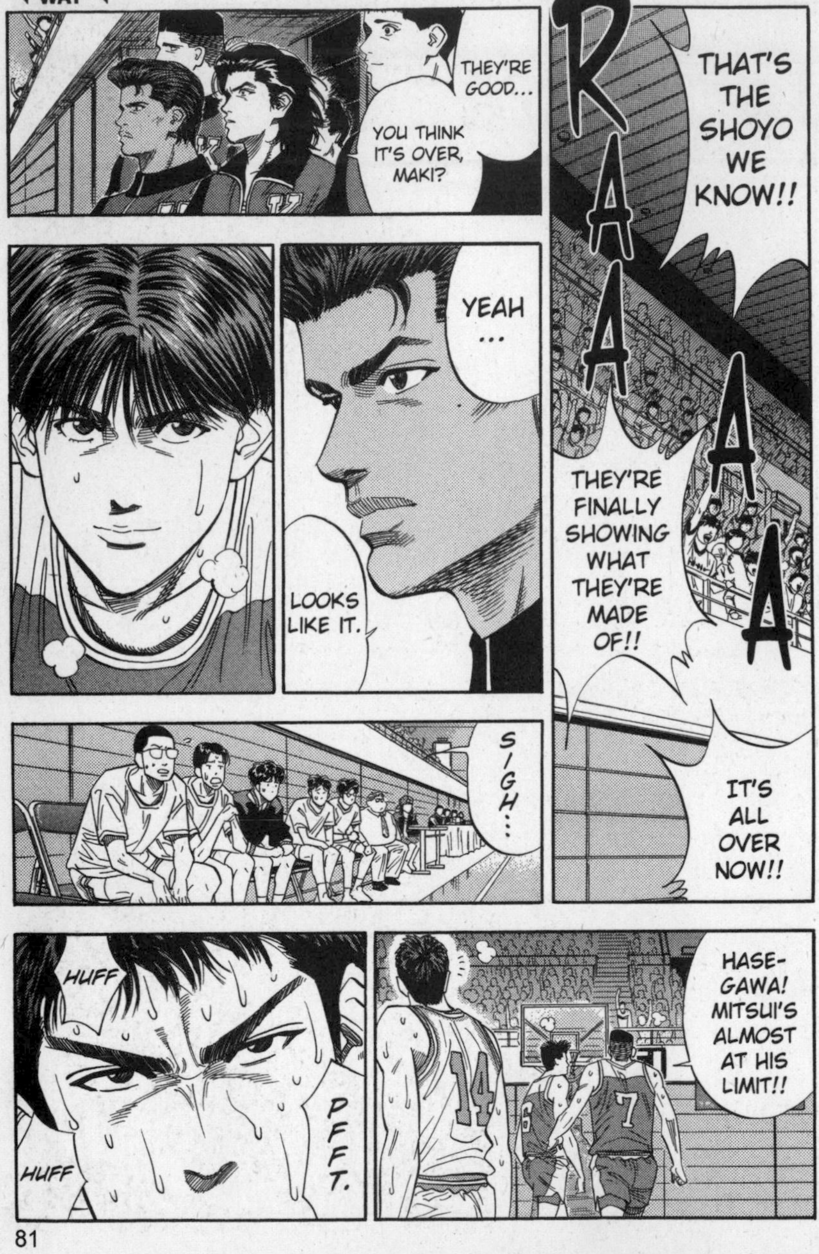
RAAAA
THAT'S THE SHOYO WE KNOW!!
THEY'RE FINALLY SHOWING WHAT THEY'RE MADE OF!!
IT'S ALL OVER NOW!!
THEY'RE GOOD...
YOU THINK IT'S OVER, MAKI?
YEAH ...
LOOKS LIKE IT.
SIGH...
HASE-GAWA! MITSUI'S ALMOST AT HIS LIMIT!!
HUFF
PFFT.
HUFF

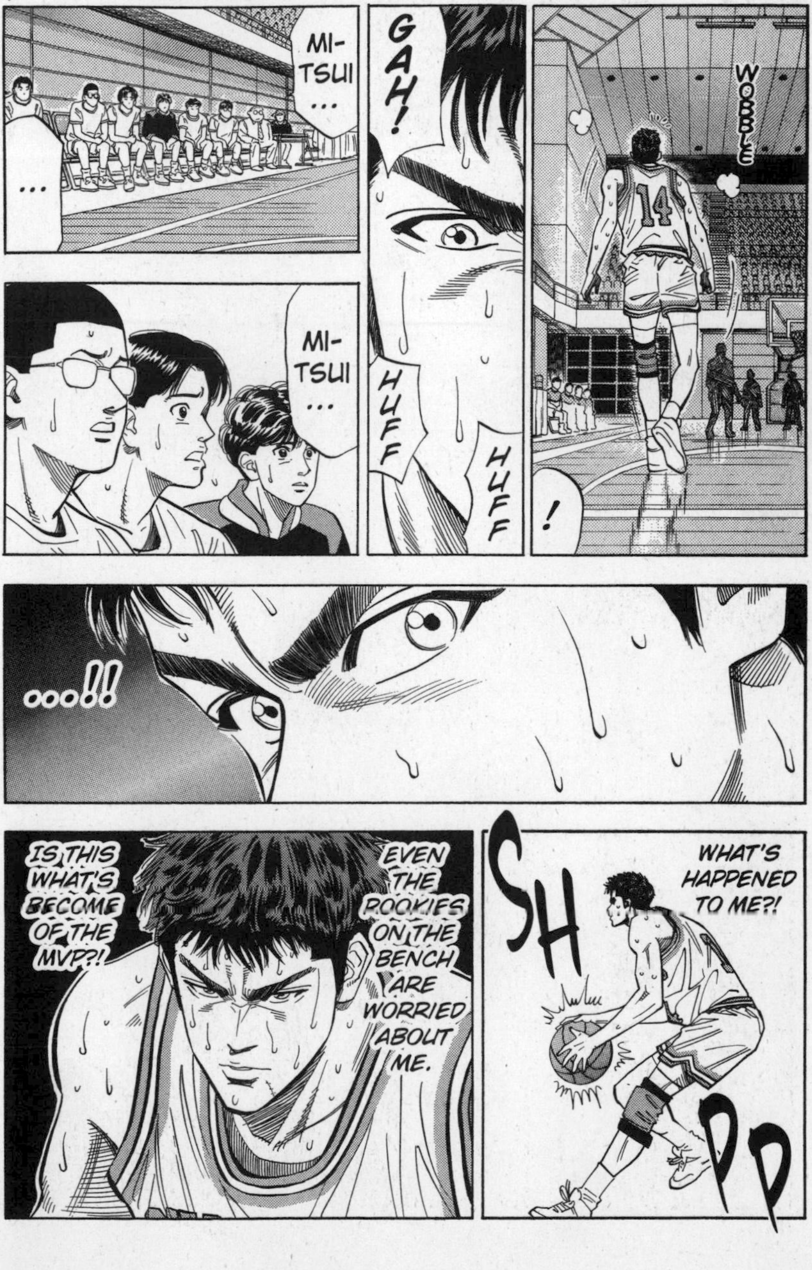
WOBBLE
!
GAH!
HUFF
HUFF
MI-TSUI...
...
MI-TSUI...
...!!
WHAT'S HAPPENED TO ME?!
SH
DD
EVEN THE ROOKIES ON THE BENCH ARE WORRIED ABOUT ME.
IS THIS WHAT'S BECOME OF THE MVP?!

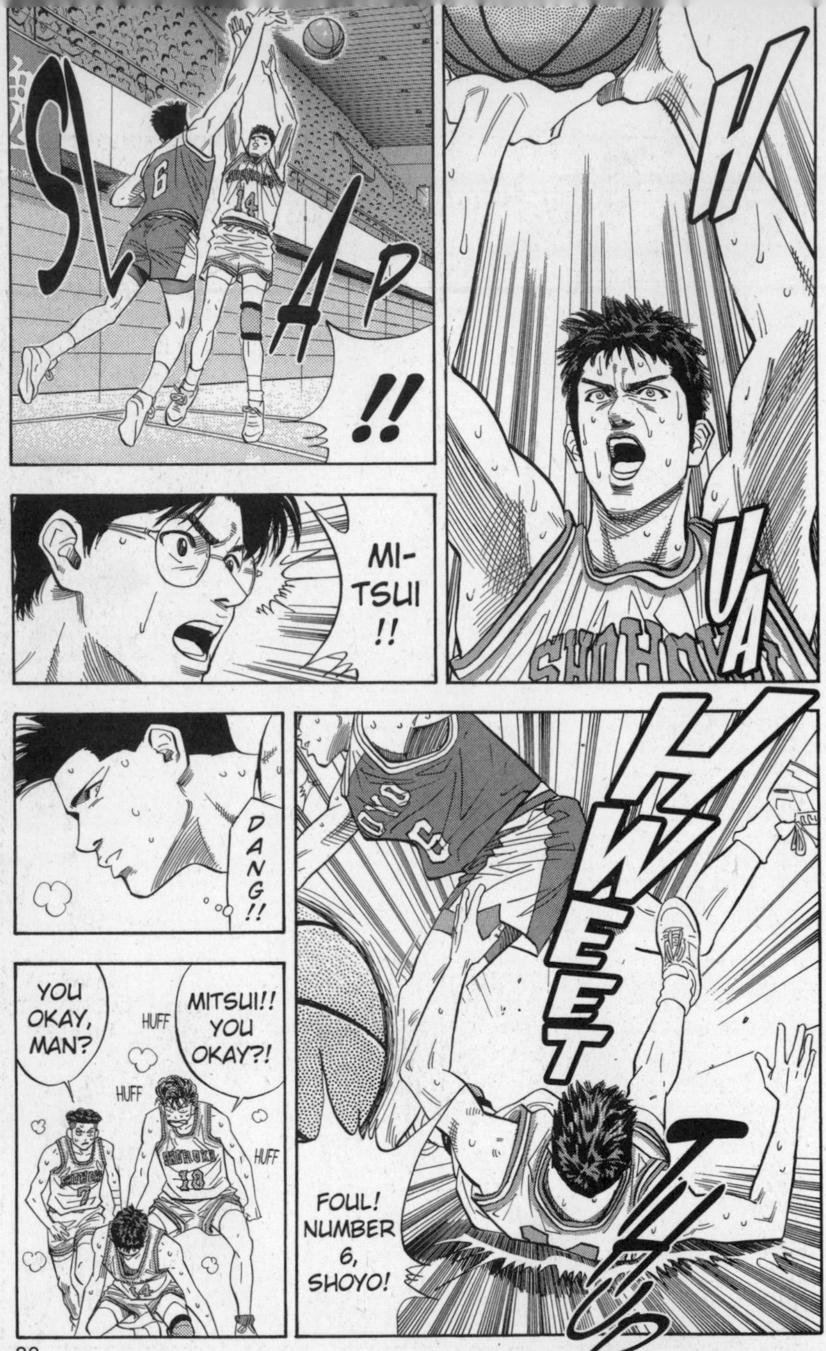

HUA
SLAP
!!
MI-
TSUI
!!
HWEEET
FOUL! NUMBER 6, SHOYO!
DANG!!
MITSUI!! YOU OKAY?!
HUFF
YOU OKAY, MAN?
HUFF
HUFF

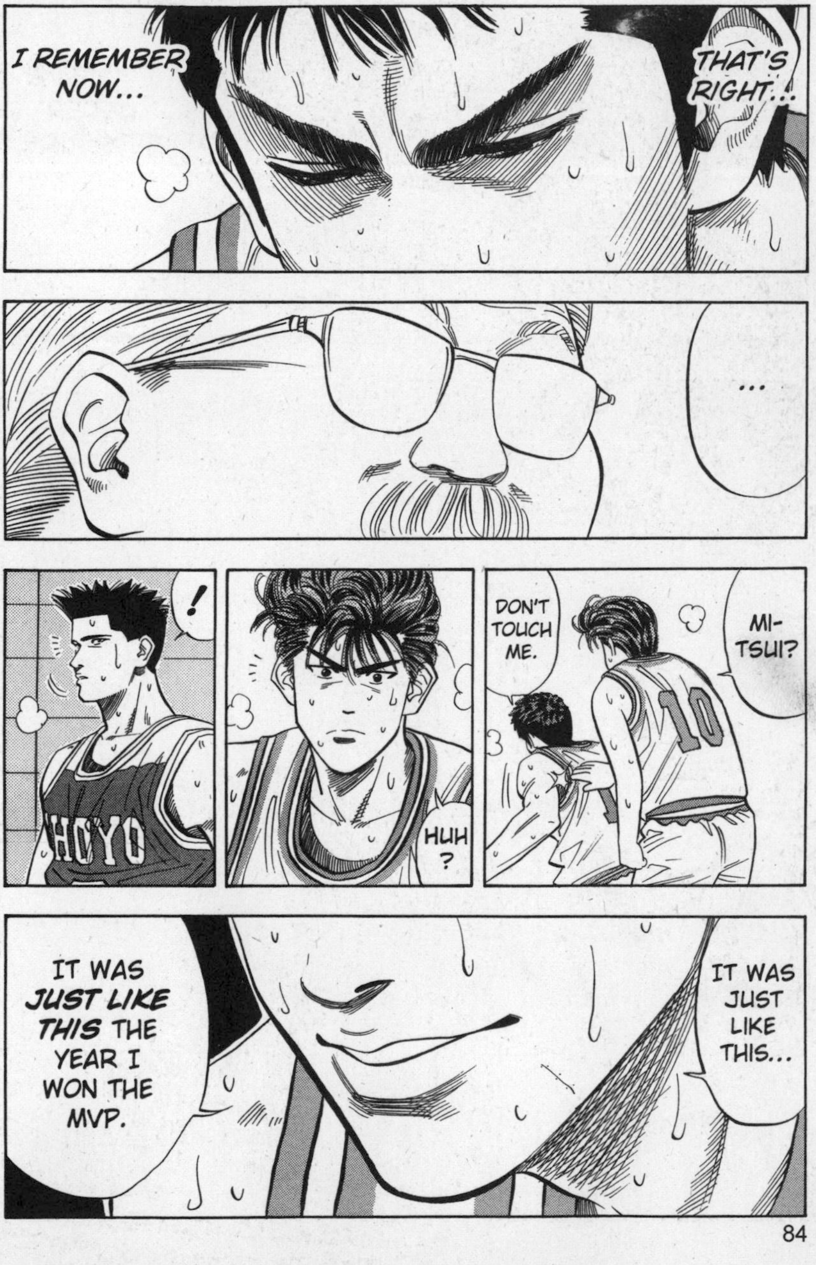
THAT'S RIGHT...
I REMEMBER NOW...
...
MI-TSUI?
DON'T TOUCH ME.
HUH?
!
IT WAS JUST LIKE THIS...
IT WAS JUST LIKE THIS THE YEAR I WON THE MVP.

READ THIS WAY

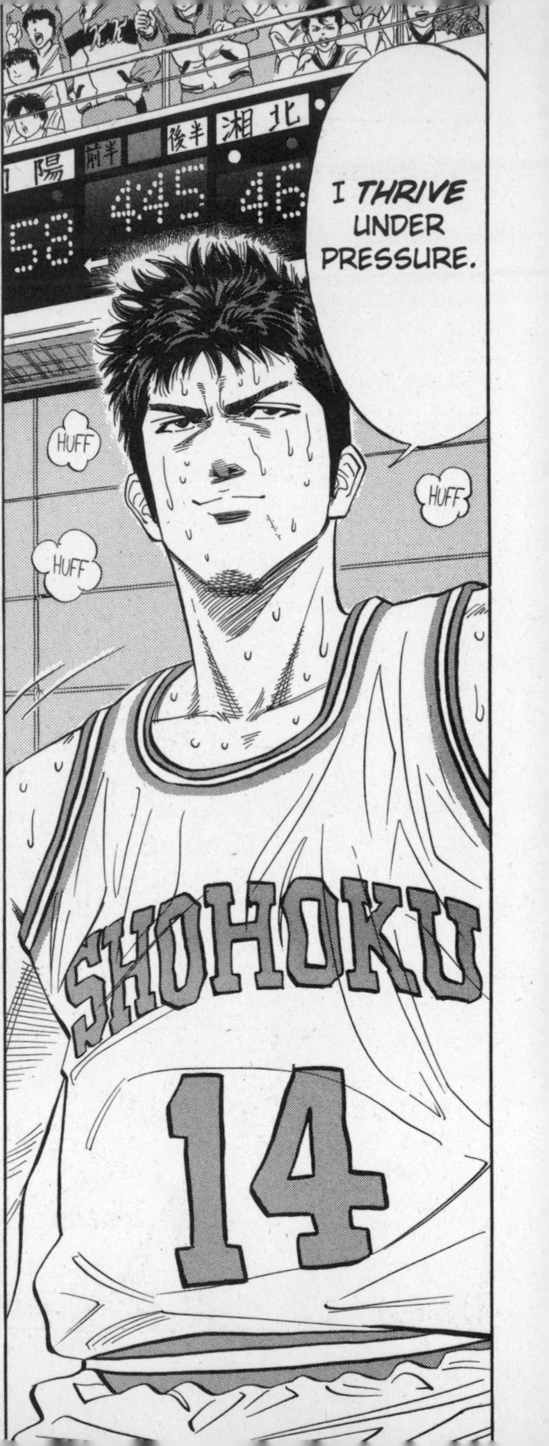
I THRIVE UNDER PRESSURE.
HUFF
HUFF
HUFF
SHOHOKU
14

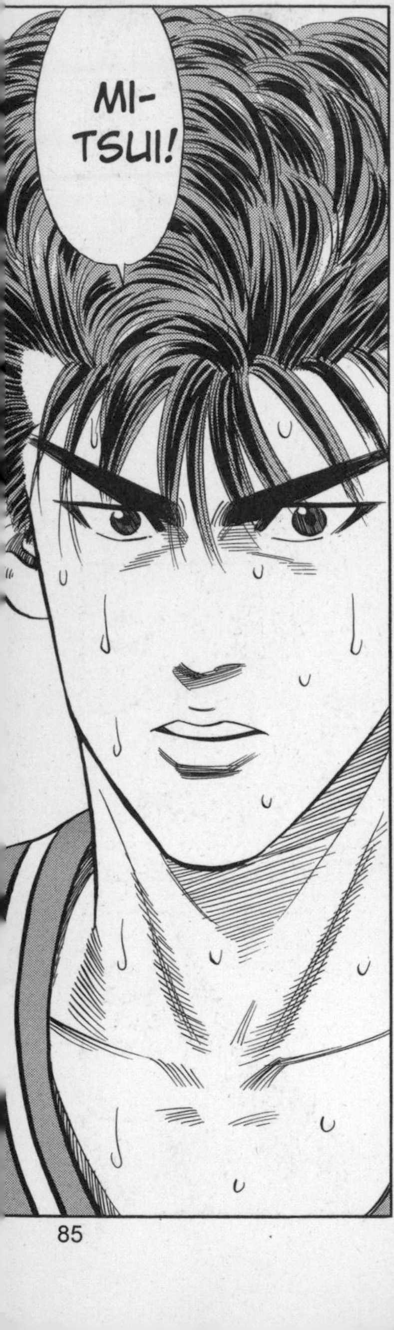
MI-
TSUI!

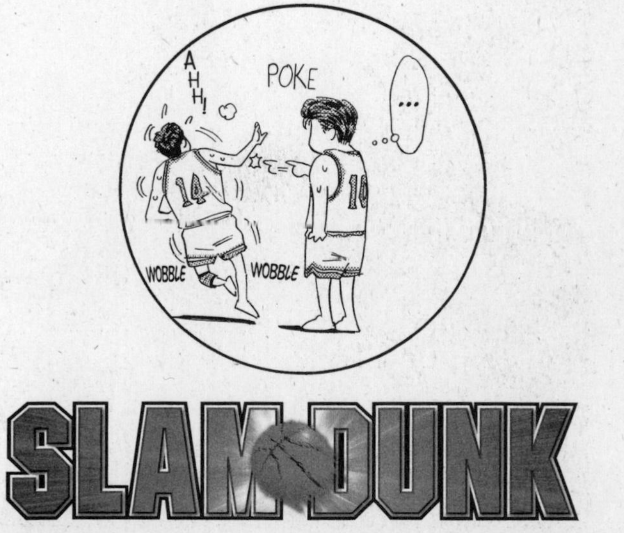
...
POKE
AHH!
WOBBLE
WOBBLE

SLAM DUNK

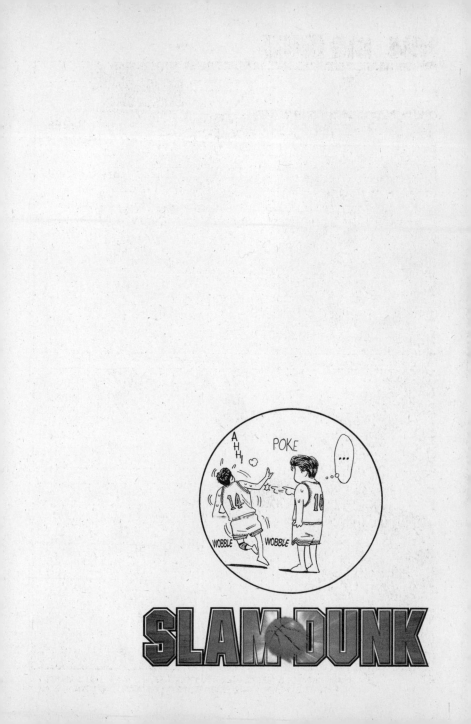

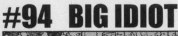

#94 BIG IDIOT

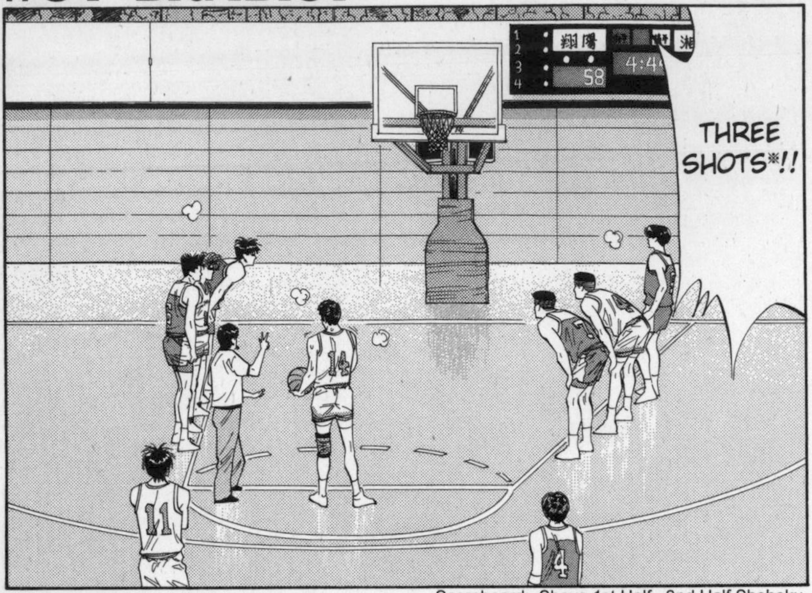

THREE SHOTS※!!

Banner: *Tokon* (fighting spirit)

Scoreboard: Shoyo 1st Half 2nd Half Shohoku

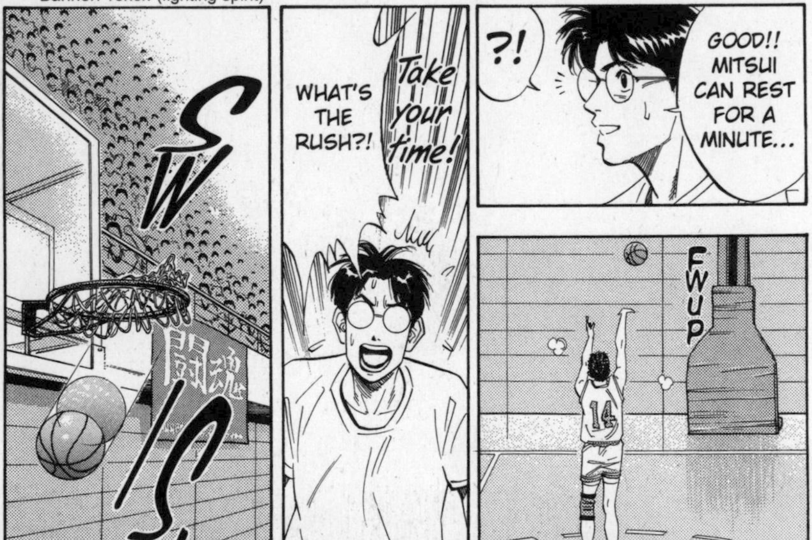

GOOD!! MITSUI CAN REST FOR A MINUTE...
?!
FWUP
Take your time!
WHAT'S THE RUSH?!
SWISH

※ NORMALLY FREE THROWS ARE AWARDED IN PAIRS, BUT IF A PLAYER IS FOULED WHILE ATTEMPTING A THREE-POINTER, THEY'RE AWARDED THREE FREE THROWS.

#94 BIG IDIOT

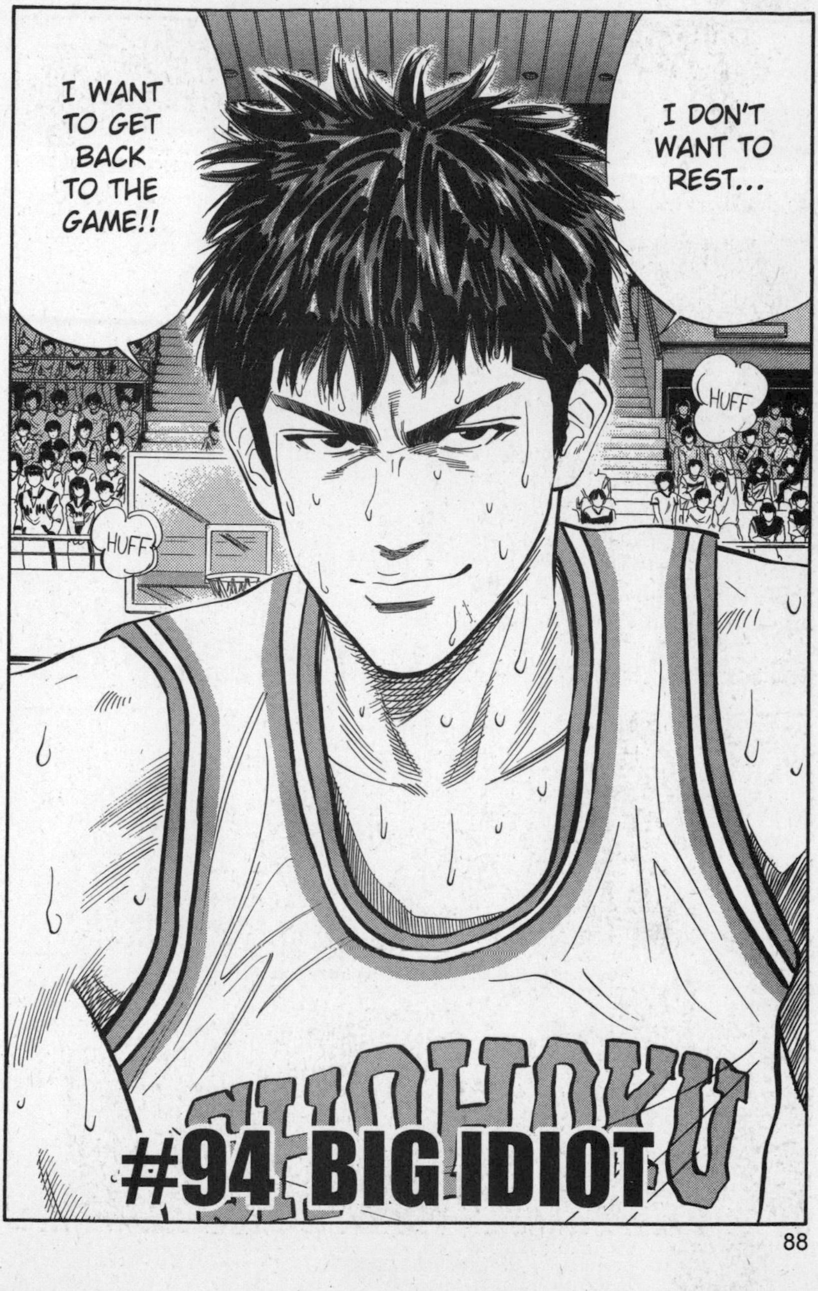
I DON'T WANT TO REST...
I WANT TO GET BACK TO THE GAME!!
HUFF
HUFF
SHOHOKU

READ THIS WAY

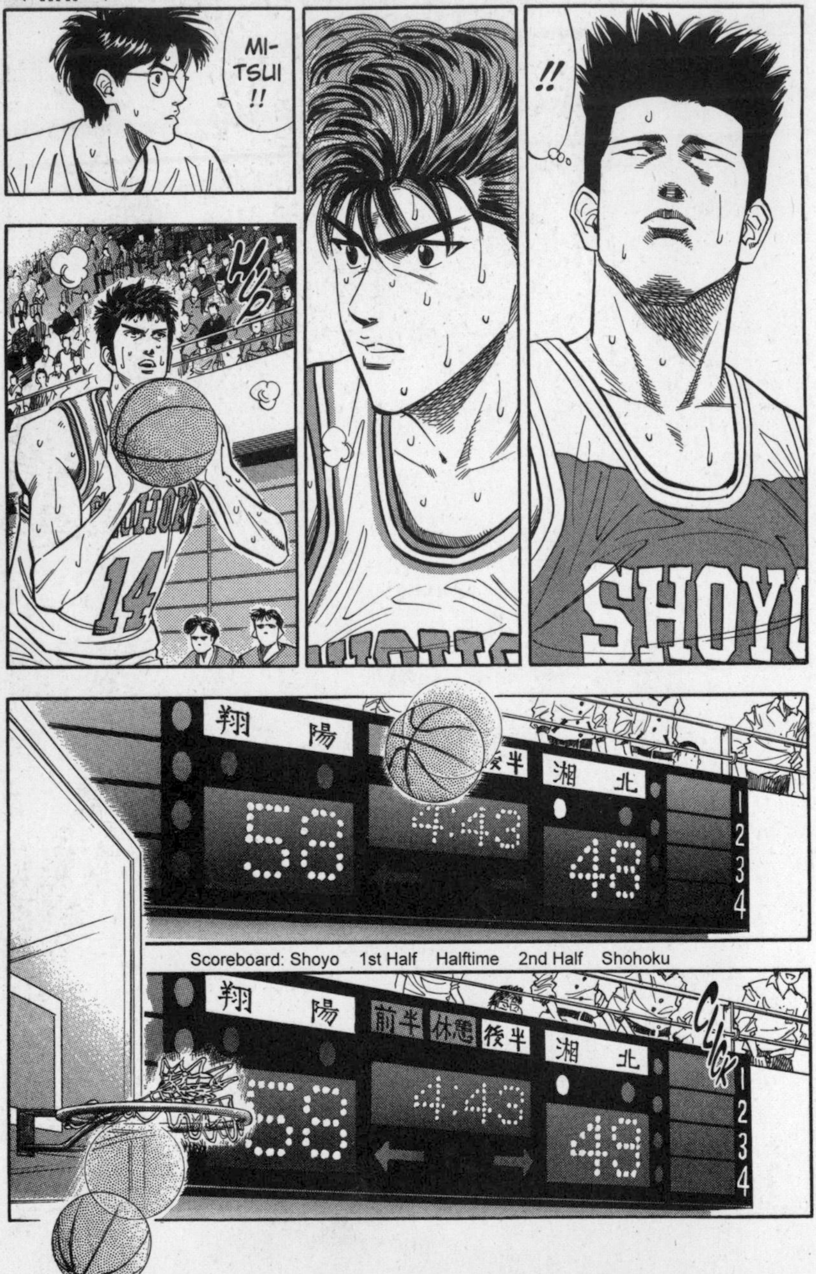
!!
MI-
TSUI
!!
HUP
翔陽
後半
湘北
58
4:43
48
1 2 3 4
Scoreboard: Shoyo 1st Half Halftime 2nd Half Shohoku
CLICK
翔陽
前半 休憩 後半
湘北
58
4:43
49
1 2 3 4

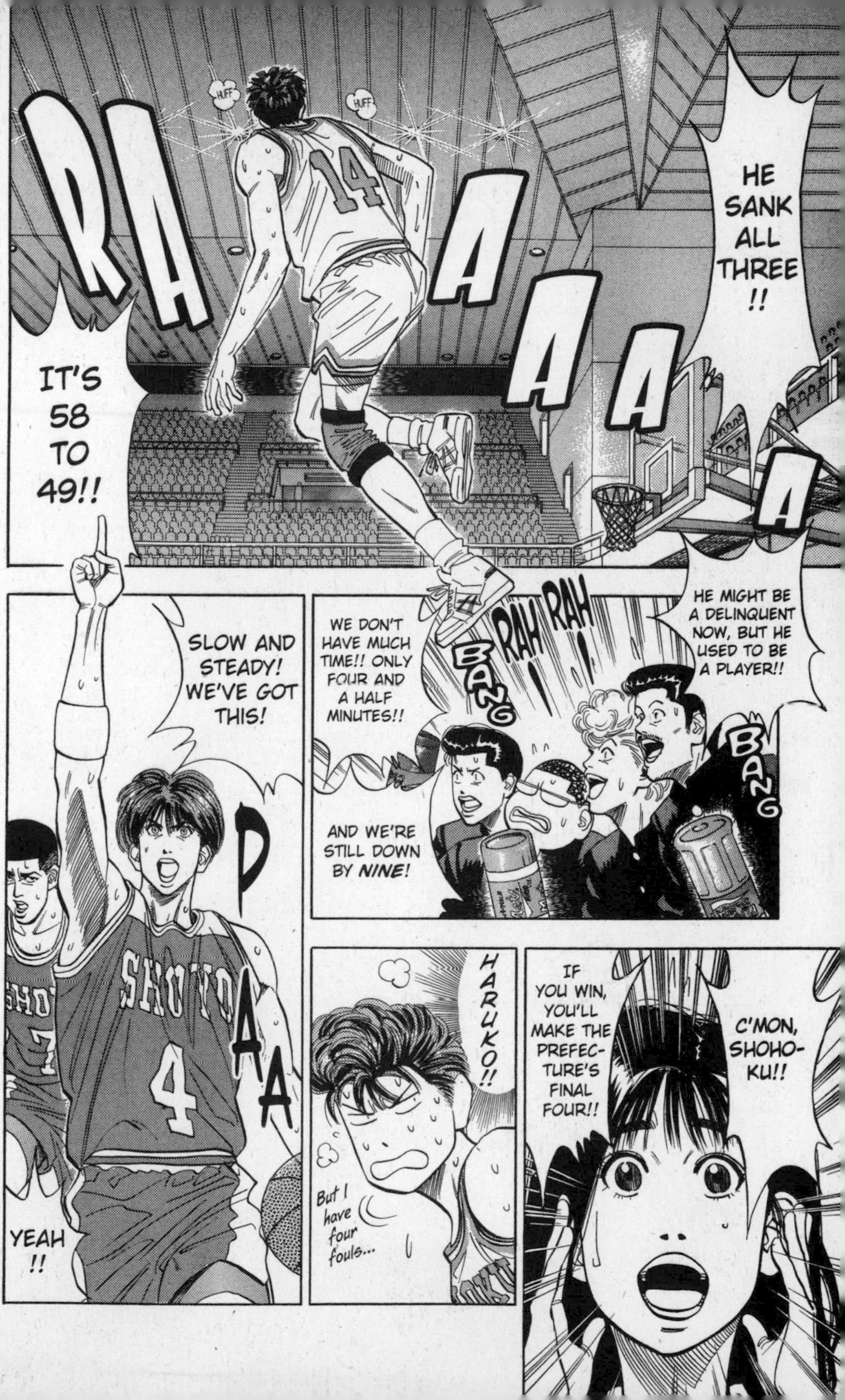
HE SANK ALL THREE!!
RAAAAAA
HUFF
HUFF
IT'S 58 TO 49!!
HE MIGHT BE A DELINQUENT NOW, BUT HE USED TO BE A PLAYER!!
BANG
RAH RAH
BANG
WE DON'T HAVE MUCH TIME!! ONLY FOUR AND A HALF MINUTES!!
AND WE'RE STILL DOWN BY ***NINE***!
C'MON, SHOHOKU!!
IF YOU WIN, YOU'LL MAKE THE PREFECTURE'S FINAL FOUR!!
HARUKO!!
But I have four fouls...
SLOW AND STEADY! WE'VE GOT THIS!
PAAA
YEAH!!

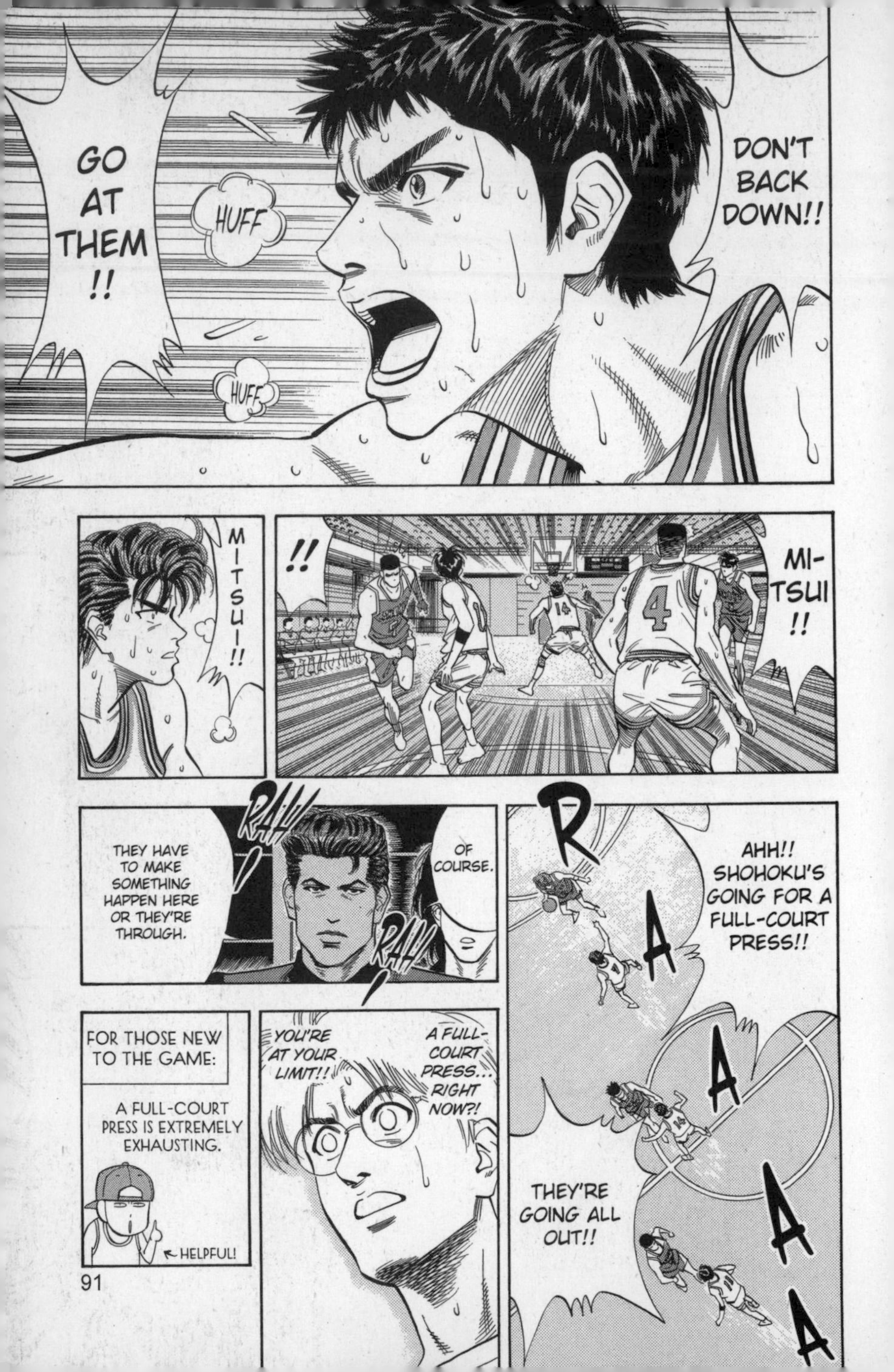
DON'T BACK DOWN!!
HUFF
GO AT THEM!!
HUFF
MI-TSUI!!
!!
MITSUI!!
R
AHH!! SHOHOKU'S GOING FOR A FULL-COURT PRESS!!
AAAAA
THEY'RE GOING ALL OUT!!
RAH
OF COURSE.
THEY HAVE TO MAKE SOMETHING HAPPEN HERE OR THEY'RE THROUGH.
RAH
A FULL-COURT PRESS... RIGHT NOW?!
YOU'RE AT YOUR LIMIT!!
FOR THOSE NEW TO THE GAME:
A FULL-COURT PRESS IS EXTREMELY EXHAUSTING.
← HELPFUL!

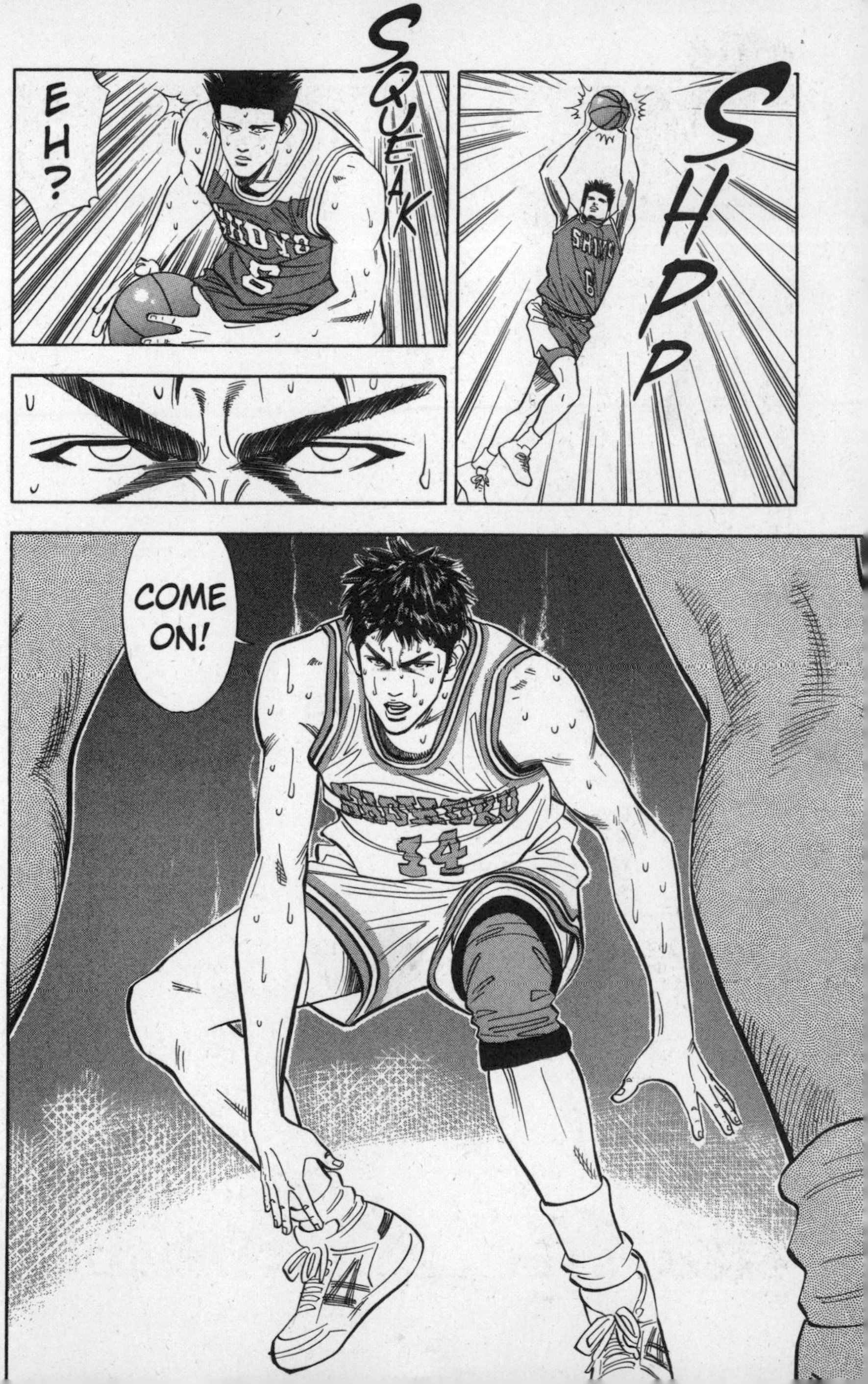
SHPP
EH?
SQUEAK
COME ON!

READ THIS WAY

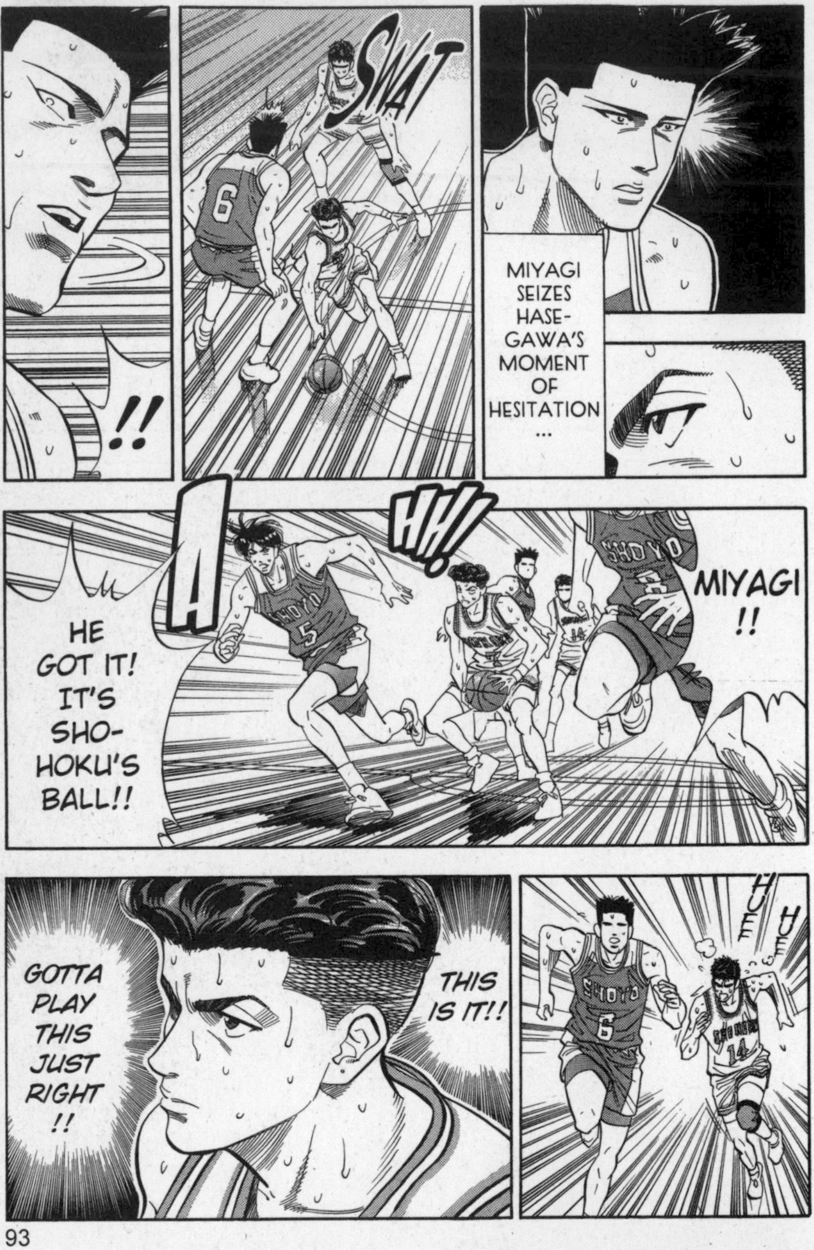

MIYAGI SEIZES HASE-GAWA'S MOMENT OF HESITATION ...
SWAT
!!
MIYAGI !!
AHH!!
HE GOT IT! IT'S SHO-HOKU'S BALL!!
HUF HUF
THIS IS IT!!
GOTTA PLAY THIS JUST RIGHT !!

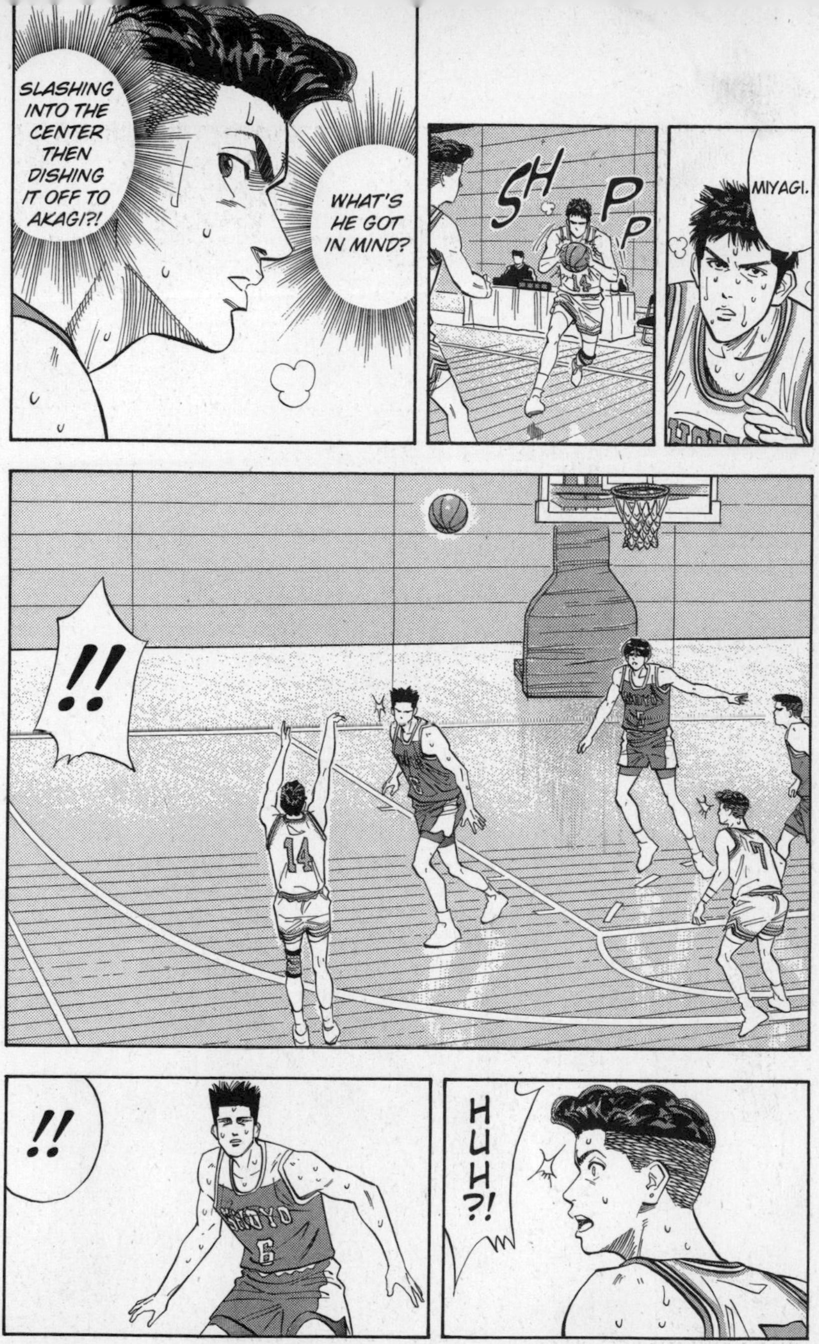
MIYAGI.
SHPP
SLASHING INTO THE CENTER THEN DISHING IT OFF TO AKAGI?!
WHAT'S HE GOT IN MIND?
!!
HUH?!
!!

READ THIS WAY

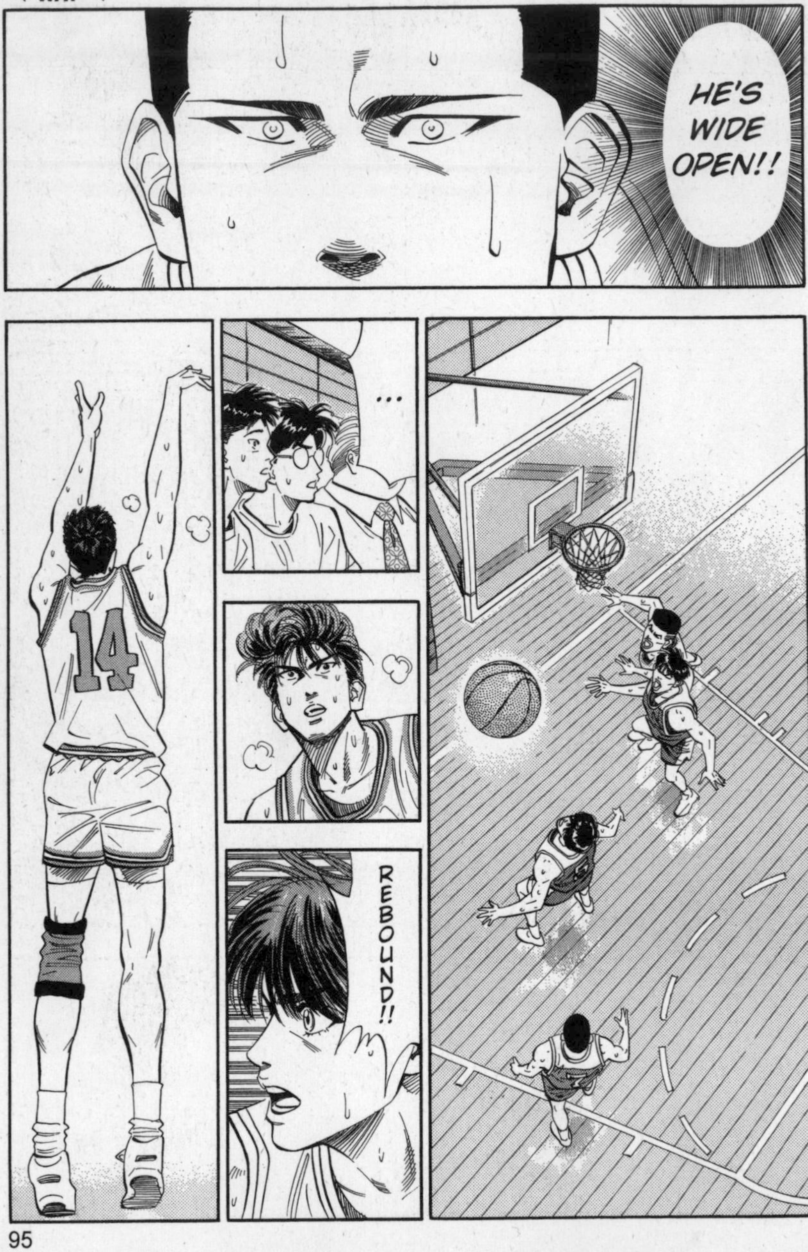
HE'S WIDE OPEN!!
...
REBOUND!!

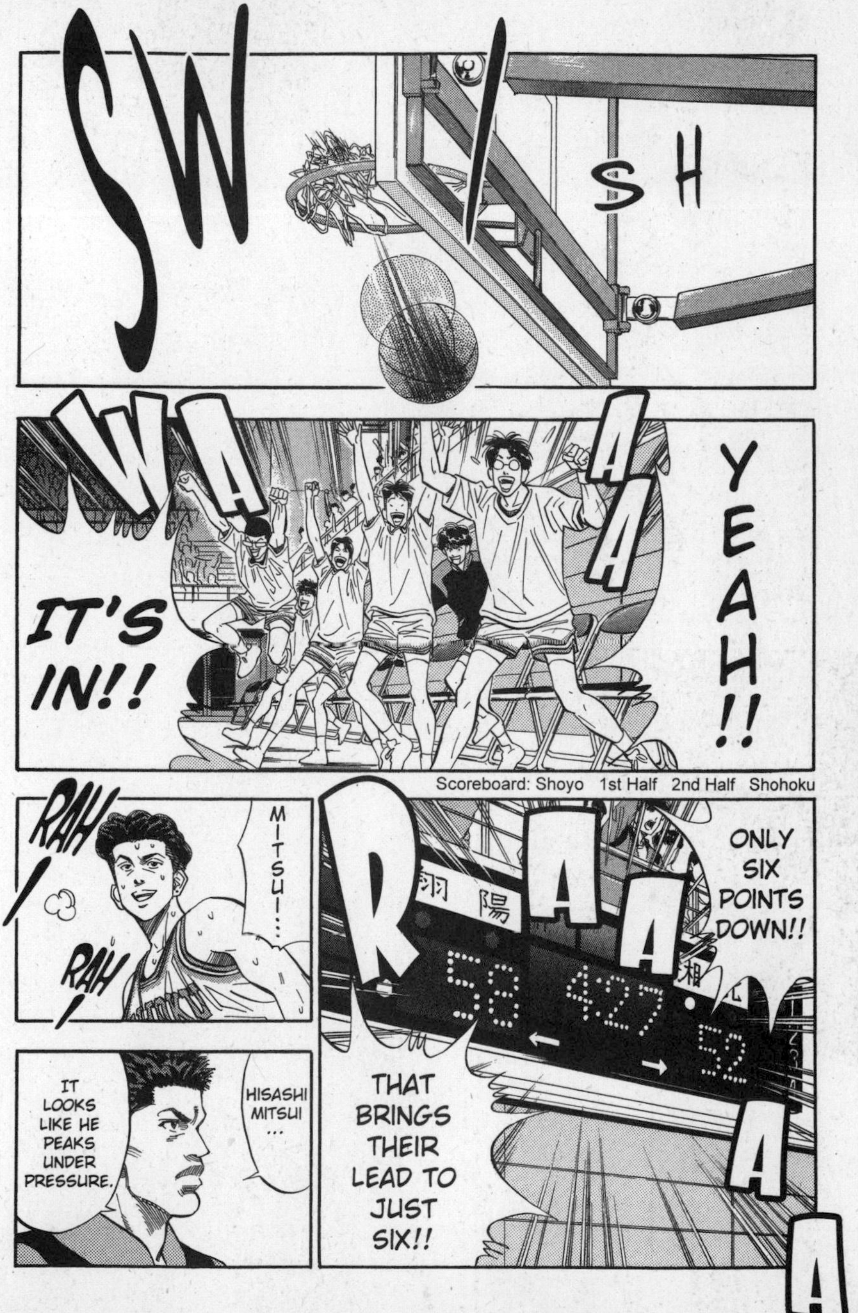
SWISH
WAAA
YEAH!!
IT'S IN!!
Scoreboard: Shoyo 1st Half 2nd Half Shohoku
RAAAA
ONLY SIX POINTS DOWN!!
58 427 52
THAT BRINGS THEIR LEAD TO JUST SIX!!
MITSUI...
RAH! RAH!
HISASHI MITSUI...
IT LOOKS LIKE HE PEAKS UNDER PRESSURE.

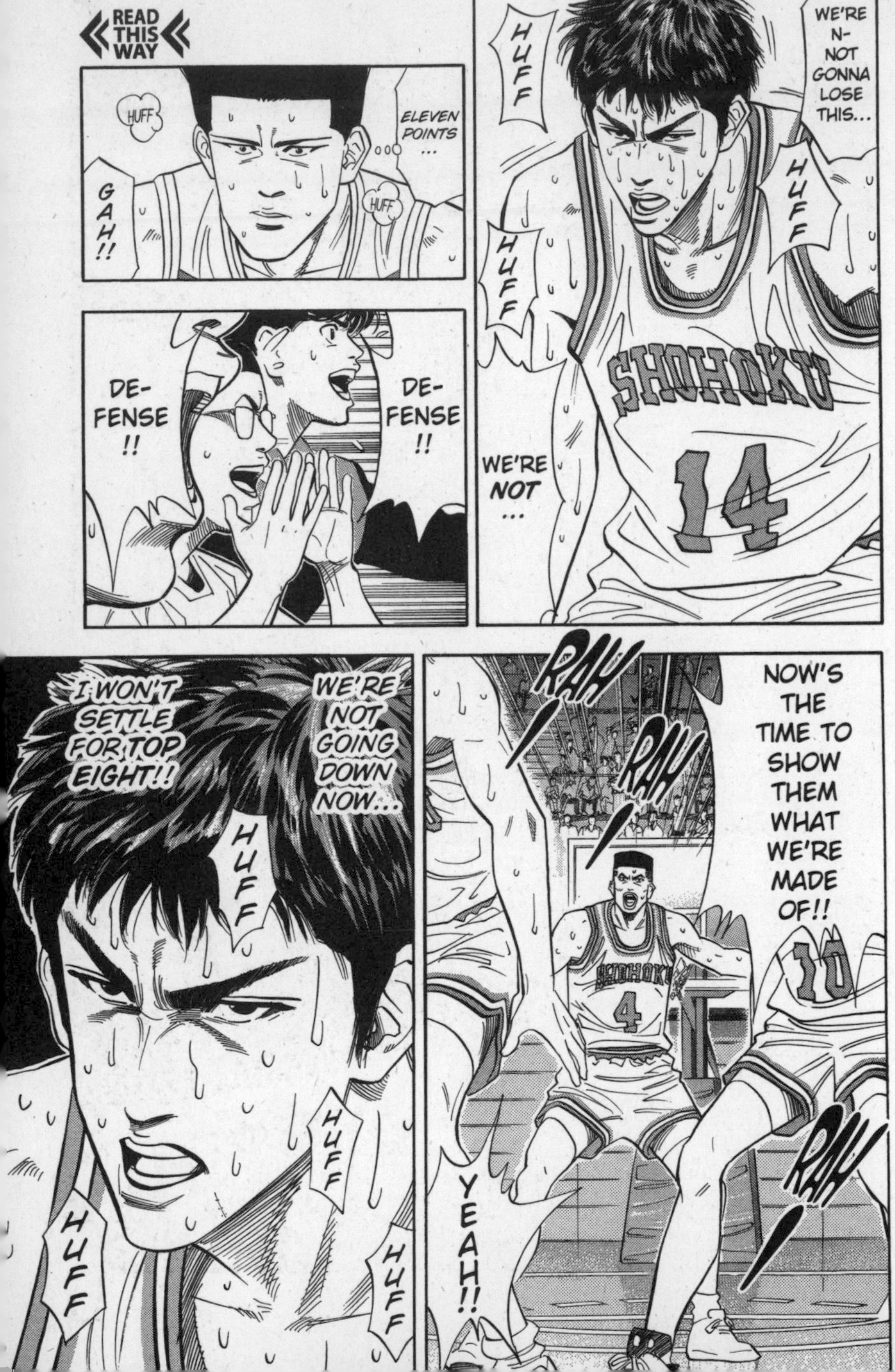
READ THIS WAY
WE'RE N-NOT GONNA LOSE THIS...
HUFF
HUFF
HUFF
WE'RE NOT ...
ELEVEN POINTS ...
HUFF
HUFF
GAH!!
DE-FENSE!!
DE-FENSE!!
NOW'S THE TIME TO SHOW THEM WHAT WE'RE MADE OF!!
RAH!
RAH!
RAH!
YEAH!!
WE'RE NOT GOING DOWN NOW...
I WON'T SETTLE FOR TOP EIGHT!!
HUFF
HUFF
HUFF
HUFF

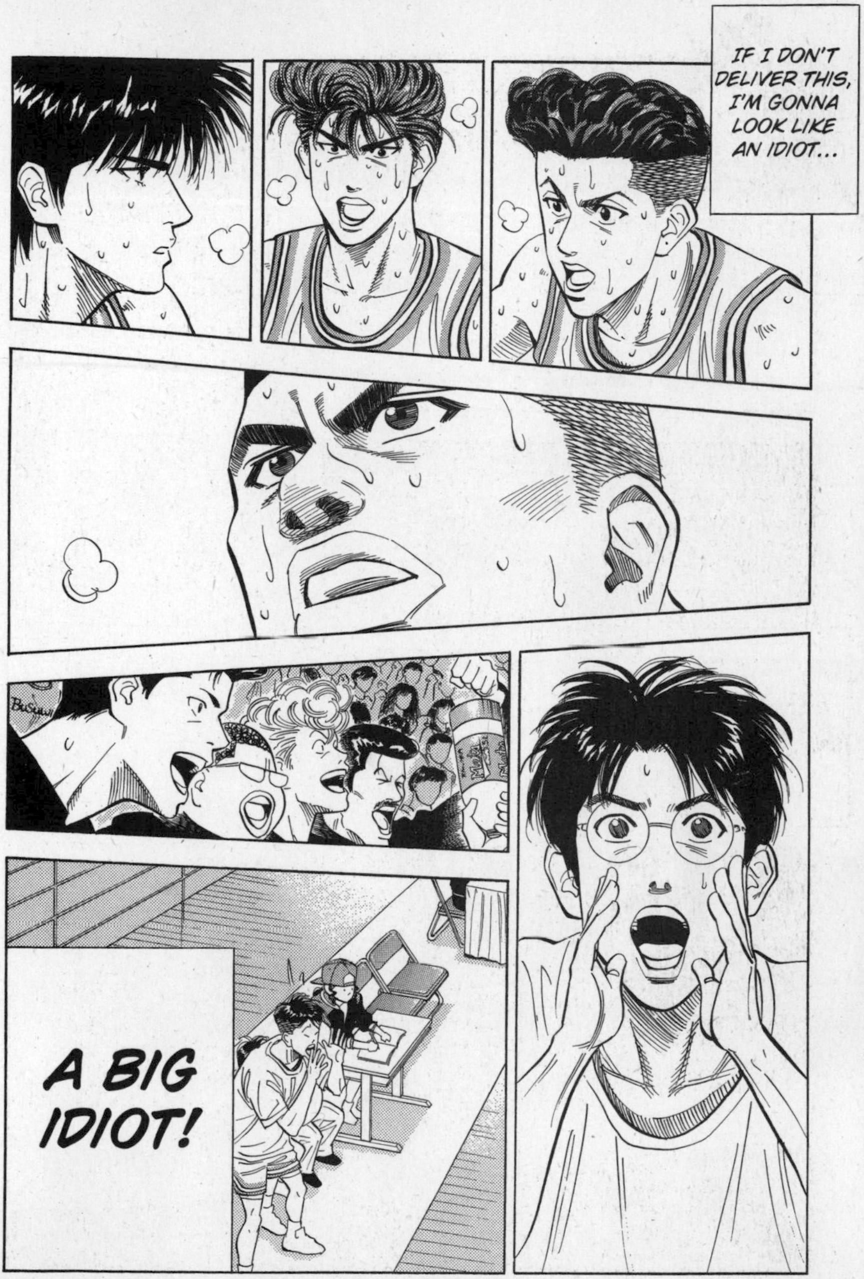
IF I DON'T DELIVER THIS, I'M GONNA LOOK LIKE AN IDIOT...
A BIG IDIOT!

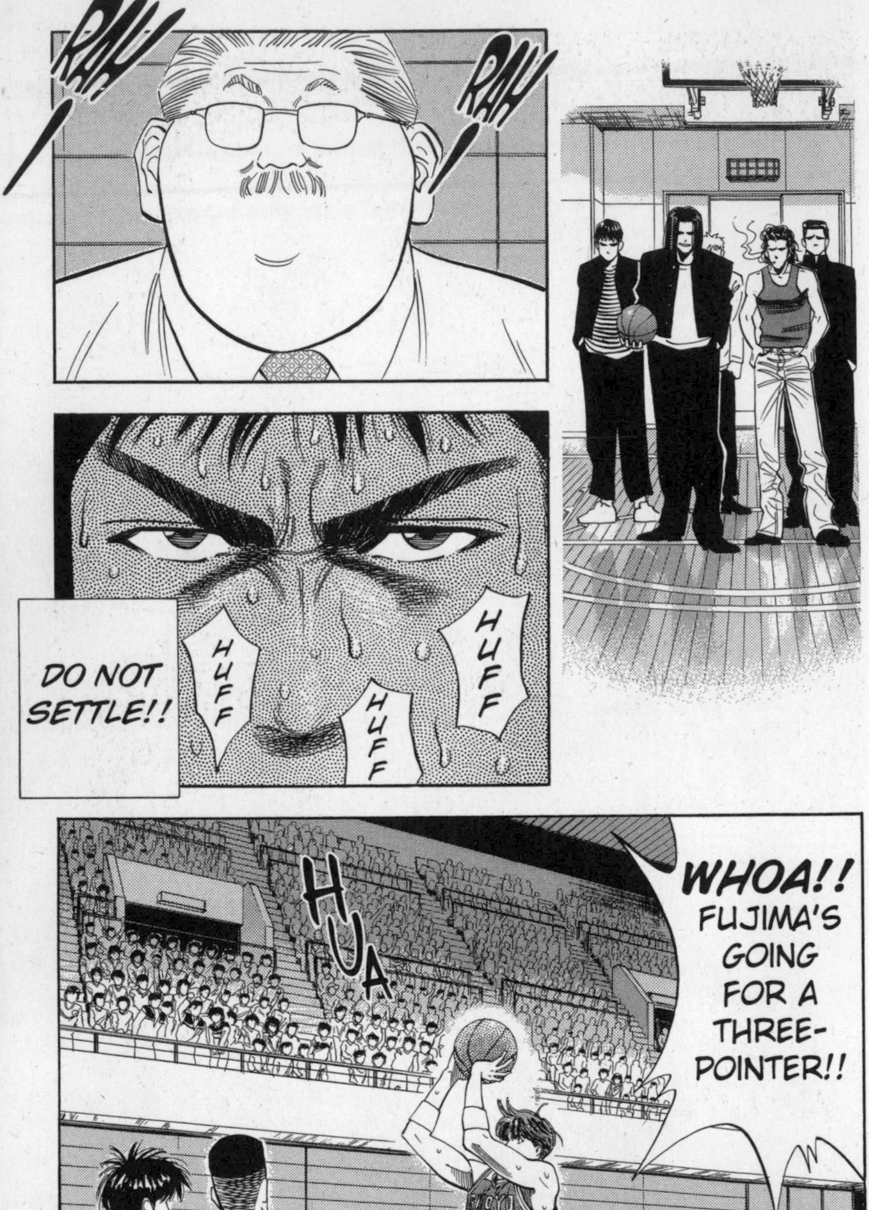
RAH!
RAH!
DO NOT SETTLE!!
HUFF
HUFF
HUFF
WHOA!! FUJIMA'S GOING FOR A THREE-POINTER!!
HUA

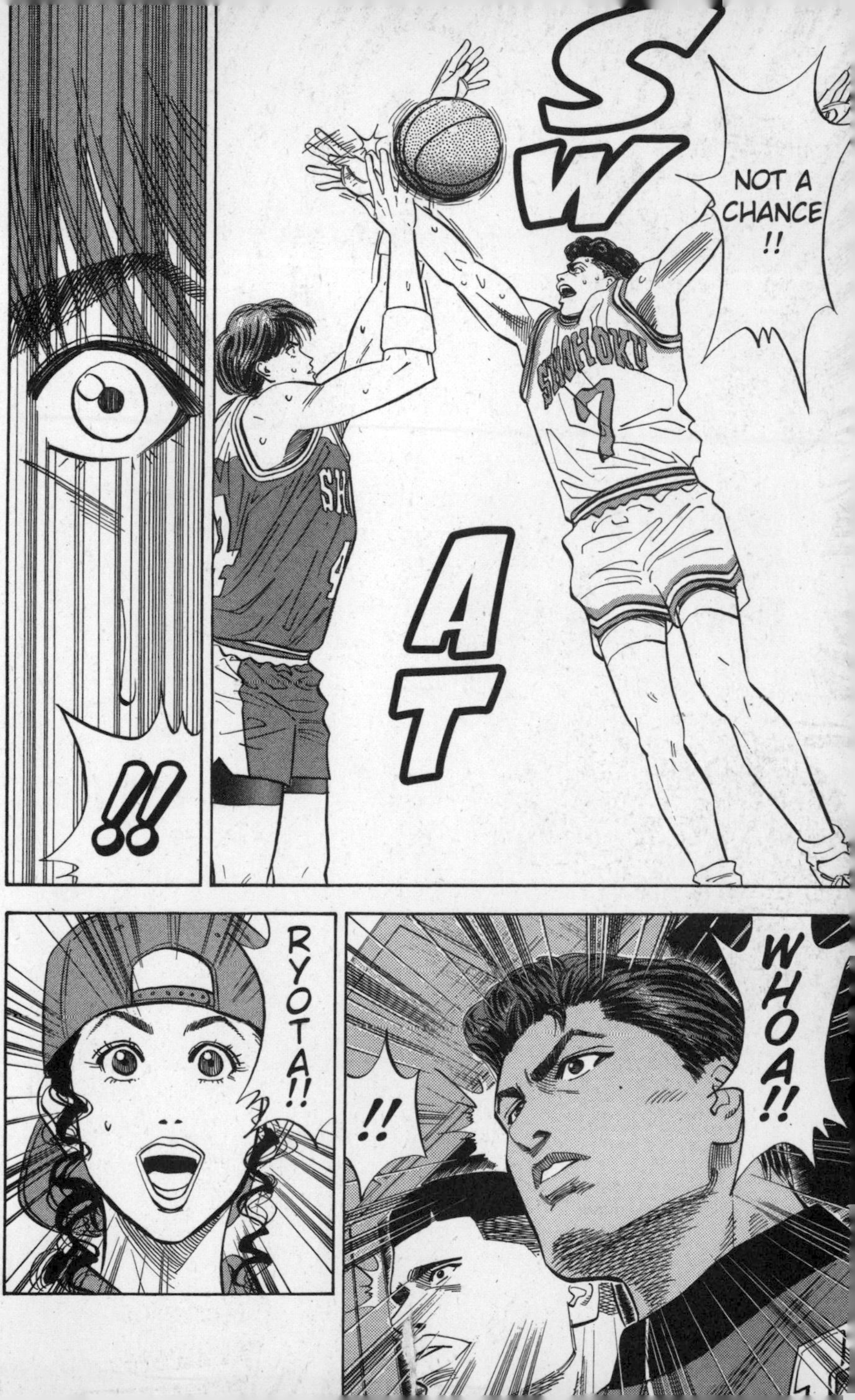
NOT A CHANCE !!
SWAT
!!
WHOA!!
!!
RYOTA!!

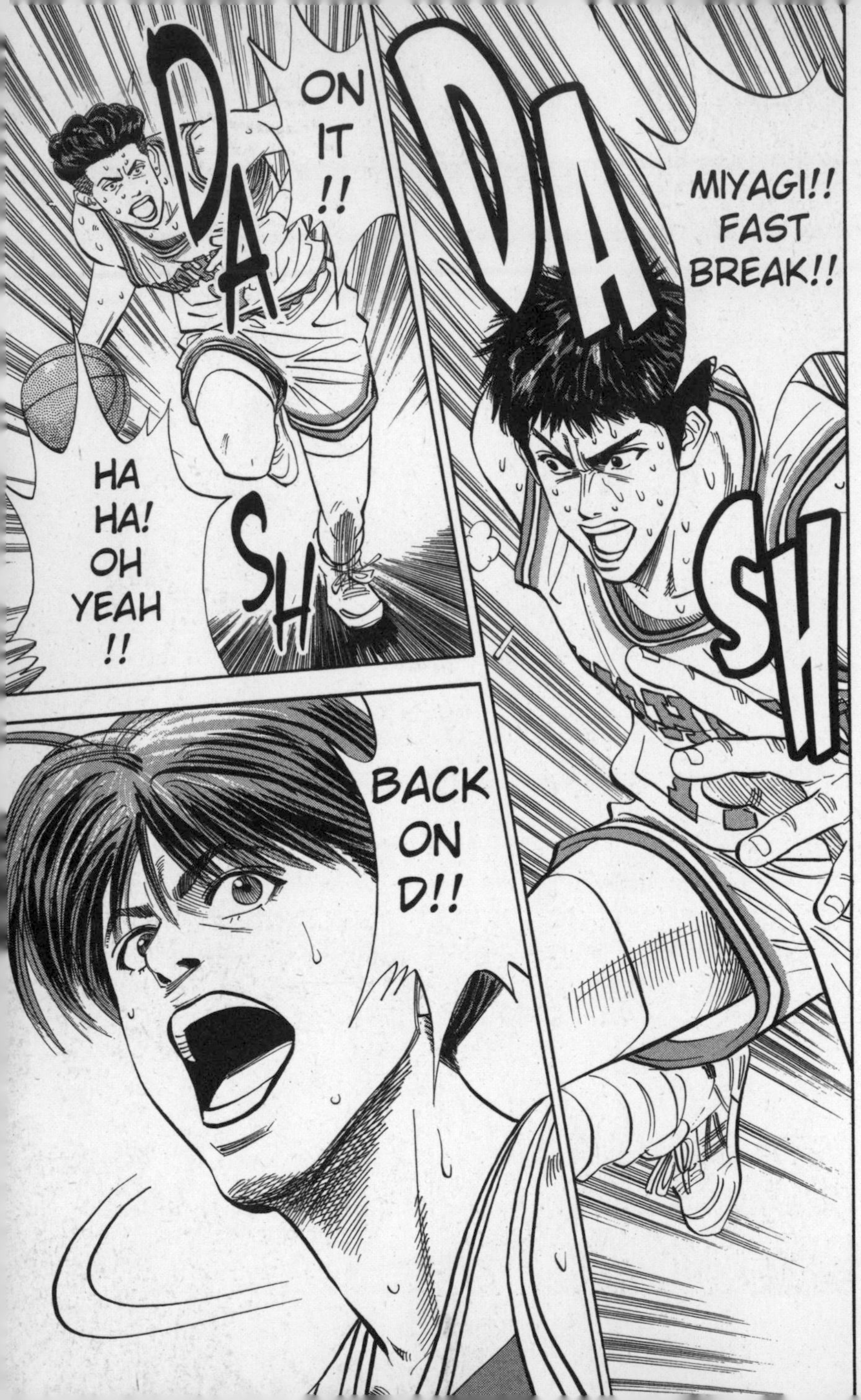
DA
MIYAGI!! FAST BREAK!!
SH
DA
ON IT!!
SH
HA HA! OH YEAH!!
BACK ON D!!

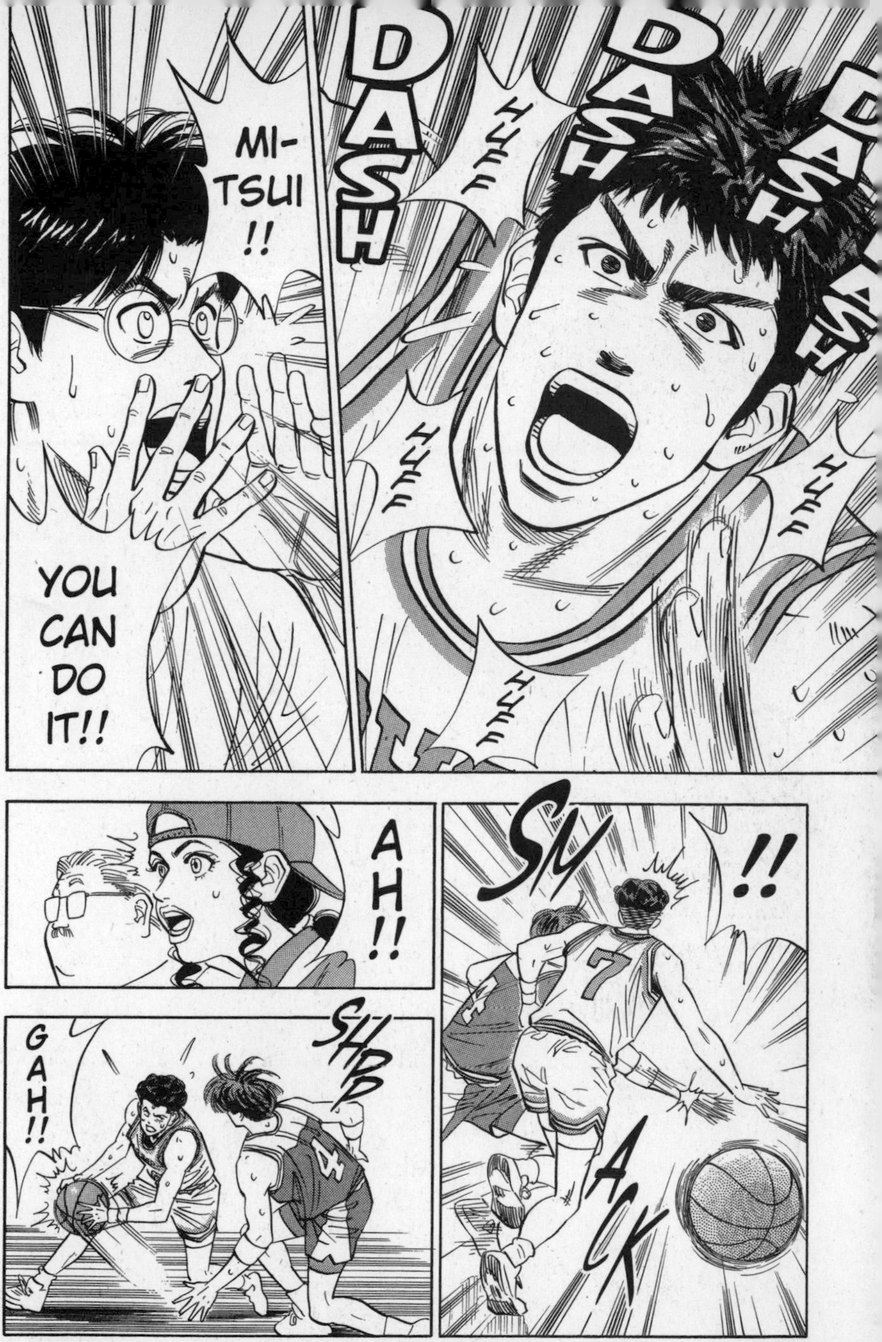
DASH
DASH
DASH
HUFF
HUFF
HUFF
HUFF
MI-
TSUI
!!
YOU
CAN
DO
IT!!
SM
ACK
!!
AH!!
SHD
GAH!!

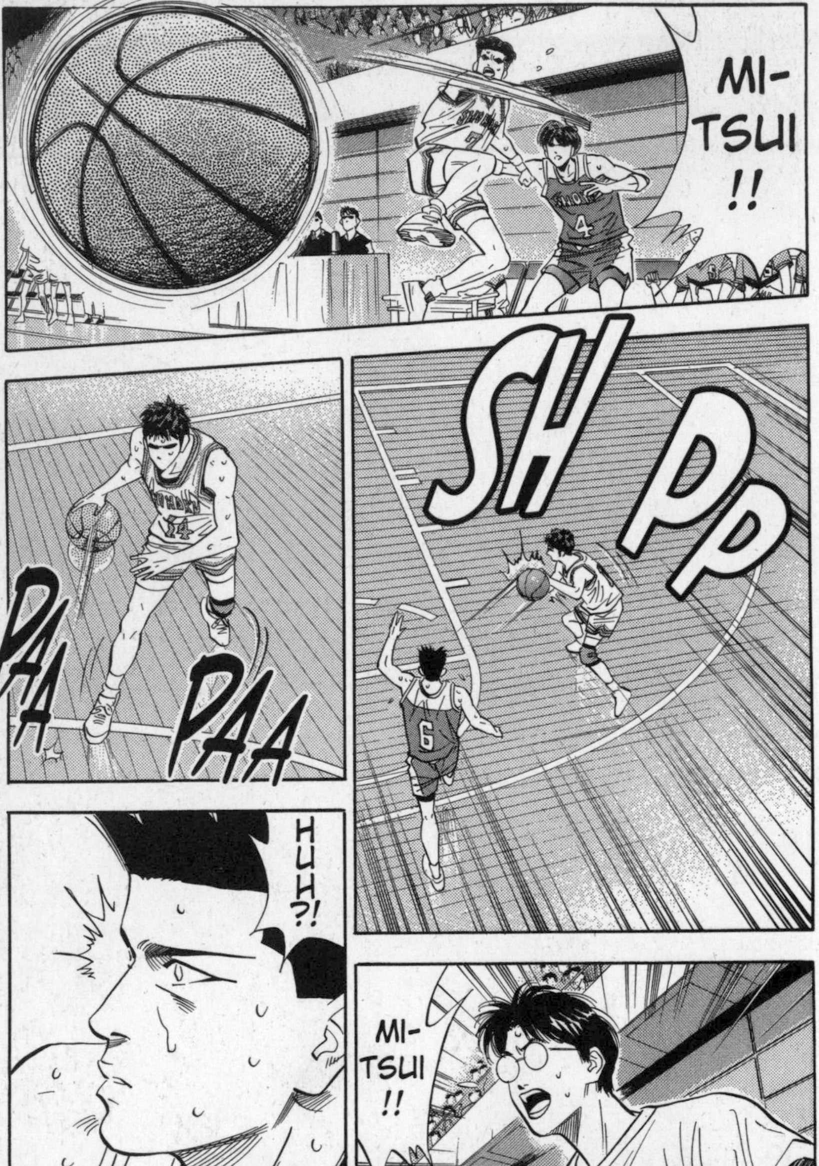
MI-TSUI!!
SHPP
PAA PAA
HUH?!
MI-TSUI!!

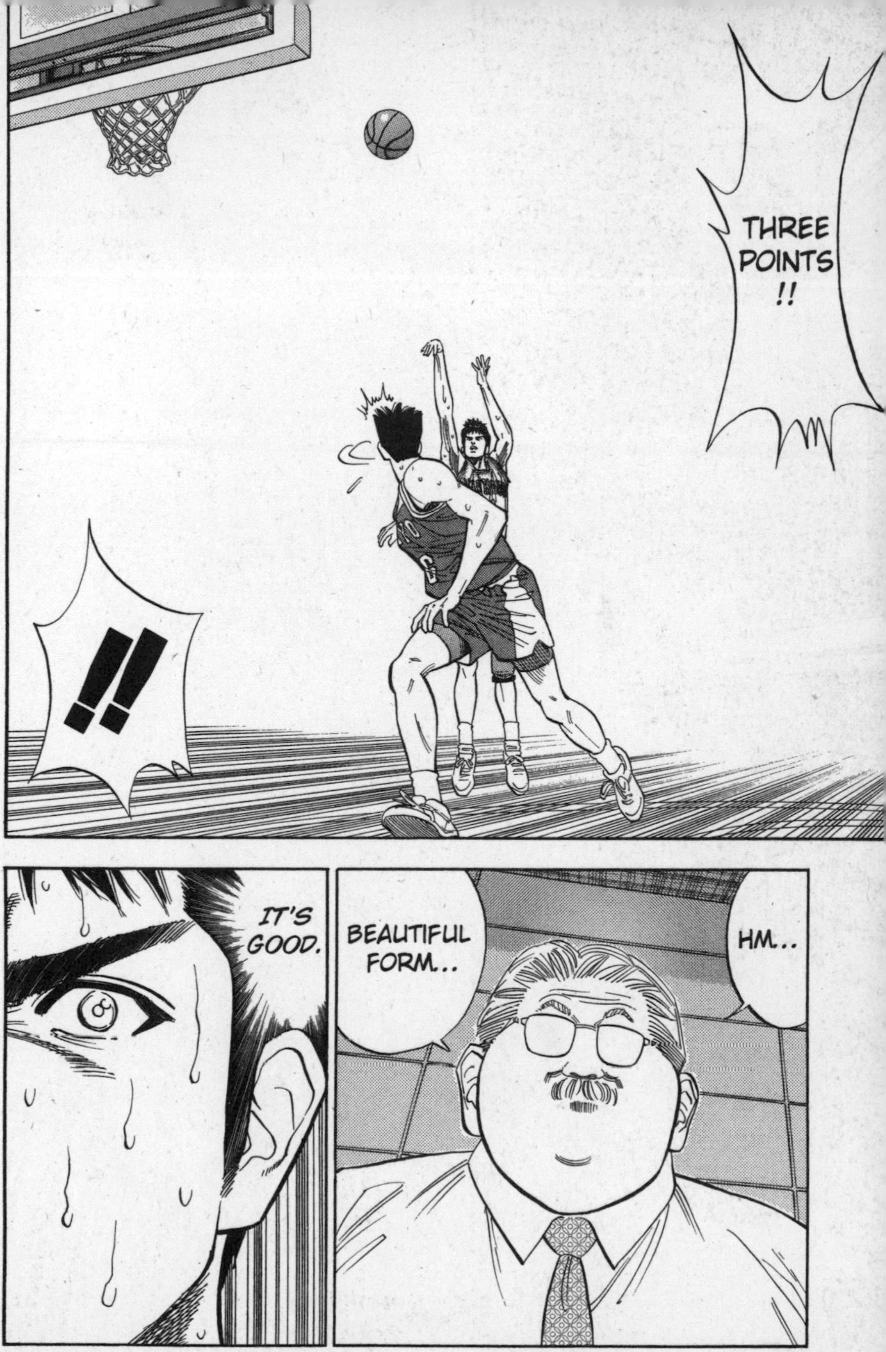
THREE POINTS !!
!!
HM...
BEAUTIFUL FORM...
IT'S GOOD.

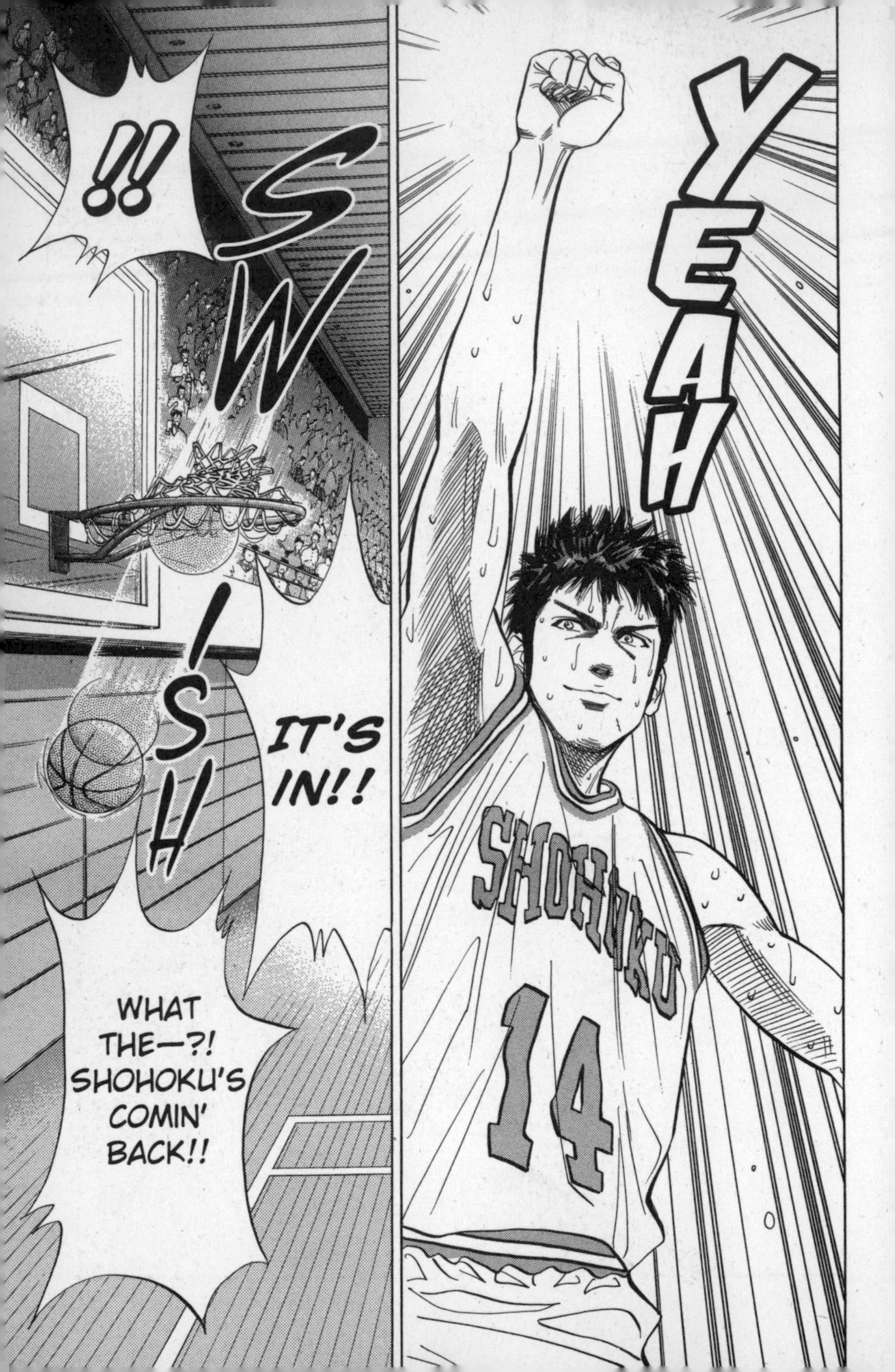
YEAH
!!
SWISH
IT'S IN!!
WHAT THE—?! SHOHOKU'S COMIN' BACK!!

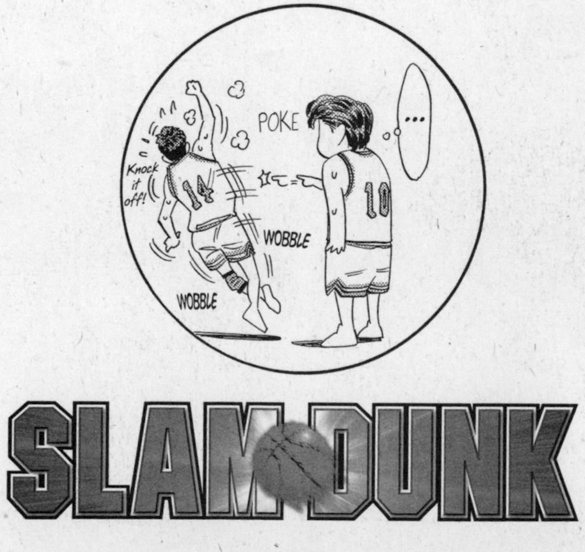

...
POKE
Knock it off!
WOBBLE
WOBBLE

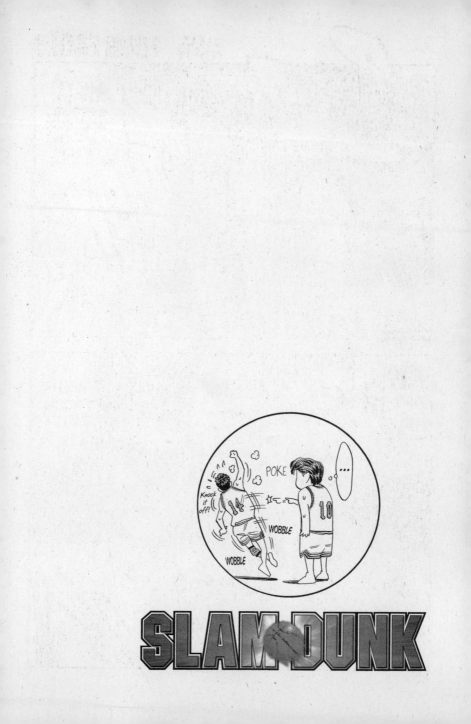

#95 FOUR FOULS

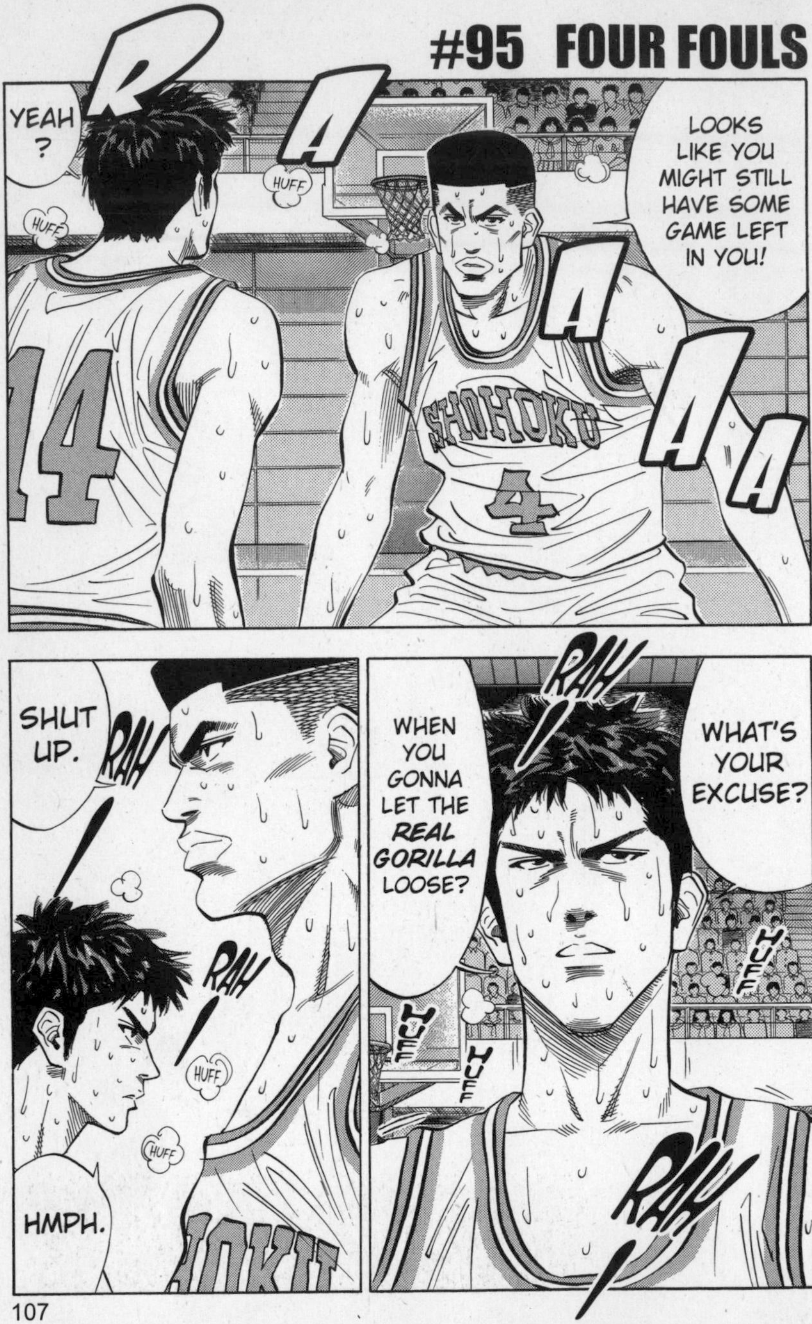
RAAAAA
LOOKS LIKE YOU MIGHT STILL HAVE SOME GAME LEFT IN YOU!
HUFF
YEAH?
HUFF
RAH
WHAT'S YOUR EXCUSE?
WHEN YOU GONNA LET THE *REAL GORILLA* LOOSE?
HUFF
HUFF
HUFF
RAH
RAH
SHUT UP.
RAH
HUFF
HUFF
HMPH.

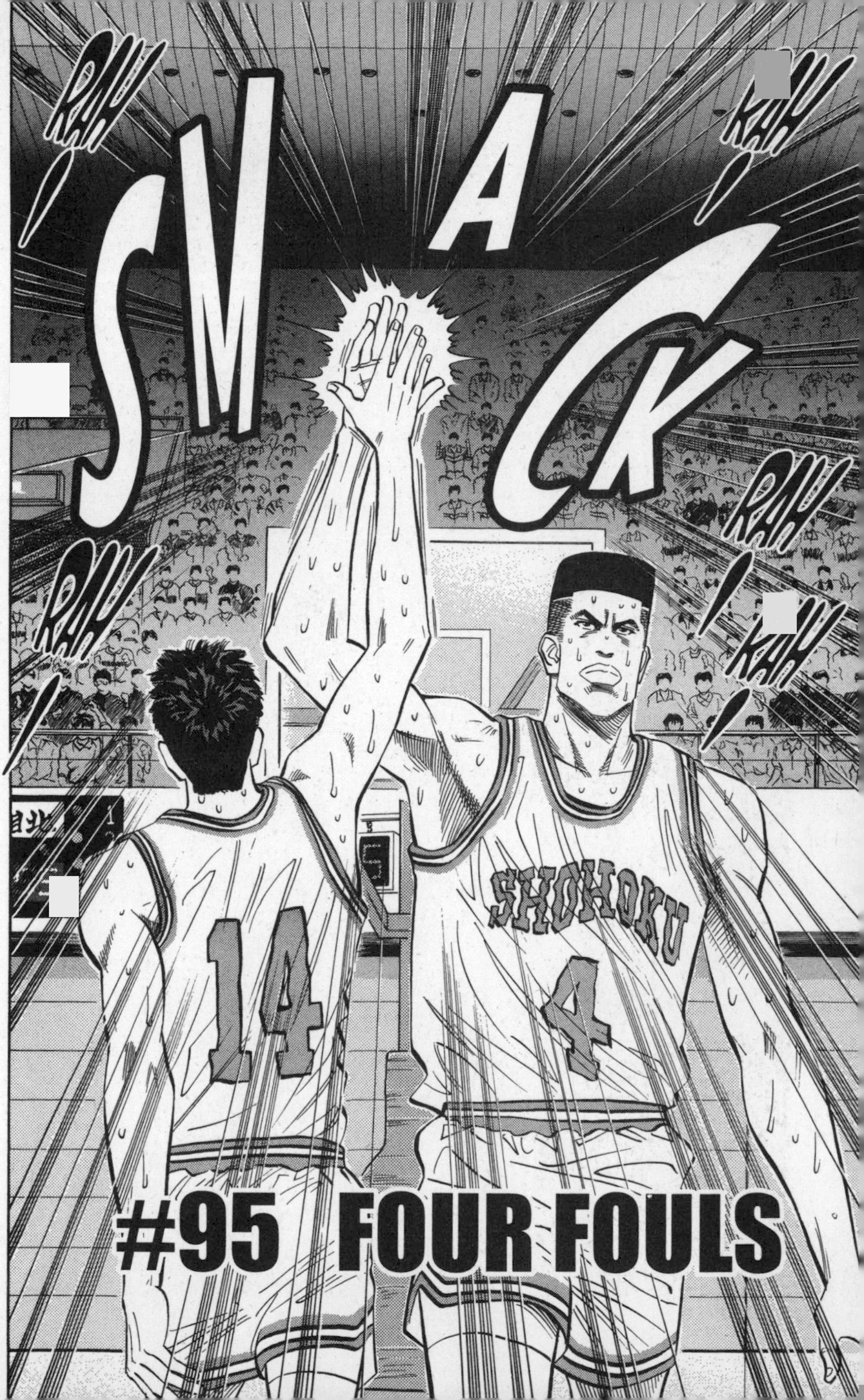
RAH!
SMACK
RAH!
RAH!
RAH!
SHOHOKU
14
4

#95 FOUR FOULS

READ THIS WAY

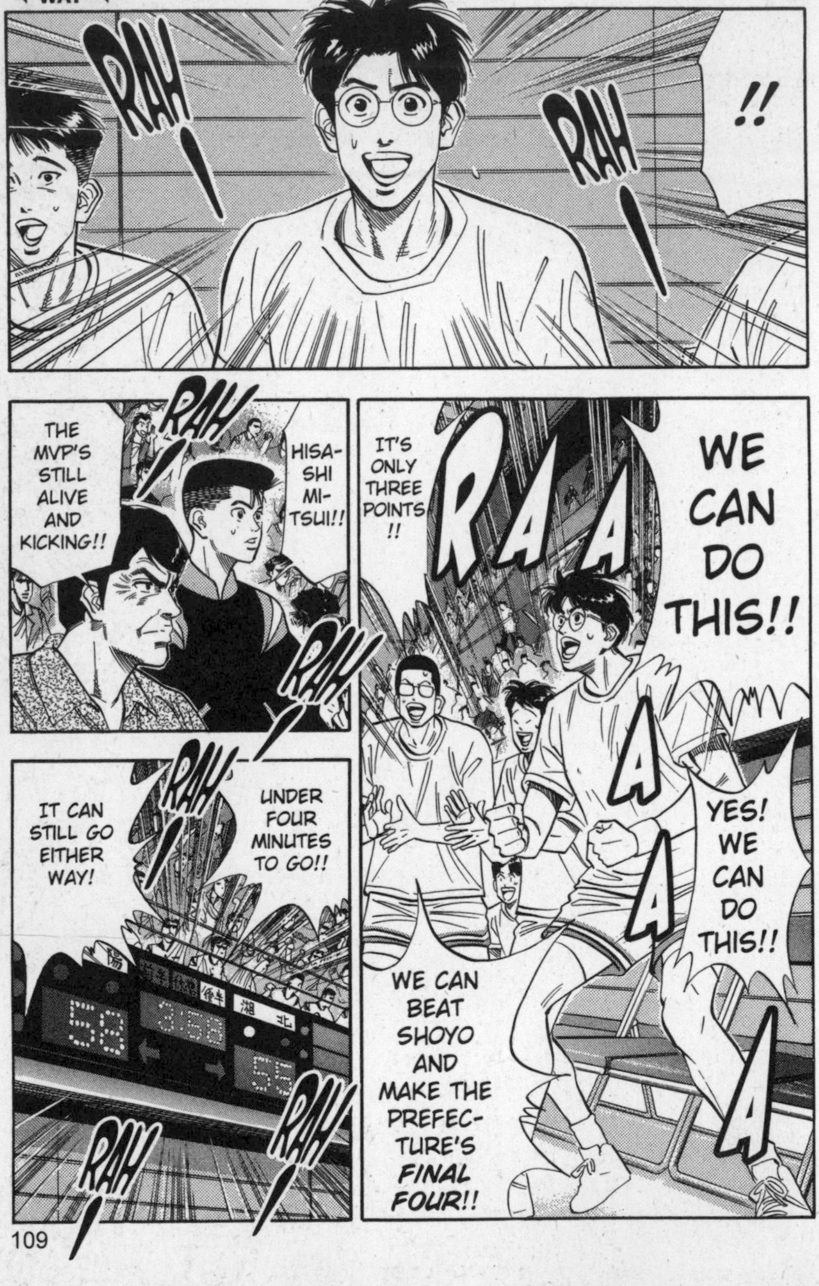
RAH!
RAH!
!!
WE CAN DO THIS!!
RAAA
IT'S ONLY THREE POINTS!!
AAAA
YES! WE CAN DO THIS!!
WE CAN BEAT SHOYO AND MAKE THE PREFECTURE'S FINAL FOUR!!
RAH!
HISASHI MITSUI!!
THE MVP'S STILL ALIVE AND KICKING!!
RAH!
RAH!
UNDER FOUR MINUTES TO GO!!
IT CAN STILL GO EITHER WAY!
58
3:58
55
RAH!
RAH!

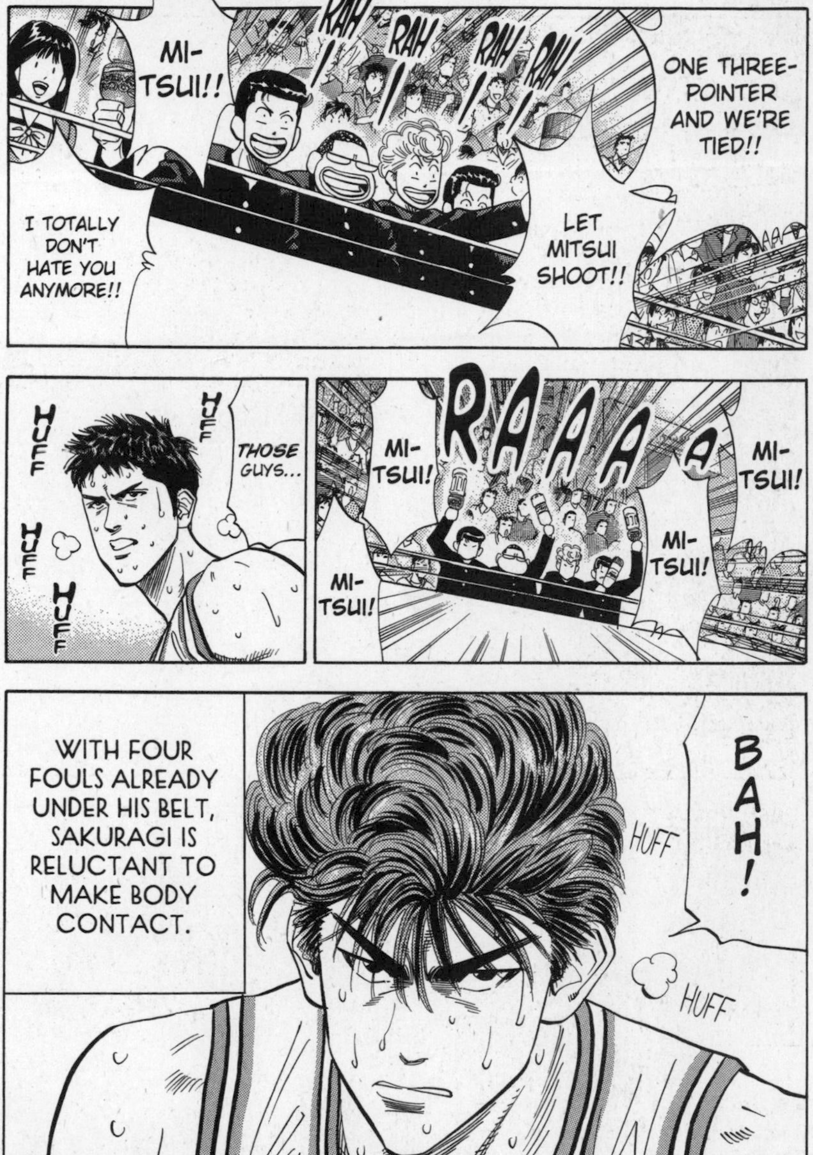
ONE THREE-POINTER AND WE'RE TIED!!
RAH!! RAH!! RAH!! RAH!!
MI-TSUI!!
LET MITSUI SHOOT!!
I TOTALLY DON'T HATE YOU ANYMORE!!
MI-TSUI!
RAAAAA
MI-TSUI!
MI-TSUI!
MI-TSUI!
HUFF
THOSE GUYS...
HUFF
HUFF
HUFF
BAH!
HUFF
HUFF
WITH FOUR FOULS ALREADY UNDER HIS BELT, SAKURAGI IS RELUCTANT TO MAKE BODY CONTACT.

READ THIS WAY

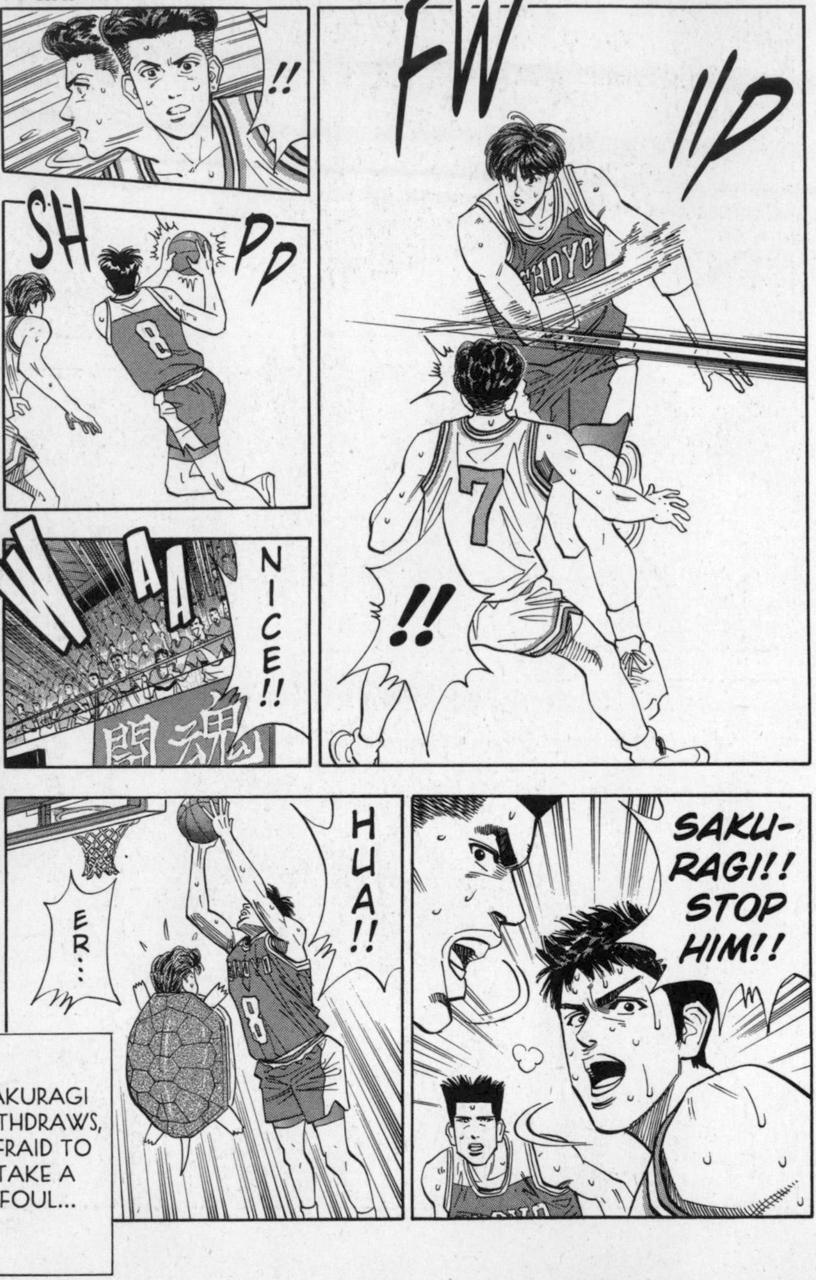
FW
IIP
!!
!!
SH
PP
WAA
NICE!!
SAKU-RAGI!! STOP HIM!!
HUA!!
ER...
SAKURAGI WITHDRAWS, AFRAID TO TAKE A FOUL...

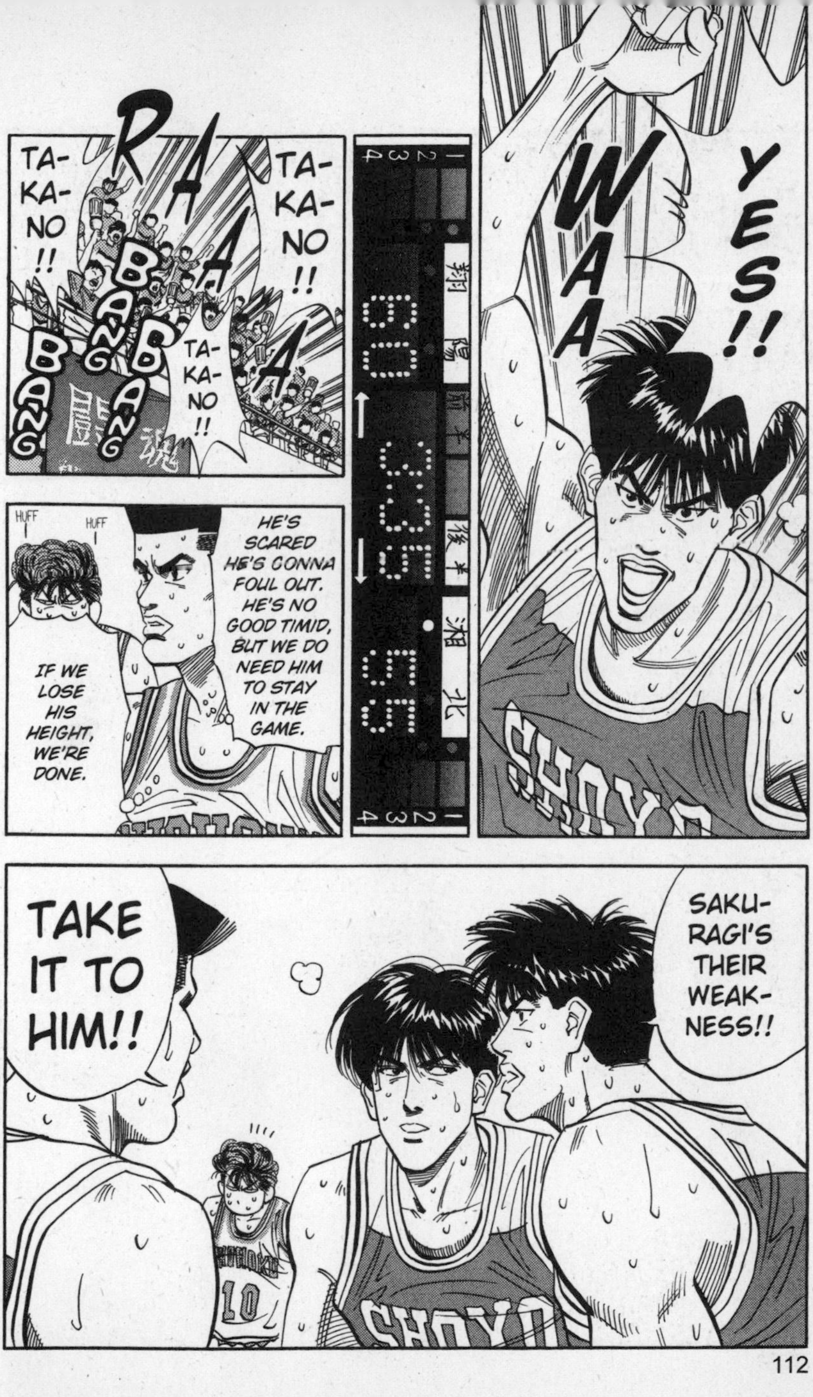
YES!!
WAAA
80
3:35
55
TA-KA-NO!!
RAAA
TA-KA-NO!!
BANG BANG BANG
TA-KA-NO!!
HUFF HUFF
HE'S SCARED HE'S GONNA FOUL OUT. HE'S NO GOOD TIMID, BUT WE DO NEED HIM TO STAY IN THE GAME.
IF WE LOSE HIS HEIGHT, WE'RE DONE.
SAKU-RAGI'S THEIR WEAK-NESS!!
TAKE IT TO HIM!!

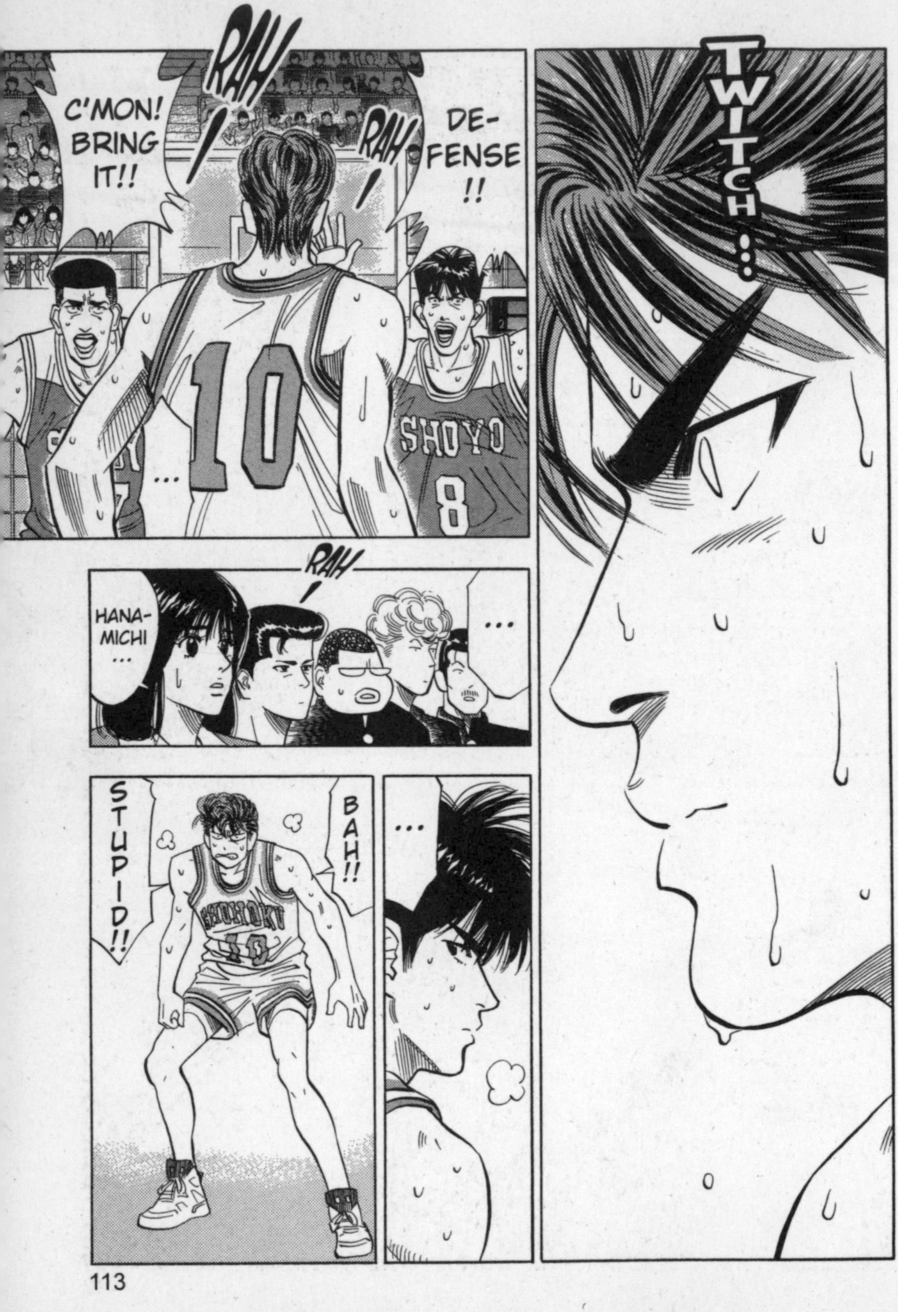
TWITCH...
DE-FENSE!!
RAH
RAH
C'MON! BRING IT!!
...
...
RAH
HANAMICHI...
...
BAH!!
STUPID!!

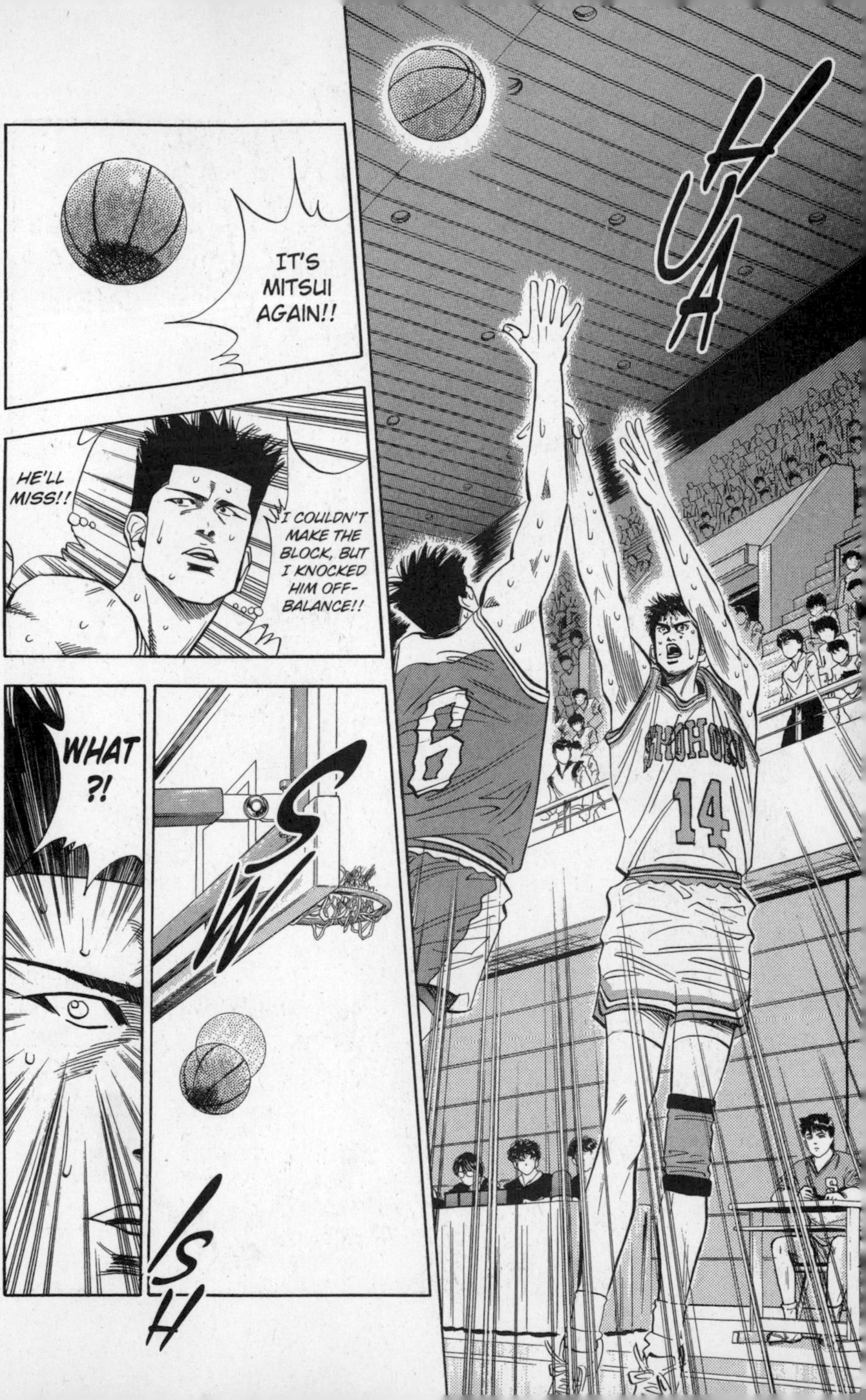
HUA
IT'S MITSUI AGAIN!!
I COULDN'T MAKE THE BLOCK, BUT I KNOCKED HIM OFF-BALANCE!!
HE'LL MISS!!
SWISH
WHAT ?!

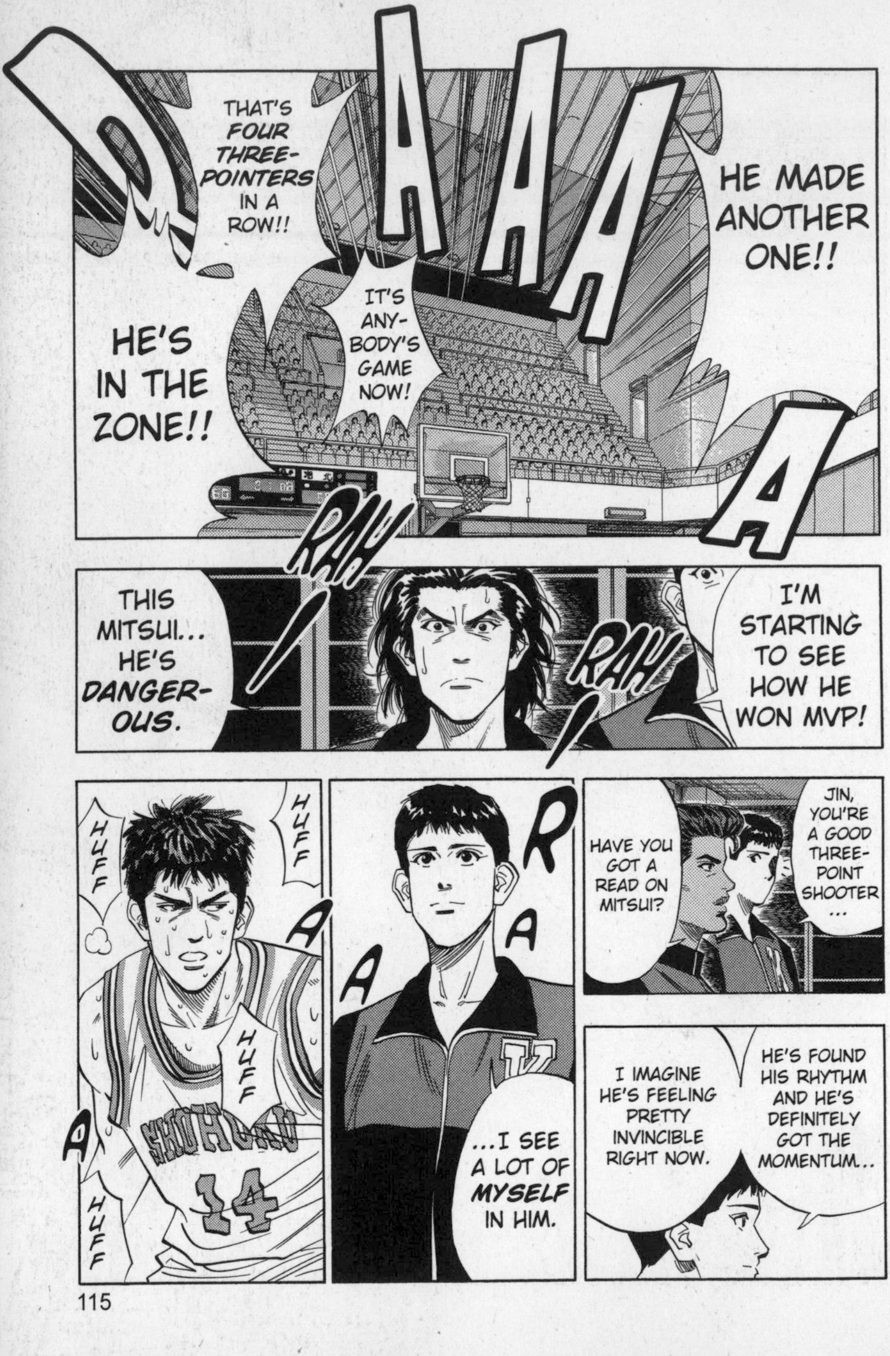

RAAAAA
HE MADE ANOTHER ONE!!
THAT'S FOUR THREE-POINTERS IN A ROW!!
IT'S ANYBODY'S GAME NOW!
HE'S IN THE ZONE!!
RAH
I'M STARTING TO SEE HOW HE WON MVP!
RAH
THIS MITSUI... HE'S DANGEROUS.
JIN, YOU'RE A GOOD THREE-POINT SHOOTER...
HAVE YOU GOT A READ ON MITSUI?
HE'S FOUND HIS RHYTHM AND HE'S DEFINITELY GOT THE MOMENTUM...
I IMAGINE HE'S FEELING PRETTY INVINCIBLE RIGHT NOW.
RAAAA
...I SEE A LOT OF MYSELF IN HIM.
HUFF HUFF
HUFF
HUFF

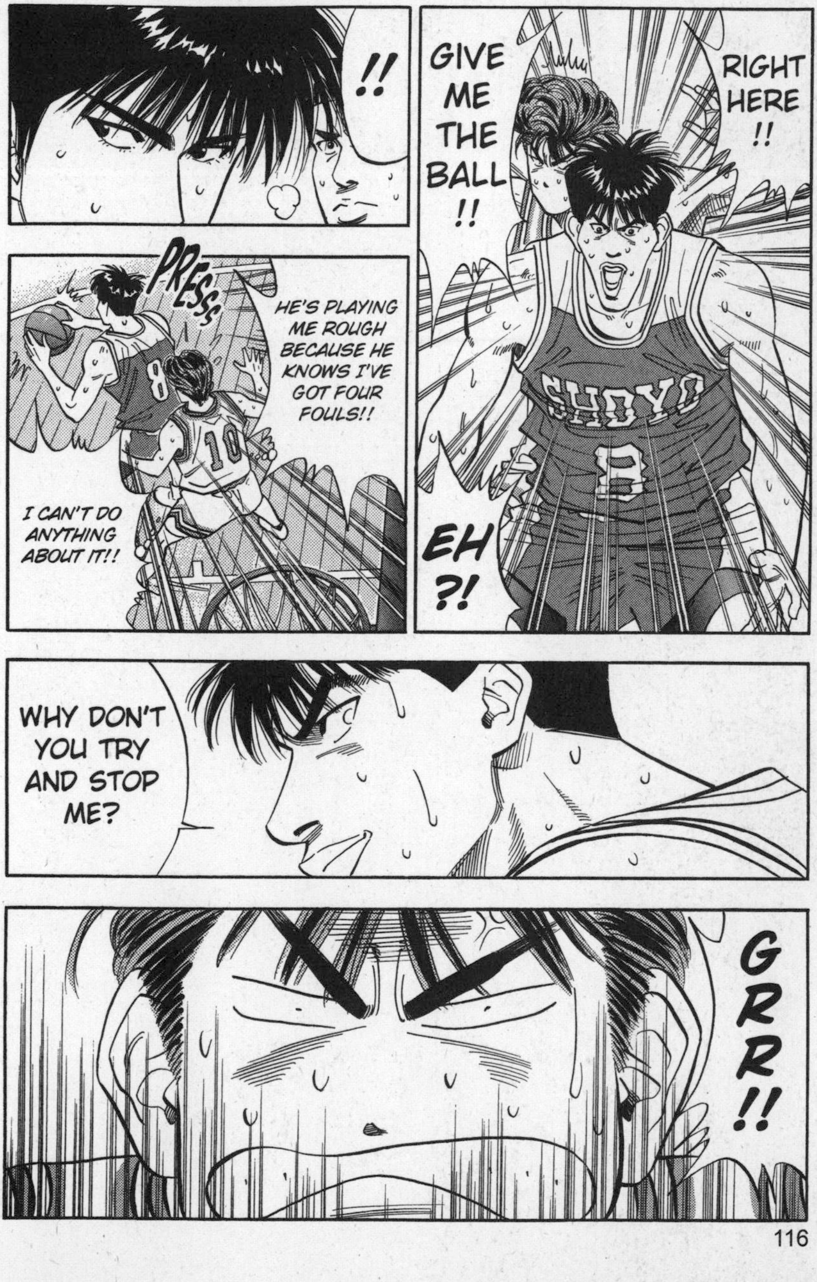
RIGHT HERE!!
GIVE ME THE BALL!!
EH?!
!!
PRESSS
HE'S PLAYING ME ROUGH BECAUSE HE KNOWS I'VE GOT FOUR FOULS!!
I CAN'T DO ANYTHING ABOUT IT!!
WHY DON'T YOU TRY AND STOP ME?
GRR!!

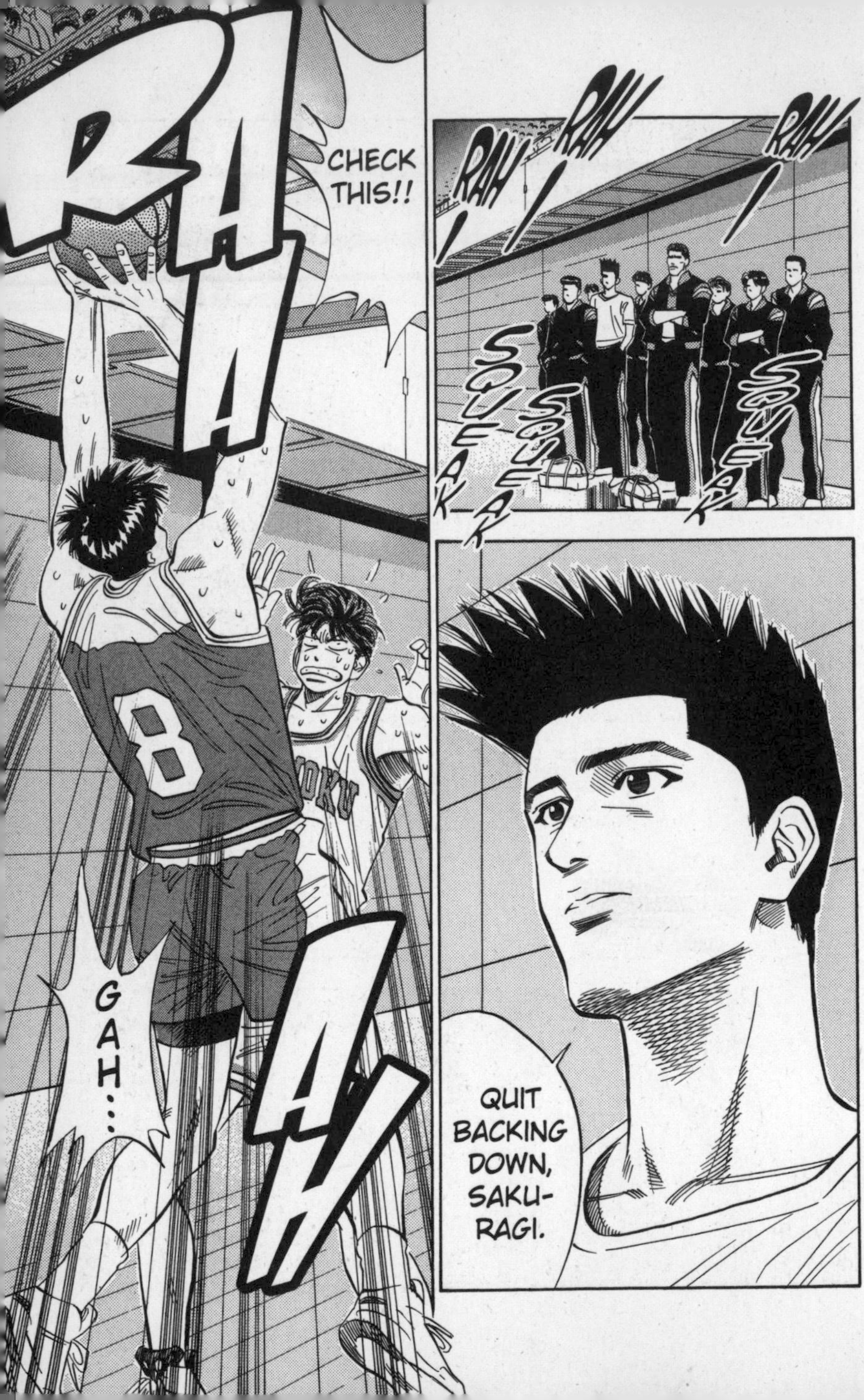
RAH
RAH
RAH
SQUEAK
SQUEAK
SQUEAK
QUIT BACKING DOWN, SAKU-RAGI.
RAAAH
CHECK THIS!!
GAH...

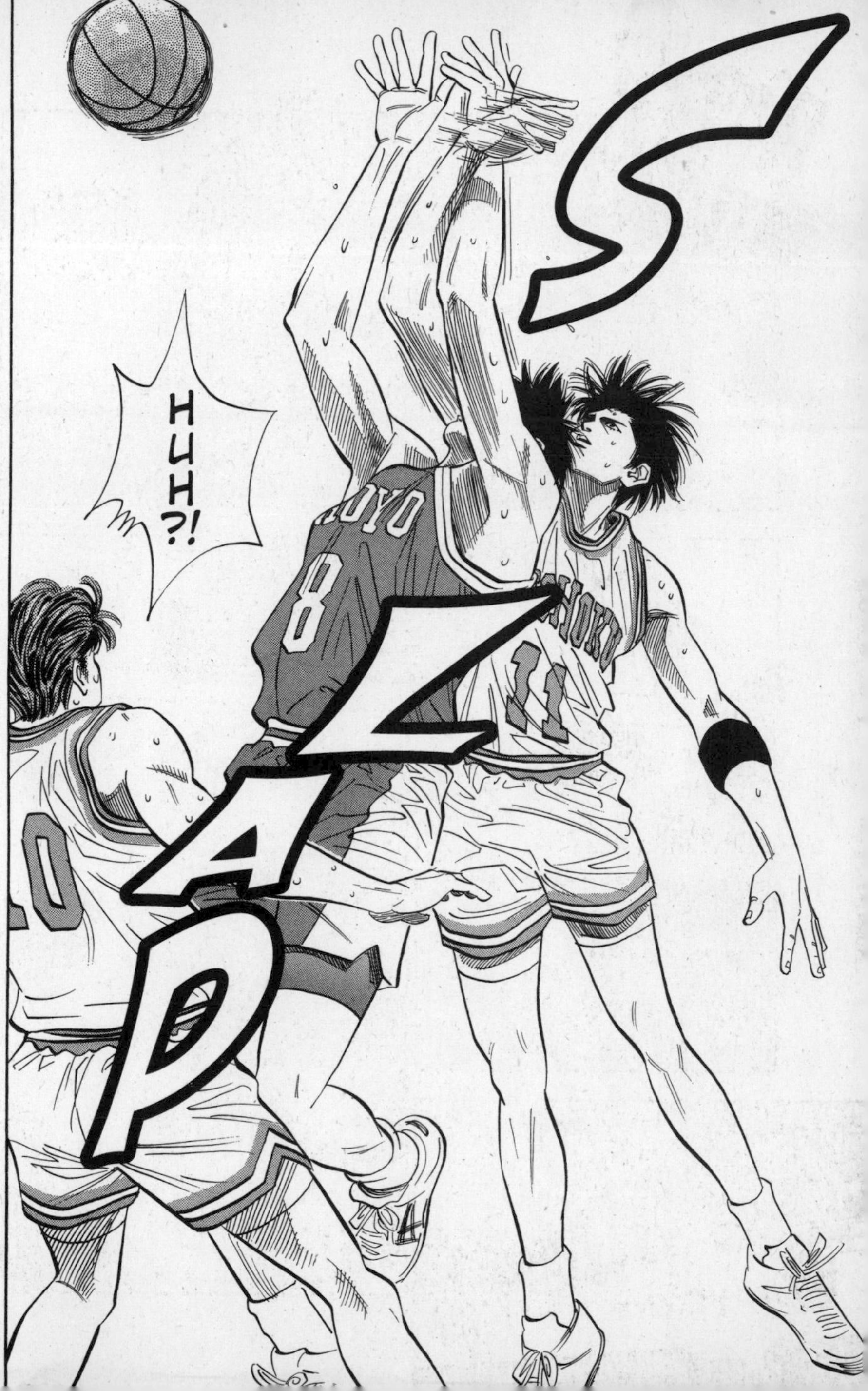
HUH?!

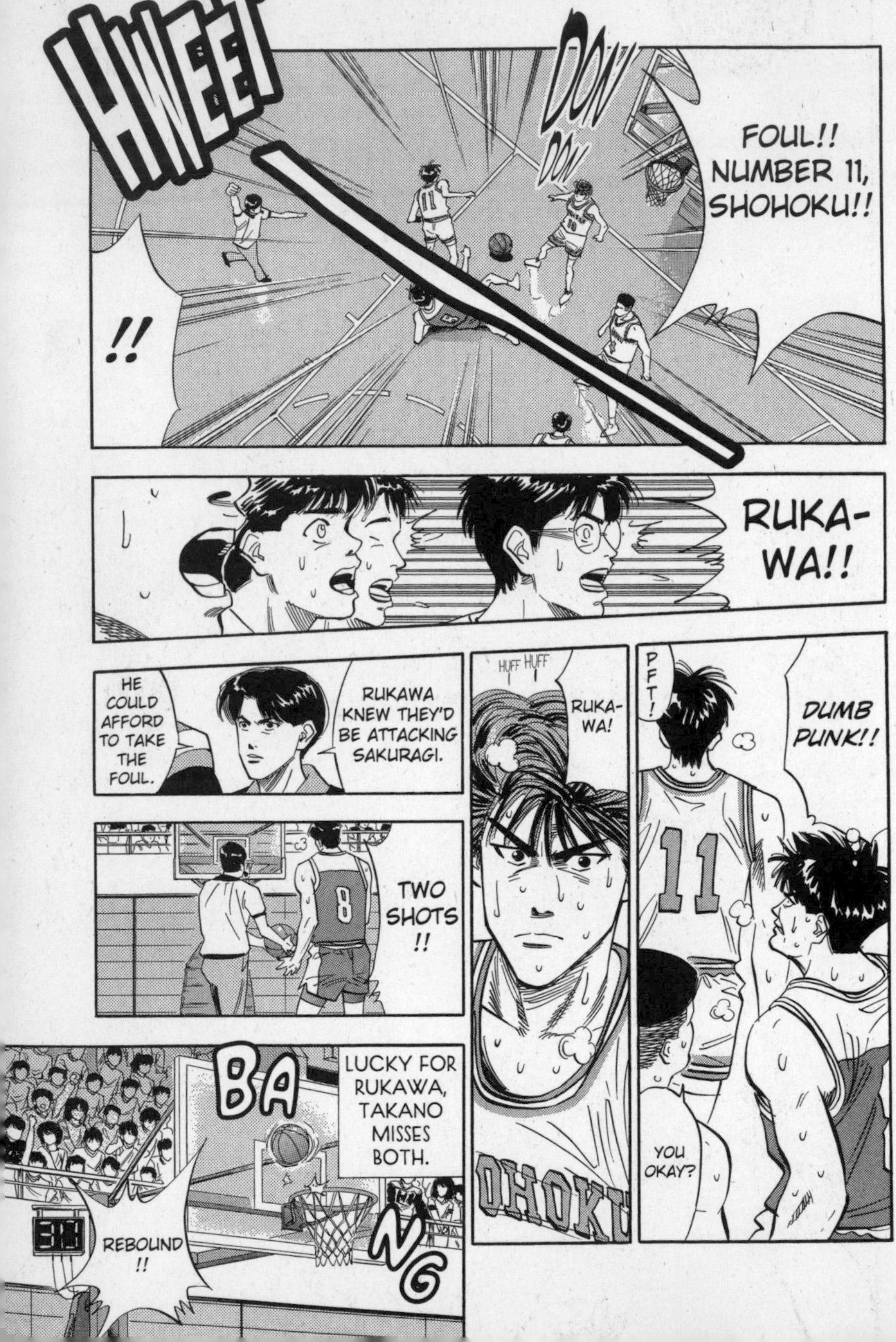
FOUL!! NUMBER 11, SHOHOKU!!
DON DON
HWEET
!!
RUKA-WA!!
DUMB PUNK!!
PFT!
YOU OKAY?
HUFF HUFF
RUKA-WA!
RUKAWA KNEW THEY'D BE ATTACKING SAKURAGI.
HE COULD AFFORD TO TAKE THE FOUL.
TWO SHOTS!!
LUCKY FOR RUKAWA, TAKANO MISSES BOTH.
BANG
REBOUND!!

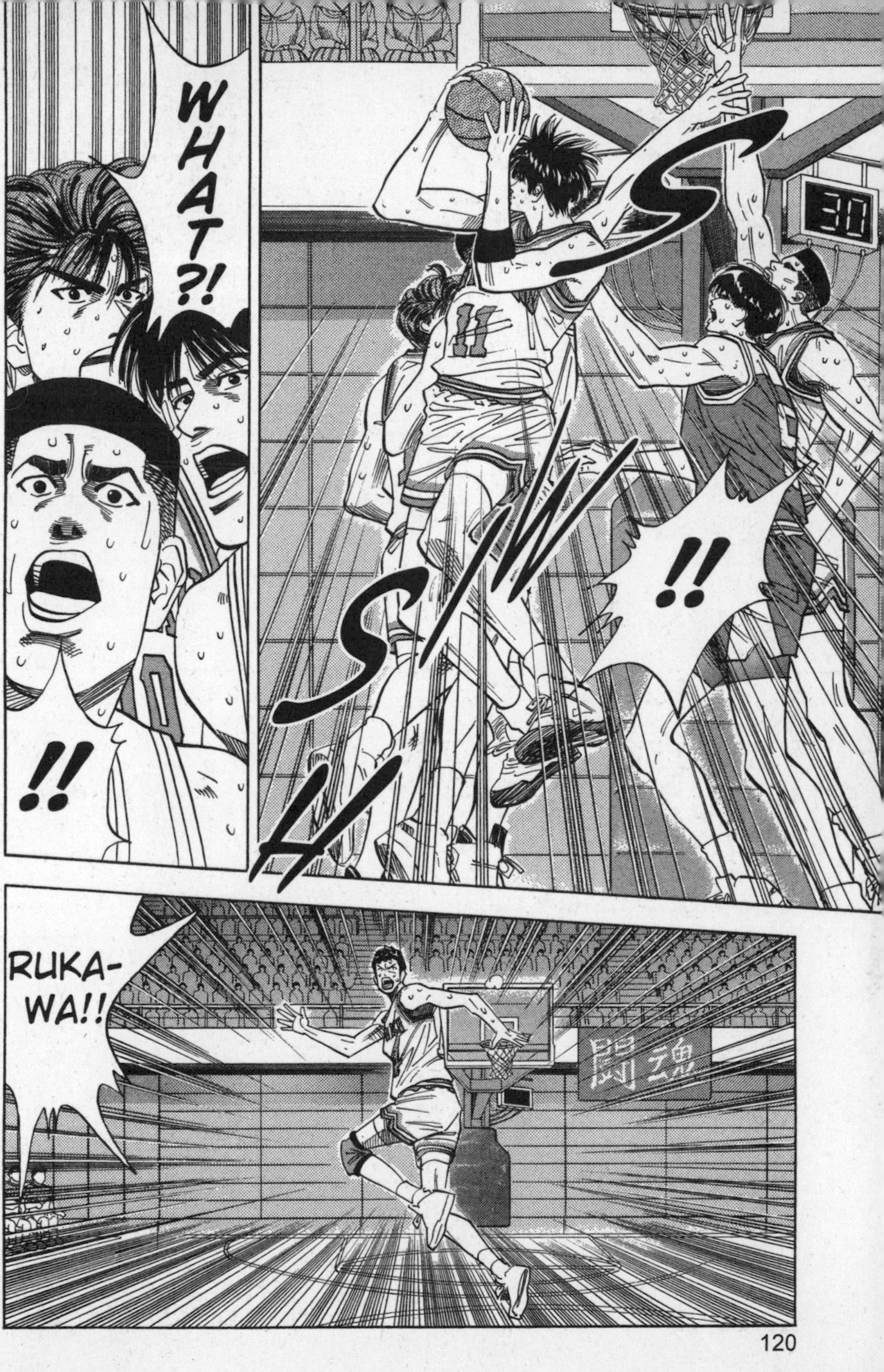
SWISH
!!
WHAT?!
!!
RUKA-
WA!!

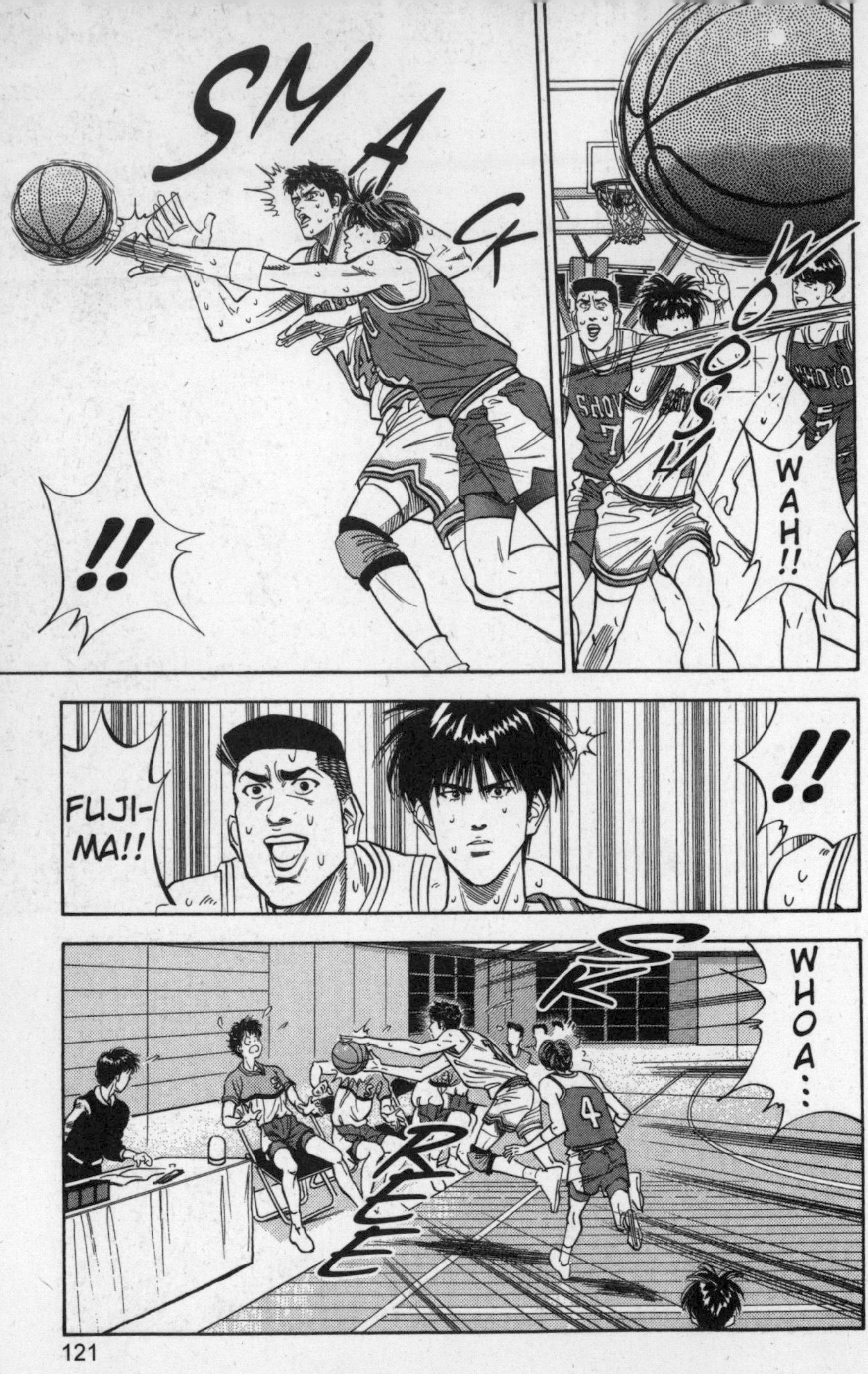
WOOOSH
WAH!!
SMACK
!!
!!
FUJI-
MA!!
WHOA...
SKRAEE

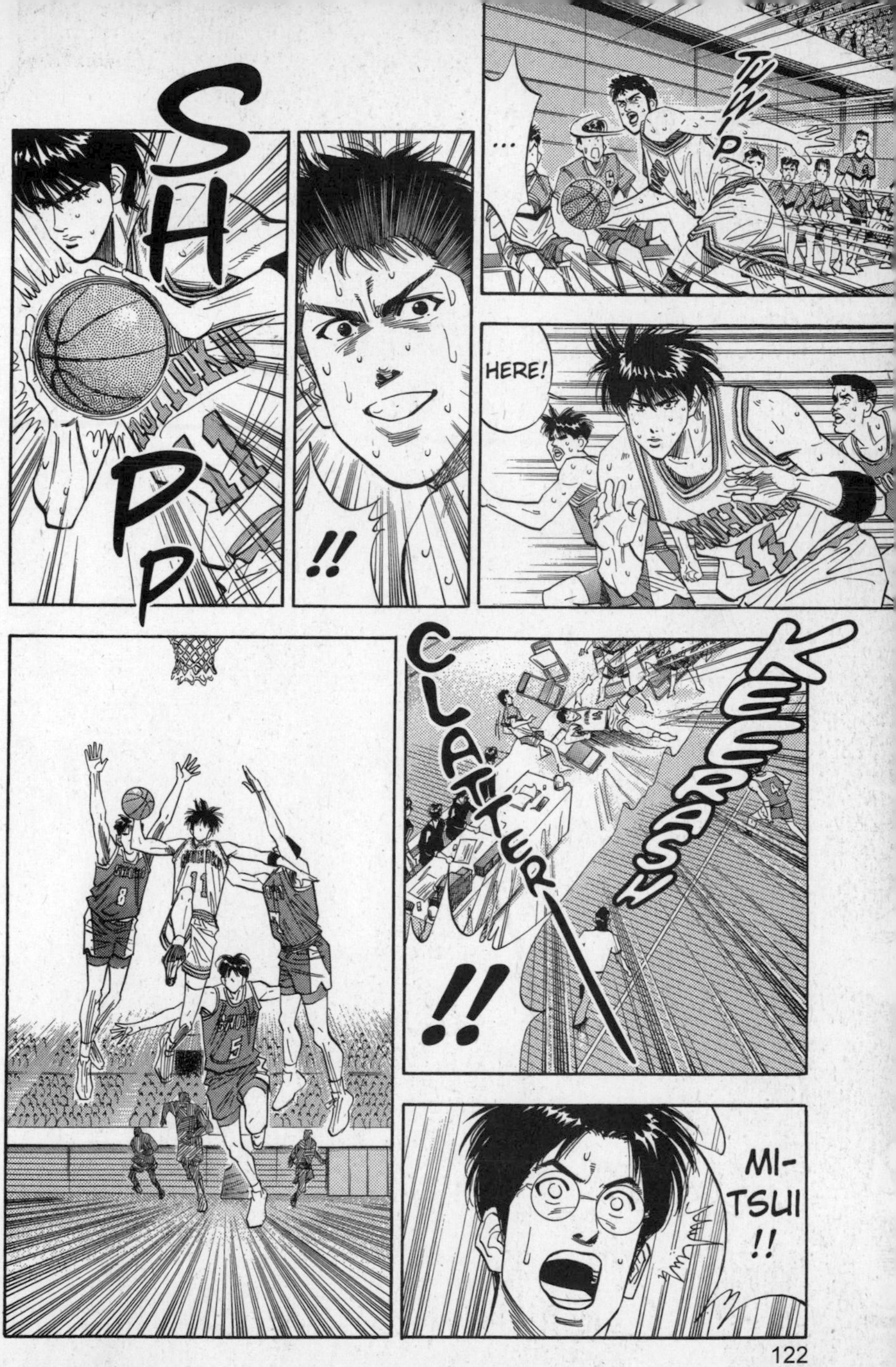
THWIP
...
HERE!
!!
SHPP
KERRASH
CLATTER
!!
MI-
TSUI
!!

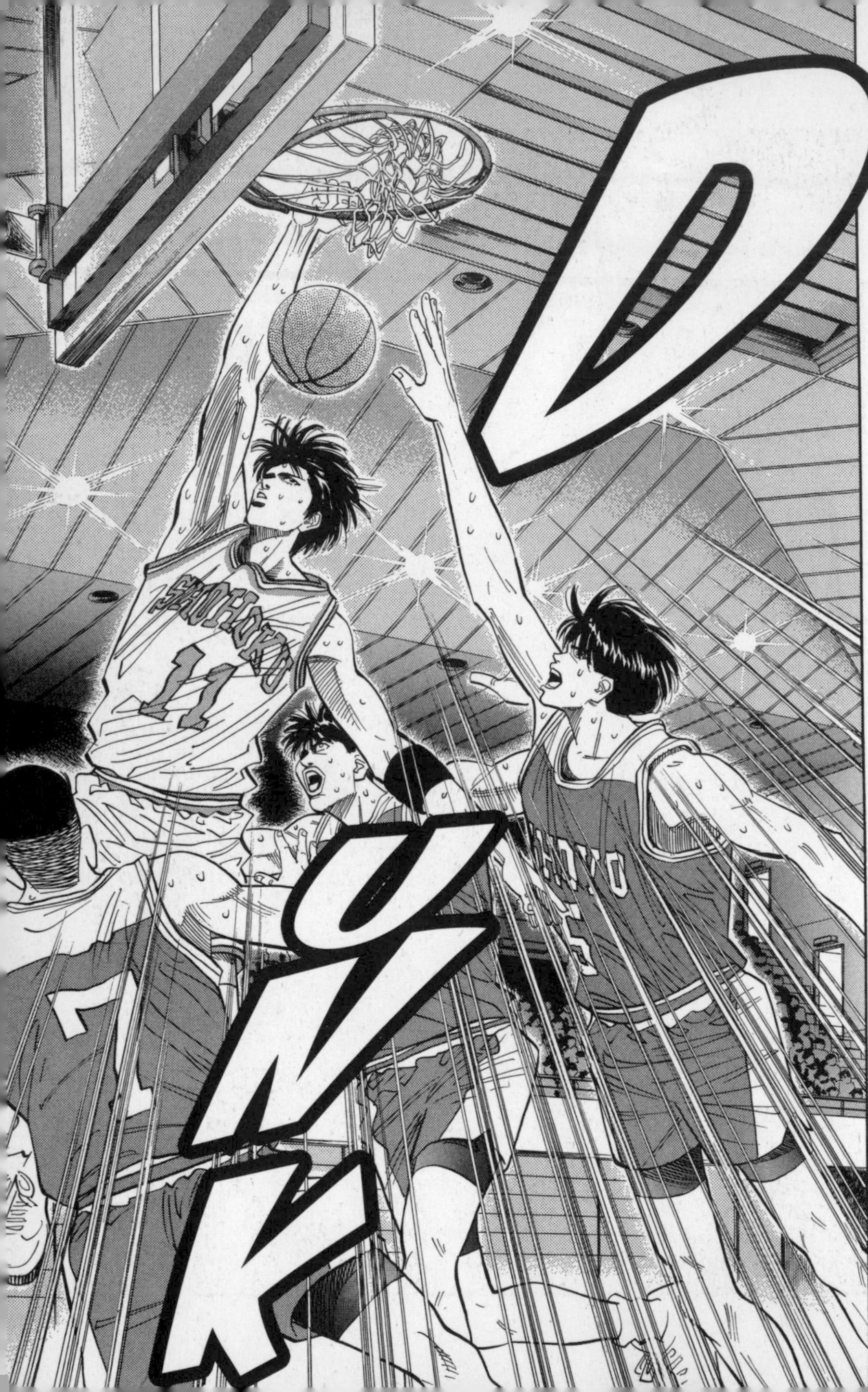
DUNK

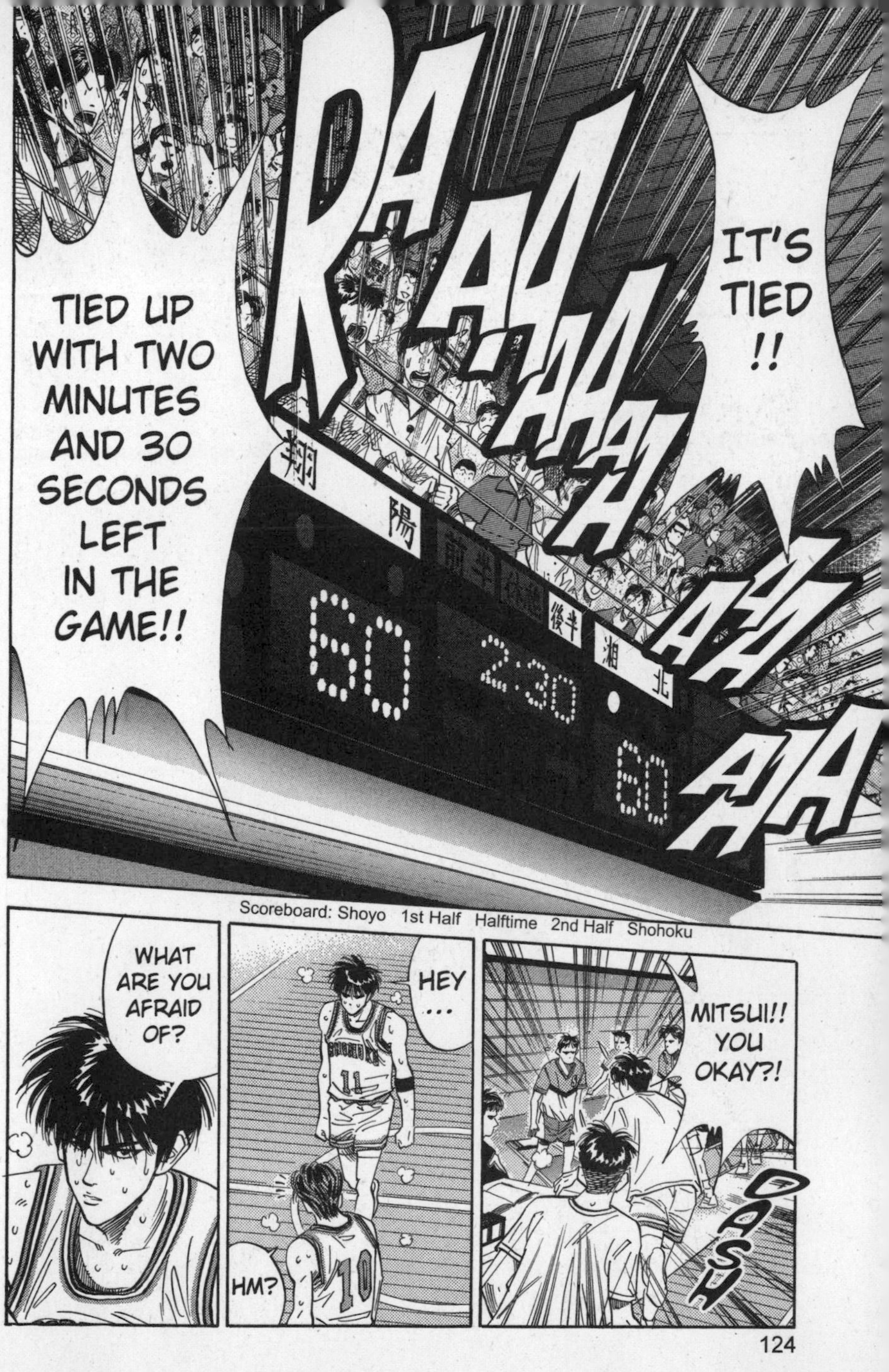
IT'S TIED!!
TIED UP WITH TWO MINUTES AND 30 SECONDS LEFT IN THE GAME!!
60
2:30
60
Scoreboard: Shoyo 1st Half Halftime 2nd Half Shohoku
MITSUI!! YOU OKAY?!
DASH
HEY...
HM?
WHAT ARE YOU AFRAID OF?

READ THIS WAY

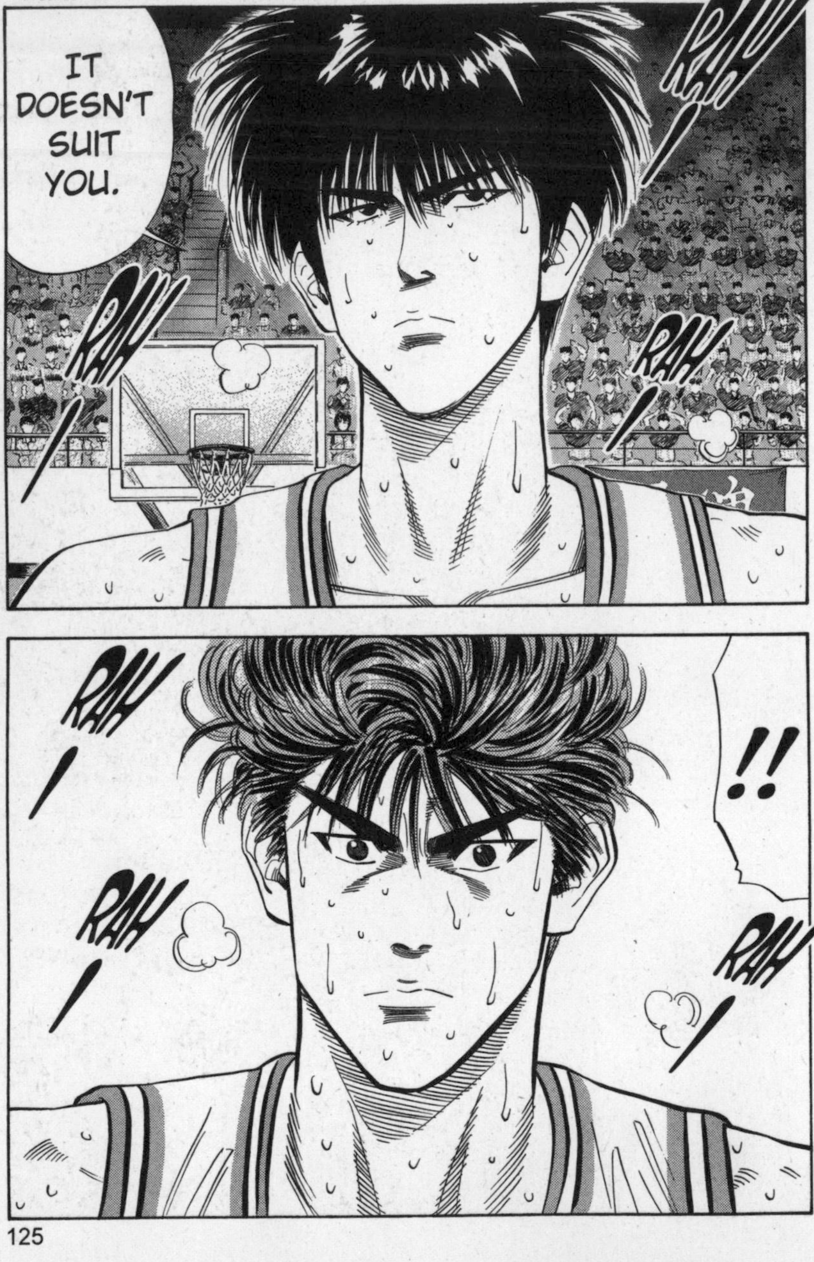
RAH!
RAH!
IT DOESN'T SUIT YOU.
RAH!
!!
RAH!
RAH!
RAH!

It doesn't suit you...
EEP

SLAM DUNK

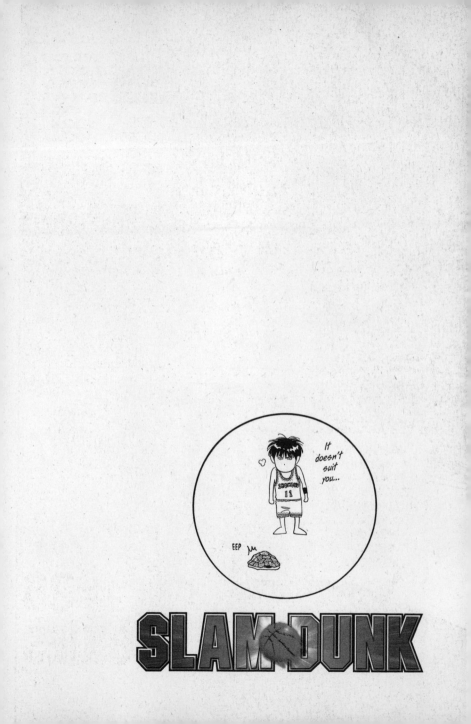

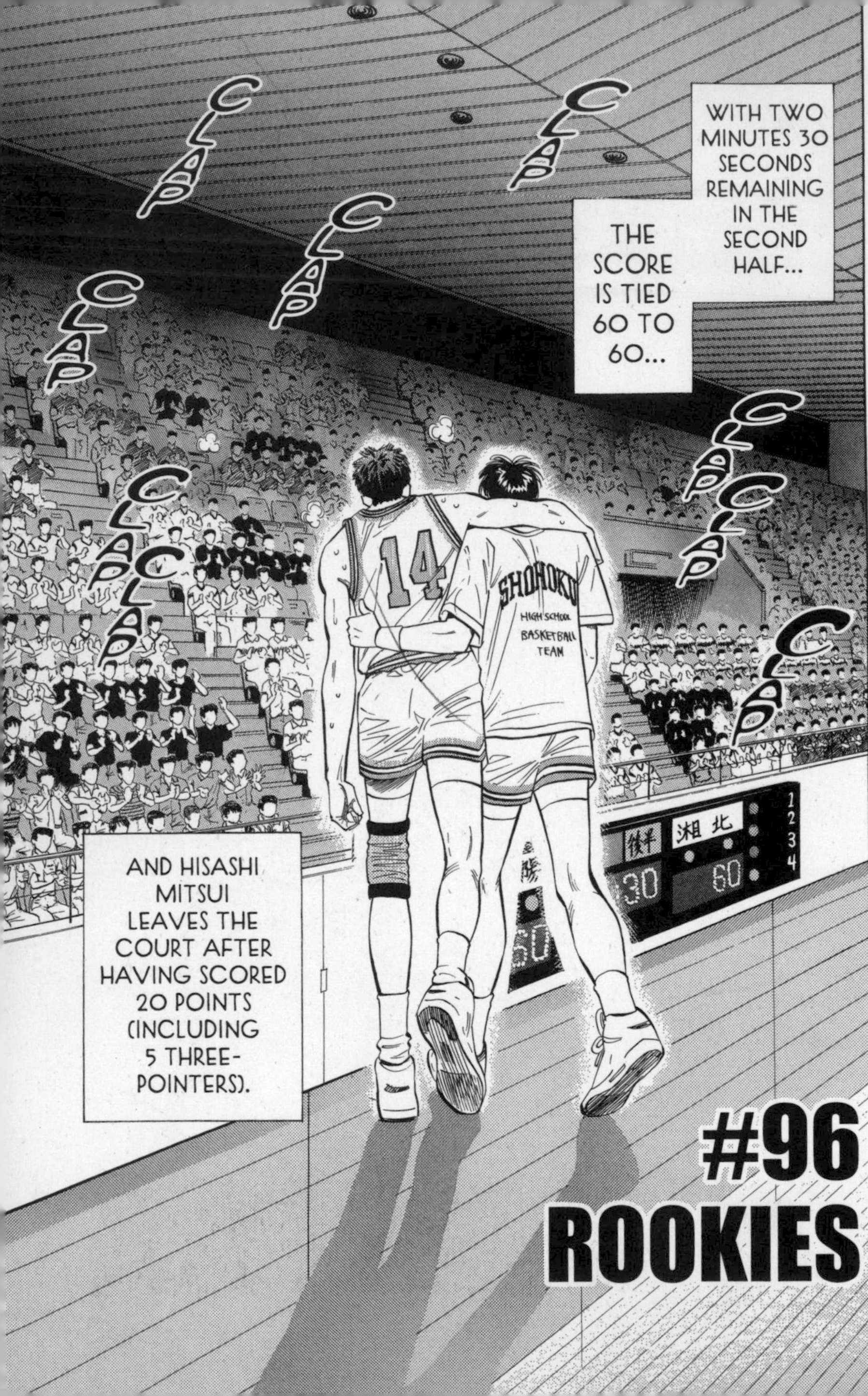

WITH TWO MINUTES 30 SECONDS REMAINING IN THE SECOND HALF...
THE SCORE IS TIED 60 TO 60...
CLAP
CLAP
CLAP
CLAP
CLAP CLAP
CLAP CLAP
CLAP
14
SHOHOKU
HIGH SCHOOL BASKETBALL TEAM
湘北
60
AND HISASHI MITSUI LEAVES THE COURT AFTER HAVING SCORED 20 POINTS (INCLUDING 5 THREE-POINTERS).
#96 ROOKIES

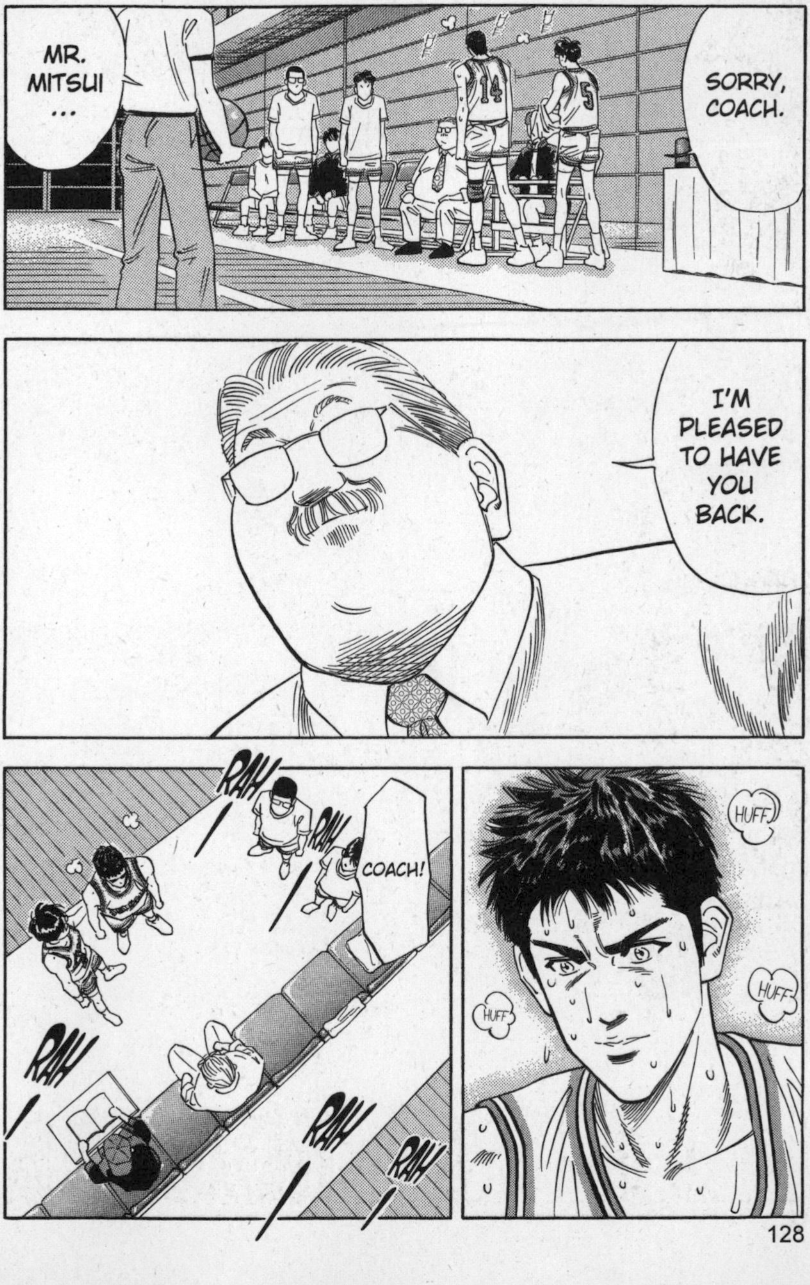

SORRY, COACH.
MR. MITSUI ...
I'M PLEASED TO HAVE YOU BACK.
HUFF
HUFF
HUFF
RAH!
RAH!
COACH!
RAH!
RAH!
RAH!

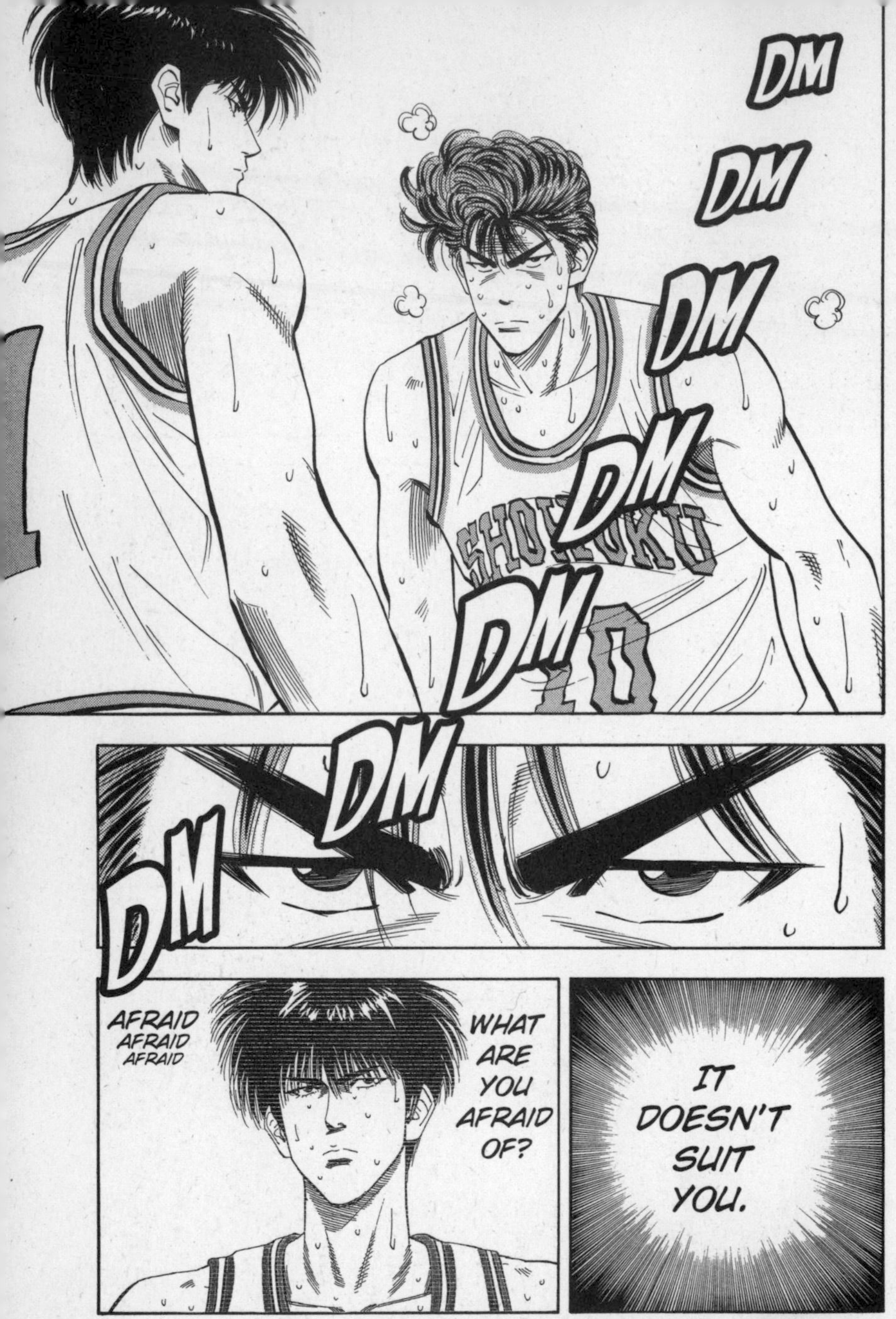

DM
DM
DM
DM
DM
DM
DM
DM
IT DOESN'T SUIT YOU.
WHAT ARE YOU AFRAID OF?
AFRAID
AFRAID
AFRAID

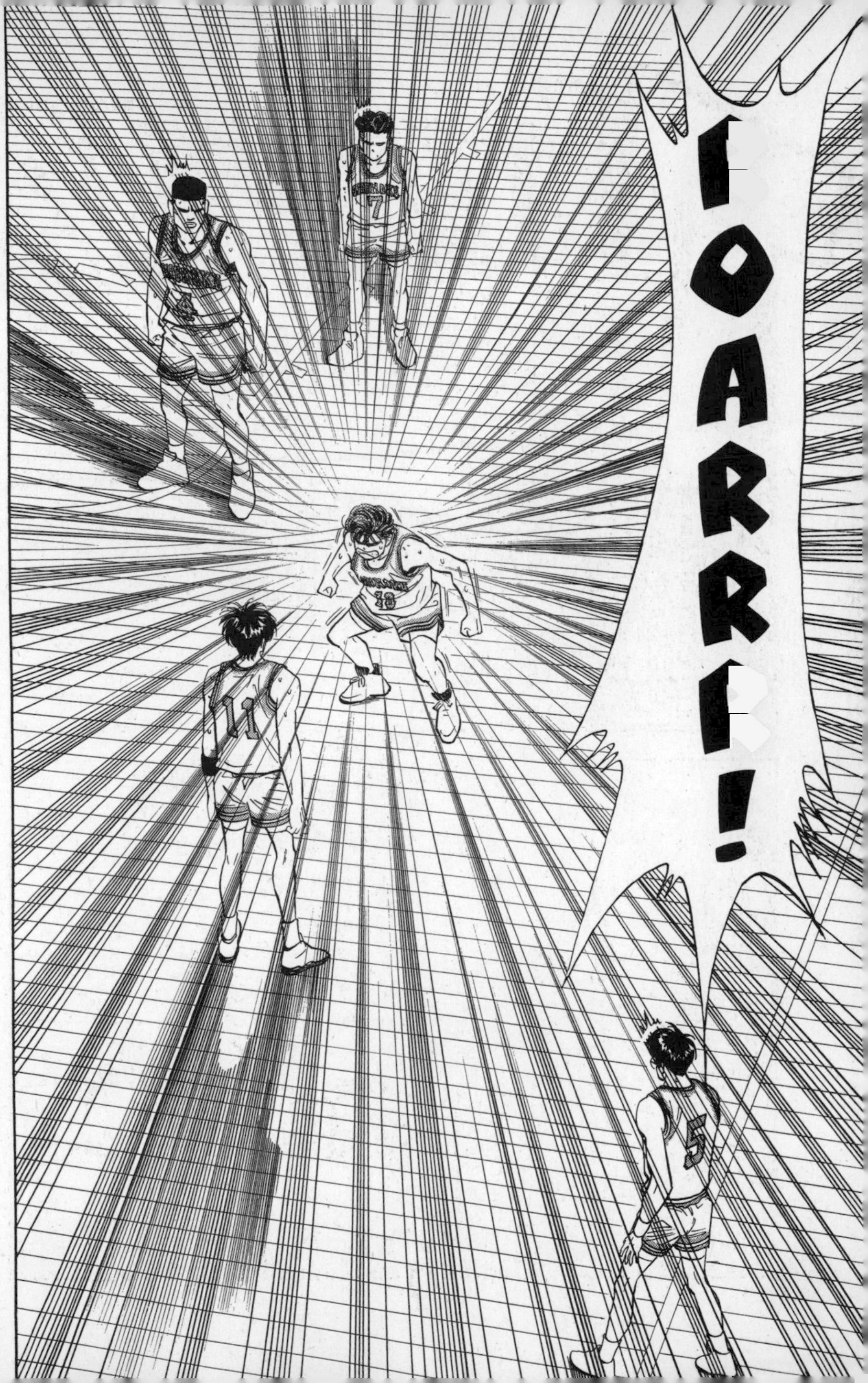
ROARRR!

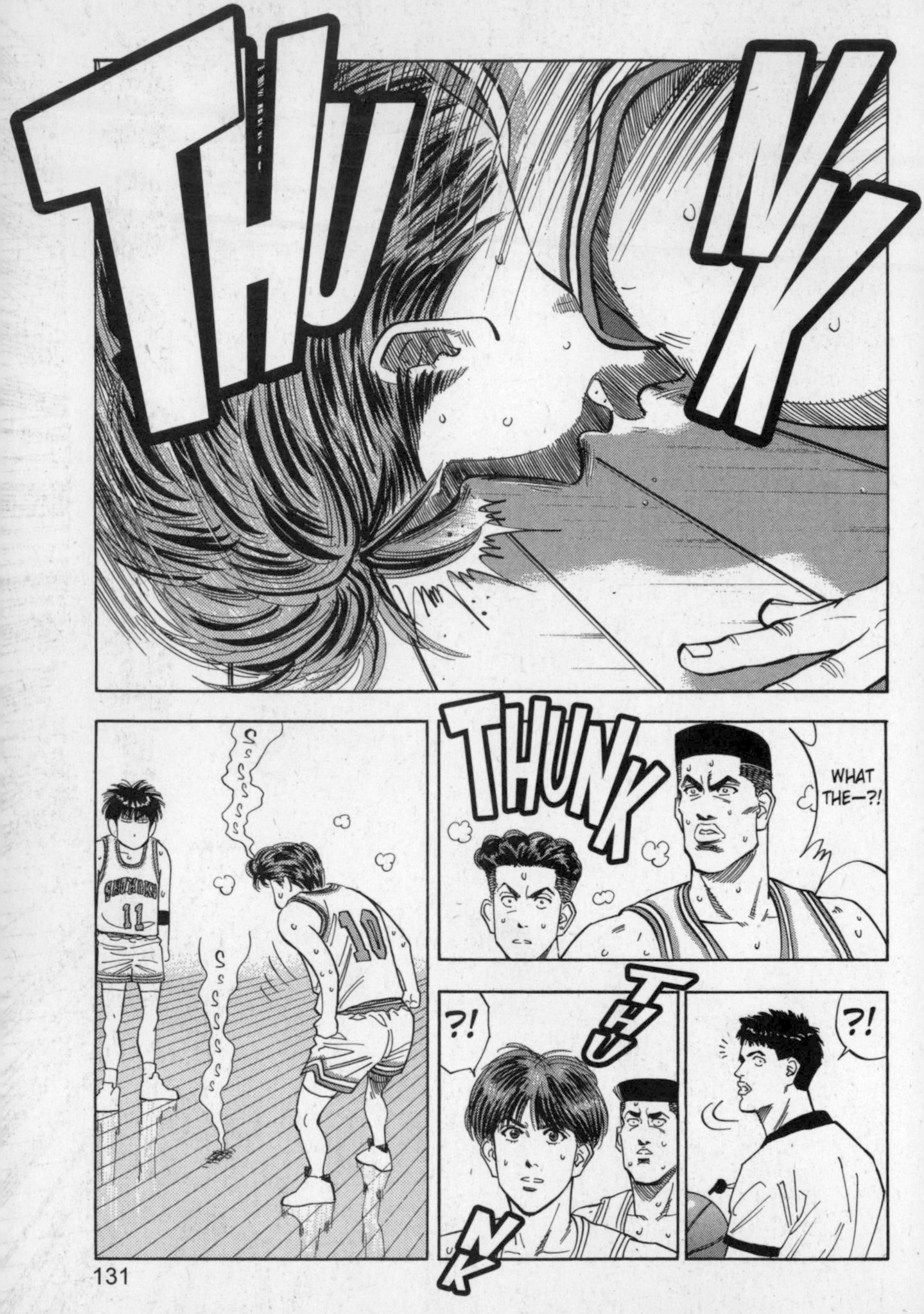
THUNK
THUNK
WHAT THE—?!
?!
?!
THUNK

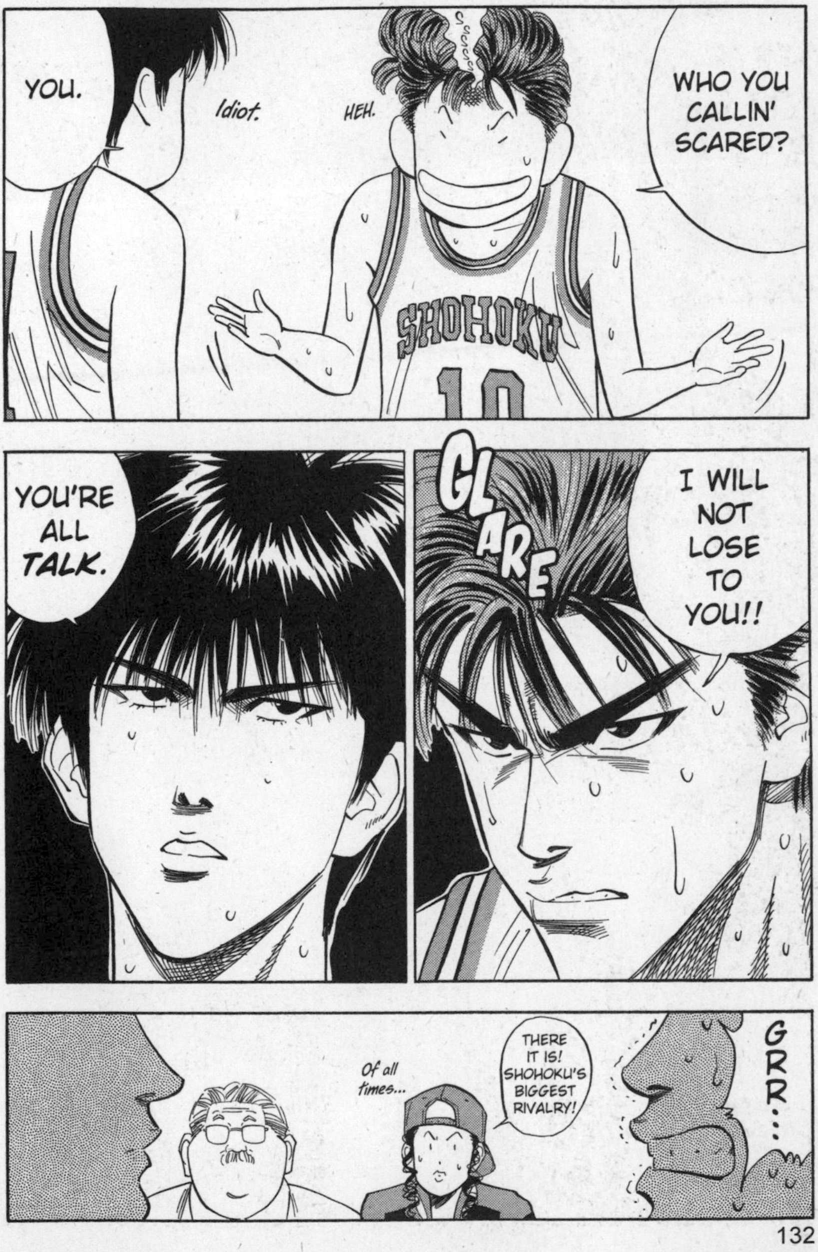
WHO YOU CALLIN' SCARED?
HEH.
Idiot.
YOU.
SHOHOKU
10
GLARE
I WILL NOT LOSE TO YOU!!
YOU'RE ALL *TALK*.
GRR...
THERE IT IS! SHOHOKU'S BIGGEST RIVALRY!
Of all times...

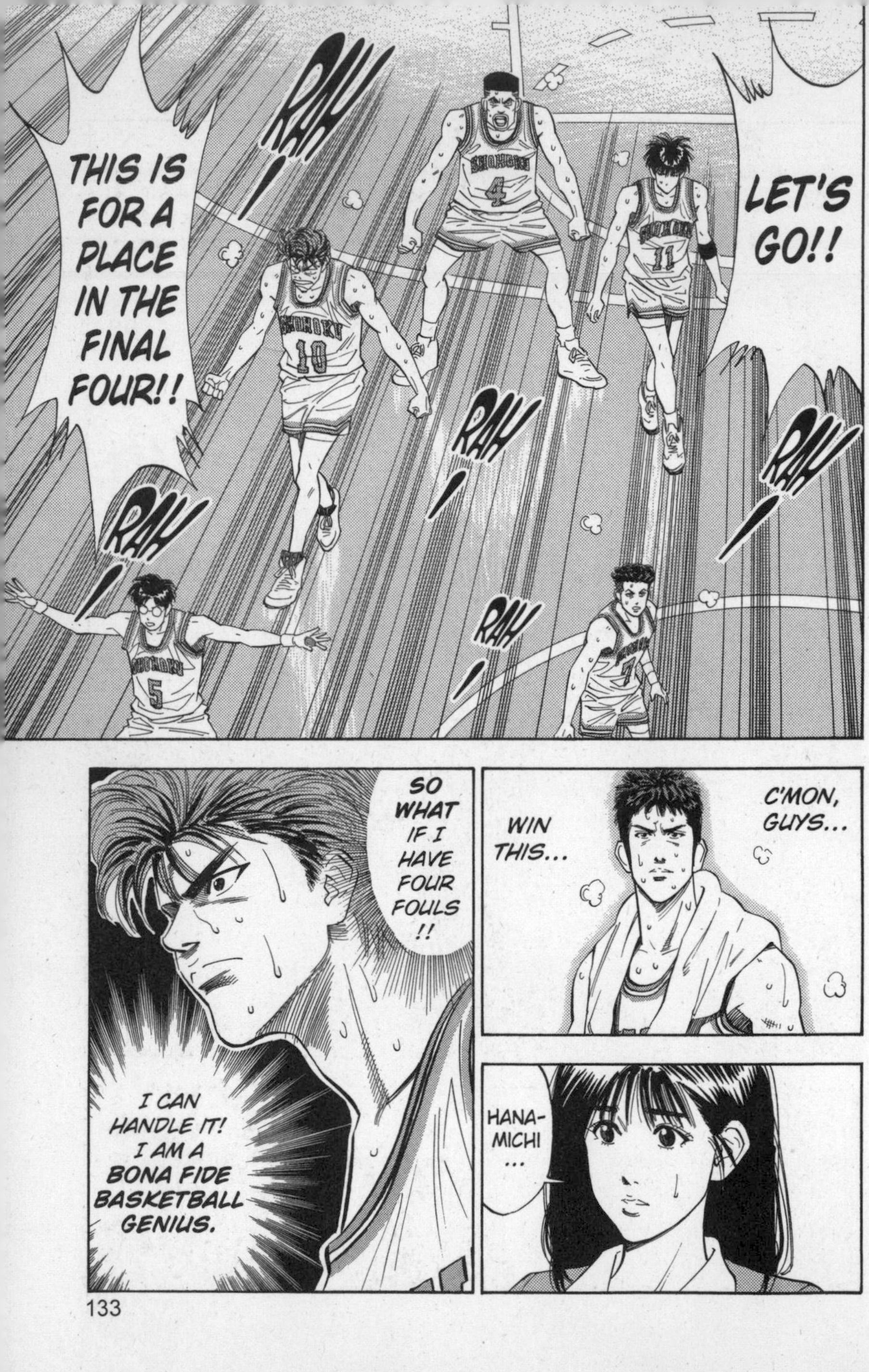
LET'S GO!!
RAH!
THIS IS FOR A PLACE IN THE FINAL FOUR!!
RAH!
RAH!
RAH!
RAH!
C'MON, GUYS...
WIN THIS...
HANA-MICHI...
SO WHAT IF I HAVE FOUR FOULS!!
I CAN HANDLE IT! I AM A BONA FIDE BASKETBALL GENIUS.

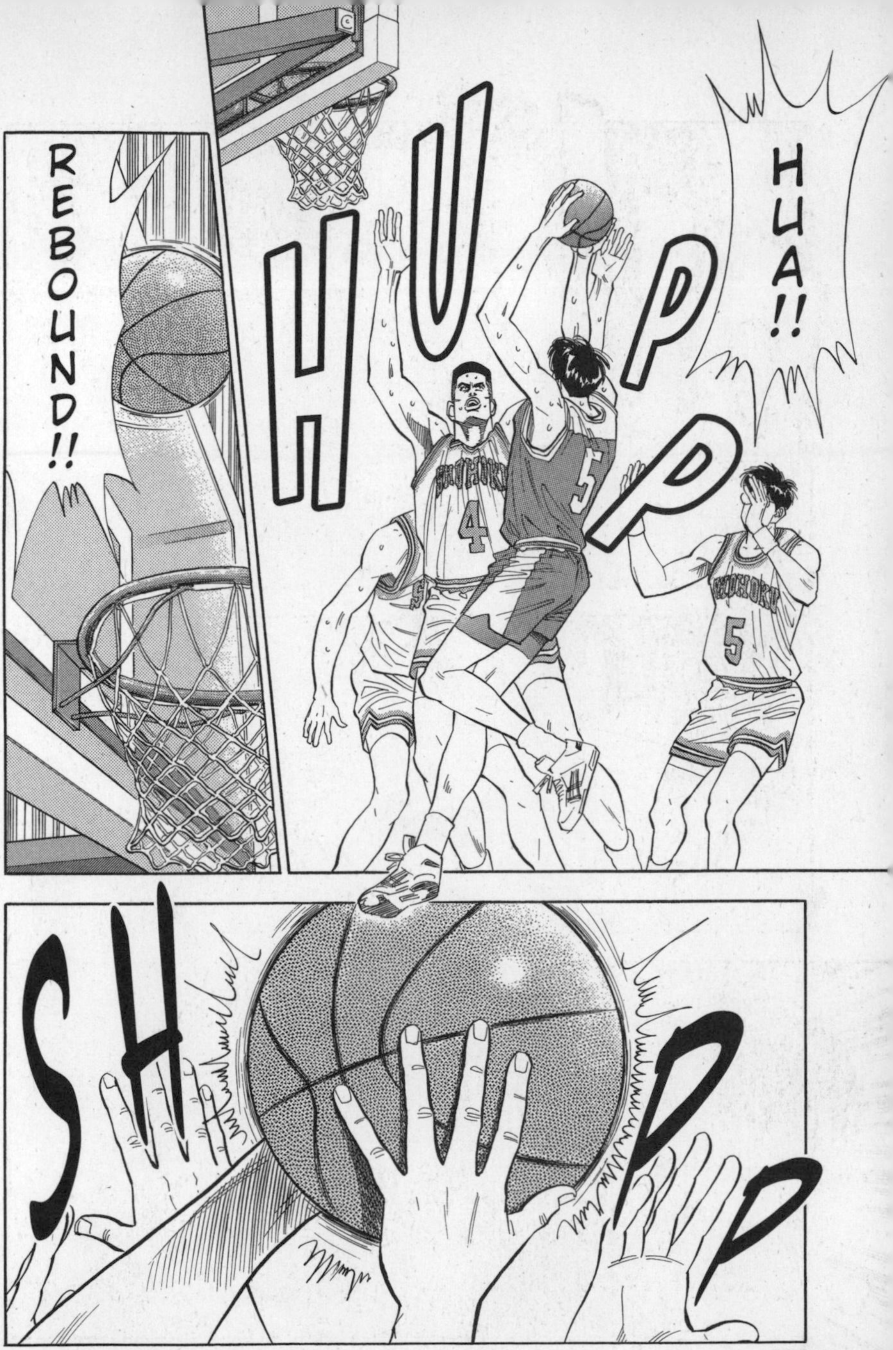
HUAA!!
HUPP
REBOUND!!
SHPP

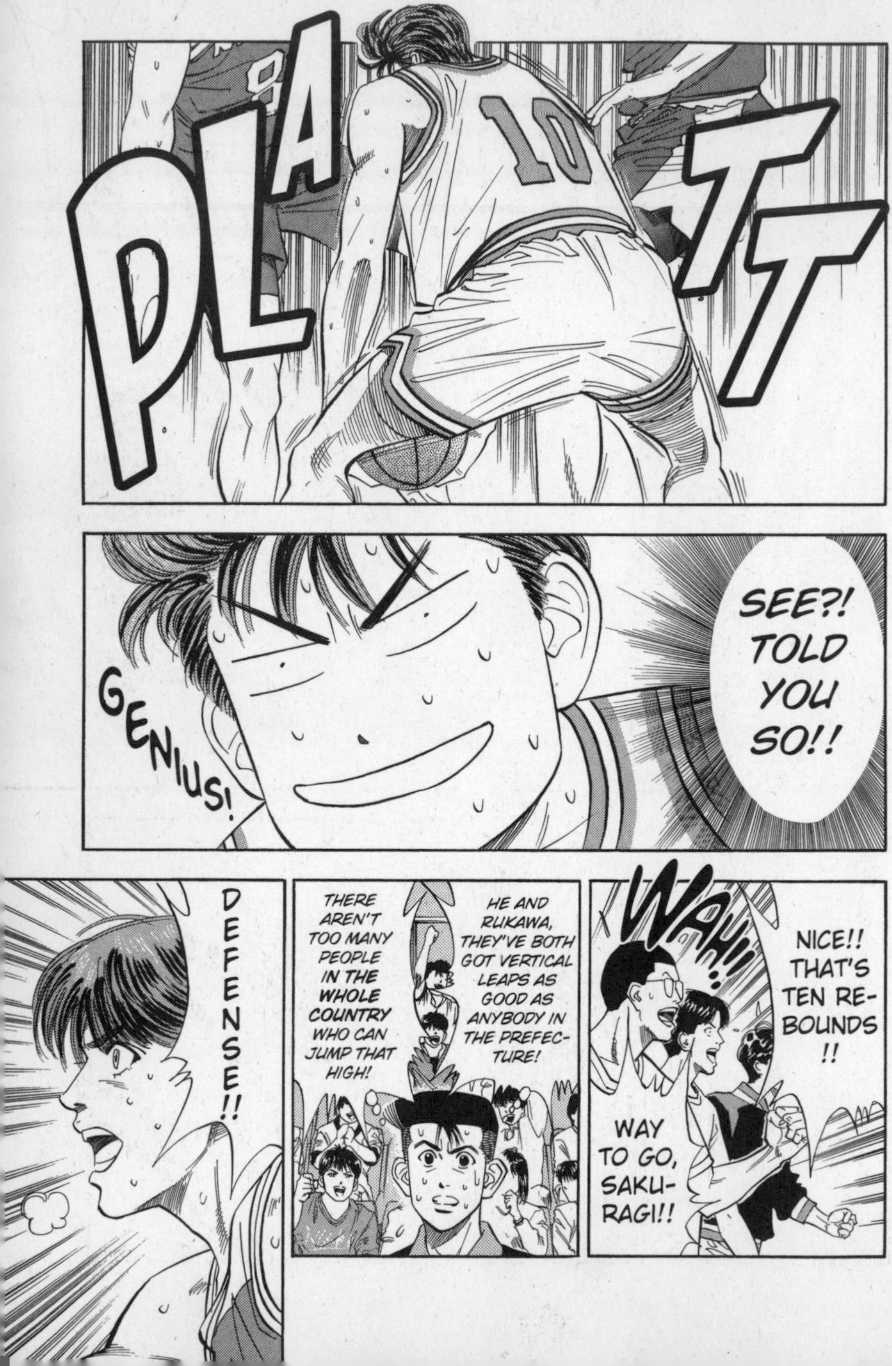
PLATT
SEE?! TOLD YOU SO!!
GENIUS!
WAH!!
NICE!! THAT'S TEN RE-BOUNDS!!
WAY TO GO, SAKU-RAGI!!
HE AND RUKAWA, THEY'VE BOTH GOT VERTICAL LEAPS AS GOOD AS ANYBODY IN THE PREFEC-TURE!
THERE AREN'T TOO MANY PEOPLE IN THE WHOLE COUNTRY WHO CAN JUMP THAT HIGH!
DEFENSE!!

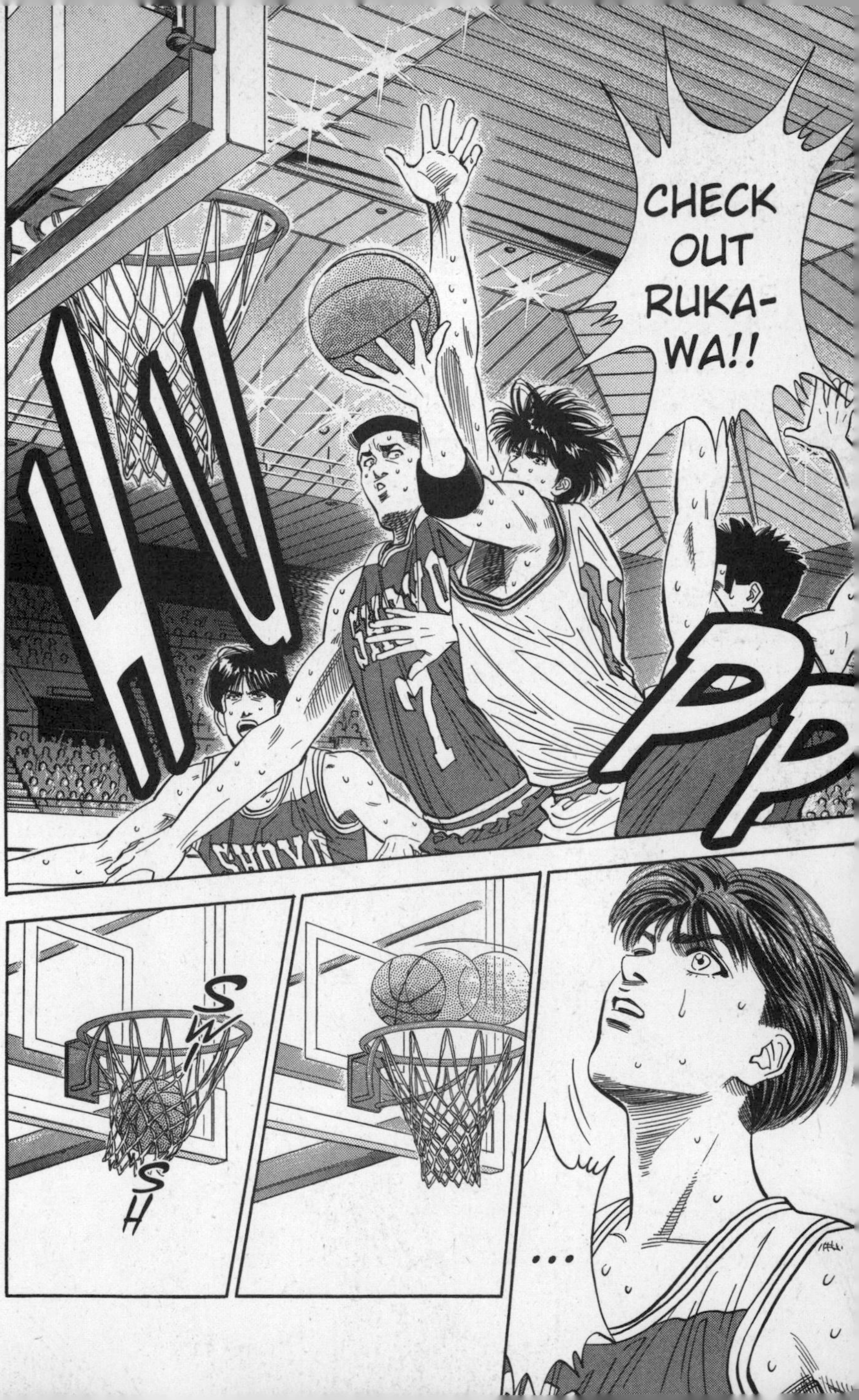
CHECK OUT RUKA-WA!!
...
SWISH

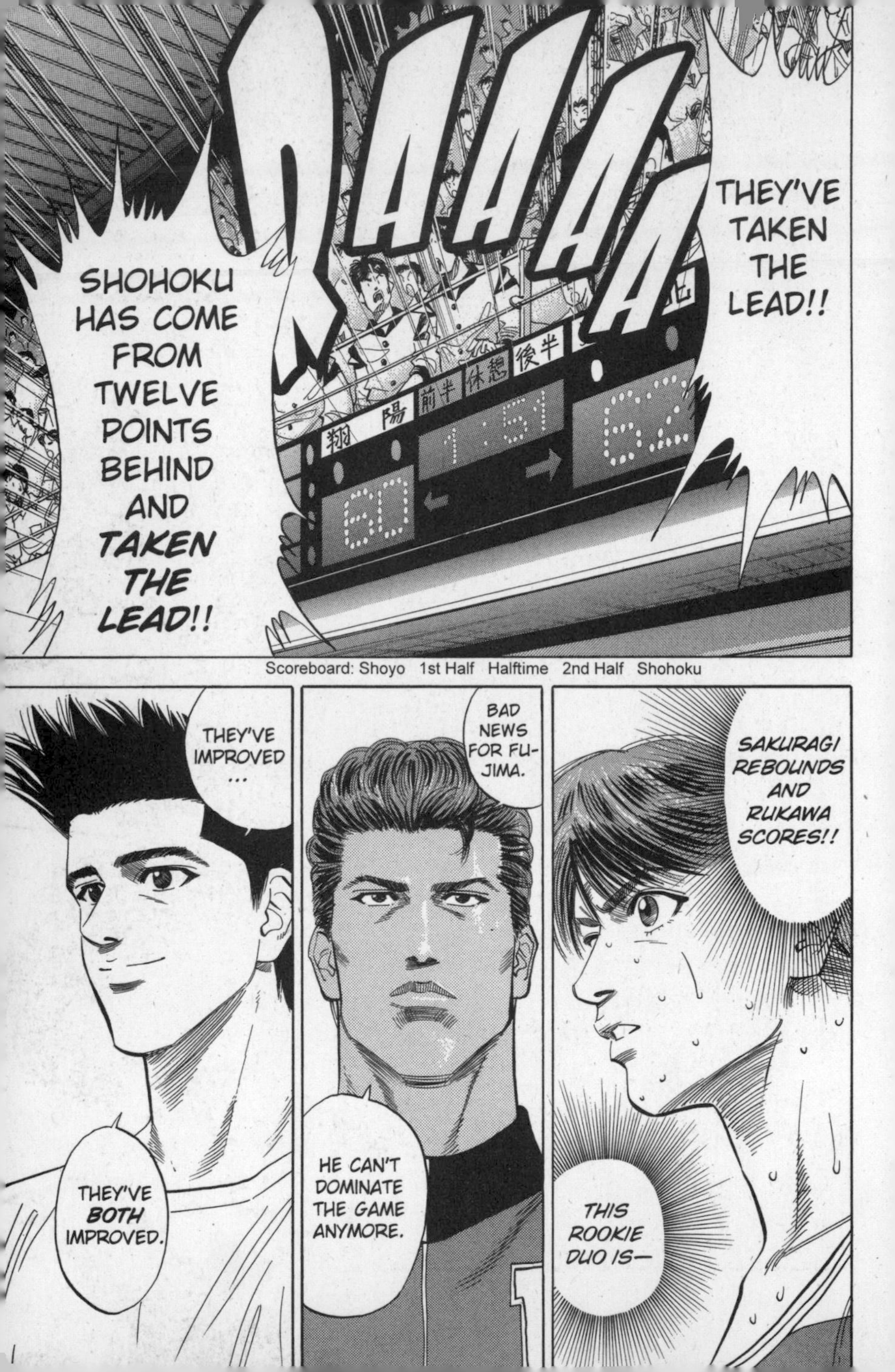
THEY'VE TAKEN THE LEAD!!
SHOHOKU HAS COME FROM TWELVE POINTS BEHIND AND *TAKEN THE LEAD!!*
Scoreboard: Shoyo 1st Half Halftime 2nd Half Shohoku
SAKURAGI REBOUNDS AND RUKAWA SCORES!!
THIS ROOKIE DUO IS—
BAD NEWS FOR FU-JIMA.
HE CAN'T DOMINATE THE GAME ANYMORE.
THEY'VE IMPROVED ...
THEY'VE *BOTH* IMPROVED.

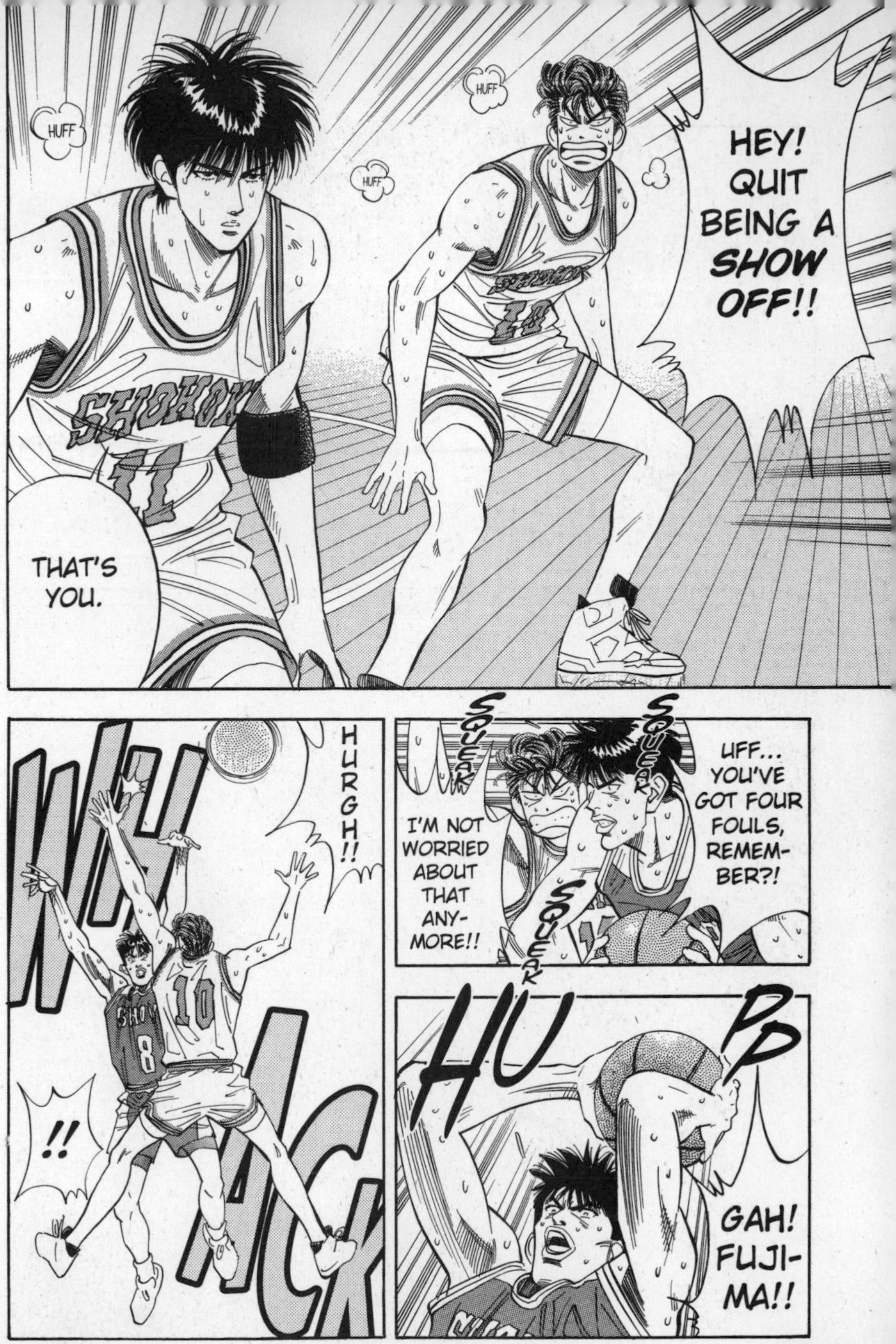
HUFF
HUFF
HUFF
HEY! QUIT BEING A SHOW OFF!!
THAT'S YOU.
SQUEAK
SQUEAK
UFF... YOU'VE GOT FOUR FOULS, REMEMBER?!
I'M NOT WORRIED ABOUT THAT ANYMORE!!
SQUEAK
HU
PP
GAH! FUJIMA!!
HURGH!!
WH
ACK
!!

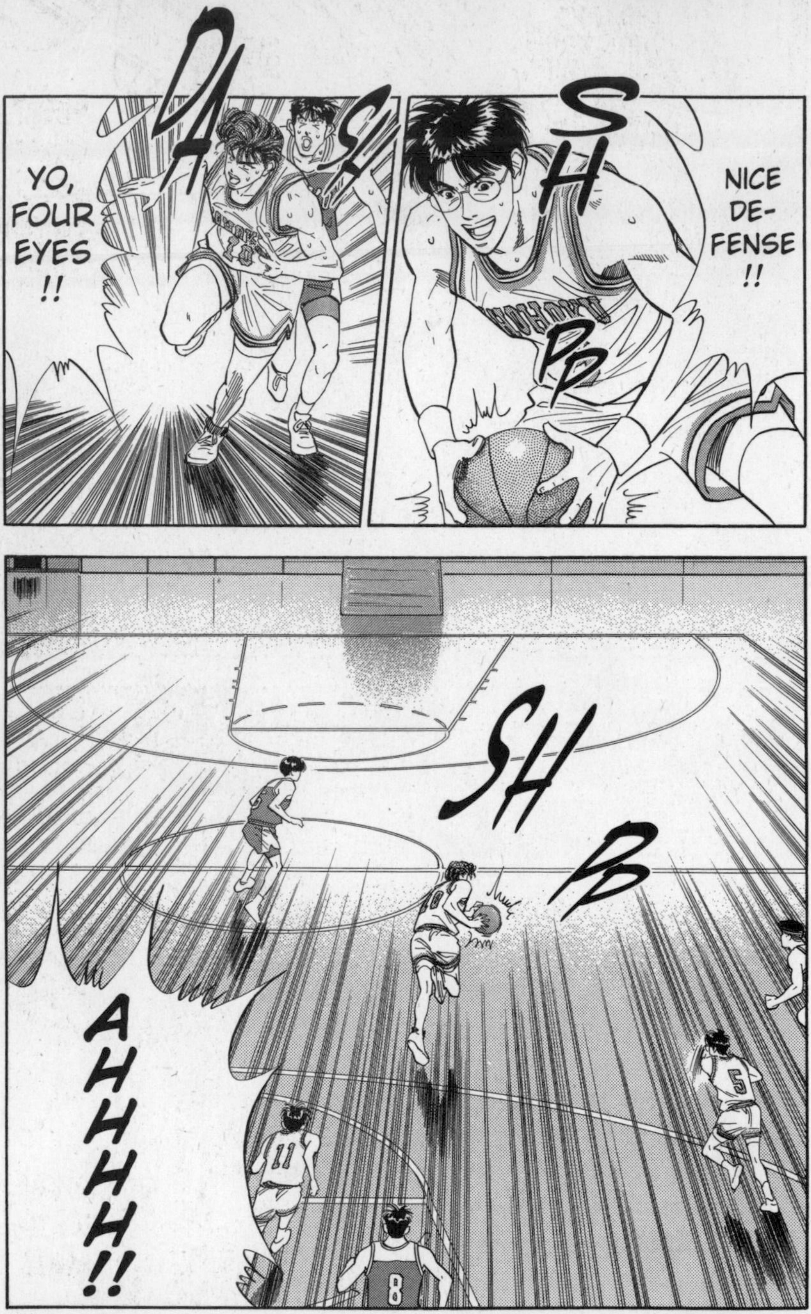
SH
NICE DE-FENSE !!
PP
DASH
YO, FOUR EYES !!
SH
PP
AHHHH!!

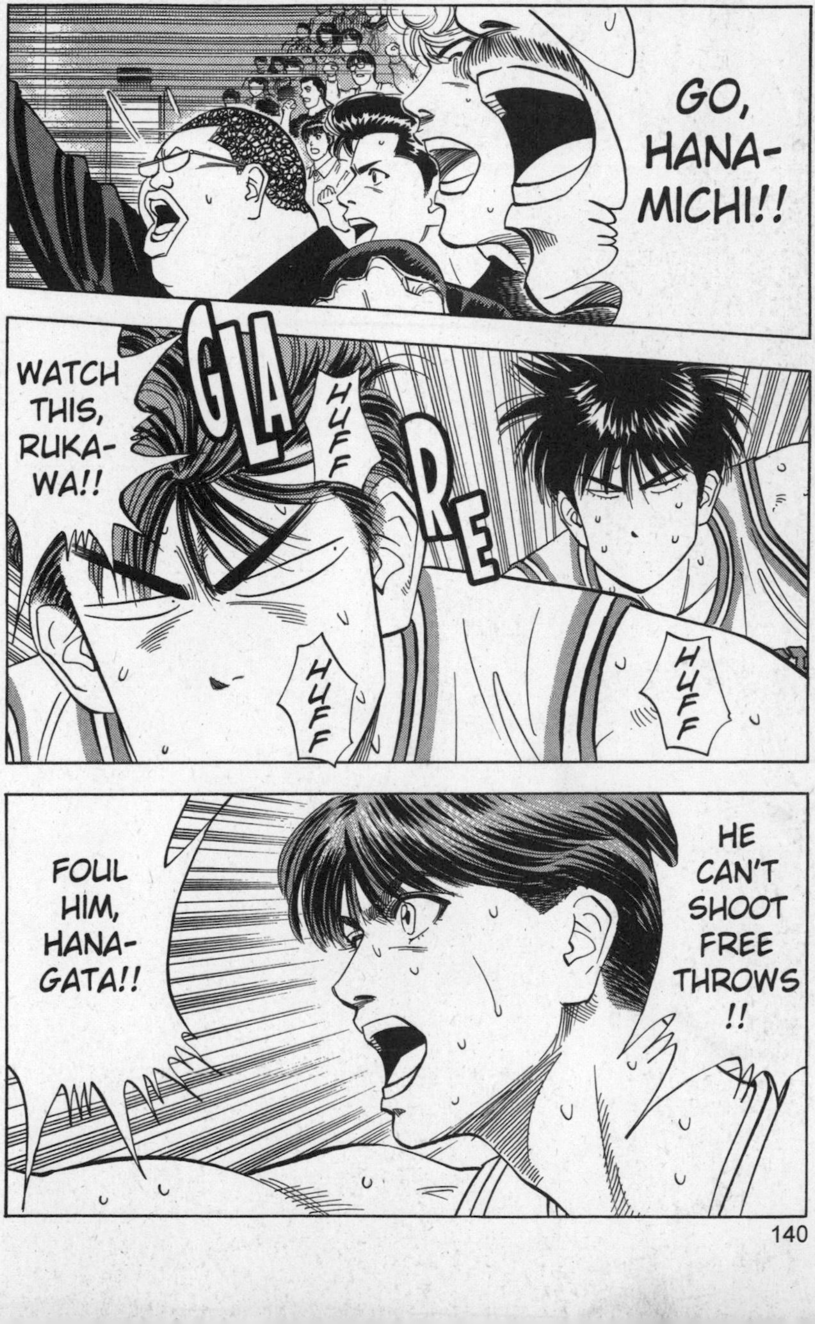
GO, HANAMICHI!!
HUFF
GLARE
HUFF
WATCH THIS, RUKAWA!!
HUFF
HE CAN'T SHOOT FREE THROWS!!
FOUL HIM, HANAGATA!!

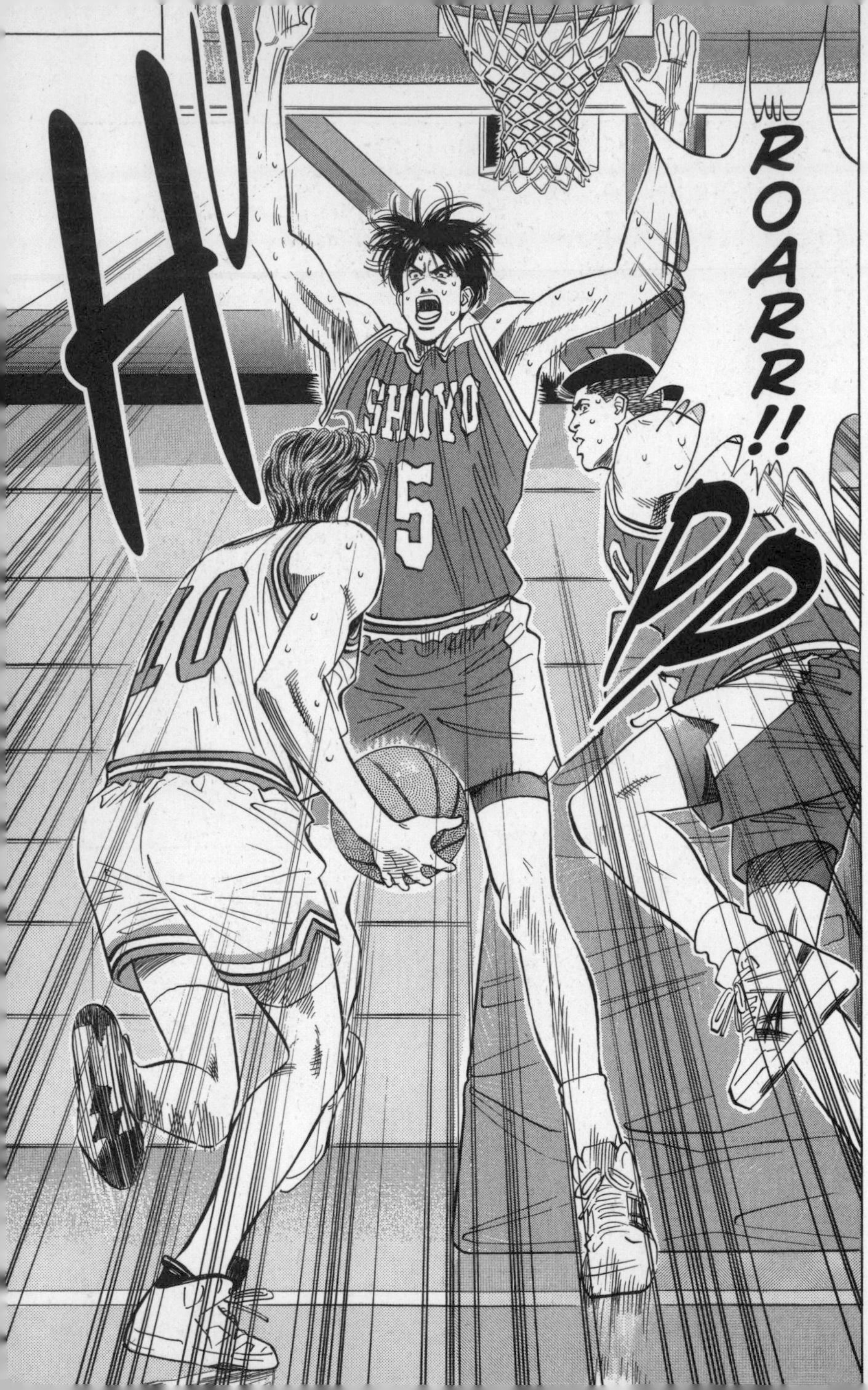
ROARR!!
SHUYO

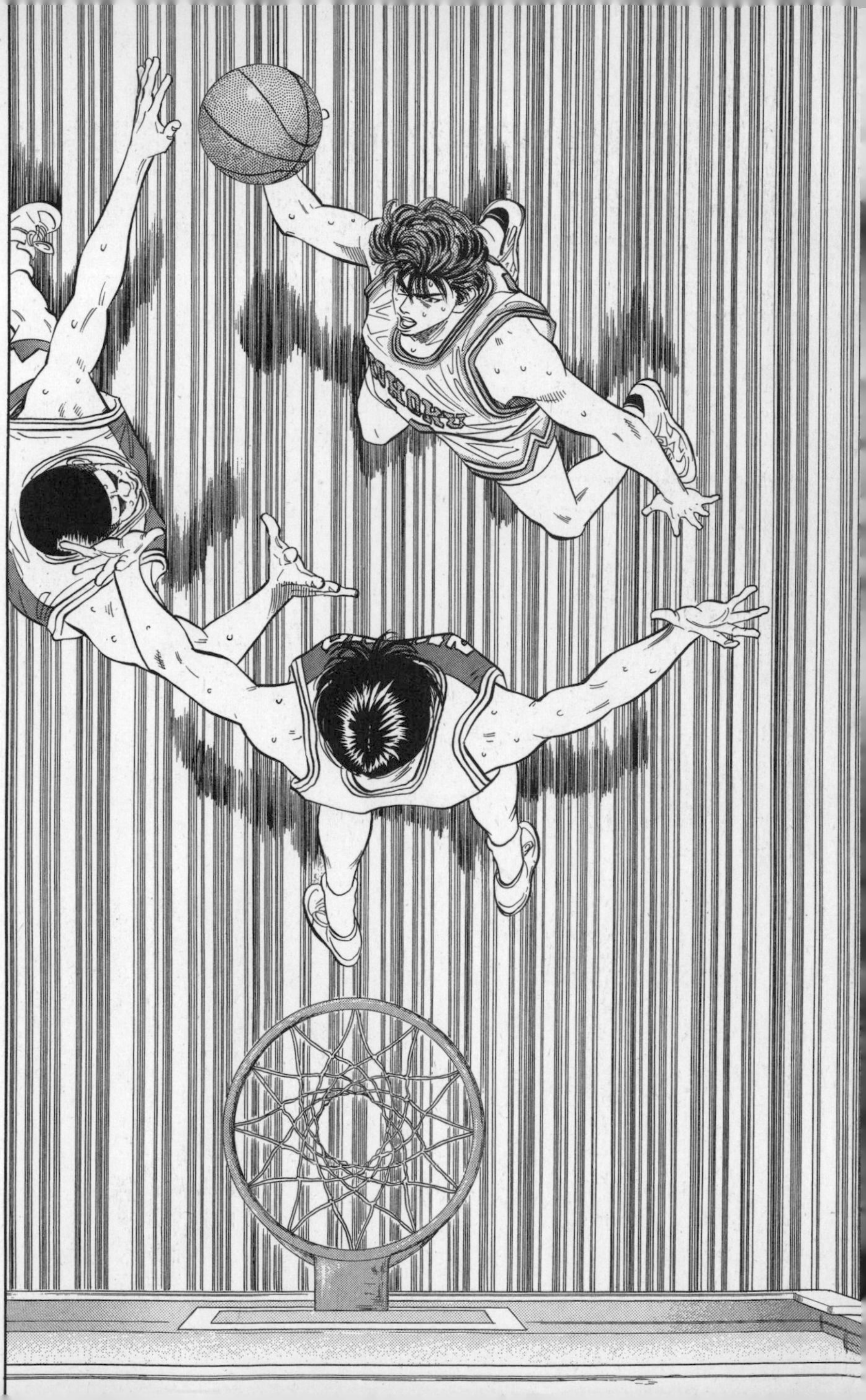

READ THIS WAY

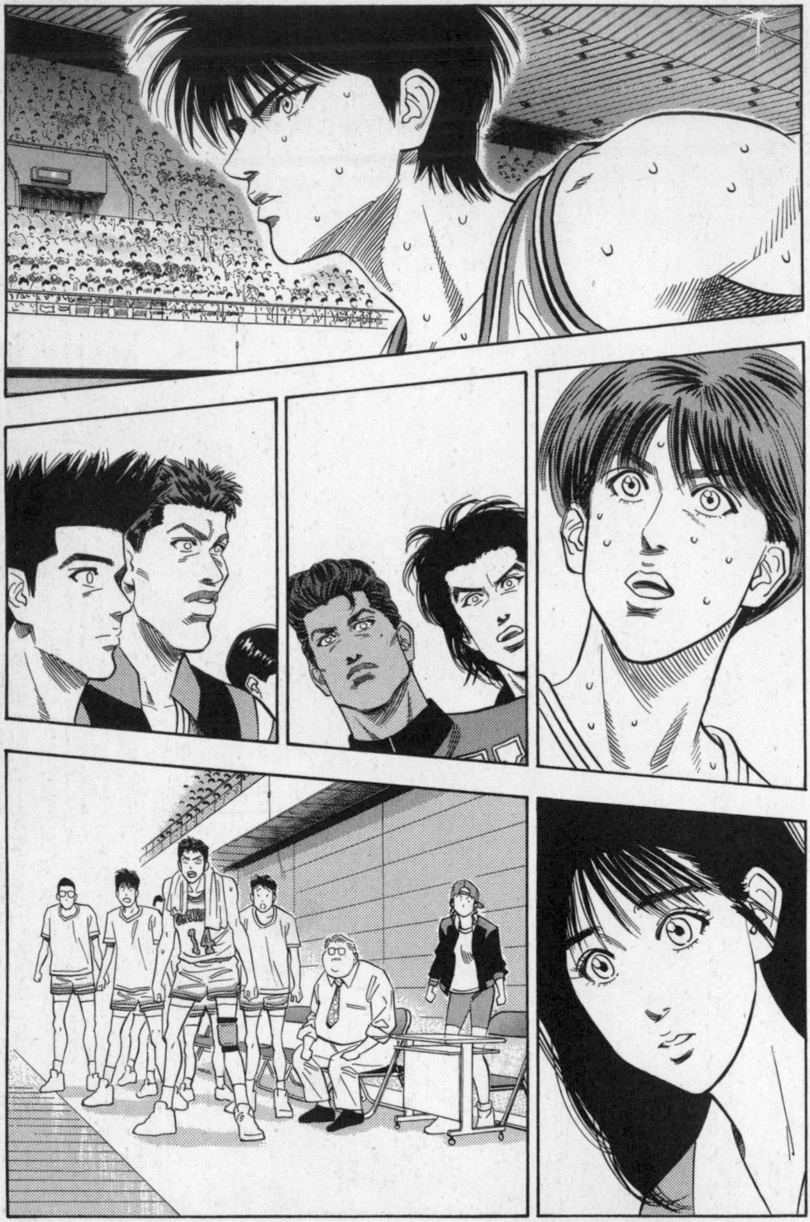

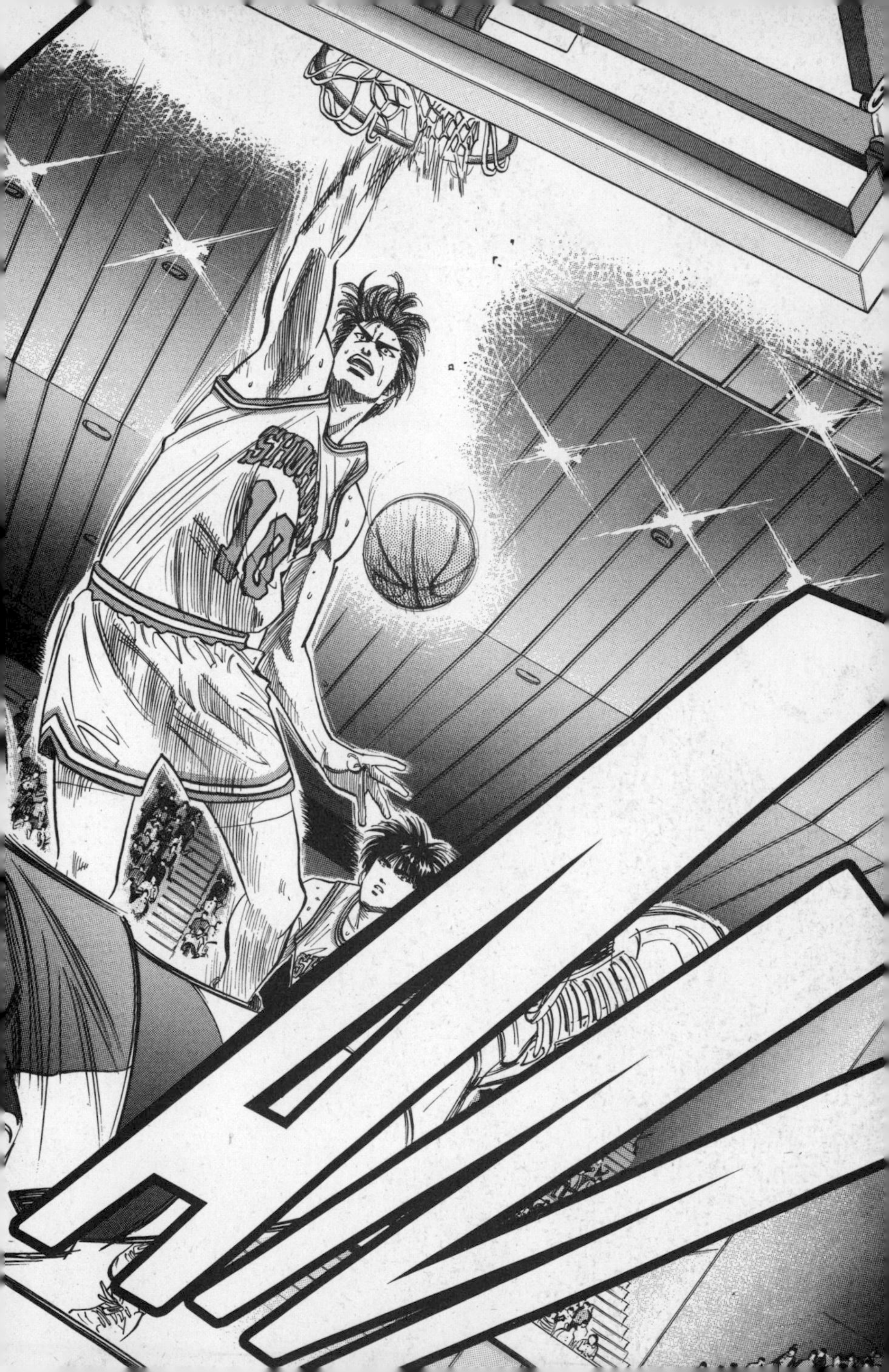

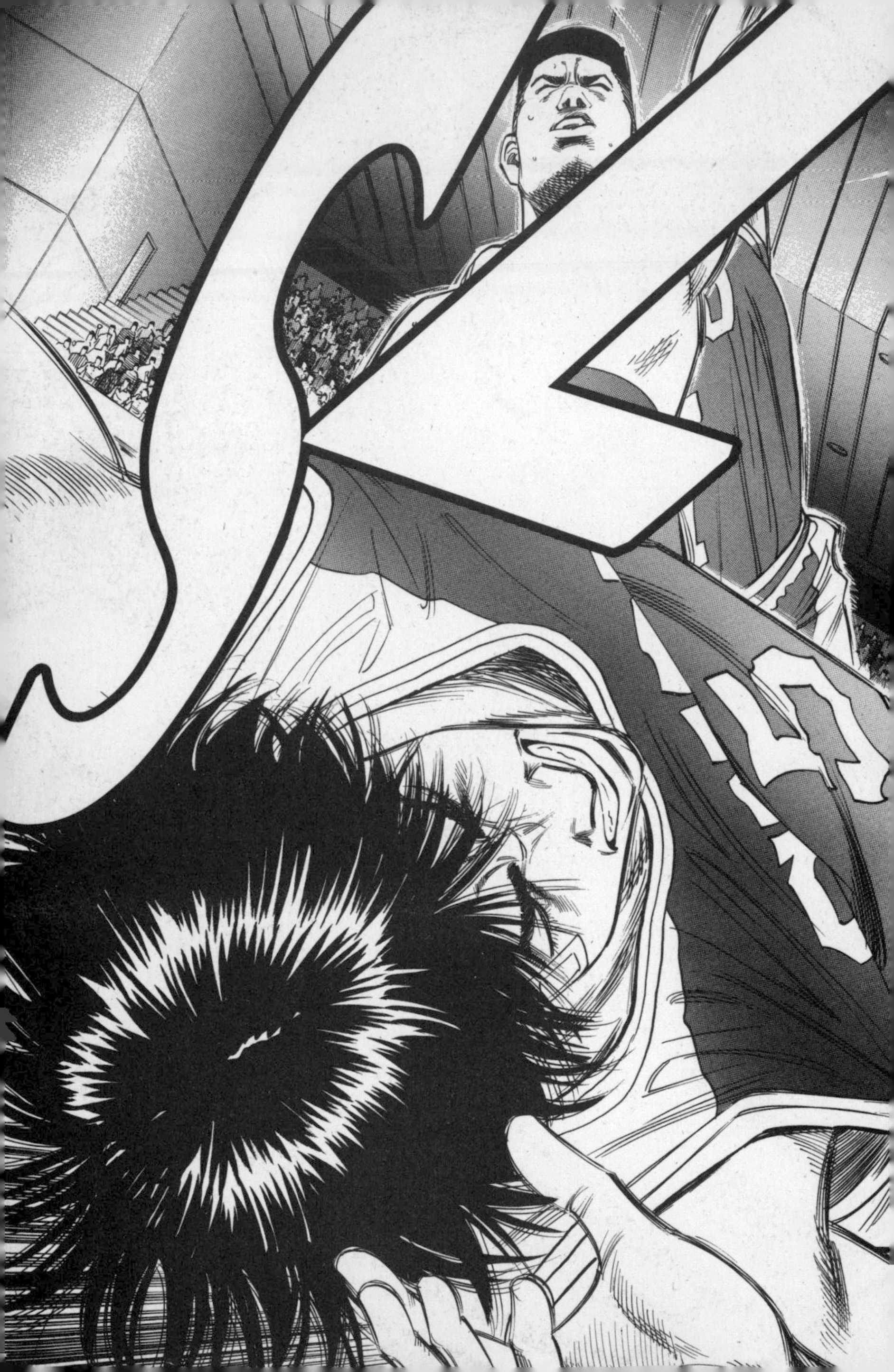

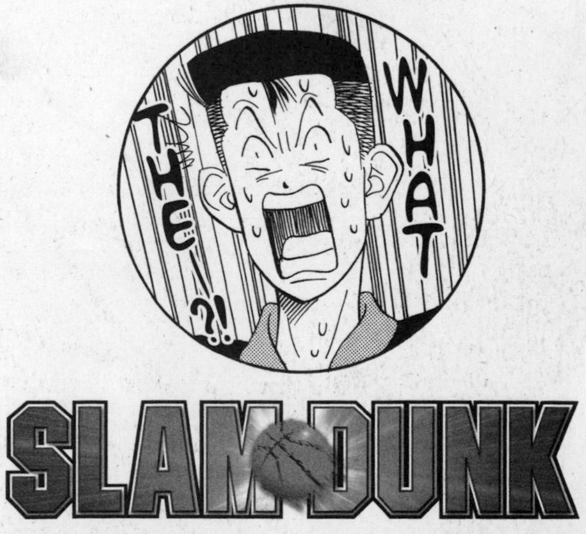
WHAT THE--?!

SLAM DUNK

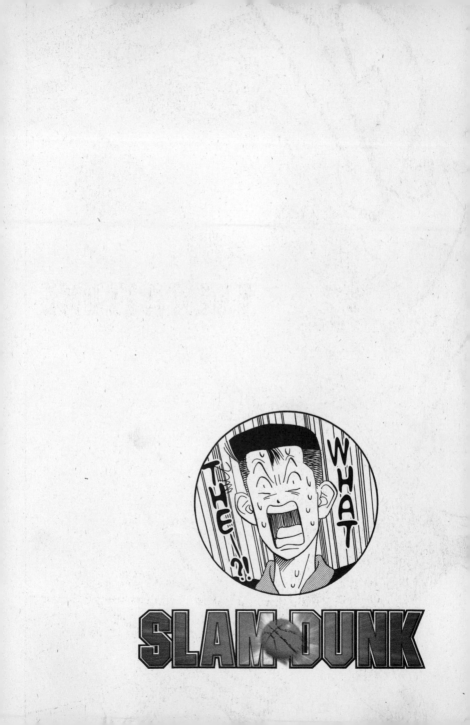

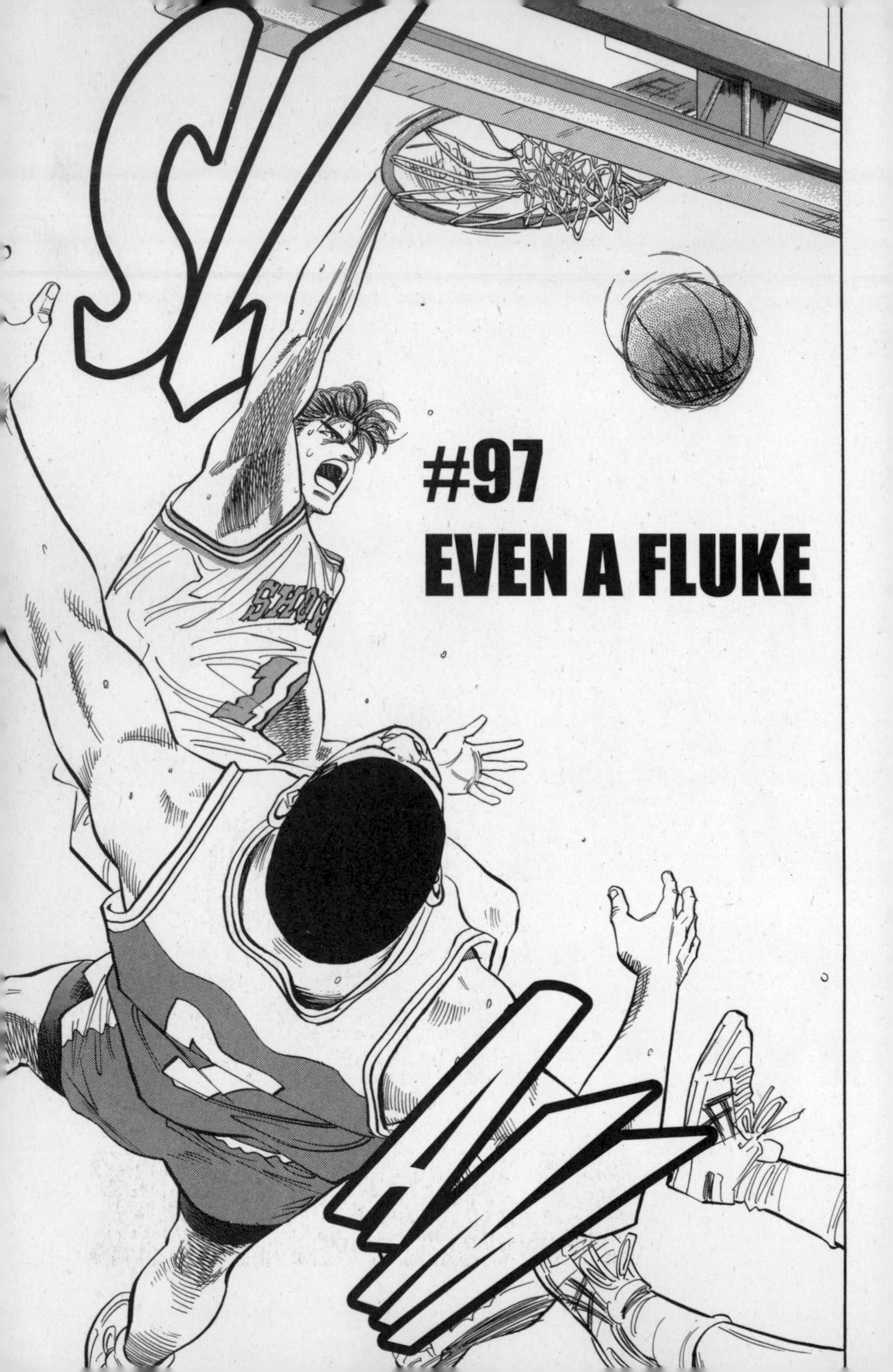

#97 EVEN A FLUKE

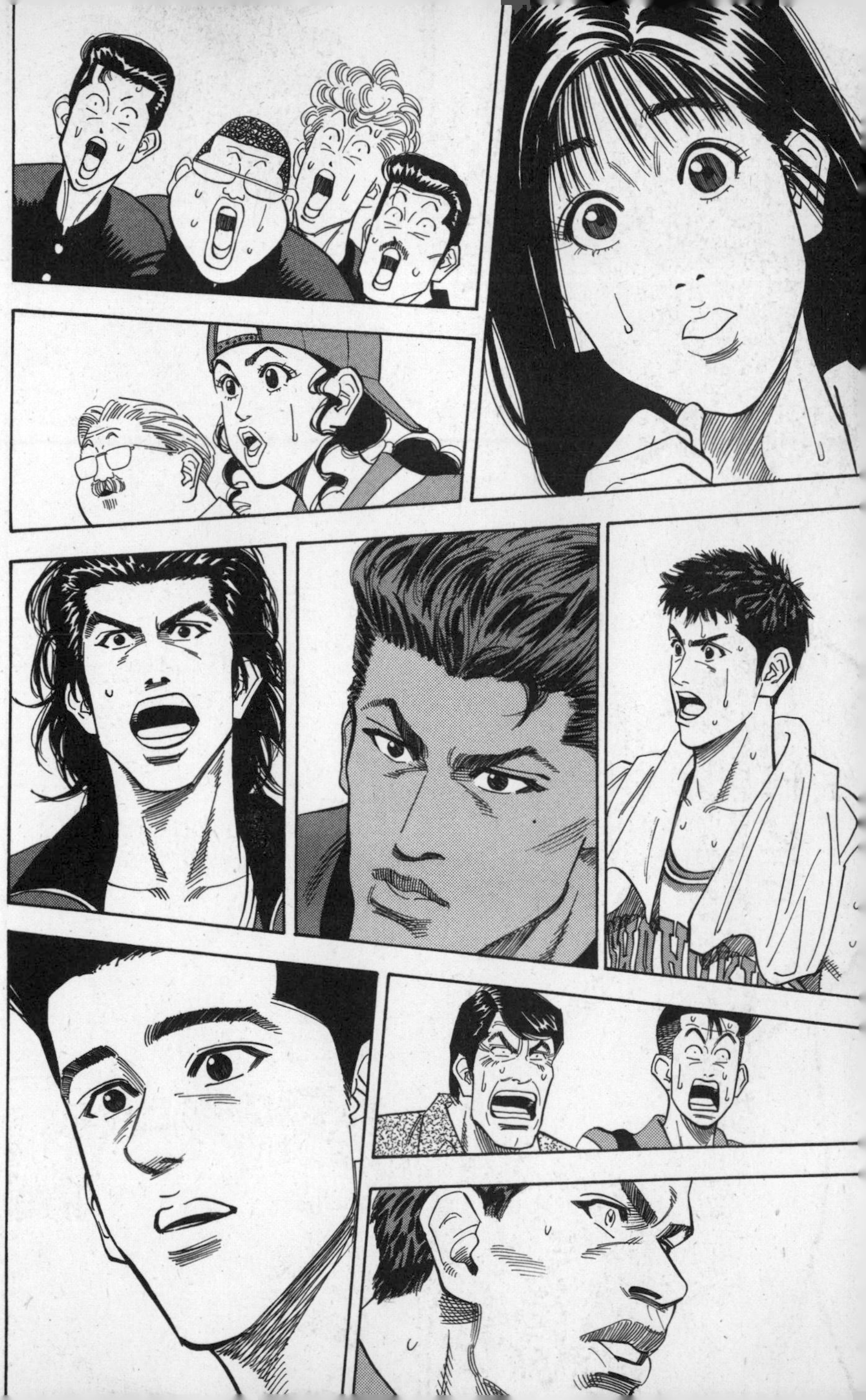

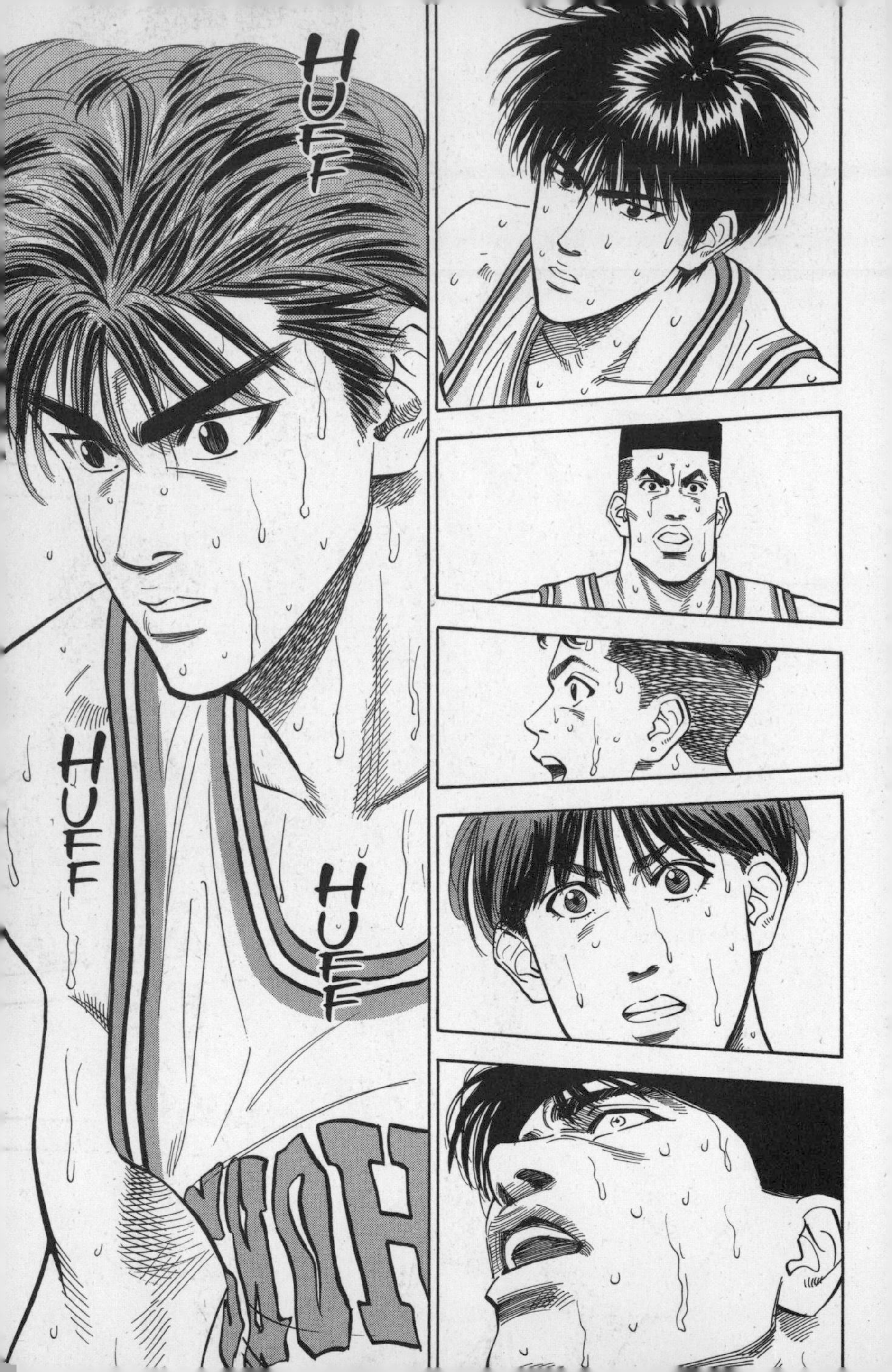
HUFF
HUFF
HUFF

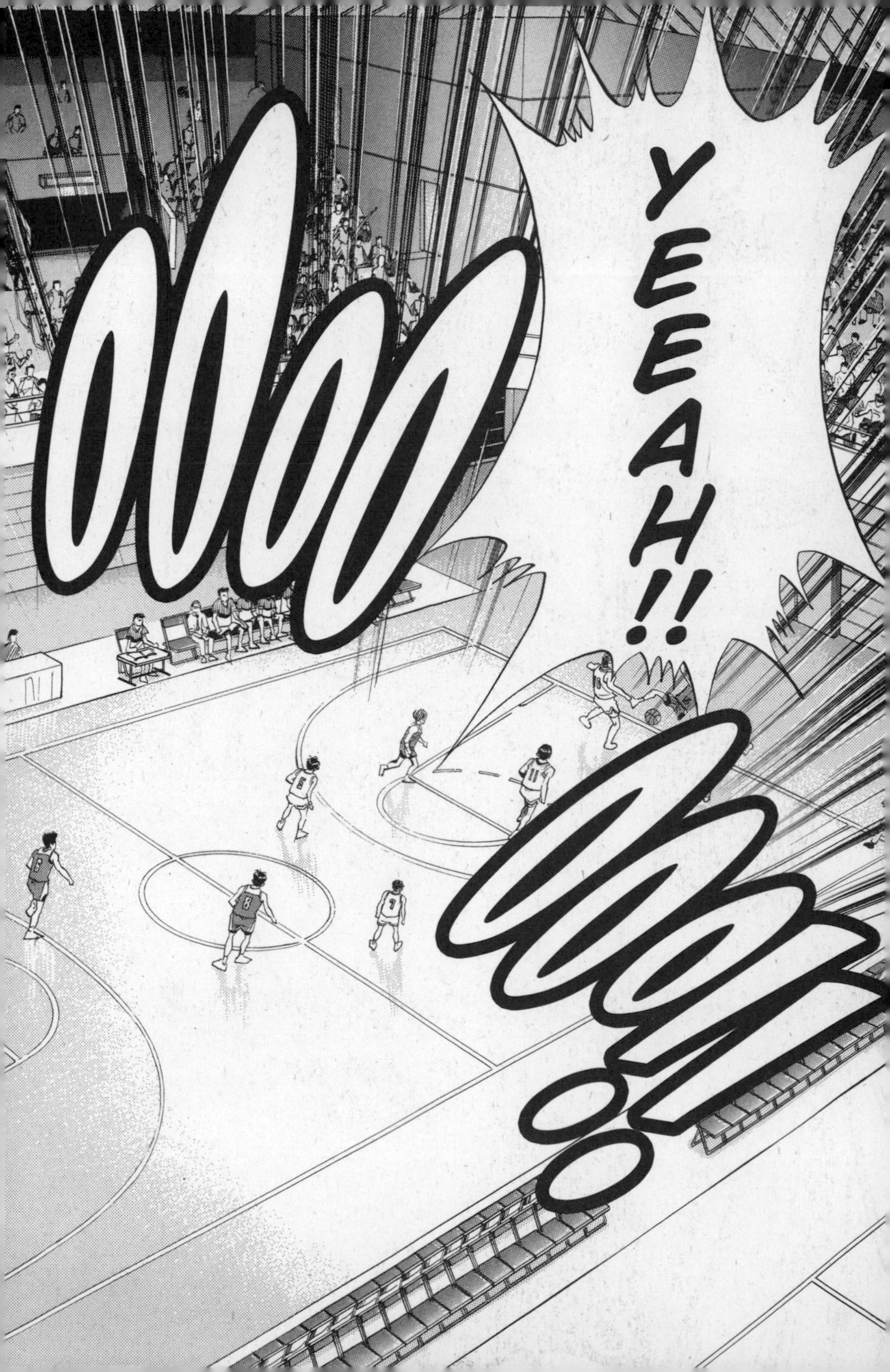
YEEAH!!

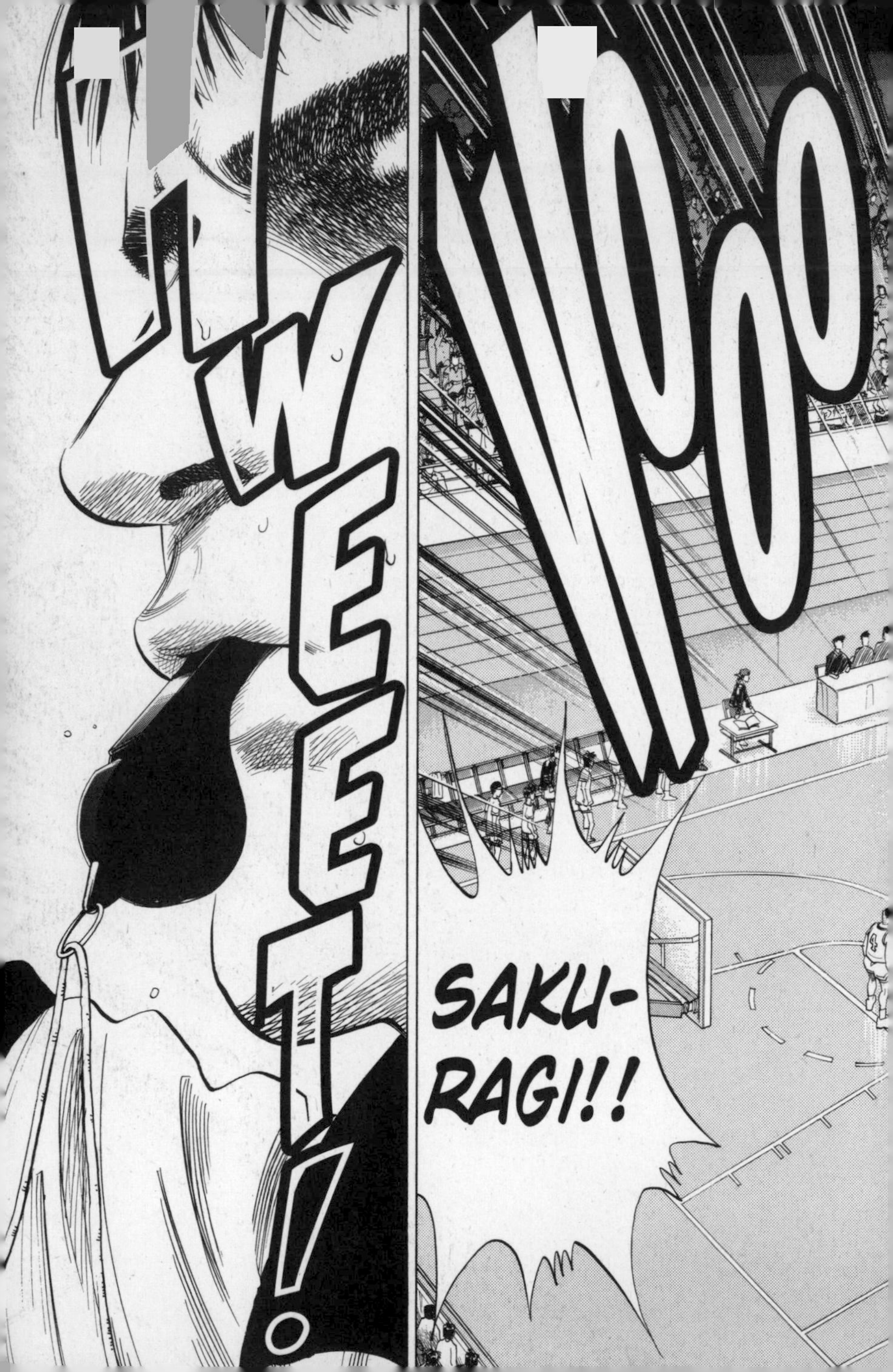
SAKU-RAGI!!
TWEET!

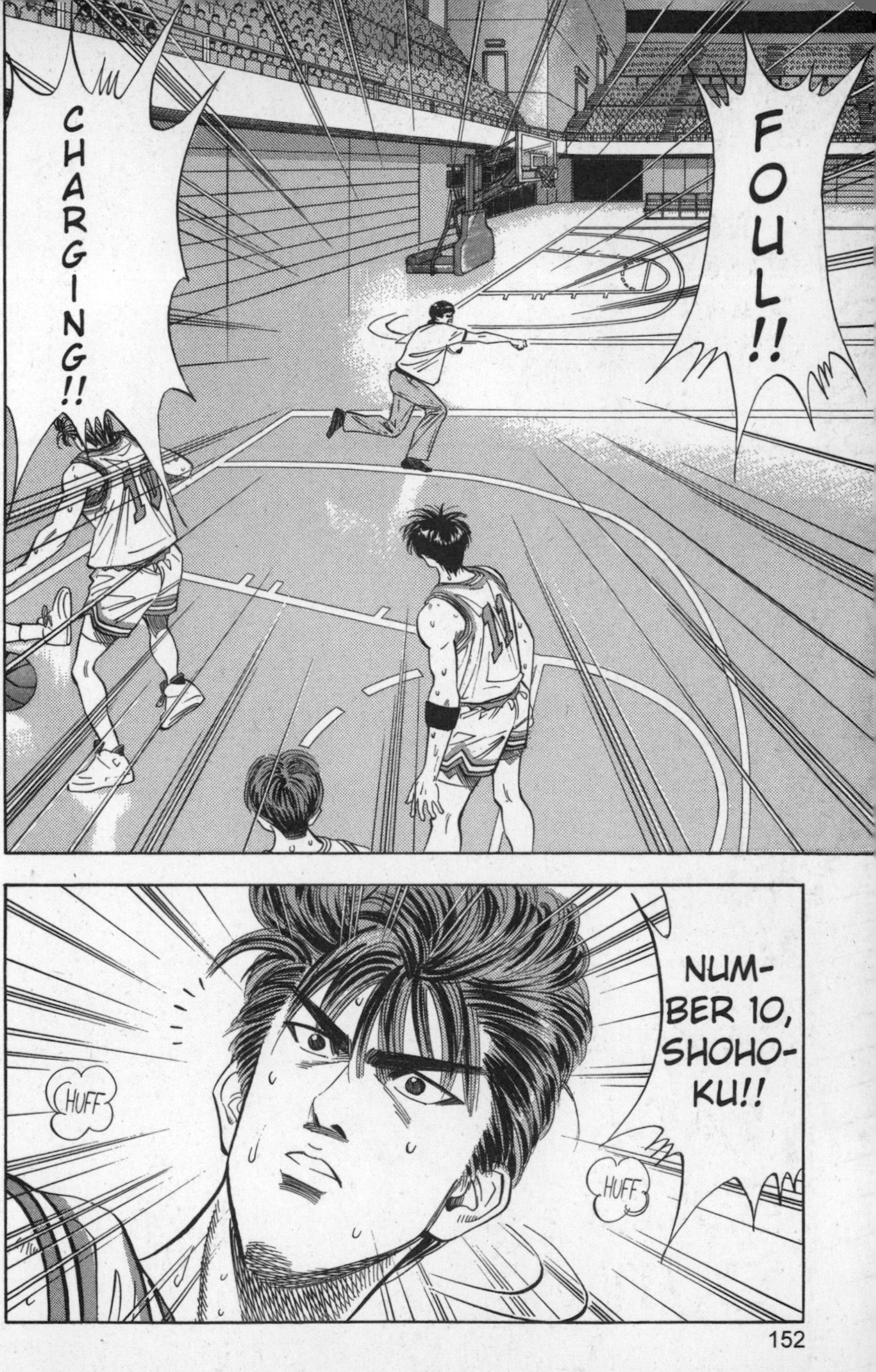
FOUL!!
CHARGING!!
NUMBER 10, SHOHOKU!!
HUFF
HUFF

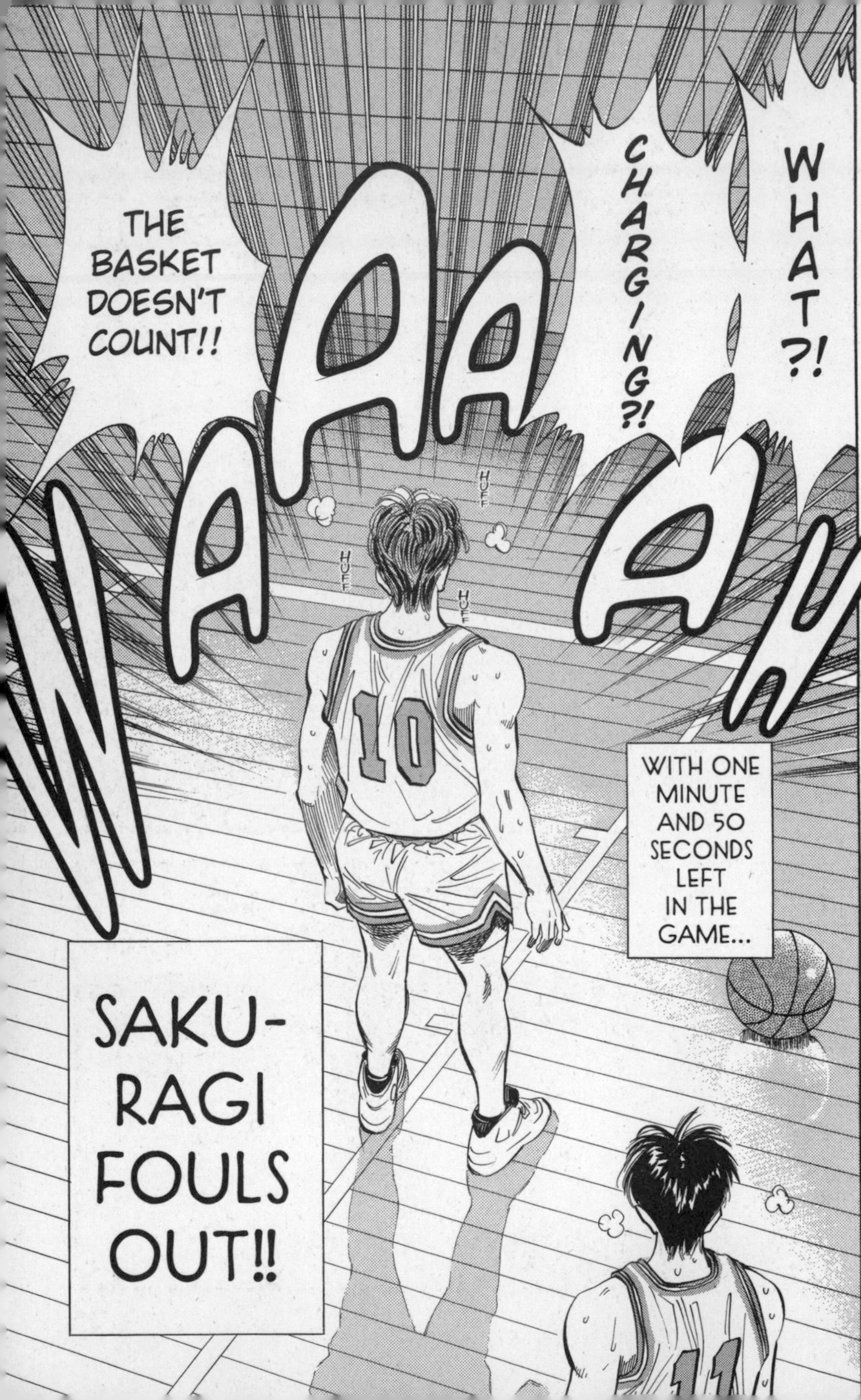
WHAT?!
CHARGING?!
WAAAAAH
THE BASKET DOESN'T COUNT!!
HUFF
HUFF
HUFF
WITH ONE MINUTE AND 50 SECONDS LEFT IN THE GAME...
SAKU-RAGI FOULS OUT!!

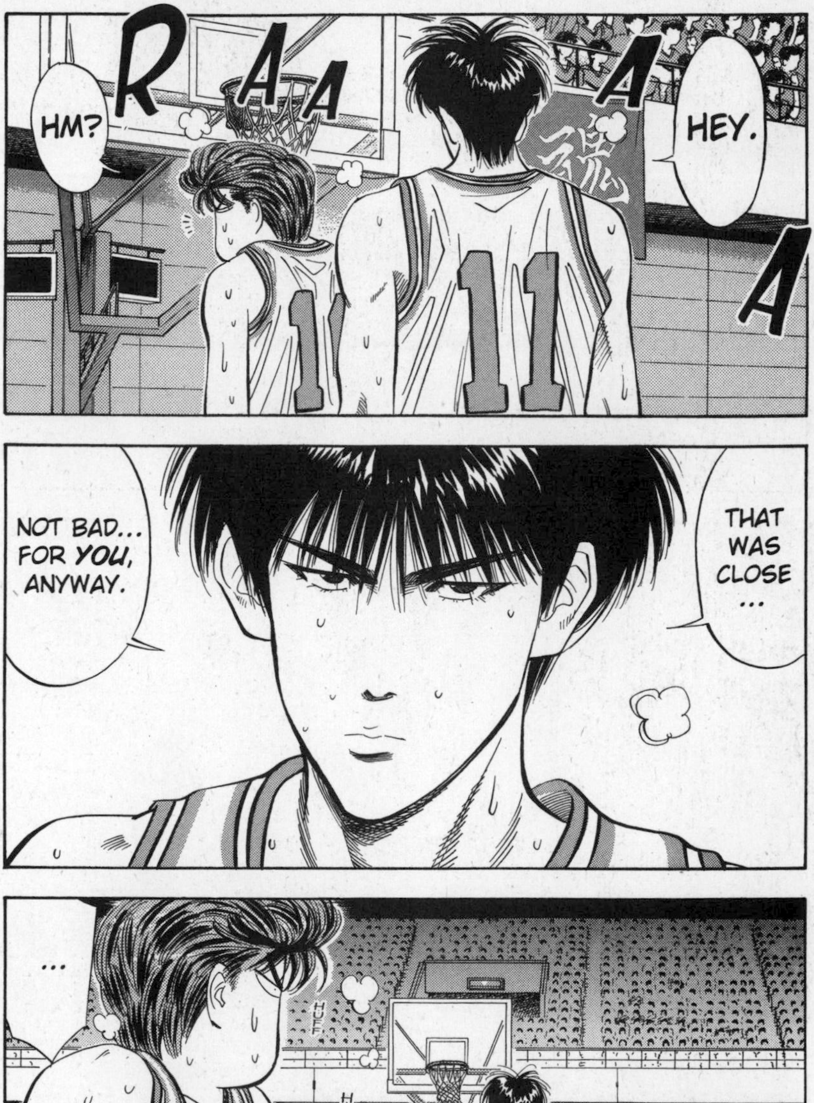
HEY.
RAAAA
HM?
THAT WAS CLOSE...
NOT BAD... FOR YOU, ANYWAY.
PAT
PAT
HUFF
HUFF
...

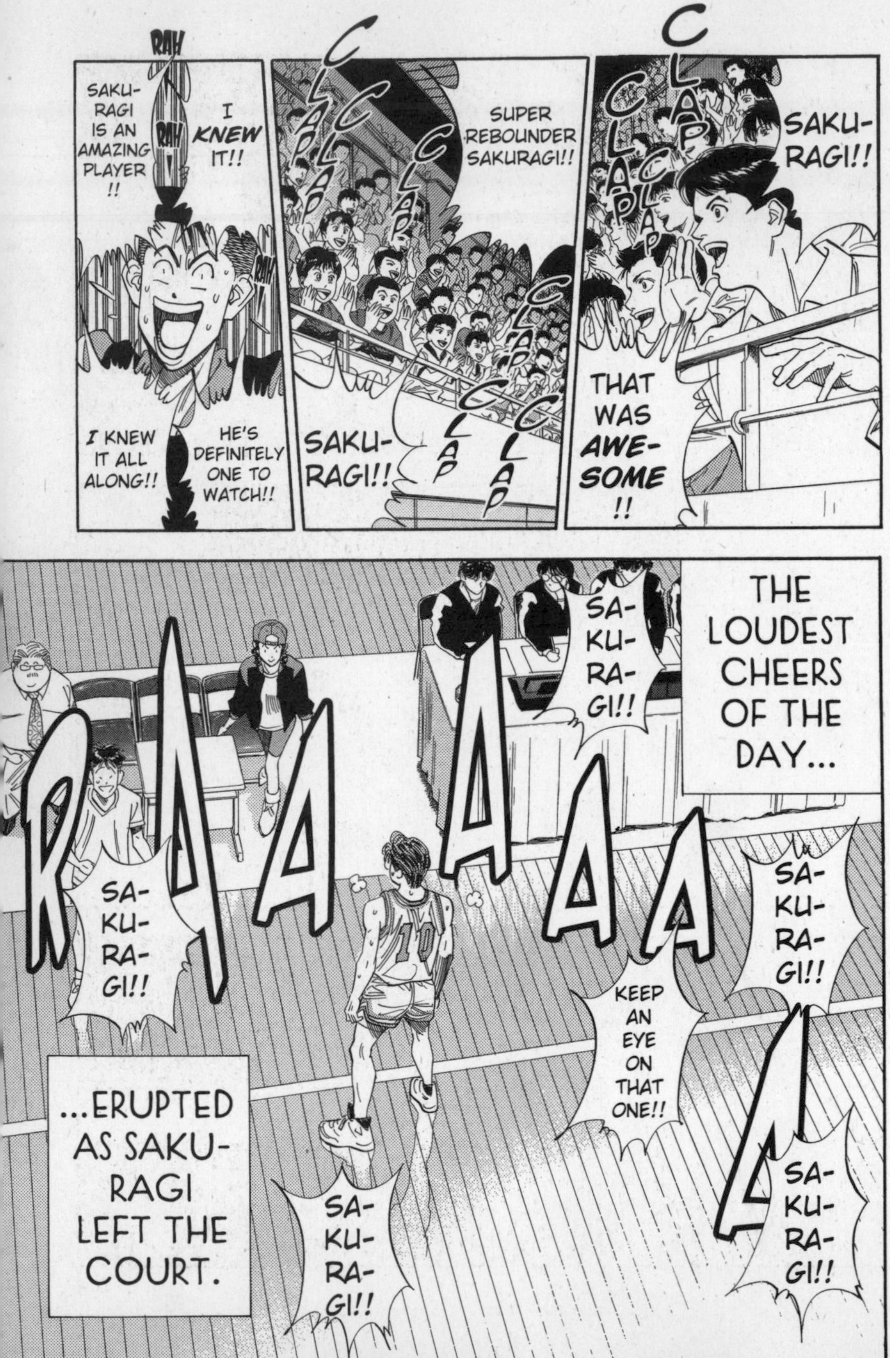
CLAP CLAP CLAP
SAKU-RAGI!!
THAT WAS AWESOME!!
CLAP CLAP CLAP CLAP
SUPER REBOUNDER SAKURAGI!!
SAKU-RAGI!!
RAH RAH
I KNEW IT!!
SAKURAGI IS AN AMAZING PLAYER!!
RAH
HE'S DEFINITELY ONE TO WATCH!!
I KNEW IT ALL ALONG!!
THE LOUDEST CHEERS OF THE DAY...
SA-KU-RA-GI!!
SA-KU-RA-GI!!
RAAAAAAA
KEEP AN EYE ON THAT ONE!!
SA-KU-RA-GI!!
SA-KU-RA-GI!!
SA-KU-RA-GI!!
...ERUPTED AS SAKURAGI LEFT THE COURT.

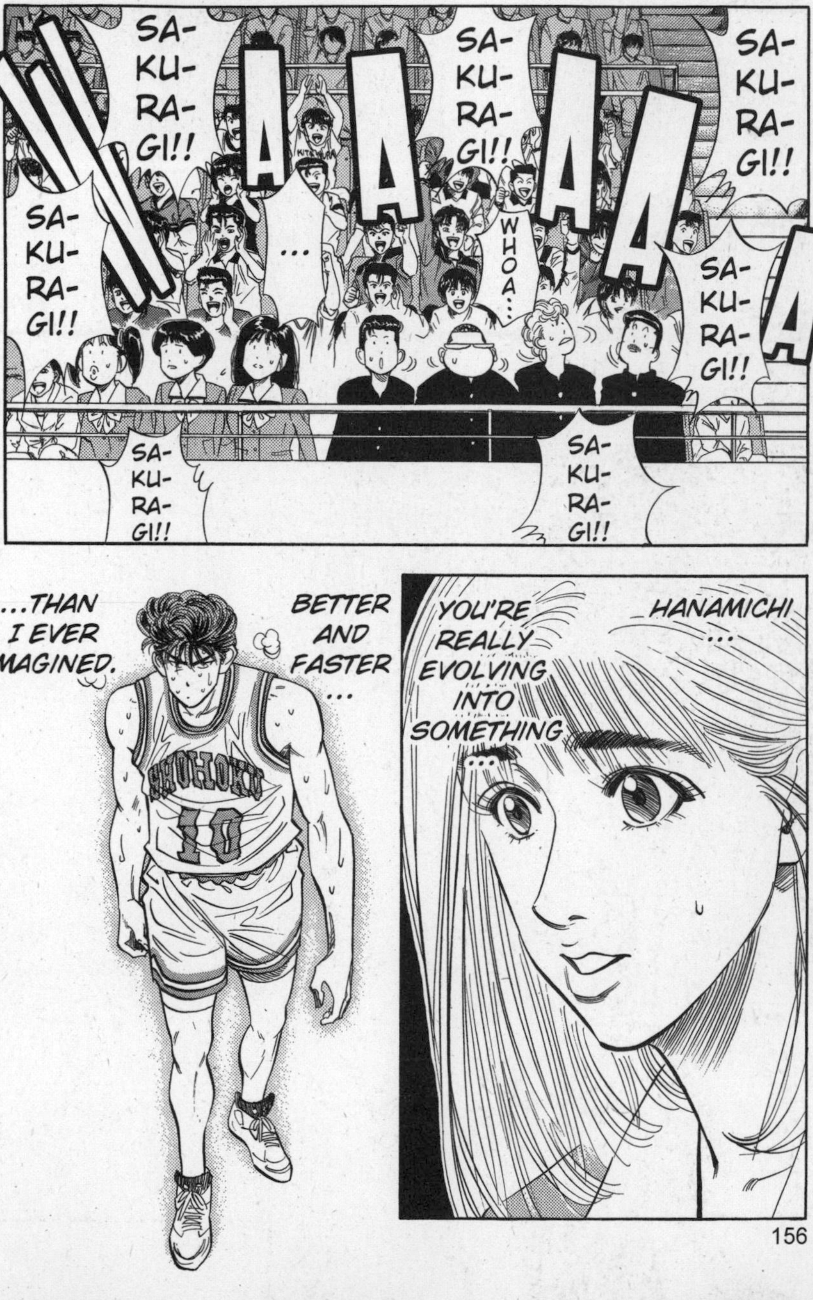
SA-KU-RA-GI!!
SA-KU-RA-GI!!
WAAAAA
SA-KU-RA-GI!!
SA-KU-RA-GI!!
WHOA...
...
SA-KU-RA-GI!!
SA-KU-RA-GI!!
SA-KU-RA-GI!!
HANAMICHI...
YOU'RE REALLY EVOLVING INTO SOMETHING...
BETTER AND FASTER...
...THAN I EVER IMAGINED.

READ THIS WAY

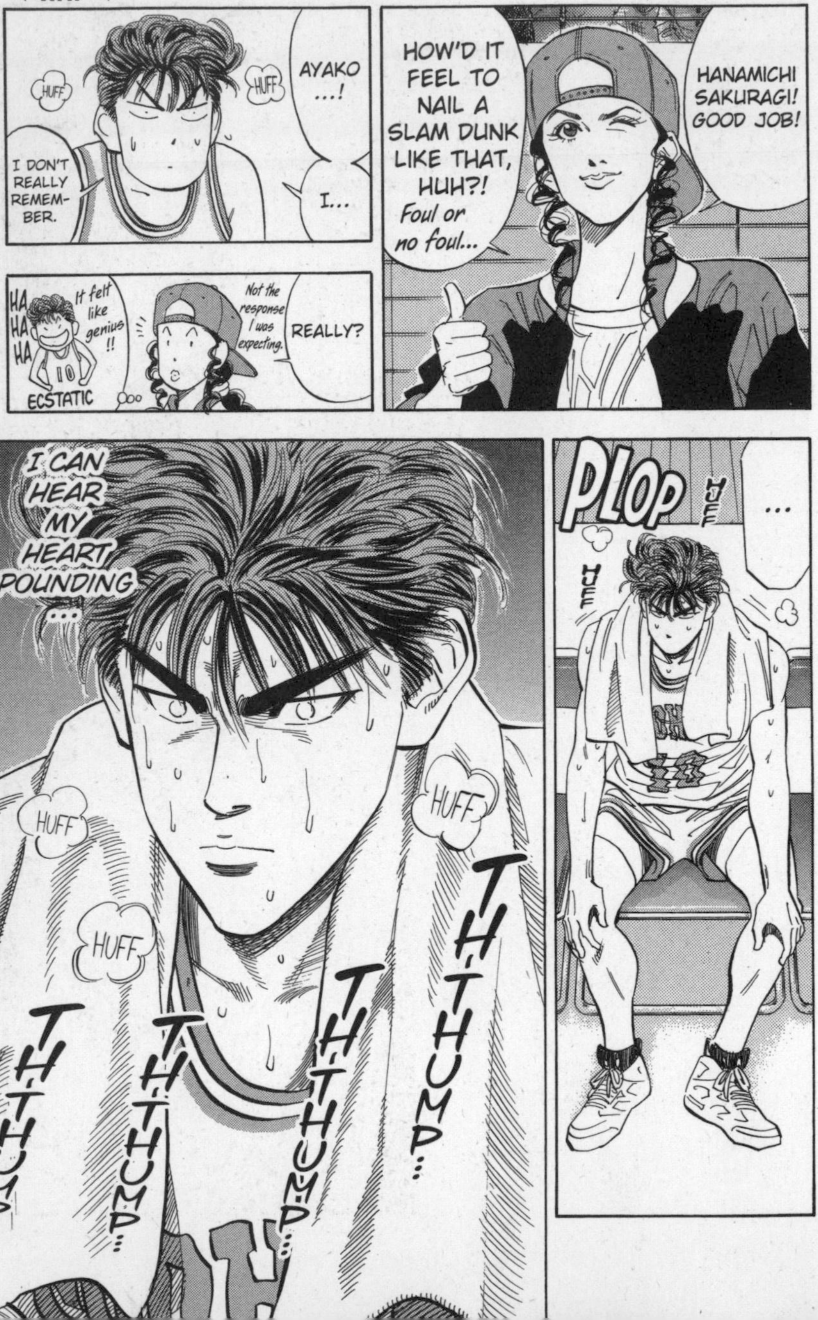
HANAMICHI SAKURAGI! GOOD JOB!
HOW'D IT FEEL TO NAIL A SLAM DUNK LIKE THAT, HUH?! Foul or no foul...
AYAKO ...!
HUFF
HUFF
I...
I DON'T REALLY REMEMBER.
REALLY?
Not the response I was expecting.
It felt like genius !!
HA HA HA
ECSTATIC
PLOP
HUFF
...
HUFF
I CAN HEAR MY HEART POUNDING...
HUFF
HUFF
HUFF
TH-THUMP...
TH-THUMP...
TH-THUMP...
TH-THUMP...

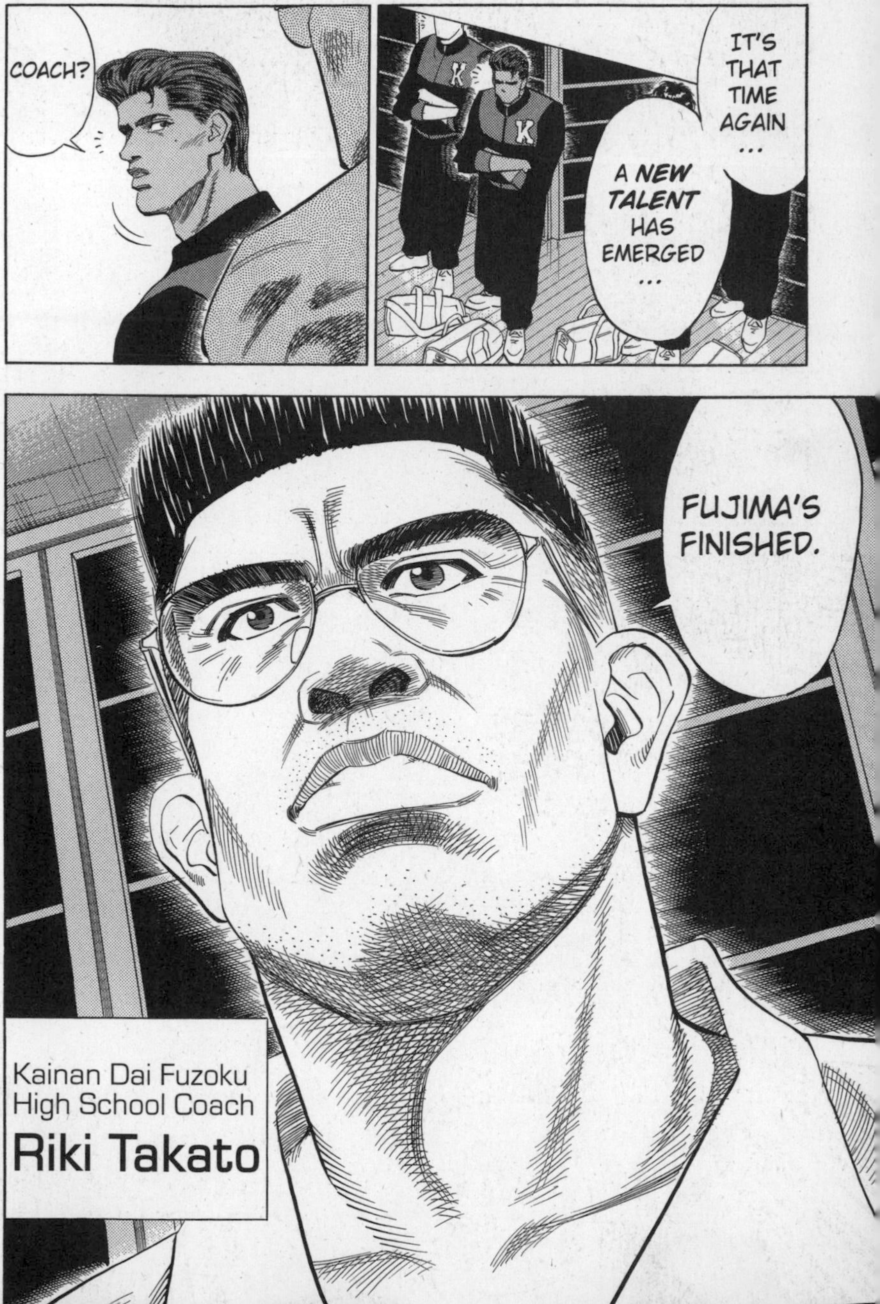
IT'S THAT TIME AGAIN ...
A NEW TALENT HAS EMERGED ...
COACH?
FUJIMA'S FINISHED.
Kainan Dai Fuzoku High School Coach
Riki Takato

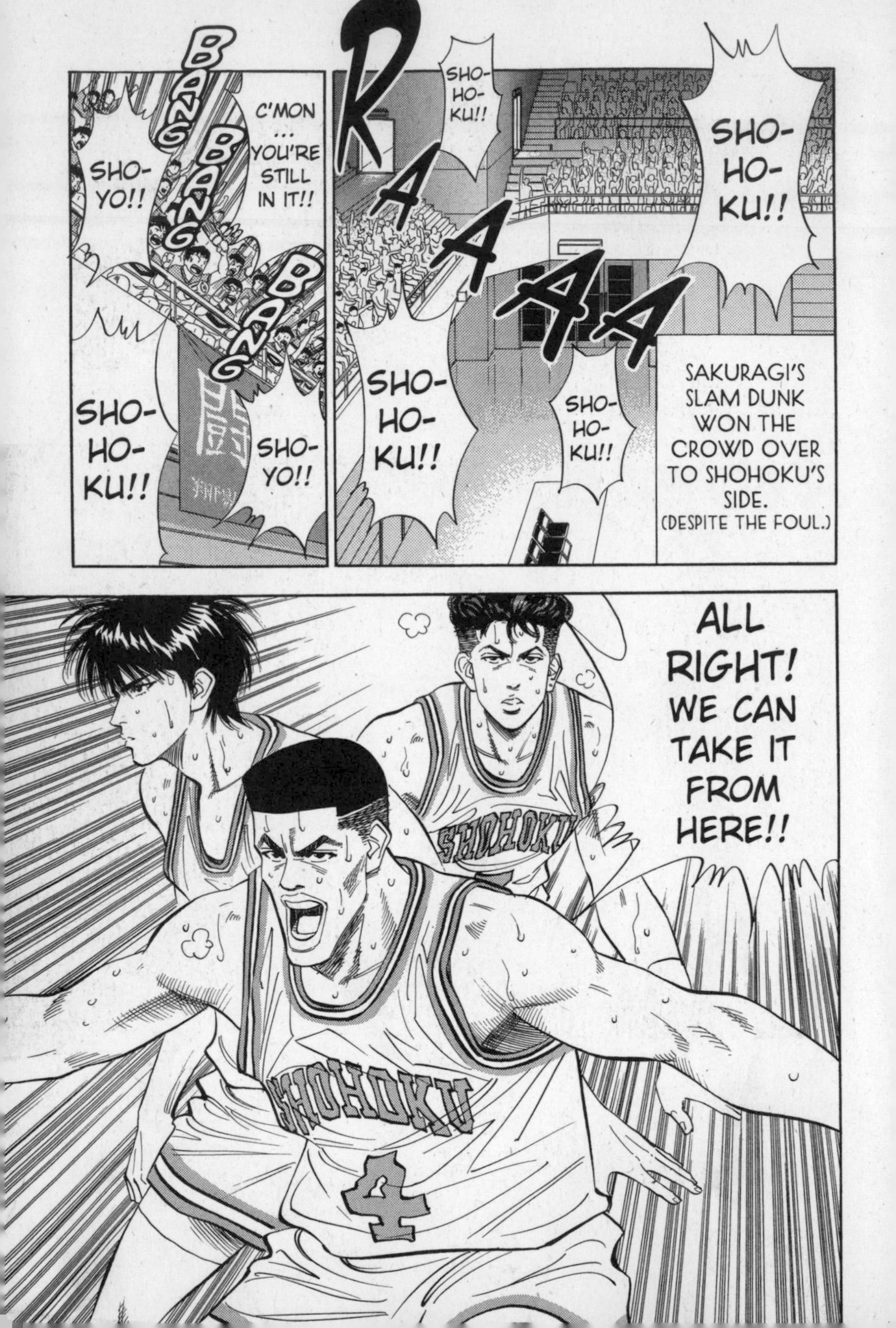
SHO-HO-KU!!
SHO-HO-KU!!
RAAAAA
SAKURAGI'S SLAM DUNK WON THE CROWD OVER TO SHOHOKU'S SIDE. (DESPITE THE FOUL.)
SHO-HO-KU!!
SHO-HO-KU!!
BANG BANG BANG BANG
C'MON ... YOU'RE STILL IN IT!!
SHO-YO!!
SHO-YO!!
SHO-HO-KU!!
ALL RIGHT! WE CAN TAKE IT FROM HERE!!

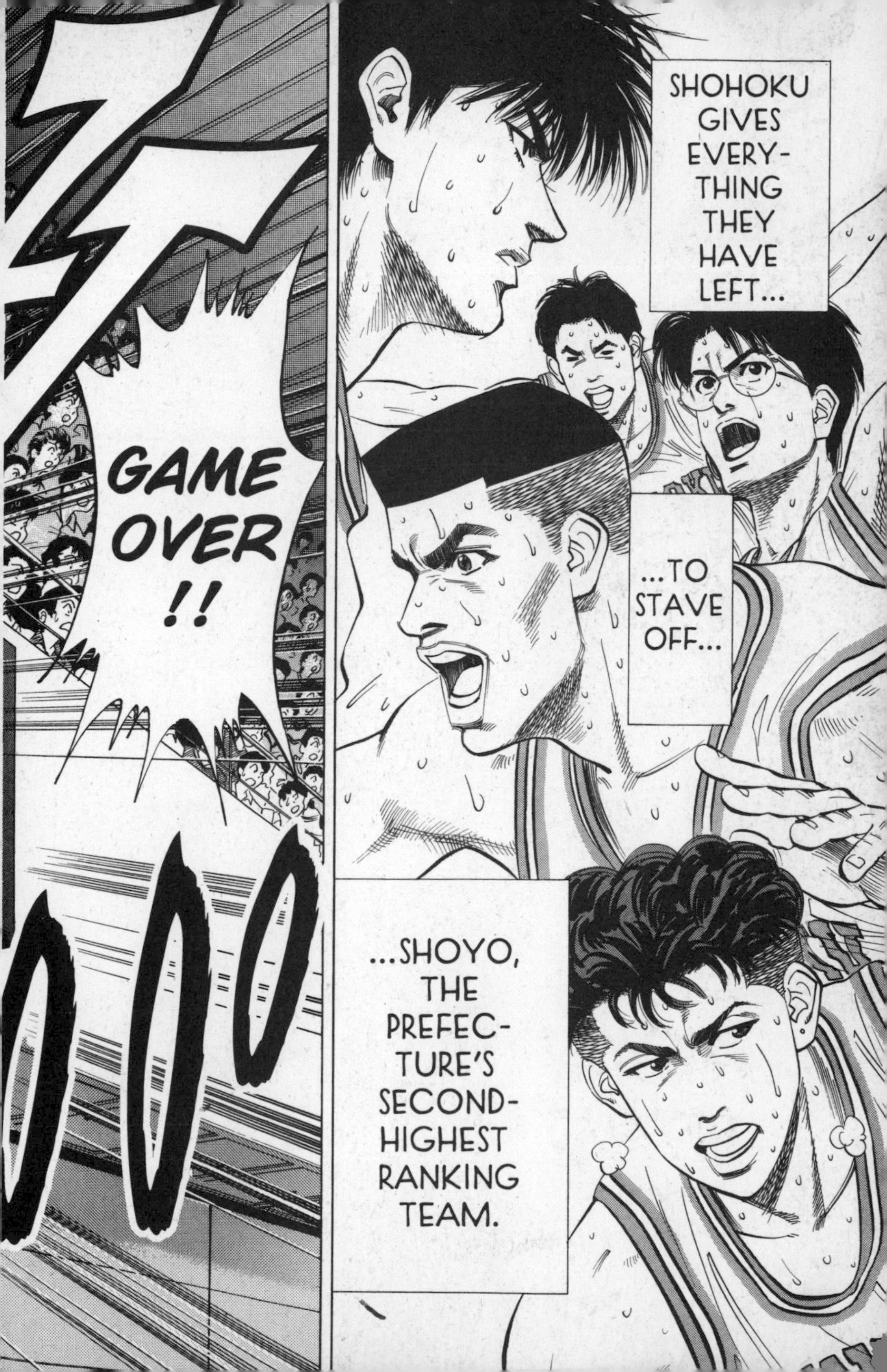
SHOHOKU GIVES EVERY-THING THEY HAVE LEFT...
...TO STAVE OFF...
...SHOYO, THE PREFEC-TURE'S SECOND-HIGHEST RANKING TEAM.
GAME OVER !!
OOO

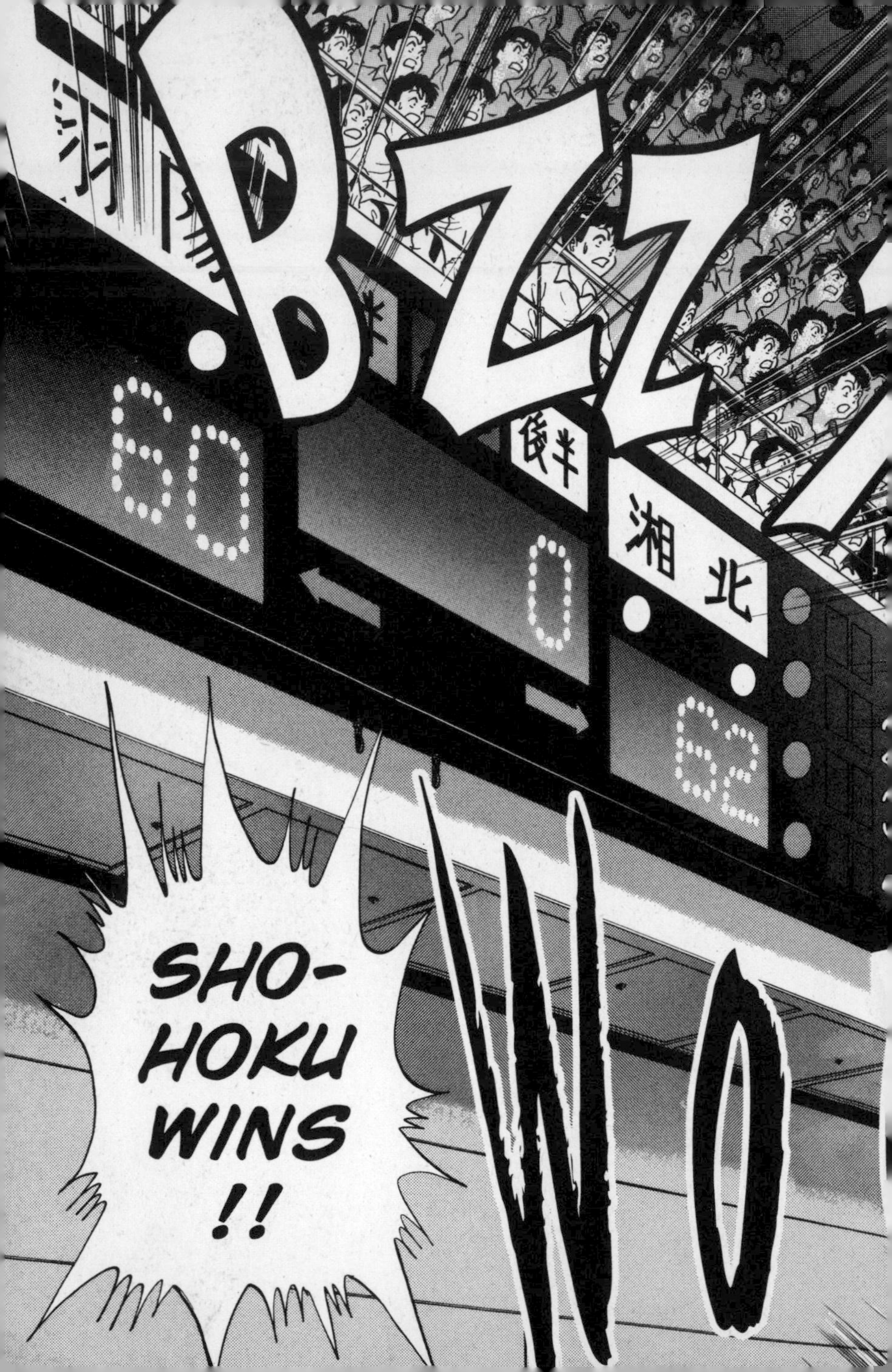
BZZ
後半
湘北
60
0
62
WO
SHO-
HOKU
WINS
!!

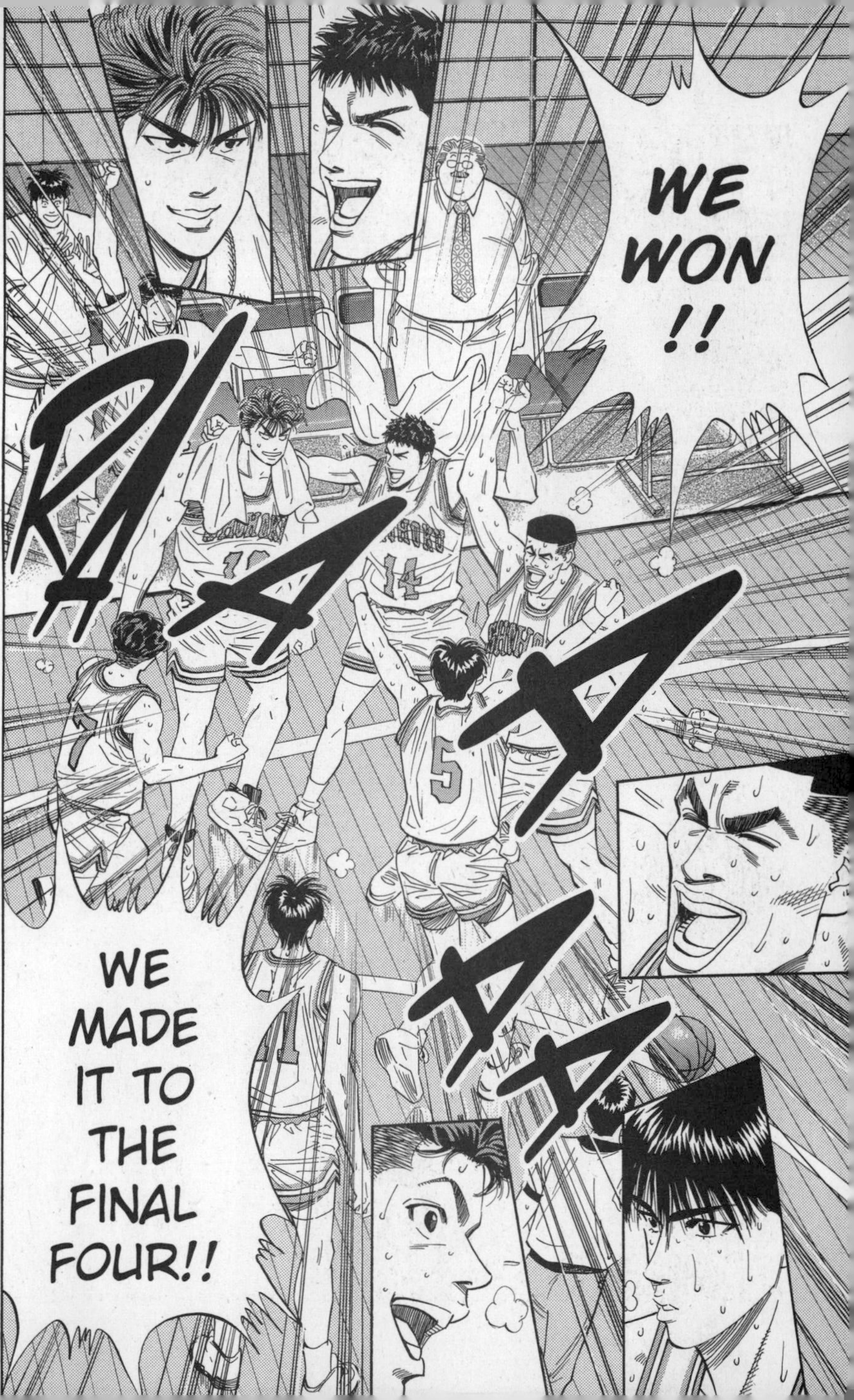
WE WON!!
RAAAAA
WE MADE IT TO THE FINAL FOUR!!

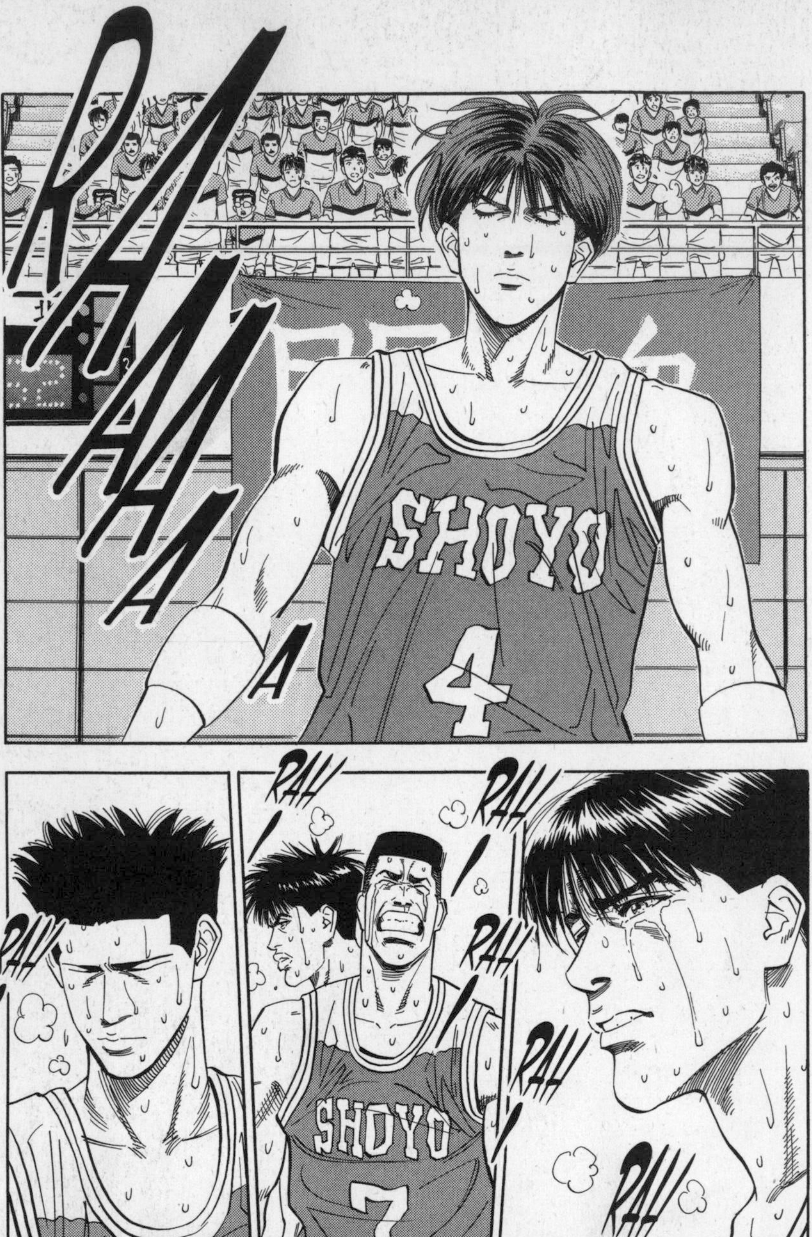
RAHAAAAA
SHOYO
4
RAH!
RAH!
RAH!
RAH!
RAH!
SHOYO
7
RAH!

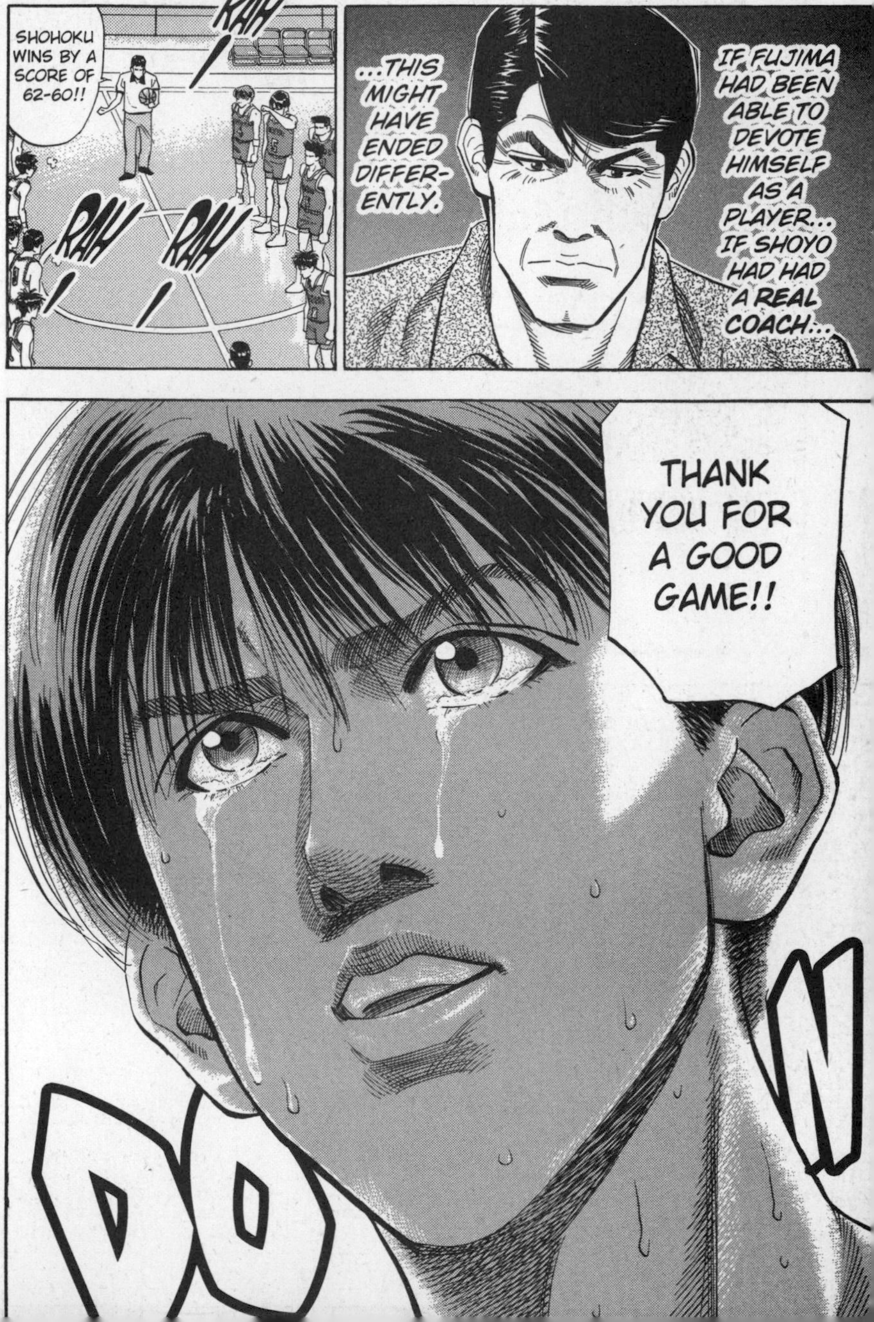
IF FUJIMA HAD BEEN ABLE TO DEVOTE HIMSELF AS A PLAYER... IF SHOYO HAD HAD A REAL COACH...
...THIS MIGHT HAVE ENDED DIFFER-ENTLY.
RAH!
SHOHOKU WINS BY A SCORE OF 62-60!!
RAH!
RAH!
THANK YOU FOR A GOOD GAME!!

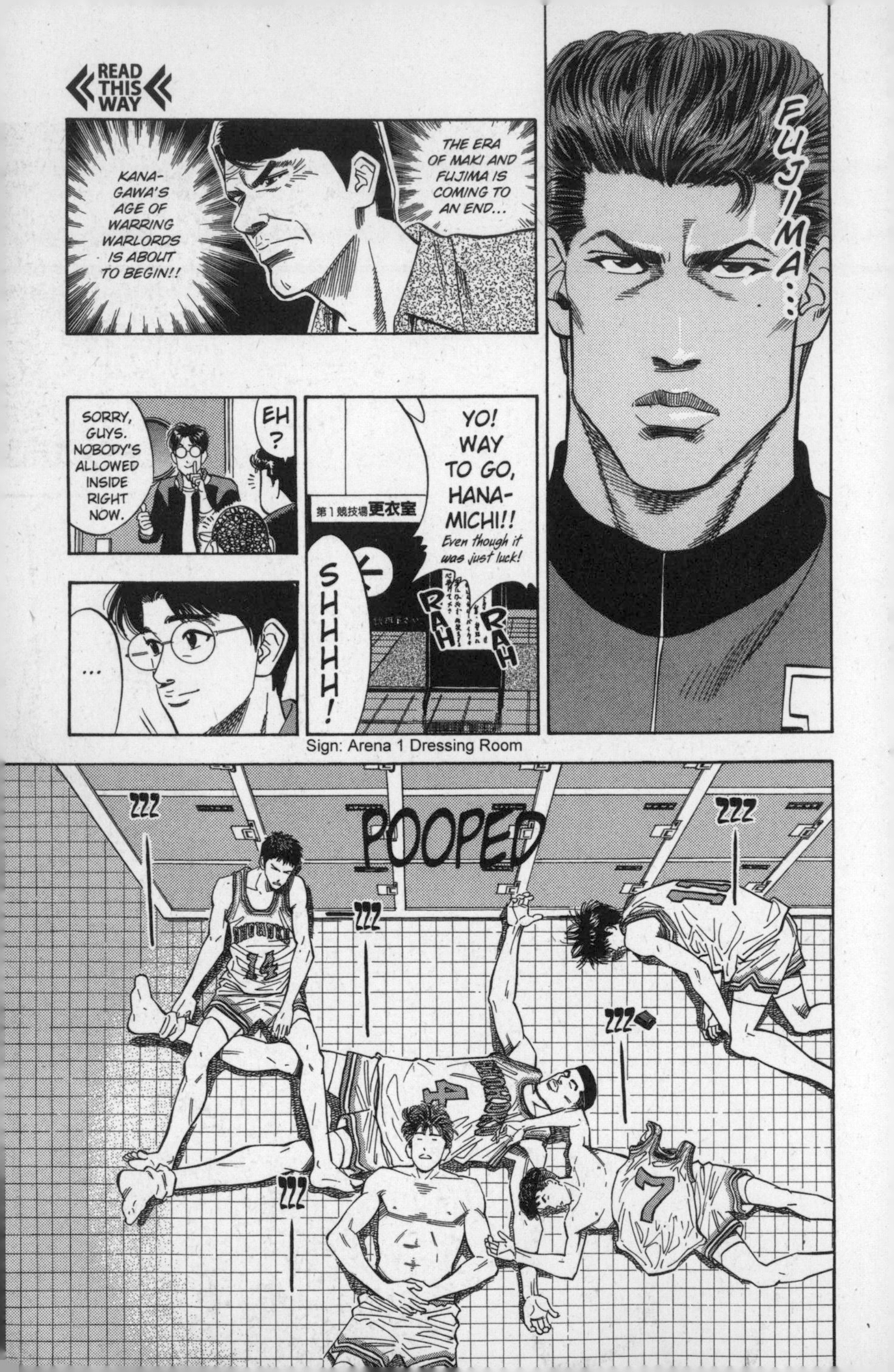
READ THIS WAY
FUJIMA...
THE ERA OF MAKI AND FUJIMA IS COMING TO AN END...
KANA-GAWA'S AGE OF WARRING WARLORDS IS ABOUT TO BEGIN!!
YO! WAY TO GO, HANA-MICHI!!
Even though it was just luck!
RAH
RAH
第1競技場更衣室
SHHHH!
EH?
SORRY, GUYS. NOBODY'S ALLOWED INSIDE RIGHT NOW.
...
POOPED
ZZZ
ZZZ
ZZZ
ZZZ
ZZZ
Sign: Arena 1 Dressing Room

MRPH...

SLAM DUNK

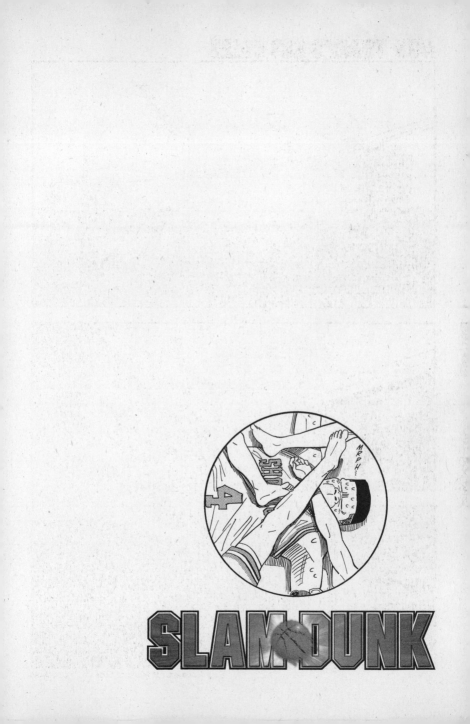

#98 TODAY'S HOT CELEB

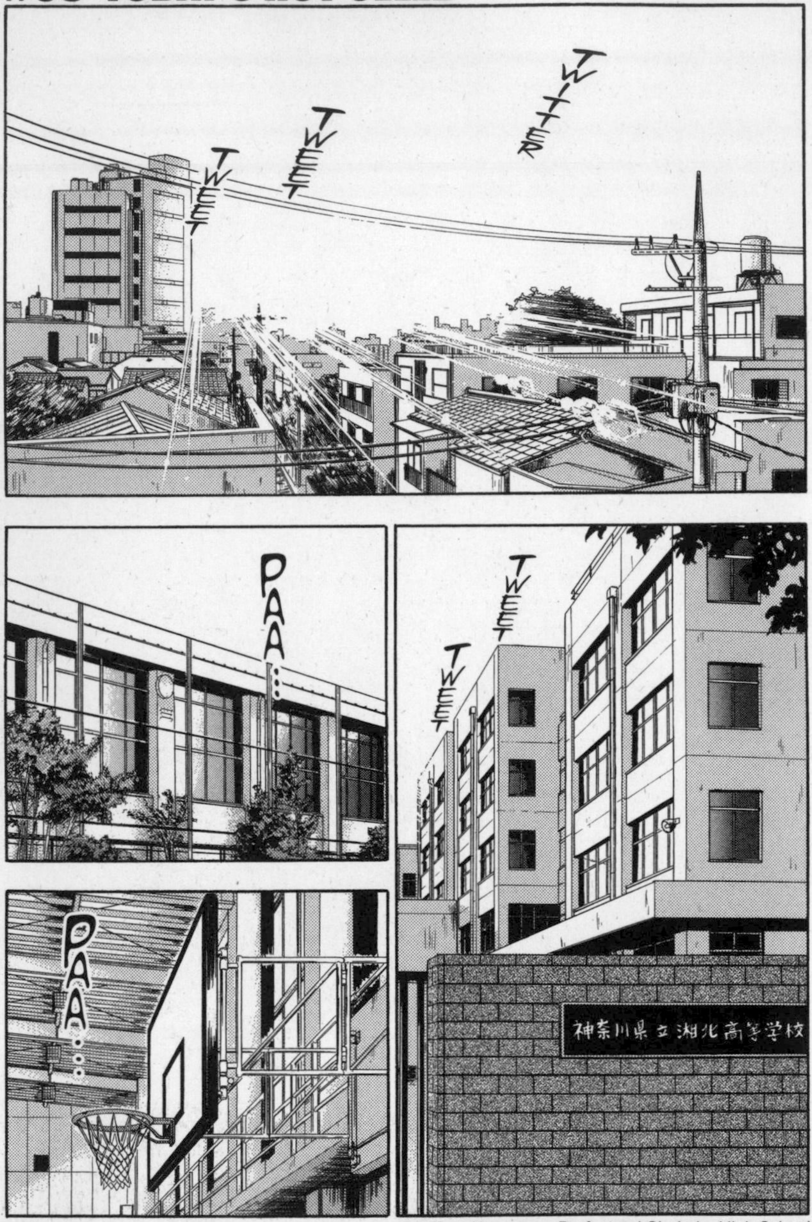
TWITTER
TWEET
TWEET
TWEET
TWEET
神奈川県立湘北高等学校
PAA...
PAA...

Sign: Kanagawa Prefectural Shohoku High School

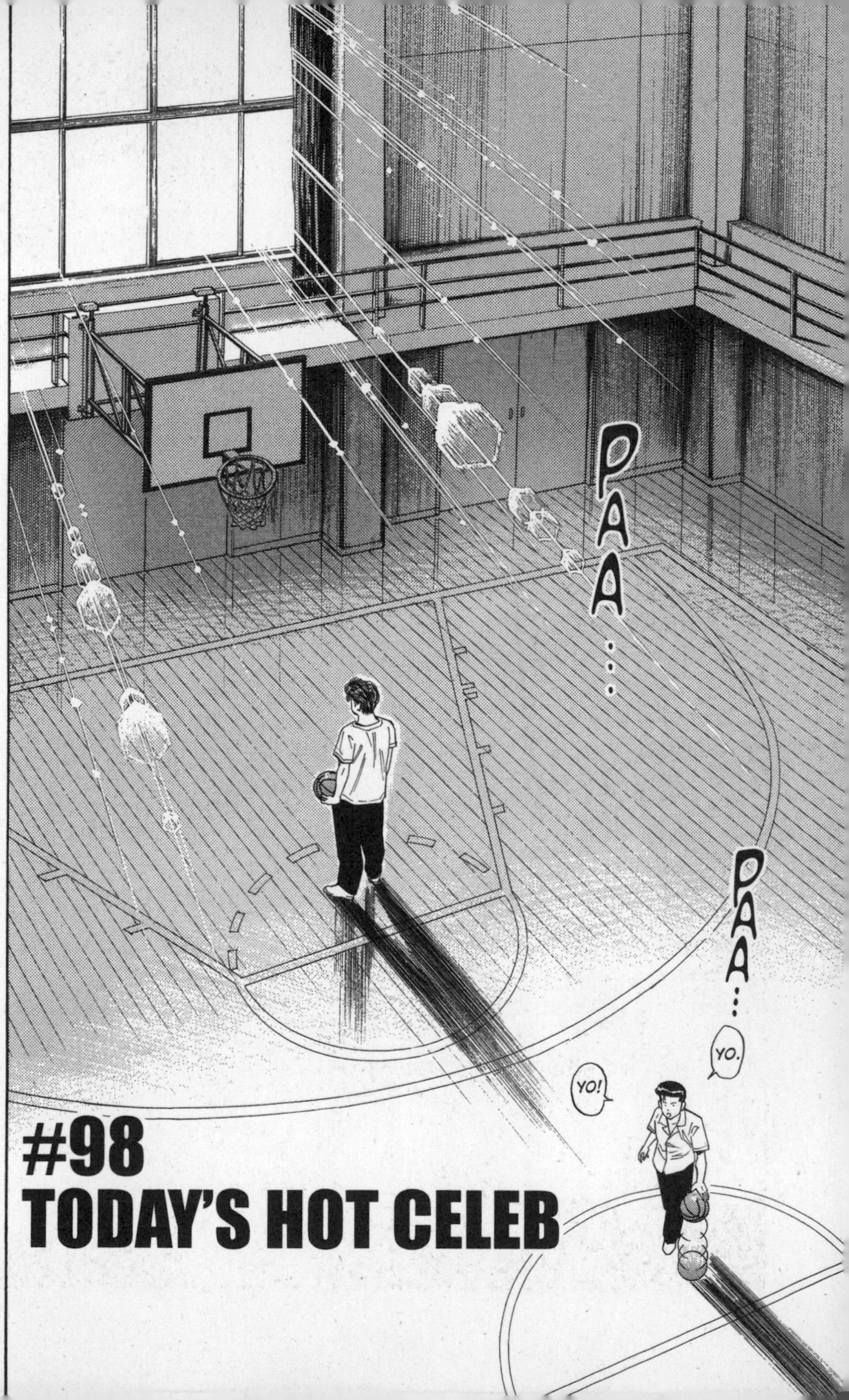
PAA...
PAA...
YO.
YO!

#98 TODAY'S HOT CELEB

READ THIS WAY

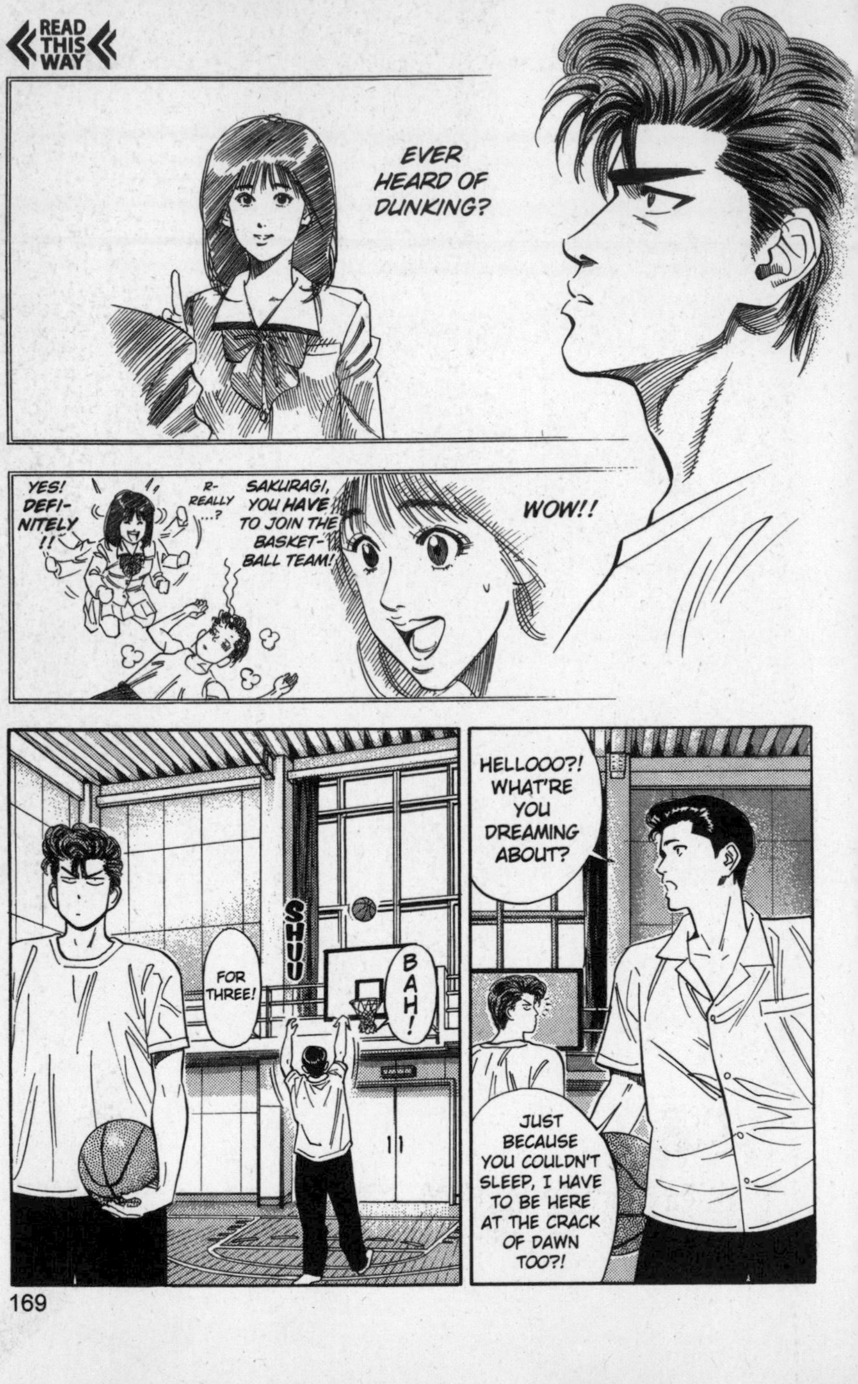
EVER HEARD OF DUNKING?
WOW!!
SAKURAGI, YOU HAVE TO JOIN THE BASKET-BALL TEAM!
R-REALLY ...?
YES! DEFI-NITELY!!
HELLOOO?! WHAT'RE YOU DREAMING ABOUT?
JUST BECAUSE YOU COULDN'T SLEEP, I HAVE TO BE HERE AT THE CRACK OF DAWN TOO?!
BAH!
SHUU
FOR THREE!

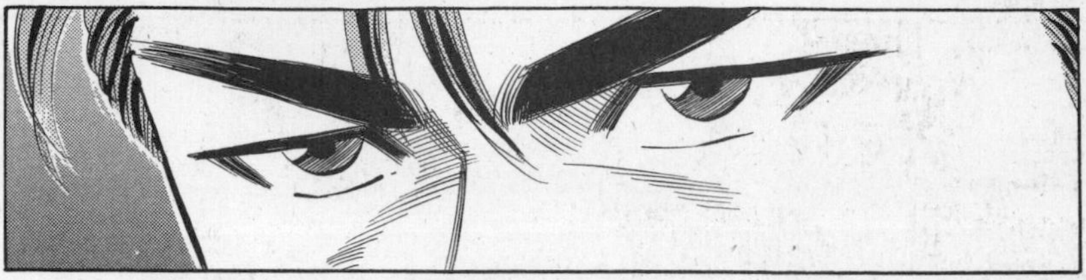

Scoreboard: Shoyo 1st Half Halftime 2nd Half Shohoku

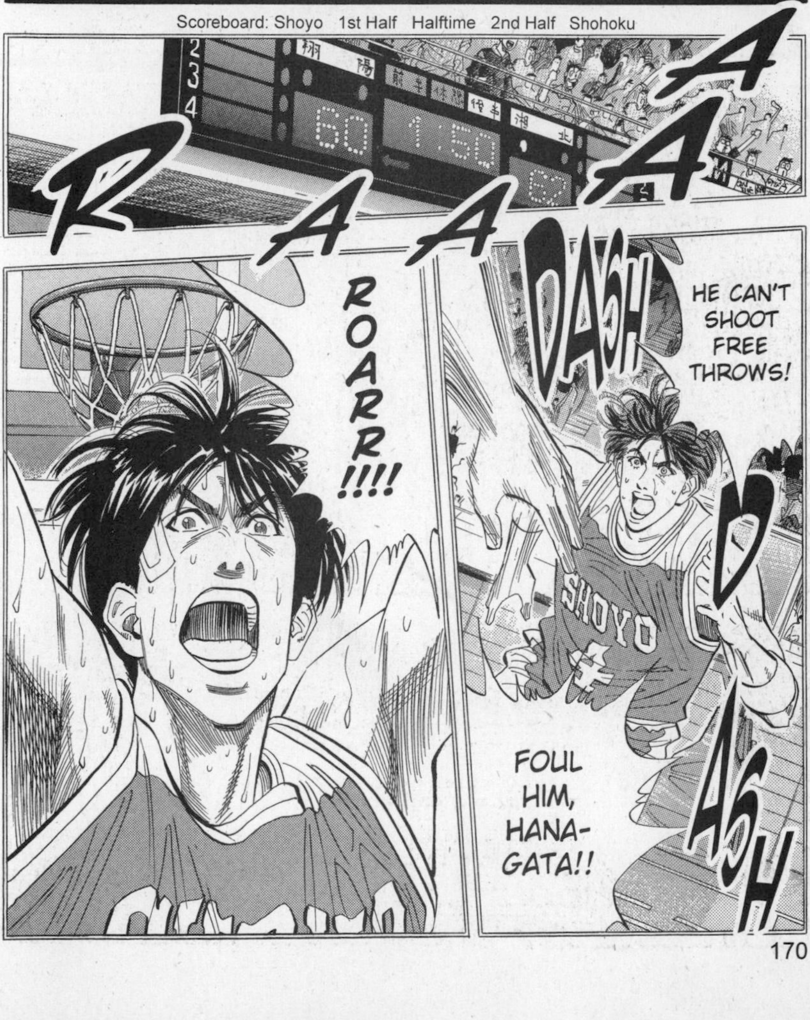
RAAAA
DASH
HE CAN'T SHOOT FREE THROWS!
FOUL HIM, HANA-GATA!!
DASH
ROARR!!!!

READ THIS WAY

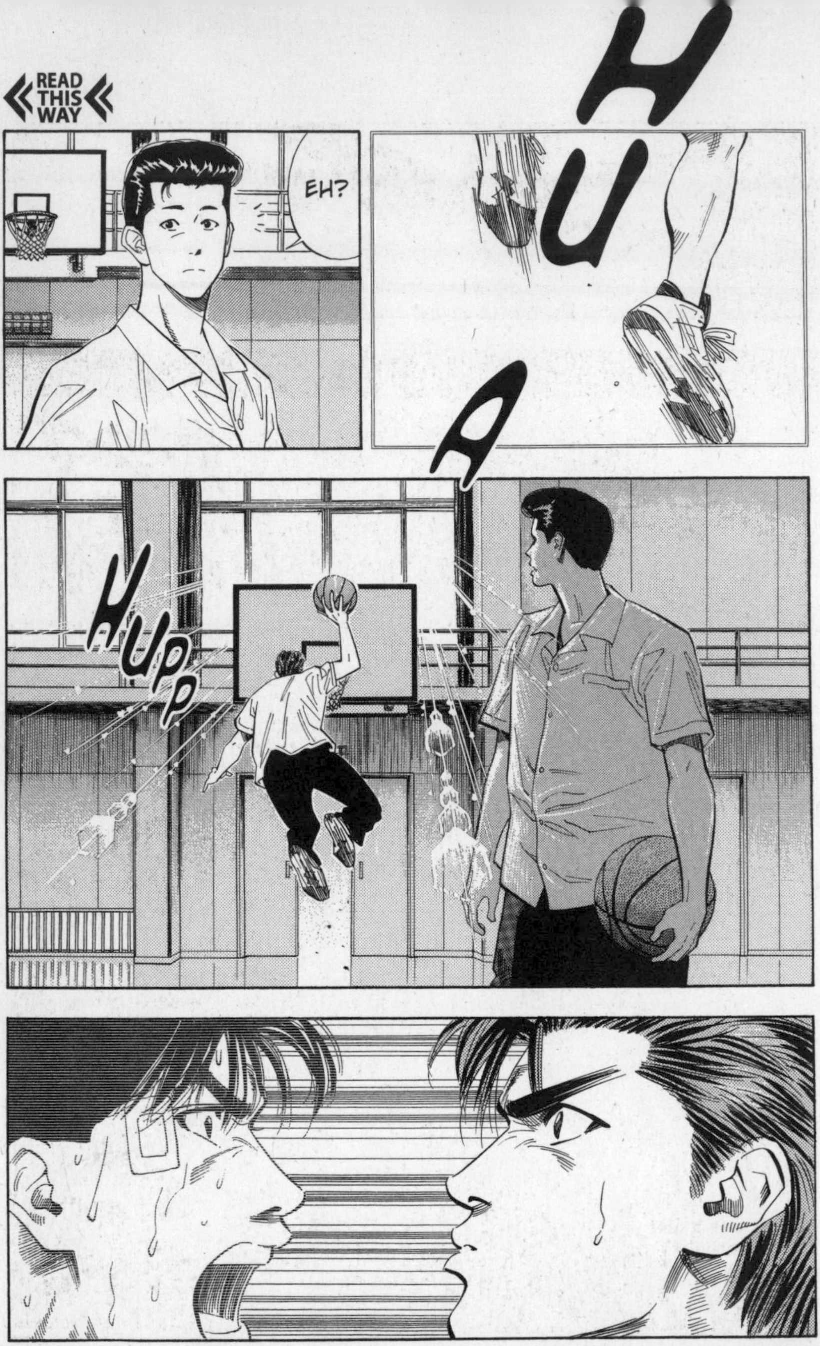
HUUA
EH?
HUPP

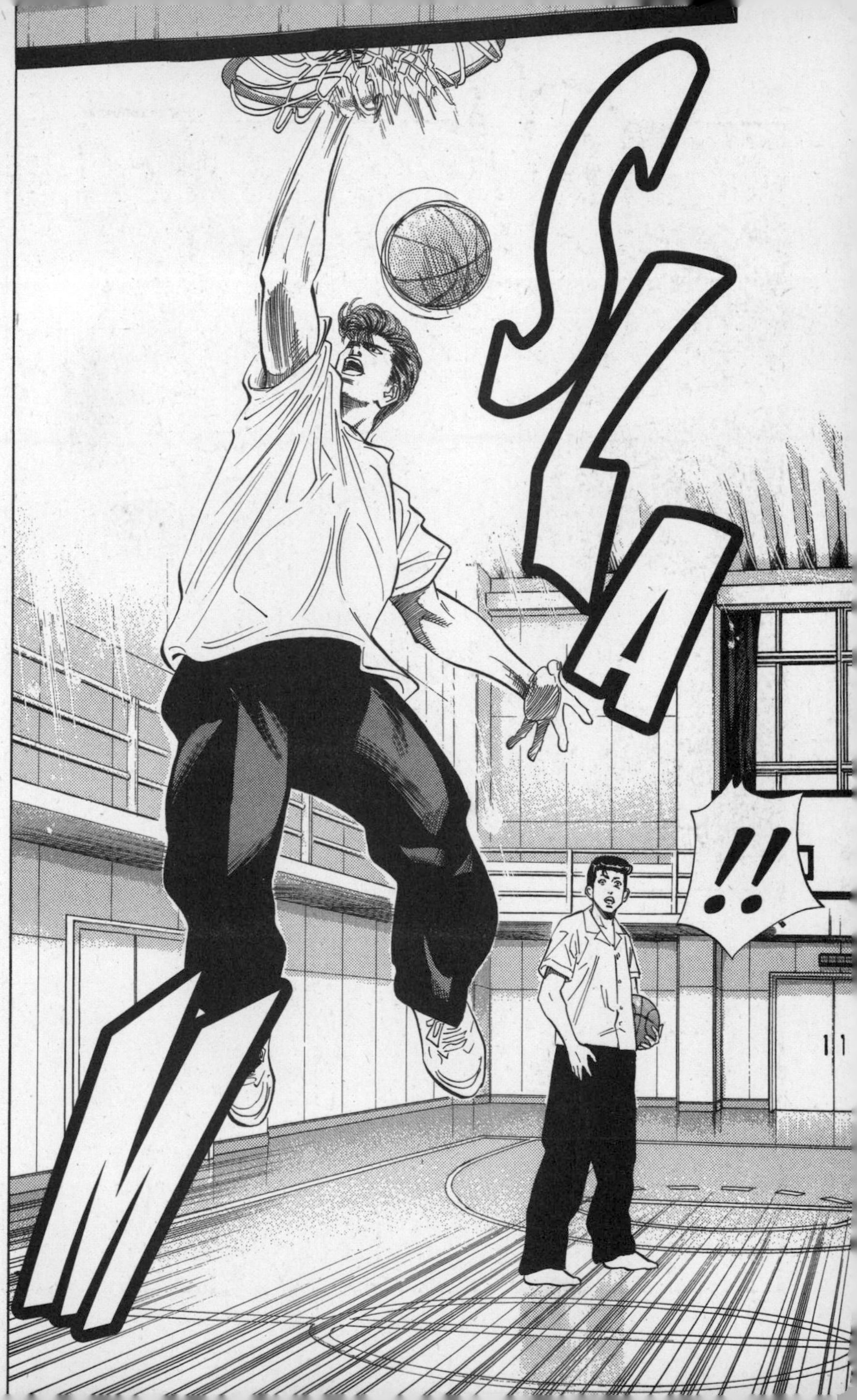
SLAM
!!

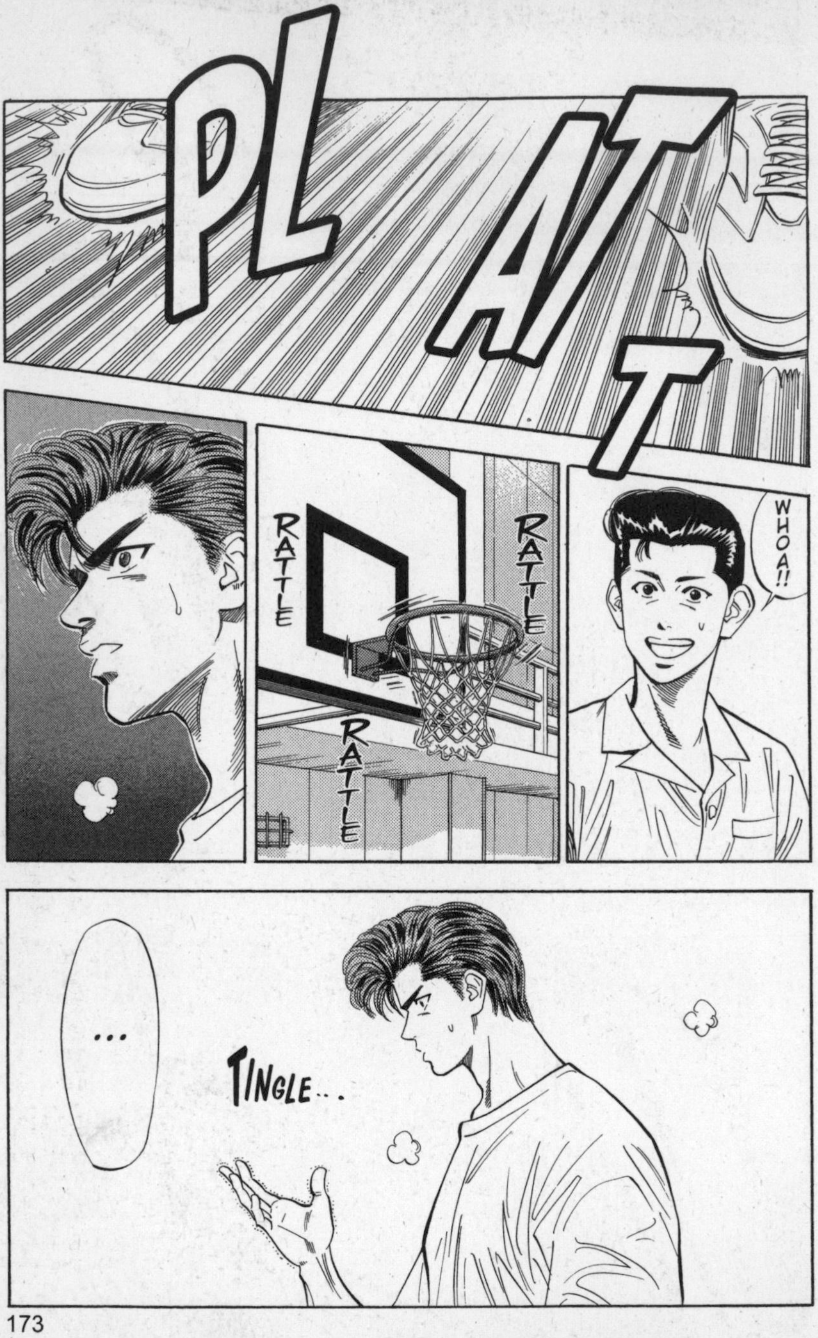
PLAT
WHOA!!
RATTLE
RATTLE
RATTLE
...
TINGLE...

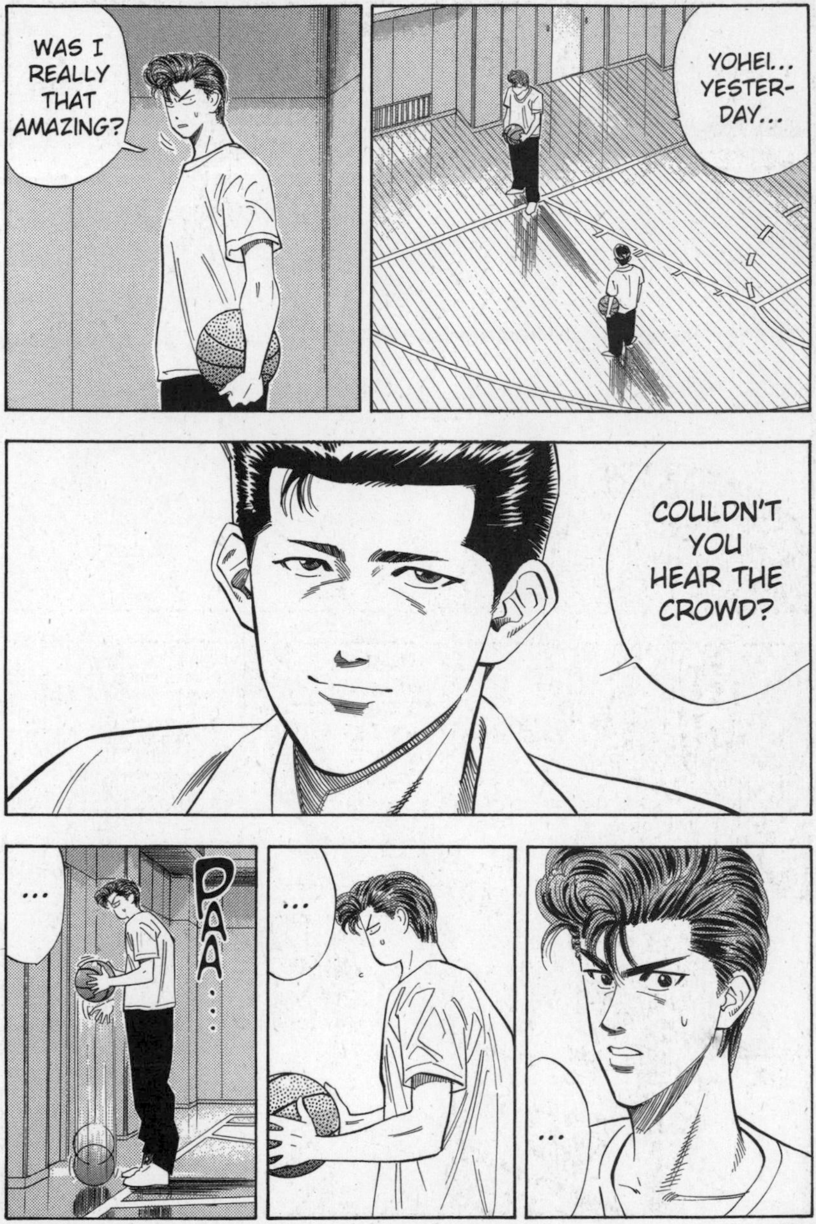
YOHEI... YESTER-DAY...
WAS I REALLY THAT AMAZING?
COULDN'T YOU HEAR THE CROWD?
...
...
PAA...
...

READ THIS WAY

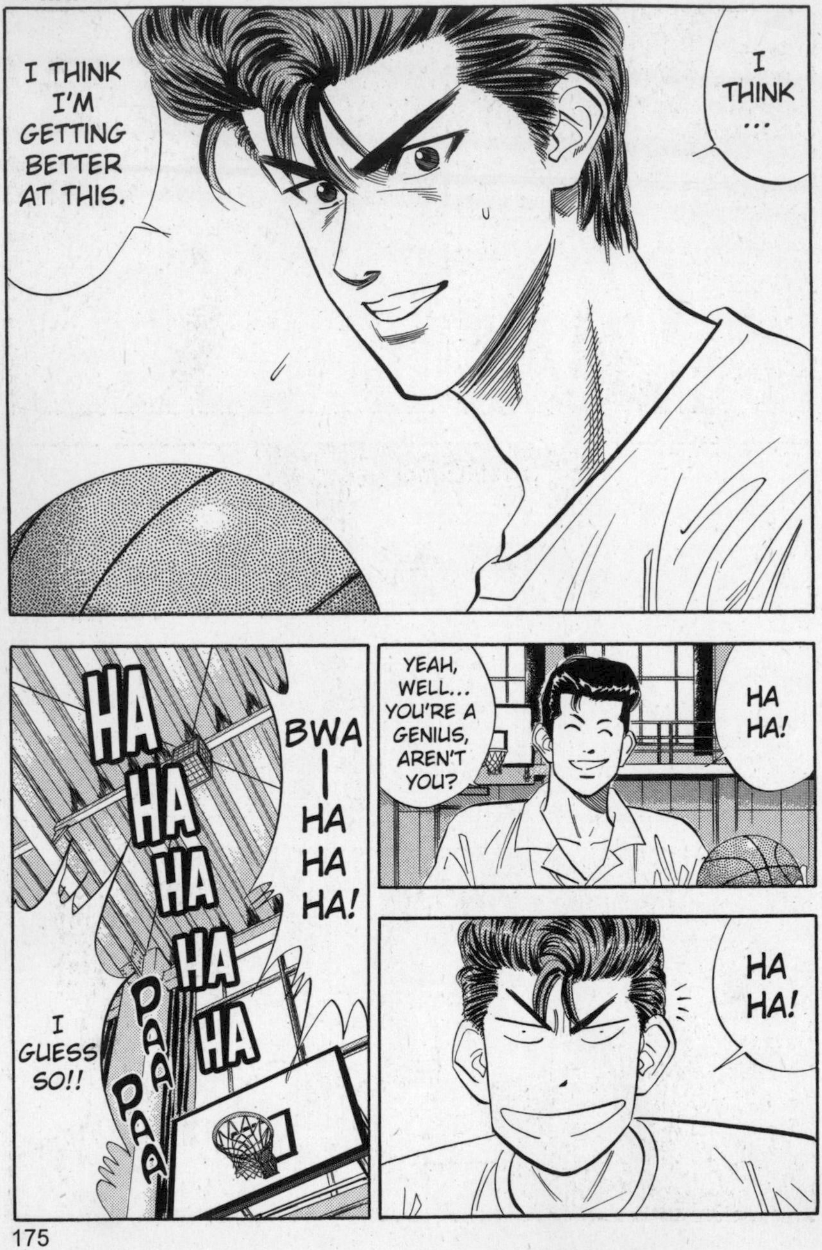
I THINK ...
I THINK I'M GETTING BETTER AT THIS.
HA HA!
YEAH, WELL... YOU'RE A GENIUS, AREN'T YOU?
HA HA!
BWA-HA HA HA HA!
HA HA HA HA HA HA
I GUESS SO!!
PAA PAA

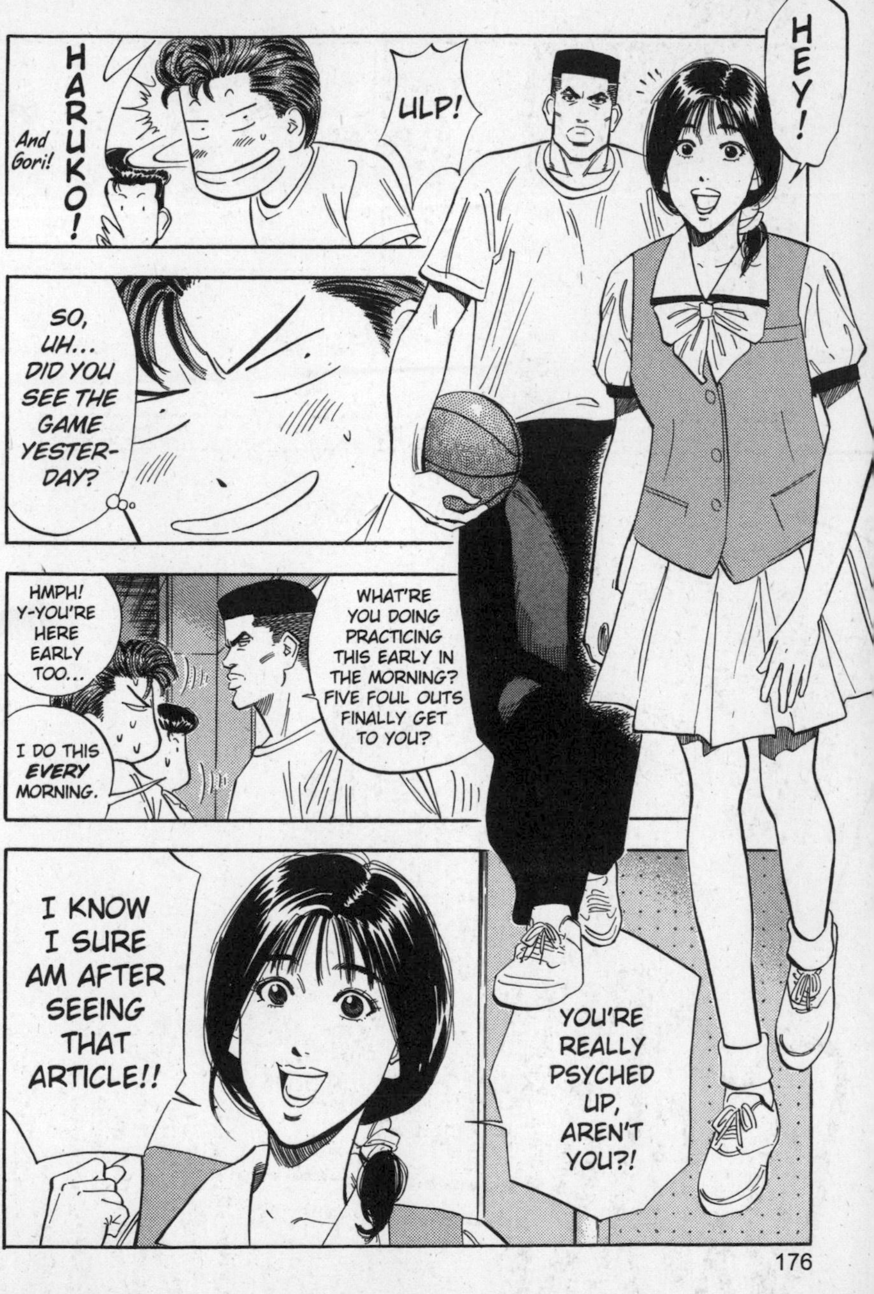
HEY!
YOU'RE REALLY PSYCHED UP, AREN'T YOU?!
ULP!
HARUKO!
And Gori!
SO, UH... DID YOU SEE THE GAME YESTER-DAY?
WHAT'RE YOU DOING PRACTICING THIS EARLY IN THE MORNING? FIVE FOUL OUTS FINALLY GET TO YOU?
HMPH! Y-YOU'RE HERE EARLY TOO...
I DO THIS *EVERY* MORNING.
I KNOW I SURE AM AFTER SEEING THAT ARTICLE!!

READ THIS WAY

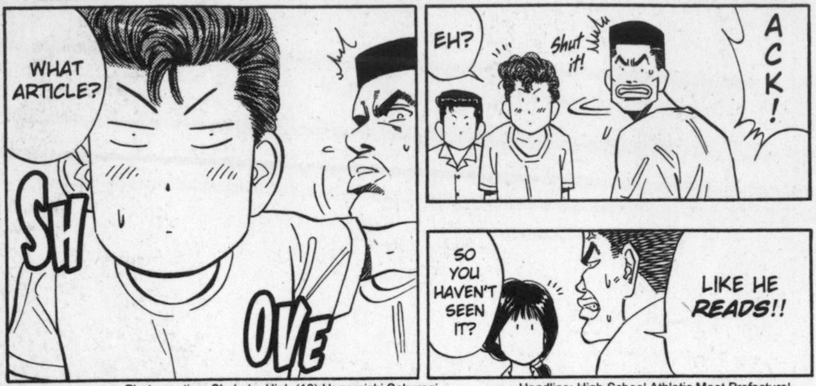
ACK!
Shut it!
EH?
LIKE HE READS!!
SO YOU HAVEN'T SEEN IT?
WHAT ARTICLE?
SHOVE

Photo caption: Shohoku High (10) Hanamichi Sakuragi with a dynamic dunk. Shoyo High (7) Nagano also pictured.

Headline: High School Athletic Meet Prefectural Qualifier Shoyo Loses Boy's Basketball

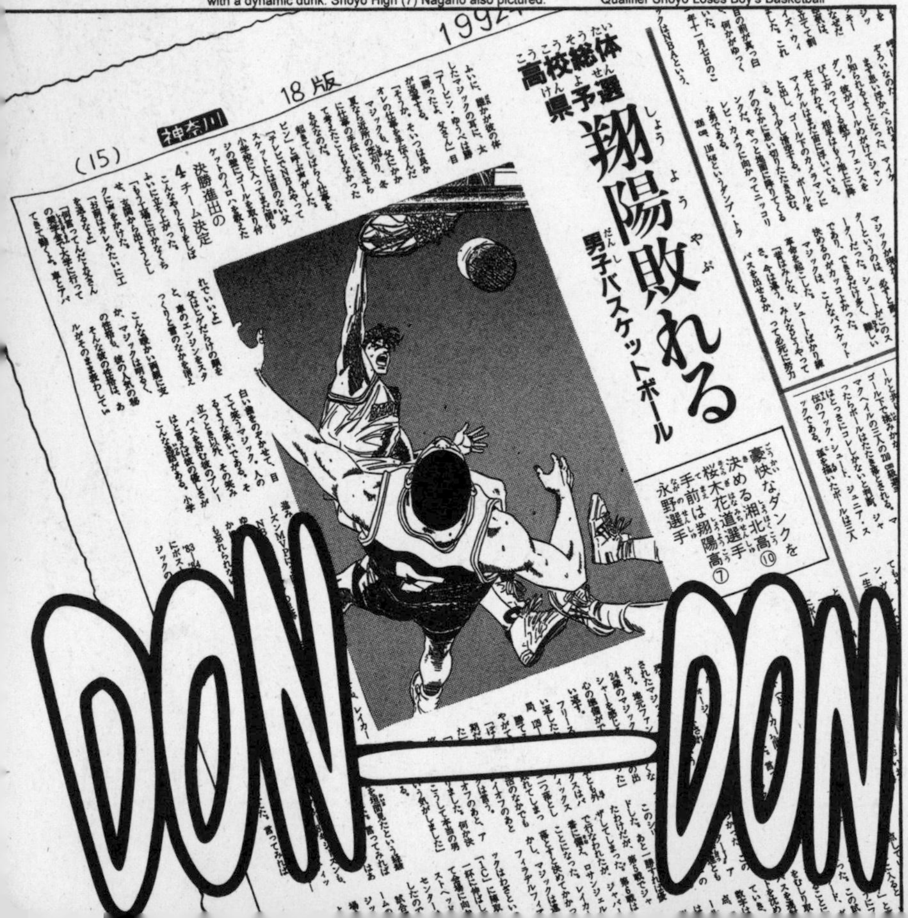
高校総体
県予選
翔陽敗れる
男子バスケットボール
豪快なダンクを決める湘北高⑩桜木花道選手
手前は翔陽高⑦永野選手
神奈川
18版
(15)
DON
DON

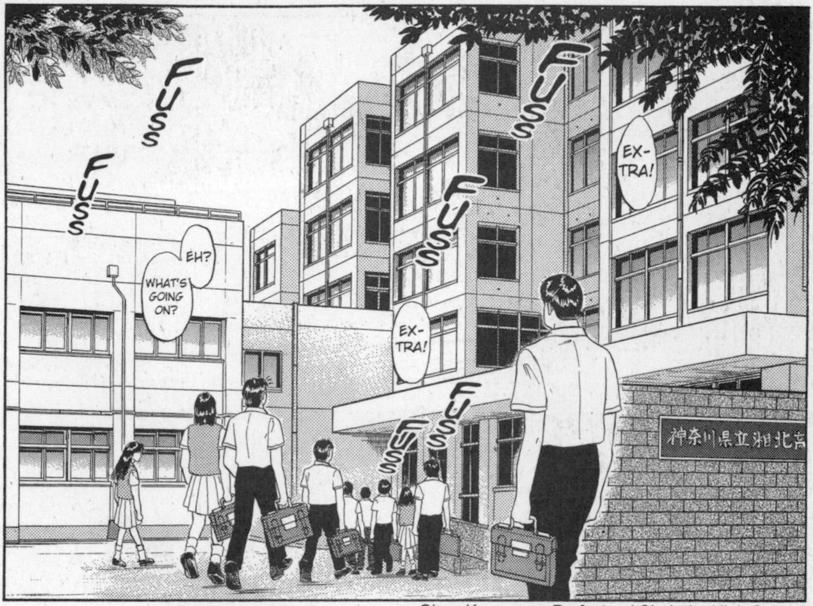
FUSS
EX-TRA!
FUSS
FUSS
FUSS
FUSS
EH?
WHAT'S GOING ON?
EX-TRA!
FUSS
FUSS
神奈川県立湘北高

Sign: Kanagawa Prefectural Shohoku High School

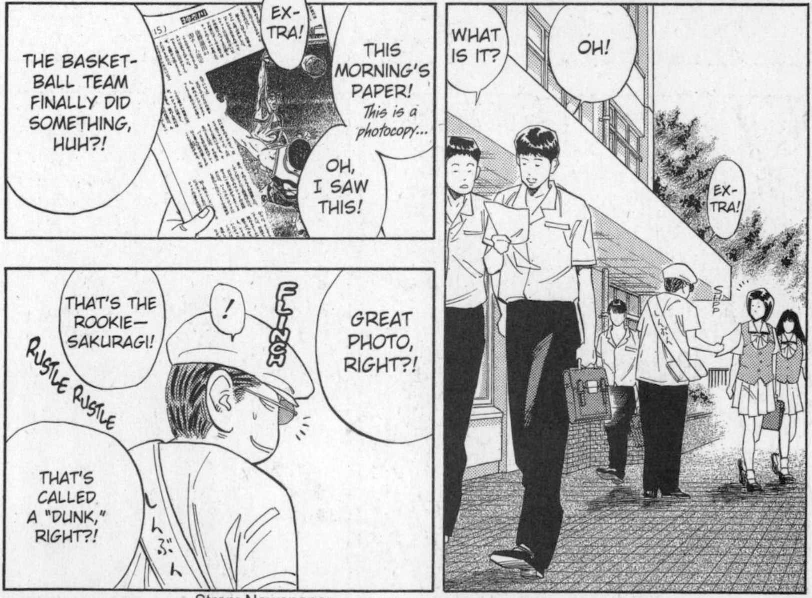
OH!
WHAT IS IT?
EX-TRA!
EX-TRA!
THIS MORNING'S PAPER!
This is a photocopy...
OH, I SAW THIS!
THE BASKETBALL TEAM FINALLY DID SOMETHING, HUH?!
GREAT PHOTO, RIGHT?!
FLINCH
!
THAT'S THE ROOKIE—SAKURAGI!
RUSTLE RUSTLE
THAT'S CALLED A "DUNK," RIGHT?!
しんぶん

Strap: Newspaper

READ THIS WAY

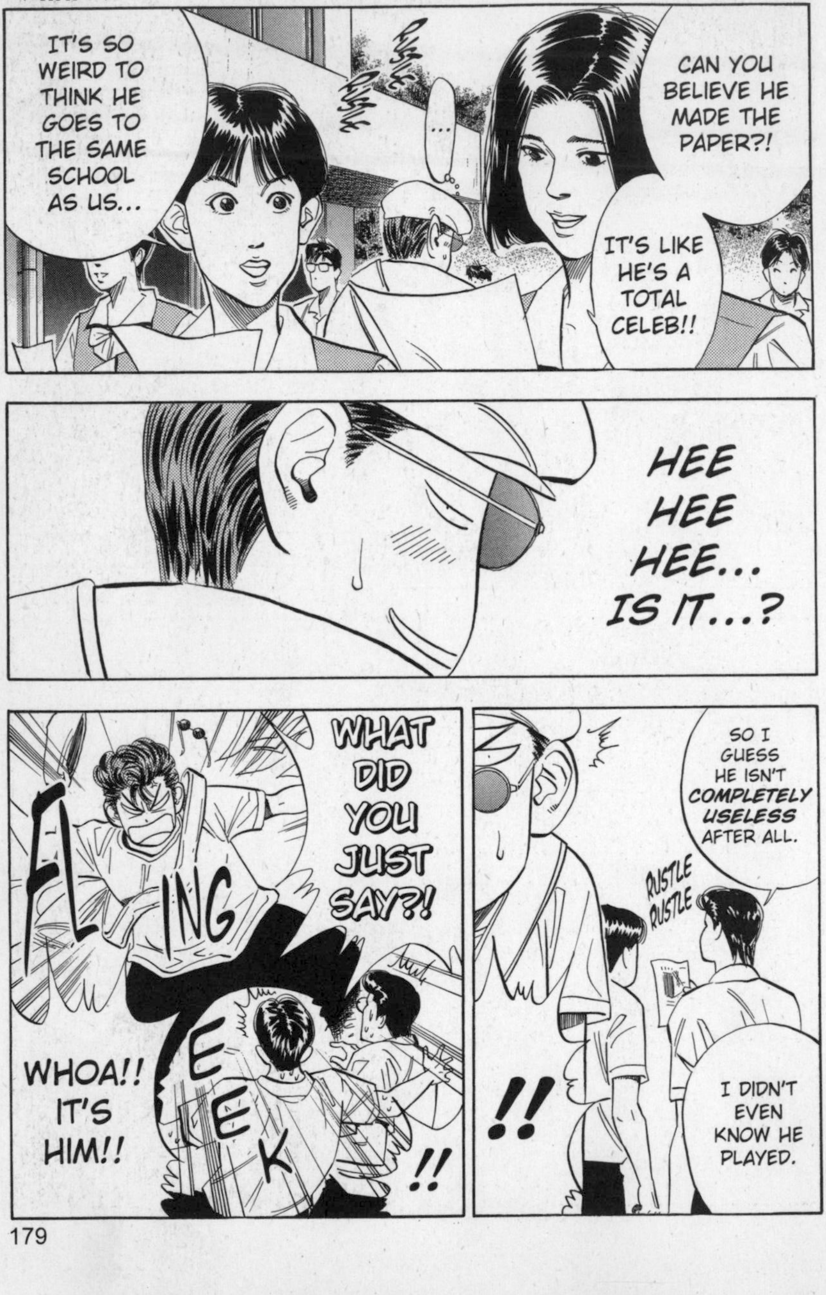

CAN YOU BELIEVE HE MADE THE PAPER?!
IT'S LIKE HE'S A TOTAL CELEB!!
...
IT'S SO WEIRD TO THINK HE GOES TO THE SAME SCHOOL AS US...
HEE HEE HEE... IS IT...?
SO I GUESS HE ISN'T COMPLETELY USELESS AFTER ALL.
RUSTLE RUSTLE
I DIDN'T EVEN KNOW HE PLAYED.
!!
WHAT DID YOU JUST SAY?!
FLING
EEEK!!
WHOA!! IT'S HIM!!

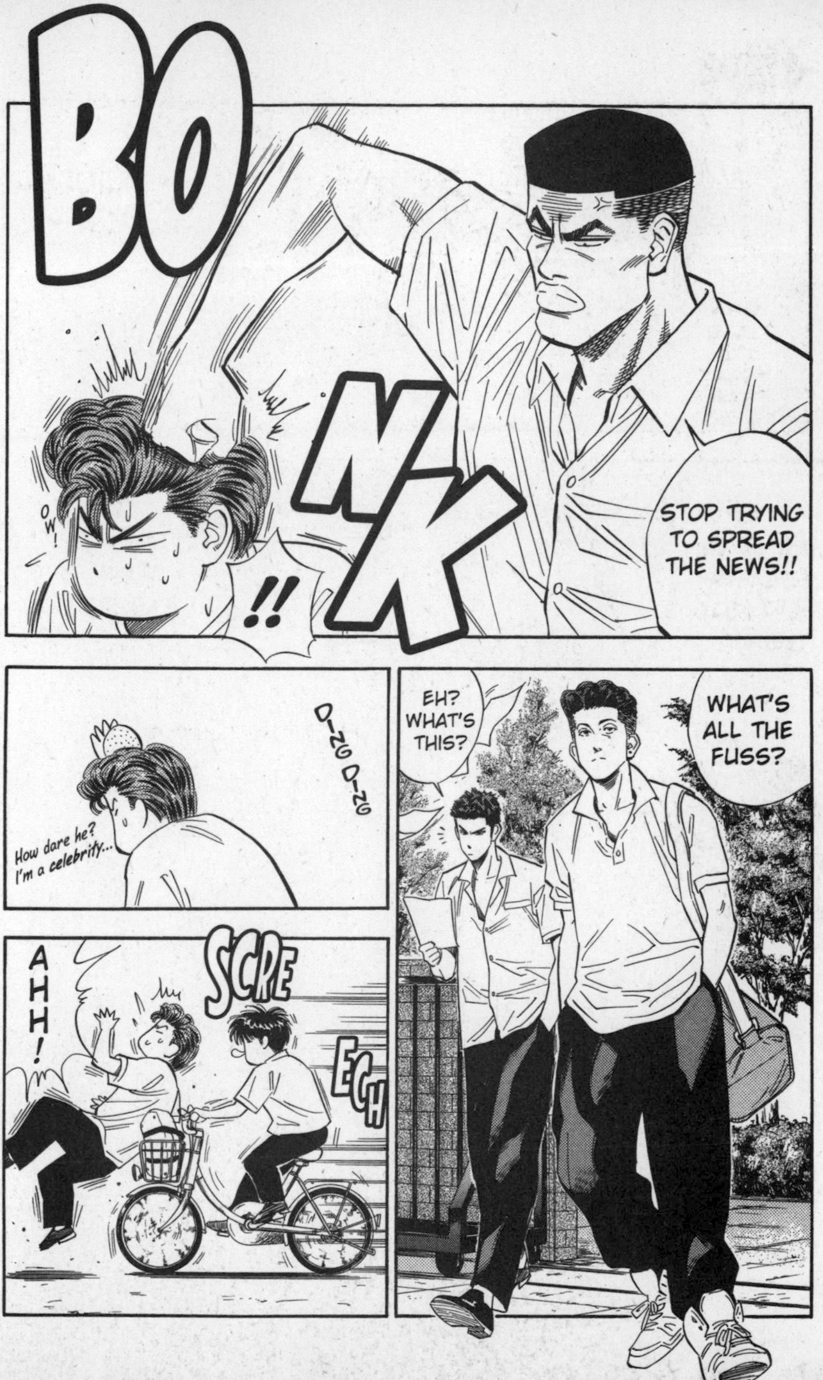
STOP TRYING TO SPREAD THE NEWS!!
BONK
OW!
!!
WHAT'S ALL THE FUSS?
EH? WHAT'S THIS?
DING DING
How dare he? I'm a celebrity...
SCREECH
AHH!

READ THIS WAY

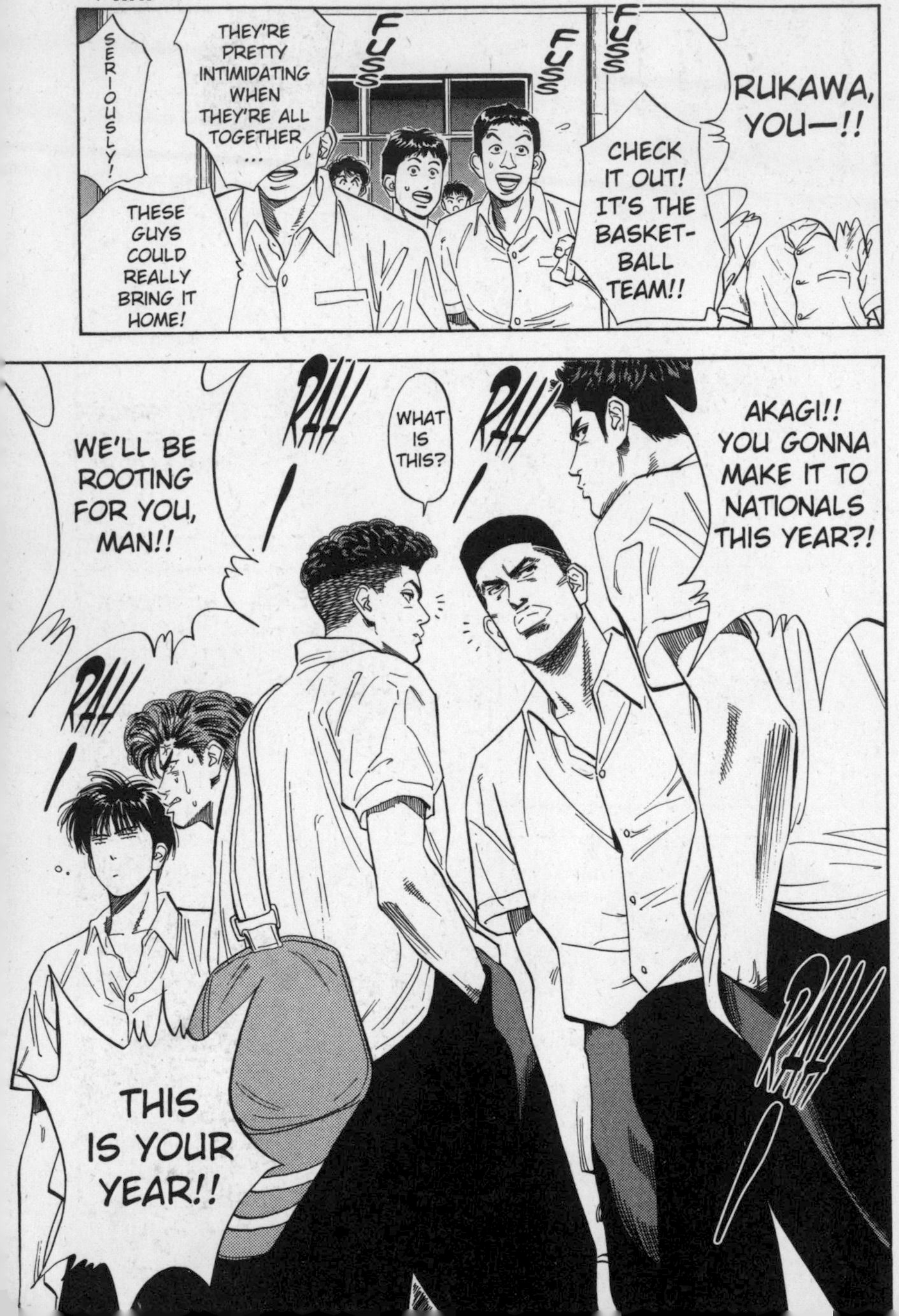
RUKAWA, YOU—!!
FUSS
CHECK IT OUT! IT'S THE BASKET-BALL TEAM!!
FUSS
FUSS
THEY'RE PRETTY INTIMIDATING WHEN THEY'RE ALL TOGETHER...
SERIOUSLY!
THESE GUYS COULD REALLY BRING IT HOME!
AKAGI!! YOU GONNA MAKE IT TO NATIONALS THIS YEAR?!
RAH!
WHAT IS THIS?
RAH!
WE'LL BE ROOTING FOR YOU, MAN!!
RAH!
RAH!
THIS IS YOUR YEAR!!

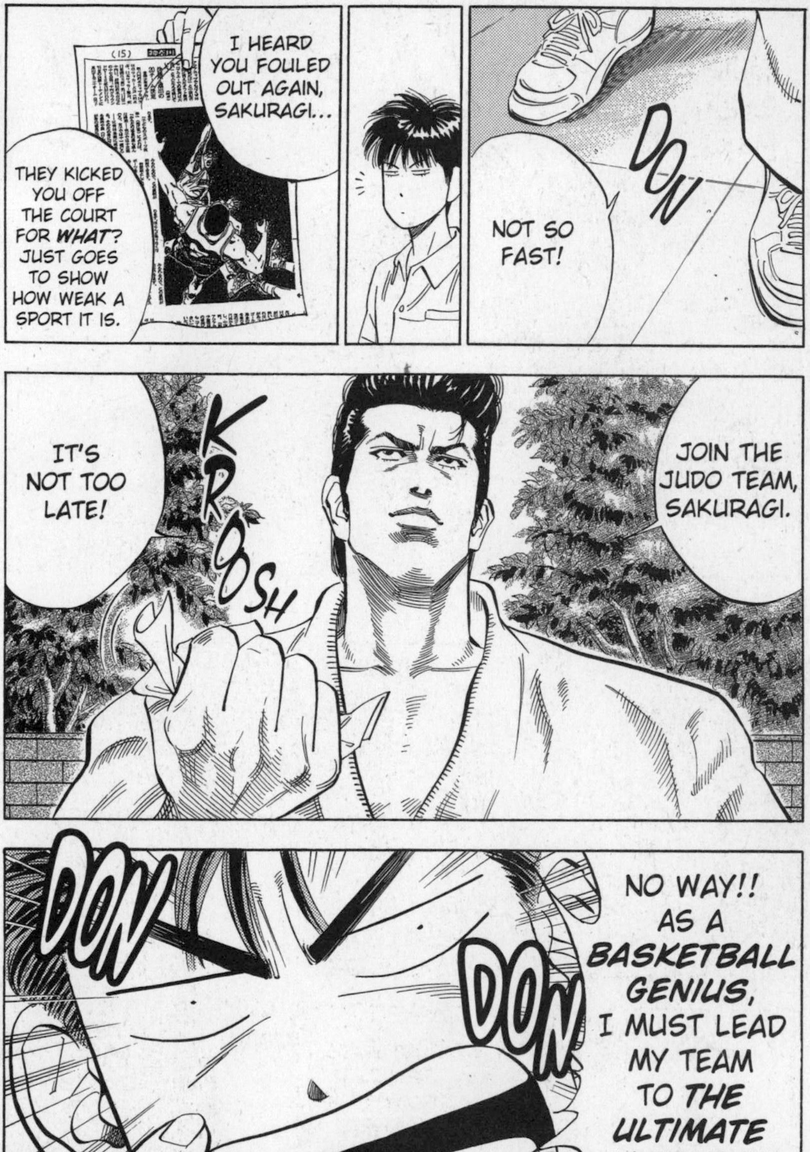
DON
NOT SO FAST!
I HEARD YOU FOULED OUT AGAIN, SAKURAGI...
THEY KICKED YOU OFF THE COURT FOR *WHAT*? JUST GOES TO SHOW HOW WEAK A SPORT IT IS.
JOIN THE JUDO TEAM, SAKURAGI.
KROOSH
IT'S NOT TOO LATE!
NO WAY!! AS A *BASKETBALL GENIUS*, I MUST LEAD MY TEAM TO *THE ULTIMATE VICTORY*!!
DON
DON

READ THIS WAY

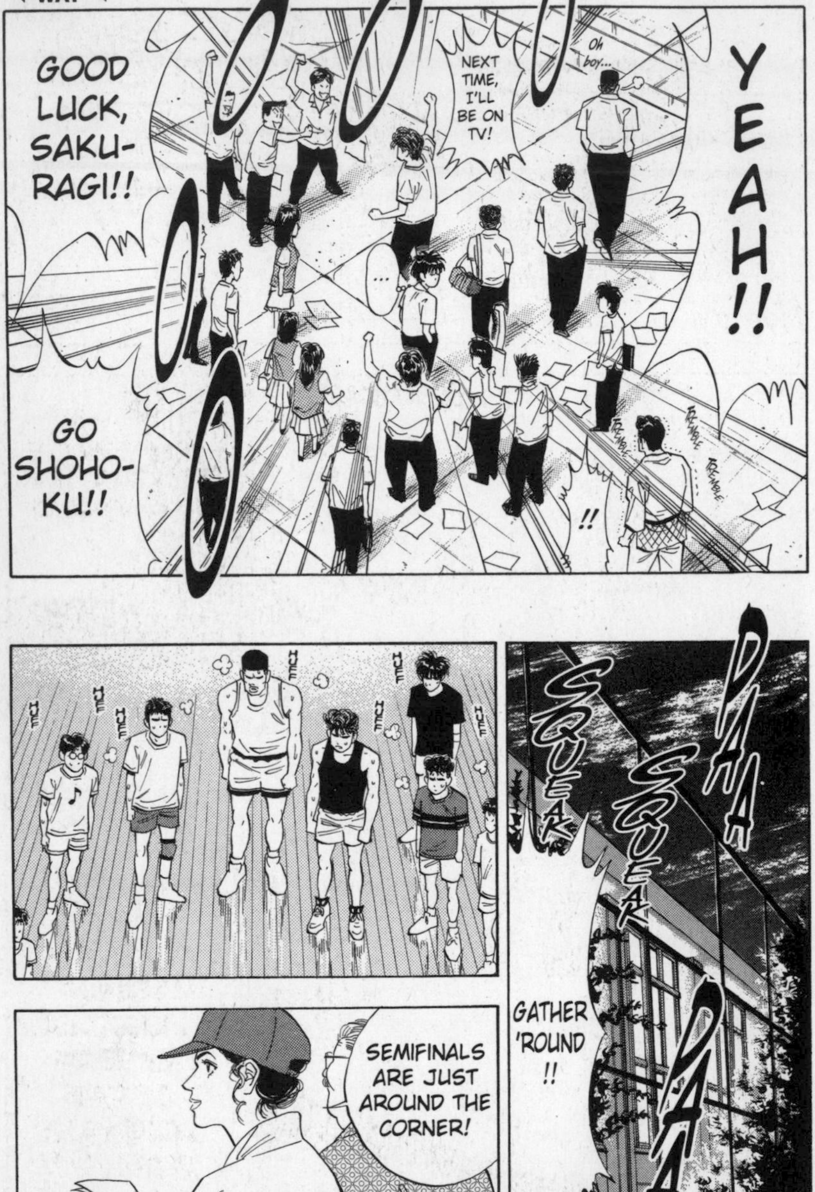
YEAH!!
Oh boy...
NEXT TIME, I'LL BE ON TV!
...
GOOD LUCK, SAKU-RAGI!!
GO SHOHO-KU!!
TREMBLE TREMBLE TREMBLE TREMBLE
!!
DAA
SQUEAK
SQUEAK
DAAA
GATHER 'ROUND!!
HUFF HUFF HUFF HUFF HUFF HUFF
SEMIFINALS ARE JUST AROUND THE CORNER!

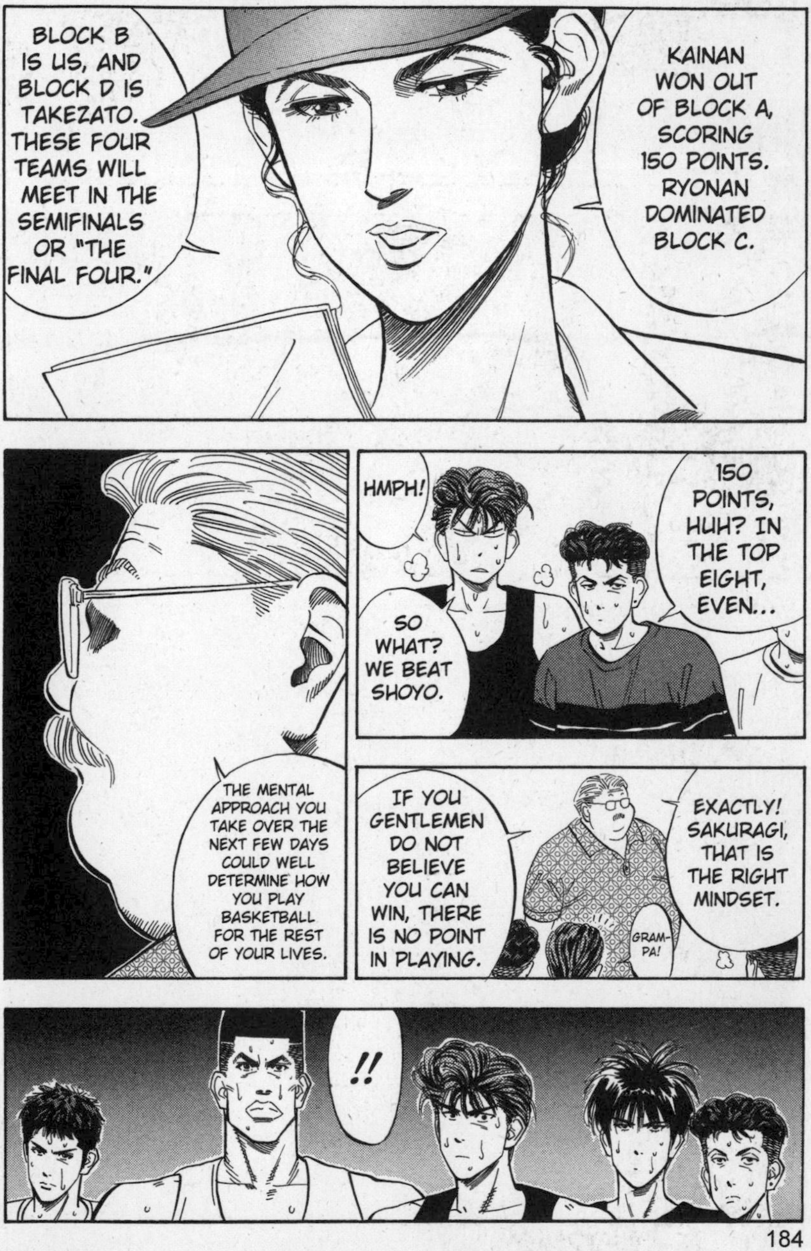
KAINAN WON OUT OF BLOCK A, SCORING 150 POINTS. RYONAN DOMINATED BLOCK C.
BLOCK B IS US, AND BLOCK D IS TAKEZATO. THESE FOUR TEAMS WILL MEET IN THE SEMIFINALS OR "THE FINAL FOUR."
150 POINTS, HUH? IN THE TOP EIGHT, EVEN...
HMPH!
SO WHAT? WE BEAT SHOYO.
EXACTLY! SAKURAGI, THAT IS THE RIGHT MINDSET.
GRAM-PA!
IF YOU GENTLEMEN DO NOT BELIEVE YOU CAN WIN, THERE IS NO POINT IN PLAYING.
THE MENTAL APPROACH YOU TAKE OVER THE NEXT FEW DAYS COULD WELL DETERMINE HOW YOU PLAY BASKETBALL FOR THE REST OF YOUR LIVES.
!!

READ THIS WAY

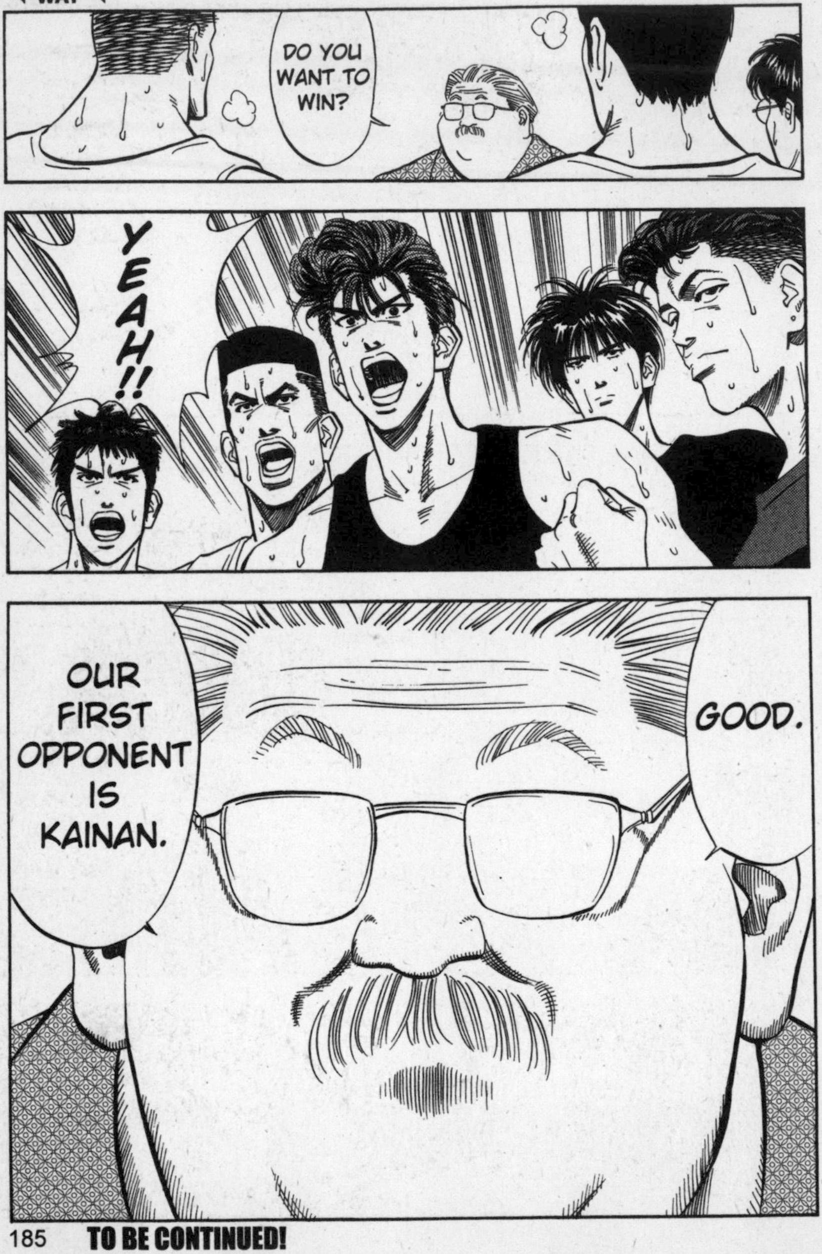
DO YOU WANT TO WIN?
YEAH!!
GOOD.
OUR FIRST OPPONENT IS KAINAN.

TO BE CONTINUED!

Coming Next Volume

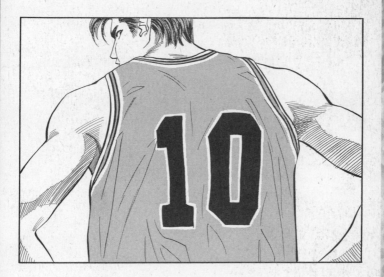

Shohoku gears up for their next match, and if they thought the game against Shoyo was tough, they're about to be put to the ultimate test against the Kings from Kainan: in the past 16 years, Kainan has not failed to make it to Nationals. Captain Akagi has dreamed of the day he'd get to lace up and take on Kainan, but does he have enough strong players on his side to see him through to victory?

ON SALE OCTOBER 2010

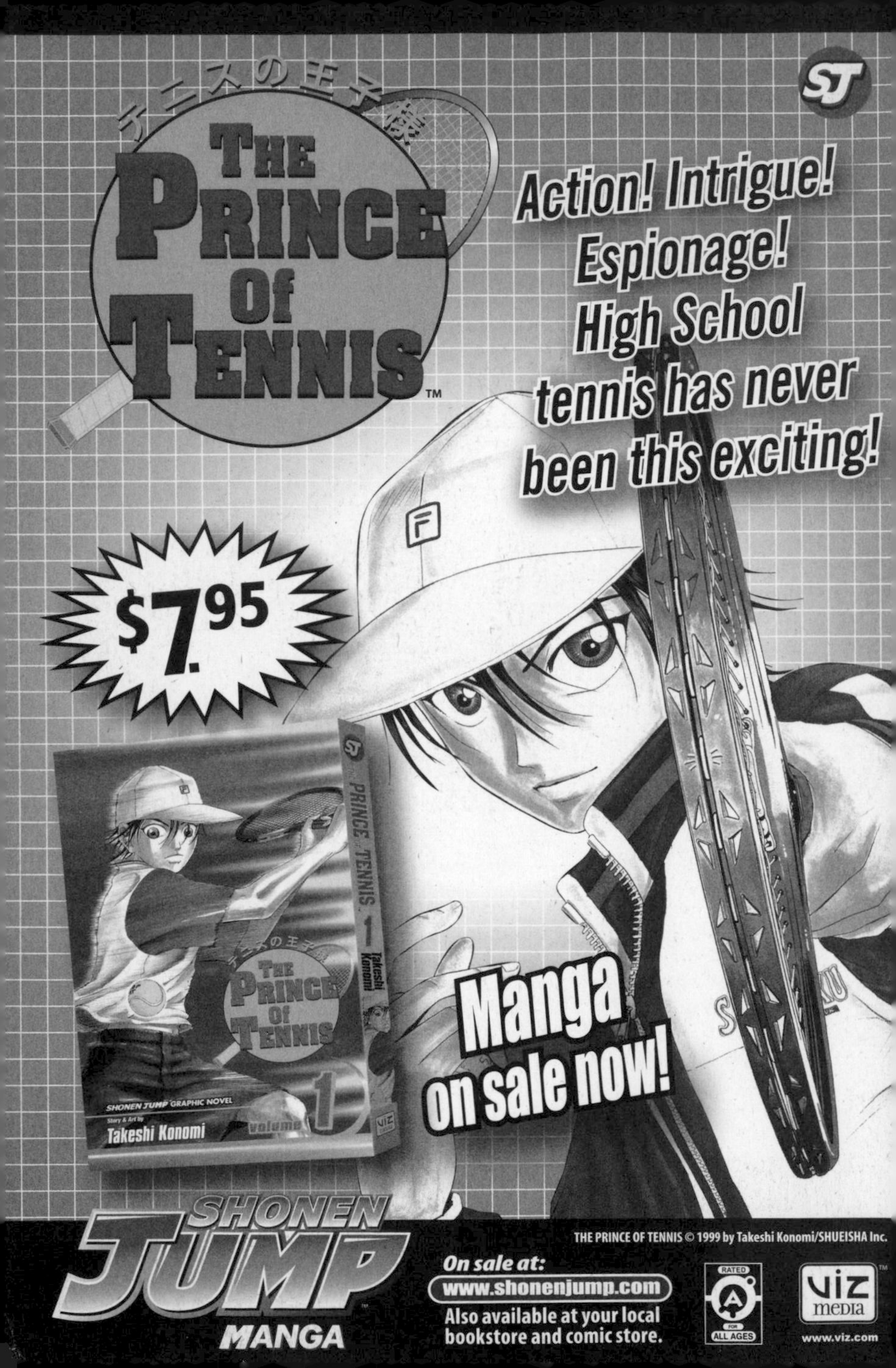
テニスの王子様
THE PRINCE OF TENNIS™
Action! Intrigue! Espionage! High School tennis has never been this exciting!
$7.95
SHONEN JUMP GRAPHIC NOVEL
Story & Art by
Takeshi Konomi
Manga on sale now!
SHONEN JUMP MANGA
THE PRINCE OF TENNIS © 1999 by Takeshi Konomi/SHUEISHA Inc.
On sale at:
www.shonenjump.com
Also available at your local bookstore and comic store.
RATED A FOR ALL AGES
VIZ media
www.viz.com

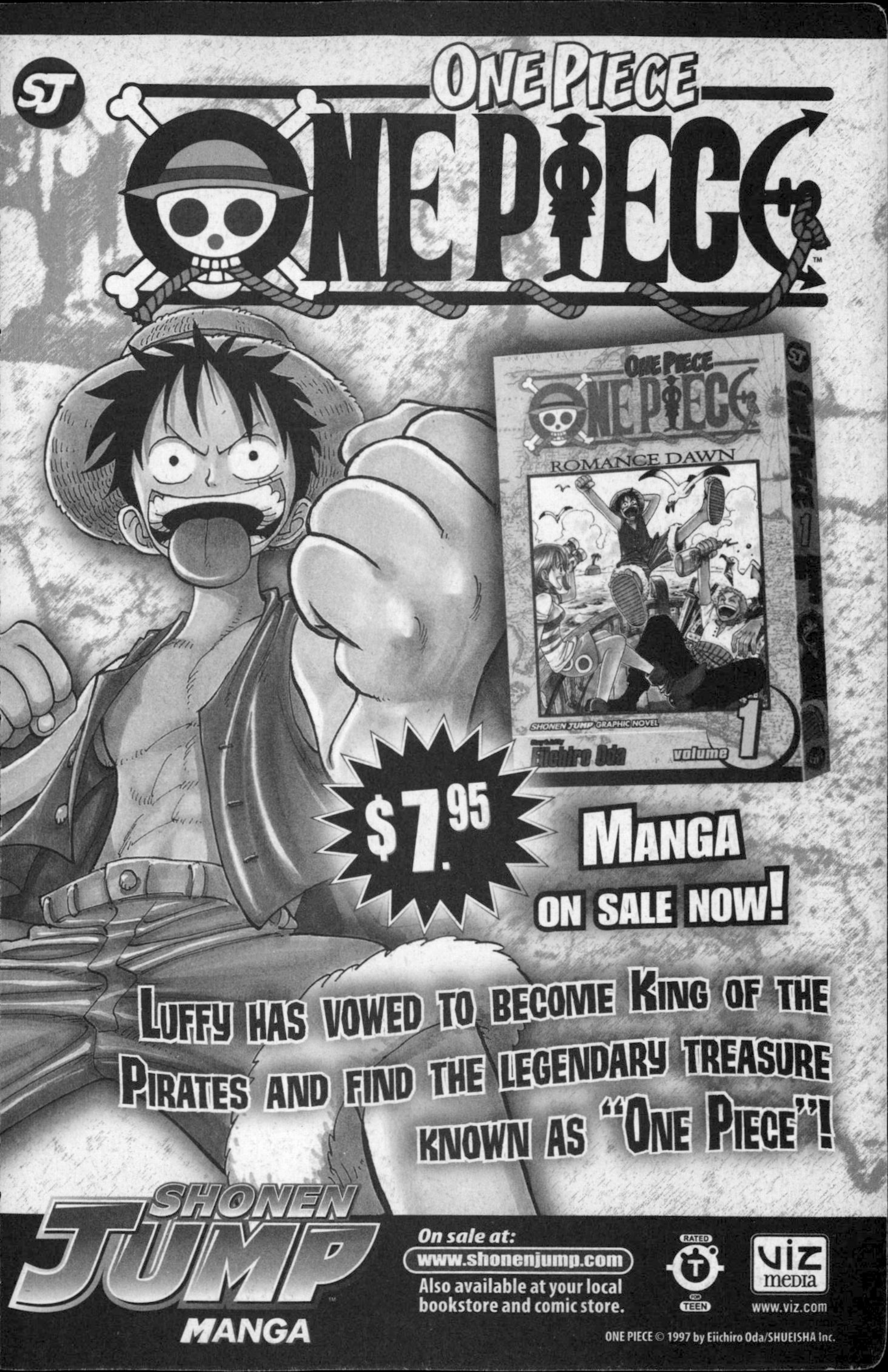
ONE PIECE
ONE PIECE
ONE PIECE
ROMANCE DAWN
SHONEN JUMP GRAPHIC NOVEL
Eiichiro Oda
volume 1
$7.95
MANGA
ON SALE NOW!
LUFFY HAS VOWED TO BECOME KING OF THE PIRATES AND FIND THE LEGENDARY TREASURE KNOWN AS "ONE PIECE"!
SHONEN JUMP
MANGA
On sale at:
www.shonenjump.com
Also available at your local bookstore and comic store.
RATED T FOR TEEN
VIZ media
www.viz.com
ONE PIECE © 1997 by Eiichiro Oda/SHUEISHA Inc.

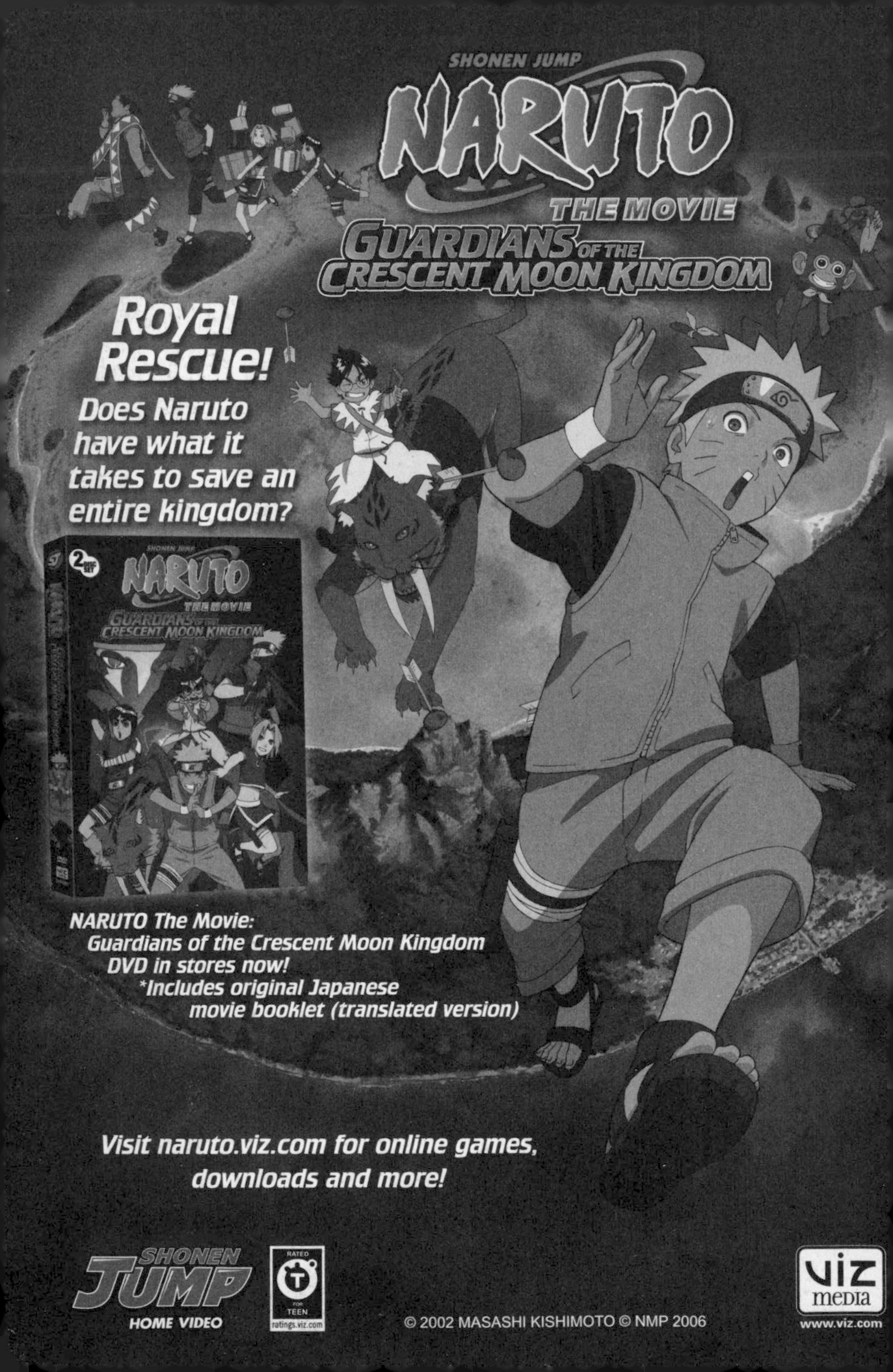
SHONEN JUMP
NARUTO
THE MOVIE
GUARDIANS OF THE CRESCENT MOON KINGDOM
Royal Rescue!
Does Naruto have what it takes to save an entire kingdom?
NARUTO The Movie: Guardians of the Crescent Moon Kingdom DVD in stores now!
*Includes original Japanese movie booklet (translated version)
Visit naruto.viz.com for online games, downloads and more!
SHONEN JUMP HOME VIDEO
RATED T FOR TEEN ratings.viz.com
© 2002 MASASHI KISHIMOTO © NMP 2006
viz media
www.viz.com

BLEACH
ブリーチ
ONE PIECE
Tegami Bachi
LETTER BEE

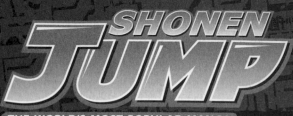

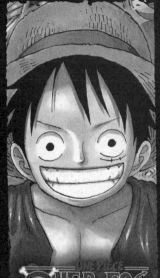

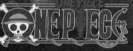

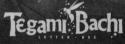

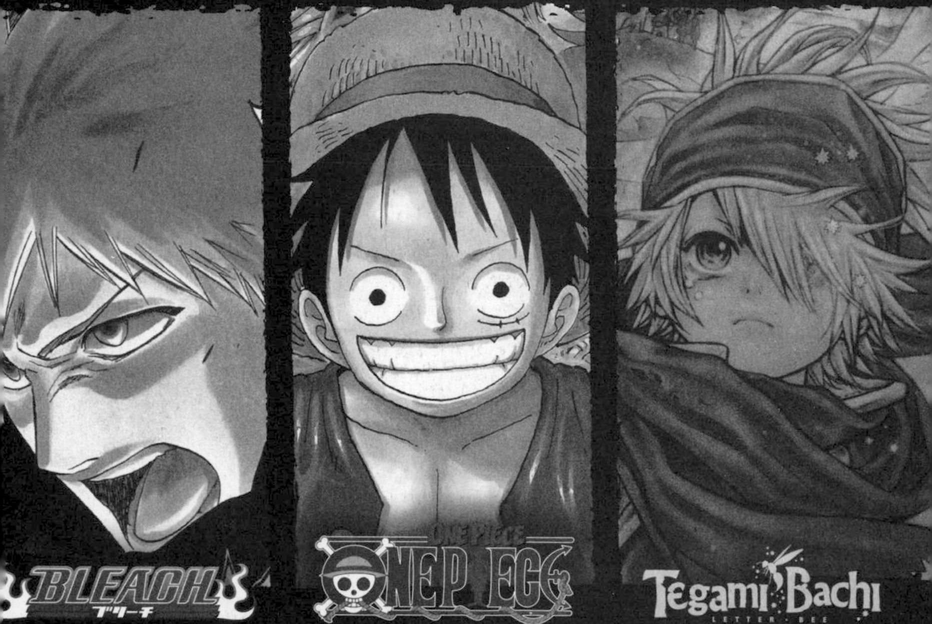

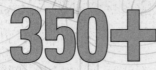
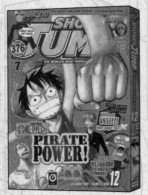
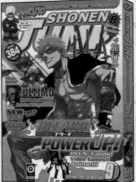
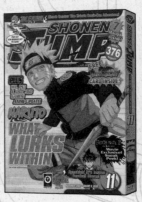

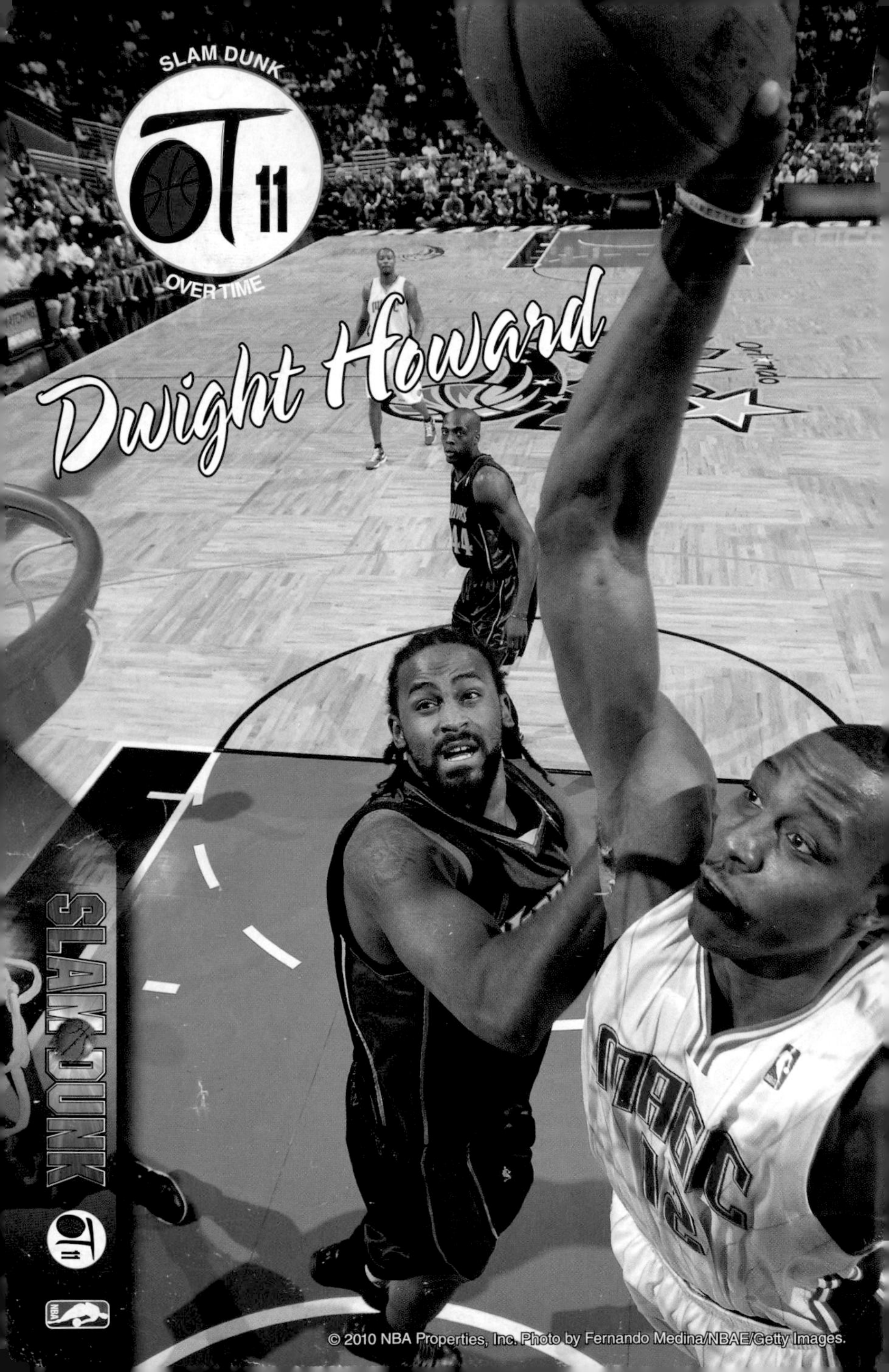
SLAM DUNK
OT 11
OVER TIME
Dwight Howard
SLAM DUNK

Hey basketball fans! Welcome to the Slam Dunk Omake-Dome, where basketball neophytes and street gamers alike learn how to ball like the pros. Today we marvel at the incredible ability of one of the hottest young stars in the game, Dwight Howard, and in the process get the skinny on what it takes to be a great center! Yes, even if you're not literally big, we'll get you to play Big Man style!

It's a Bird! It's a Plane! No, It's...

He doesn't have a cape (or at least, he only wears one when he's throwing down thunderous dunks at the NBA All-Star game), but everything else about Dwight Howard's game is larger than life—no wonder he's earned the nickname "Superman"! He wrote several goals down when he was in eighth grade, including leading his high school team to a state championship and becoming the first overall selection in the NBA Draft. Done and done!

The physically imposing center is one of the brightest young stars in today's NBA. Voted Defensive Player of the Year and an NBA All-First Team selection, Howard also set a record in 2009 when he was voted to the NBA All-Star team with an all-time-best 3,151,181 votes!

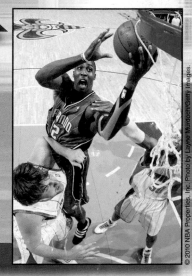

Rule-Changer

Playing one of the most physically demanding positions on the court, Howard has wowed spectators and opponents alike with his athleticism. Extremely quick and agile for a man who's 6' 11" and weighs 265 pounds, he can soar out of nowhere to block a shot or grab a rebound, and he's known for his active, aggressive team defense. He also has the underrated knack of drawing fouls, as he ranks at the top of the league for foul shots every year. As one opponent said in admiration in 2009, "If he gets any more athletic or jumps any higher, they're going to have to change the rules."

He's the straw that stirs the drink for the Orlando Magic, and a major reason why the team made it to the 2009 NBA Finals, but he's also well-known for his unselfish play and his lovable personality off the court—he's been known to crack up his teammates by dancing to popular Beyoncé songs, and on the more serious side, he regularly contributes to charities that help underprivileged kids.

CAREER SEASON AVERAGES

Year	Team	G	GS	MPG	FG%	3P%	FT%	OFF	DEF	RPG	APG	SPG	BPG	TO	PF	PPG
04-05	ORL	82	82	32.6	0.520	0.000	0.671	3.5	6.5	10.0	0.9	0.9	1.7	2.01	2.83	12.0
05-06	ORL	82	81	36.8	0.531	0.000	0.595	3.5	9.0	12.5	1.5	0.8	1.4	2.65	3.38	15.8
06-07	ORL	82	82	36.9	0.603	0.500	0.586	3.5	8.8	12.3	1.9	0.8	1.9	3.87	2.99	17.6
07-08	ORL	82	82	37.7	0.599	0.000	0.590	3.4	10.8	14.2	1.3	0.9	2.2	3.21	3.34	20.7
08-09	ORL	79	79	35.7	0.572	0.000	0.594	4.3	9.6	13.8	1.4	1.0	2.9	3.04	3.42	20.6
09-10	ORL	74	74	34.9	0.607	0.000	0.603	3.5	9.8	13.3	1.7	1.0	2.7	3.46	3.54	18.6
Career	--	481	480	35.8	0.574	0.056	0.601	3.6	9.1	12.7	1.5	0.9	2.1	3.03	3.24	17.5
All-Star	--	5	4	24.8	0.633	0.250	0.412	3.4	4.8	8.2	1.0	1.4	1.8	1.60	2.60	14.0

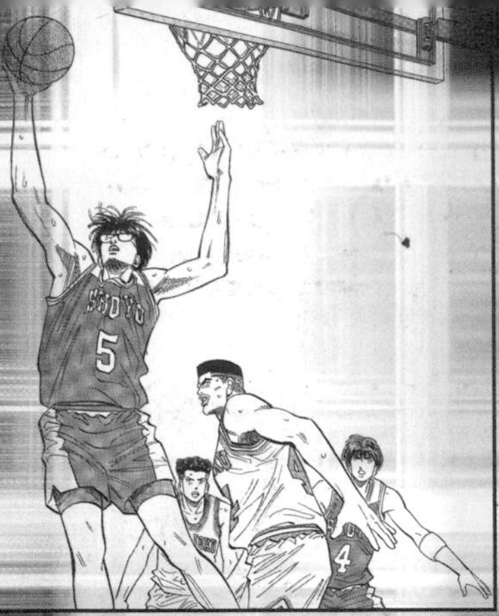

Hitting the Big Time, Big Man Style

Whether you're a genuine big man or happen to be manning the middle in a pick-up game, don't forget these valuable pointers about center play! You'll open things up for your teammates as well as take advantage of your own skills!

1. Reading is Fundamental
When you get the ball down low on offense, take a moment to "read" what's happening on the court around you. If the other team is double-teaming you, someone should be open! Or if the defense is "rotating" to keep up with your teammates, you might spot someone coming open. Or if you're played straight up, one-on-one, it could be your opportunity to take the ball to the hoop, or put the player guarding you off-balance with an unexpected shot (see point #3 ahead). In any case, learning to read what's happening around you will give you the knowledge to take your best option.

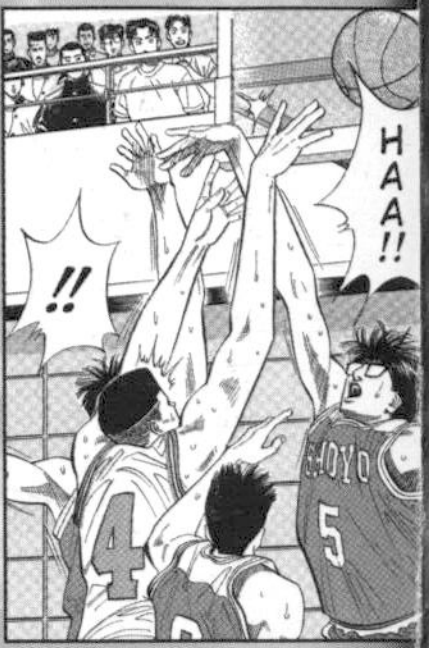
HAAA!!
!!

2. Free Throws
When you're mixing it up down low, chances are you're going to get fouled often. Make your opponent pay by hitting a high percentage of free throw shots! Need a free throw refresher? Check out *Slam Dunk* vol. 2!

3. Your Shot Arsenal
When most people think of centers, they think of thundering slam dunks and power moves to the basket. (Hanamichi sure does!) You can bet that your opponents think the same way too, so they'll focus on "packing it in" and not giving you an easy jam. Use that to your advantage and develop your other shots, like banking the ball off the glass for a basket (Tim Duncan is a master at this), or using the skyhook shot (a Kareem Abdul-Jabbar specialty). If the other team is too intent on stopping a jam, you'll be left open for these and other shots!

4. Passing the Rock
There's a reason why they call the center position a "pivot" position—the action swings around you. Just because you're a big man doesn't mean that passing skills aren't important. Develop your passing skills (see *Slam Dunk* vol. 7) so when the other team focuses on you, you can befuddle 'em with a slick pass to your teammate! True double-threat players (shooting and passing) are doubly tough to defend!

5. Protecting the Paint
When you're down in the box with the other big boys, there's going to be contact and spirited competition for rebounds. Remember all the tips of the trade we told you about blocking shots and getting rebounds in *Slam Dunk* vol. 4 and 5? Time to put them in use. Your tough, resilient play in the middle can set the tone for your entire defense, so don't slack it out there! And don't forget all the team defense tips we taught you in *Slam Dunk* vol. 9!

Bonus Tip: Post Moves

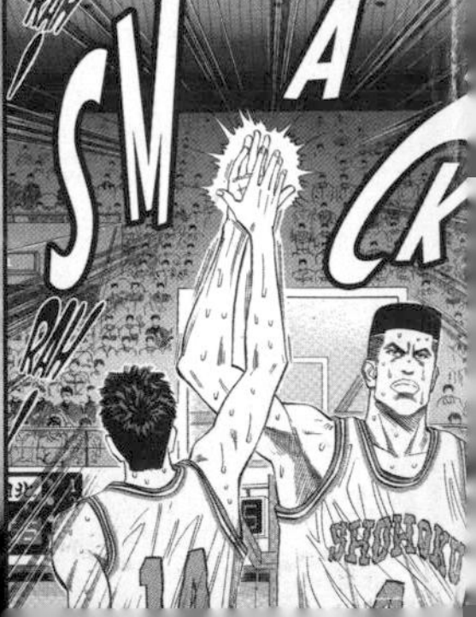
SMACK

Moving with the ball down low is different than moving with it in the open court—be sure to develop your positioning and footwork. Precise, quick movements are essential. Learn how to "back down" your defender by dribbling closer to the basketball with your back to your opponent (think boxing out, but heading the other way). Pump fakes, when you fake going up for a shot, can be useful too, as well as spin moves, where you can fake going one way for a moment (usually with a head bob) and then take it to the basket in the other direction. Be sure to keep a good handle on the ball—with so many people down low, you can be sure a few steal attempts will be made!

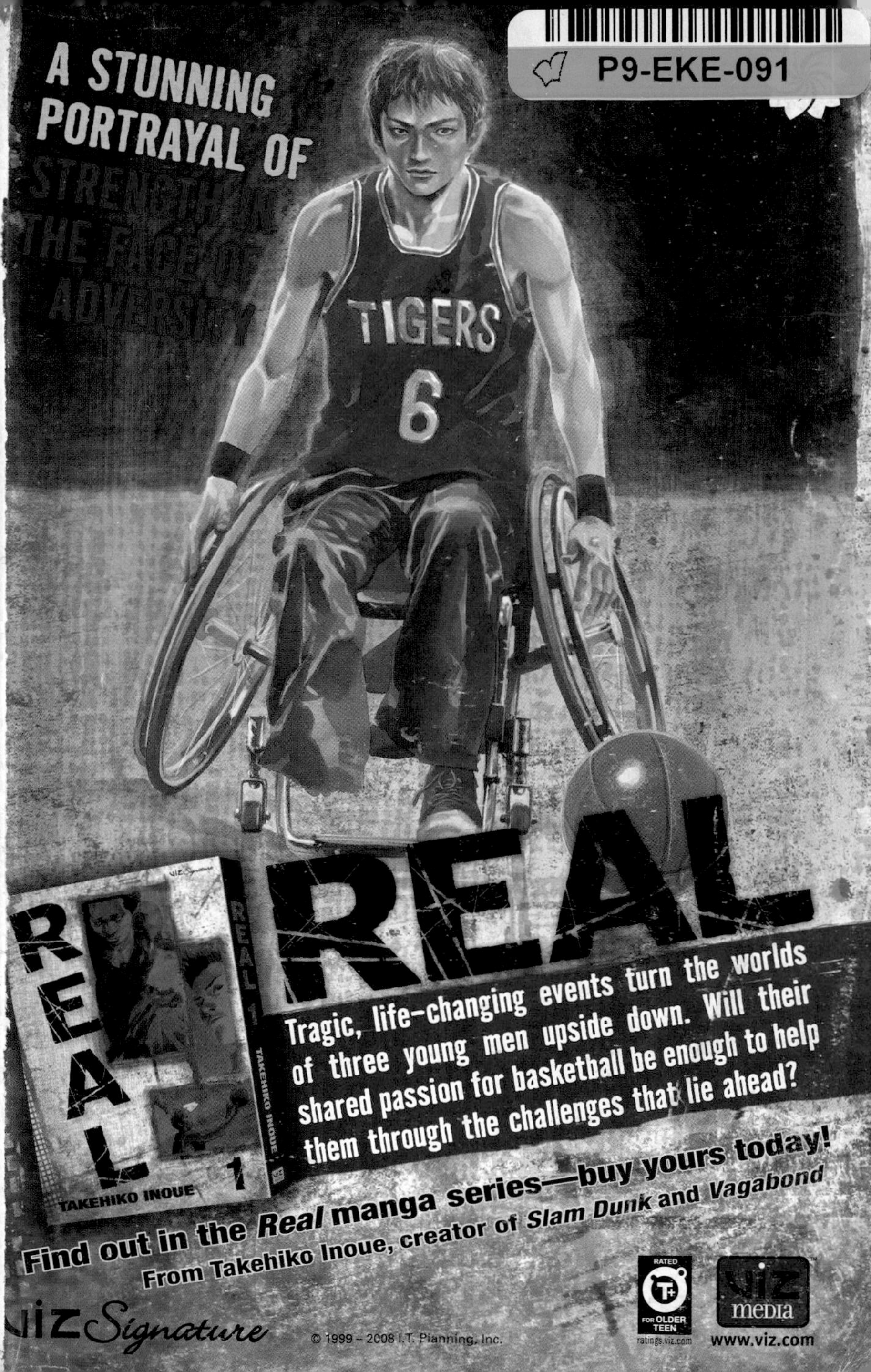
P9-EKE-091
A STUNNING PORTRAYAL OF
STRENGTH IN THE FACE OF ADVERSITY
TIGERS
6
REAL
REAL
REAL 1
TAKEHIKO INOUE
1
Tragic, life-changing events turn the worlds of three young men upside down. Will their shared passion for basketball be enough to help them through the challenges that lie ahead?
Find out in the Real manga series—buy yours today!
From Takehiko Inoue, creator of Slam Dunk and Vagabond
VIZ Signature
© 1999 – 2008 I.T. Planning, Inc.
RATED T+ FOR OLDER TEEN
ratings.viz.com
VIZ media
www.viz.com